T0355215

Free Speech and Turbulent Freedom

Free Speech and Turbulent Freedom

The Dangerous Allure of Censorship in the Digital Era

MICHAEL J. GLENNON

Oxford University Press is a department of the University of Oxford. It furthers
the University's objective of excellence in research, scholarship, and education
by publishing worldwide. Oxford is a registered trade mark of Oxford University
Press in the UK and certain other countries.

Published in the United States of America by Oxford University Press
198 Madison Avenue, New York, NY 10016, United States of America.

CIP data is on file at the Library of Congress

ISBN 978-0-19-763676-3

DOI: 10.1093/oso/9780197636763.001.0001

Printed by Sheridan Books, Inc., United States of America

To my students

Citizens of feudal states are alarmed at our democratic institutions lapsing into anarchy; and the older and more cautious among ourselves are learning from Europeans to look with some terror at our turbulent freedom.

—Ralph Waldo Emerson, "Politics" (1844)

Contents

Preface

Years ago, when I worked as legal counsel for the Senate Foreign Relations Committee, we occasionally pulled all-nighters reconciling the House and Senate versions of a bill. Inevitably, we haggled over the wording, each side trying to preserve the language that would please our respective bosses. One evening, as we were toiling over a bill that contained provisions on foreign aid, human rights, and arms sales of keen interest to the State Department and the Pentagon, I set off through the warrenlike offices of the Rayburn Building in search of coffee. Opening the wrong door, I was surprised to find a State Department lawyer sitting at a desk in front of a typewriter. He should have been at home, in bed, but here he was, typing away, writing language that he was quietly slipping to the House staffers, who presented it as their own.

Back then—even then—the influence of national security bureaucrats pervaded the lawmaking process. They drafted legislation that members of Congress introduced. They endorsed or opposed measures at hearings and markups. They presented views to conference committees that were laid out next to the House and Senate positions. They lobbied tirelessly, waiting outside the chambers during floor debates, ready with arguments and data to back them up, pushing to inscribe their positions into law.[1]

I was reminded of that experience when reading the Twitter Files[2] and the opinion of the federal district court in *Missouri v. Biden*. In that case, the states of Missouri and Louisiana joined several private plaintiffs who sought to bar the federal government from encouraging, pressuring, or inducing the major social media platforms to suppress constitutionally protected speech. The court handed them an initial victory on July 4, 2023. In issuing a preliminary injunction,[3] the court found that "the United States Government seems to have assumed a role similar to an Orwellian 'Ministry of Truth.'"[4] It detailed the evidence: "Opposition to COVID-19 vaccines; opposition to COVID-19 masking and lockdowns; opposition to the lab-leak theory of COVID-19; opposition to the validity of the 2020 election; opposition to President Biden's policies; statements that the Hunter Biden laptop story was true; and opposition to policies of the government officials in power. All were suppressed."[5] In these and other areas, the court found, the government coerced, significantly encouraged, or jointly participated in the platforms' censorship. Government officials

> used meetings and communications with social-media companies to pressure those companies to take down, reduce, and suppress the free speech of American citizens. They flagged posts and provided information on the type of posts they wanted suppressed. They also followed up with directives to the social-media companies to provide them with information as to action the company had taken with regard to the flagged post. This seemingly unrelenting pressure . . . had the intended result of suppressing millions of protected free speech postings by American citizens.[6]

The case, the court concluded, "arguably involves the most massive attack against free speech in United States' history."[7]

It was bad enough that the security state had dominated Congress, which is supposed to be an independent branch of the government.[8] Unlike Congress, however, the internet companies were not created to be part of the government. They are, or were supposed to be, *private* entities, not arms of the security state. When the government joins with private actors to censor speech, as it has clearly done in coercing and colluding with these platforms, that joint enterprise becomes subject to First Amendment limits. Their action is then constitutionally akin to a sheriff's giving the Ku Klux Klan kerosene and directions to the homes of civil rights activists. The government cannot do indirectly what it cannot do directly; it cannot escape constitutional limits by contracting out censorship to intermediaries. Yet that is what it has done with social media platforms—and that has escaped the attention of a large segment of the American public. Many Americans do not realize that the government has actively joined with private companies to close the nation's marketplace of ideas to viewpoints and information that they do not want the public to see or hear. Many do not realize that the nation's legendary ability to "self-correct" depends upon hearing discomfiting viewpoints and information to spot mistakes that need to be corrected. And many who do realize that do not seem to care.

It is no exaggeration to say that a sea change has occurred in American attitudes toward free speech. I first saw that change among students. Since leaving the Hill, I've taught constitutional and international law in U.S. graduate and law schools. When I entered teaching, freedom of speech was regarded as sacrosanct, the heartbeat of the American political order. In the past few years, however, many students, like much of the public, have come to see freedom of speech as unnecessary or even objectionable. Many see no reason to protect speech that spreads seeming misinformation, advocates violence, encourages hate, or is otherwise harmful. These problems, some believe, are better addressed not by the U.S. Constitution, which they view as flawed, but by new, yet-to-be-defined standards or by those of other countries or international institutions. Many embrace this view with an unyielding moral certainty.

I did not write this book to argue that rights are God-given or that harmful speech is in fact harmless or that the Constitution is without defects. I did write it to at least plant the seeds of three propositions. First, whether or not one accepts freedom of speech as an unalienable, natural right, there are overwhelming practical reasons to protect it. Second, those reasons undergird the Supreme Court's interpretation of the First Amendment as protecting ideas we hate, including advocacy of violence, offensive speech, and apparent falsehood. Third, the bedrock principles of the First Amendment are a better safeguard of Americans' digital speech than are porous international standards. I conclude that the courts, in applying the First Amendment's framework, will need to invigorate earlier precepts of its jurisprudence if free speech is to survive the gravest threat it now confronts: the newly emerged censorship regime jointly forged by the security state and major social media platforms.

I write in the hope that students and others committed to social justice might profit from the experience and intellectual odyssey of another young idealist, Oliver Wendell Holmes Jr. In equally turbulent times, he too was committed to social justice. He nearly lost his life fighting for that commitment. He survived, however, to point the way for a safer method of resolving competing visions of justice. If this volume seems, at times, to be three different books tackling those three propositions, it is in this larger purpose united: to suggest that moral certitude and the censorship it engenders will pave the road to a violent end game for American democracy and that the safer route is a road of humility, pluralism, and free speech.

1

Introduction

In August 1864, twenty-three-year-old Oliver Wendel Holmes Jr., stepped off the train from Boston in Concord, Massachusetts. He had come to seek the advice of a family friend, Ralph Waldo Emerson, the Sage of Concord. Holmes was unsure what to do with his life. His father, a prominent poet and doctor, had "put the screws on him"[1] to go to law school, he said. Yet he still felt a pull toward the philosophical and literary career exemplified by Emerson. More important, Holmes no doubt wondered whether the momentous ideas he had earlier taken from Emerson still made sense. Over the previous three years he had, in a way, put some of those ideas to the test.

Holmes made his way from the station down Concord's gravel streets, under the shady elms of Main Street, past the yellow house where Emerson's friend Henry David Thoreau had died two years earlier, past the shops of Concord's bustling village and Wright's Tavern, where the British army made its headquarters on April 19, 1775. He passed the square with the Concord Lyceum, where his father would lecture; passed the meeting house of the First Parish Church, where Emerson's grandfather had been pastor; walked through the pine and chestnut trees Emerson had planted; and stepped up to the front door of Emerson's big white house on the road to Lexington, twenty minutes from the station. When he had last seen Emerson, before the war, Holmes had cut a memorable figure, six feet two and strikingly handsome. Now he was thin and gaunt, and he walked with a slight limp. Holmes found Concord's tranquility unsettling. Days before, on July 17, he had been discharged as a captain from the Union army; a year earlier, in the run-up to the battle of Chancellorsville, an iron ball had ripped through his boot and entered his heel, which took eight months to heal. After the war, he later said, the world never seemed quite right again.[2] One can understand why.

Of the nearly two thousand regiments in the Union army, only four had suffered more battle deaths than his.[3] Nearly every officer he knew or cared for, he wrote, was either dead or wounded.[4] Wracked continually by dysentery and lice, he had barely survived some of the war's bloodiest battles. In October 1861, at Ball's Bluff, of seventeen hundred Union soldiers, nine

Free Speech and Turbulent Freedom. Michael J. Glennon, Oxford University Press. © Oxford University Press 2024. DOI: 10.1093/oso/9780197636763.003.0001

hundred perished.[5] Holmes, shot through the chest and bleeding from the mouth, was taken from the battlefield to a hut filled with groaning men and sawed-off limbs and told he might die. Eleven months later, at Antietam, where Union casualties exceeded those of the U.S. Army on D-day,[6] Holmes was shot through the neck and taken to a field hospital. The surgeon shook his head and walked away, saying he was obliged to attend to patients who could recover and leaving the still-conscious Holmes unattended.[7] ("I'm glad it's not a case for amputation," Holmes quipped, "for I don't think you'd be equal to it.")[8] Yet he recovered, fighting again in the Wilderness, where he reported watching fellow staff members spattered with brains when a shell exploded in their headquarters, and, later, encountered bodies piled five or six deep, the wounded writhing under the dead.[9] In one of his final letters home, Holmes wrote that his "narrowest escape"[10] came in May 1864 when, confronted suddenly by twenty Confederate horsemen, he spurred his horse to a gallop, ducked down on the side of his horse, and bolted through the line unscathed.[11] He had then had enough. The next day he wrote his parents that the "wear and tear" on his "mind and body" was a "greater strain on both than I am called to endure."[12] "[T]hese last few days have been very bad.... I tell you many a man has gone crazy since this campaign begun from the terrible pressure.... I hope to pull through but don't yet know."[13]

"I may not," he cryptically concluded, "have quite the same ideas."[14]

The chief source of his earlier ideas was the man Holmes had come to Concord to see. Emerson, Holmes recalled half a century later, "set me on fire."[15] Emerson had set many minds on fire. One of the most famous men in the United States, Emerson spent months every year lecturing captivated audiences around the country and then revising and publishing his words for eagerly awaiting readers. His eminence afforded easy access to leading literary and political figures of the day, in the United States and abroad. When he became impatient during the Civil War at the delay in emancipation, he visited Lincoln in the White House and urged him to proclaim the freedom of the slaves. A fervid abolitionist, Emerson had become de facto head of what was not only a literary, philosophical, and religious movement; transcendentalism, as it was called, was also a social and political movement—one that aspired "to provide a soul for modern liberalism."[16] Transcendentalism's core teaching was that absolute, objective, universal truth not only exists but that it can be accessed directly and intuitively by every individual. "To believe your own thought," Emerson wrote, "to believe that what is true for you in your private heart is true for all men,—that is genius."[17] Truth is for the "well awake," the citizen who "links himself naturally to his brothers."[18]

Holmes's wartime experience convinced him that that sentiment was not only wrong but dangerous. It blocks discussion, he believed, derails democracy, and leads to the kind of bloodletting he had just endured. He never regretted fighting for the Union army. Years afterward he regarded himself as having had the "great good fortune" to serve.[19] Recognizing that different people have different intuitions, however, he concluded that absolute certainty is an illusion. The route to truth, such as it is, lies in *questioning* your own thought and matching it against thoughts that lie in the hearts of *others*— not in assuming that what is true for you is necessarily true for everyone else. Seven decades later and three decades after his appointment to the Supreme Court by President Theodore Roosevelt, Holmes would retire as the most esteemed American jurist since John Marshall, having fought every step of the way against illusory certitude. In the course of that journey, Holmes looked to uncertainty itself as the rationale for the diamond he planted in the crown of American jurisprudence: the notion of the marketplace of ideas. In myriad cases, Holmes's pragmatist image of that marketplace has animated the Court's interpretation of the First Amendment's prohibition against the abridgment of freedom of speech or the press. As recently as June 2021, in upholding a cheerleader's right to criticize her high school in social media posts sent outside of school hours from off-campus, the Court said:

> Our representative democracy only works if we protect the "marketplace of ideas." This free exchange facilitates an informed public opinion, which, when transmitted to lawmakers, helps produce laws that reflect the People's will. That protection must include the protection of unpopular ideas, for popular ideas have less need for protection.[20]

As noted in the preface, this book unfolds in three parts: past, present, and future. The first describes how Holmes moved from moral absolutism to a pragmatist respect for the free exchange of ideas. It defends the concept of the marketplace of ideas against familiar critiques. The second part describes how that concept is reflected in three foundational, distinctive realms of First Amendment law: advocacy of law violation, hate speech, and disinformation. And the third suggests that the Amendment's historically accepted scope is now too narrow to vindicate that vision, that in the globalized, digitized world in which government and private social media companies have become intertwined, hazy international limits will replace the constraints of the First Amendment unless the Amendment is recognized as protecting the free speech interests of all who participate in the modern marketplace of ideas—not simply government and corporate "speakers" but also social media users, listeners, bystanders, and society at large.

It scarcely requires noting that moral certitude is ubiquitous in contemporary American society, inflaming racial and cultural animosities on all sides. A former vice president spoke for many when he said, "We don't negotiate with evil; we defeat it."[21] Domestic political opponents, like foreign adversaries, are routinely regarded as the physical embodiment of evil. A respected 2021 public opinion survey of Trump and Biden voters revealed that substantial majorities of each group view elected officials from the opposing party as presenting a clear and present danger to American democracy. Nearly half agreed at least somewhat that red or blue states should secede from the Union to form their own country.[22] It's easy, in our fast-changing country, to see such animosities as unprecedented. I write this book as a reminder that they are not, that we have been here before, that we know where absolutism can lead, and that we know *part of* the solution: an unwavering commitment to freedom of speech, without which our ailing political system will never correct itself. My hope is that, in beginning with Holmes's journey from certitude to humility, we may recall a lesson that allows us to avert calamity.

Let us return momentarily, then, to Holmes and Emerson.

PART I
THE PAST

2

Prophet and Disciple

From left to right: Ralph Waldo Emerson, Photograph by Josiah Johnson Hawes (1857); Oliver Wendell Holmes Jr., Photograph by Silsbee, Case & Co., Photograph Artists (between 1861 and 1865).
Source: Wikimedia Commons.

Ralph Waldo Emerson was what would today be called a public intellectual. Indeed, he was easily the most visible public intellectual in nineteenth-century America. Emerson came to instant prominence in 1838 with a provocative lecture at the Harvard Divinity School. His remarks on the failure of institutionalized Christianity and doubts about the reality of miracles sparked such notoriety that he was not invited back for decades. The deeper significance of the address lay in two themes Emerson would expound over the course of his life: individualism and certainty. Together,

Free Speech and Turbulent Freedom. Michael J. Glennon, Oxford University Press. © Oxford University Press 2024.
DOI: 10.1093/oso/9780197636763.003.0002

these combined to form a belief in unmediated revelation, accessible universally through personal intuition. "Man is the wonderworker," he had told the graduating seniors. Trust in your own hearts, "go alone . . . refuse the good models, even those which are sacred to the imagination. . . . [C]ast behind you all conformity, and acquaint men at first hand with Deity." These individual intuitions, he taught, tapped into a universal moral code that embraced all humanity, binding upon individuals and governments alike as against any contrary human-made law. These instincts, to Emerson, were not hunches to be debated or hypotheses to be tested empirically or postulates to be weighed against competing postulates—they were final insights into absolute, universal, objective truth.

As Emerson often acknowledged, much of this was not new. Strands traced at least to Plato, Emerson's most oft-cited authority.[1] Emerson's view was also given wide currency by his friend Henry David Thoreau, who argued the rightness of civil disobedience. Yet as the nation's racial fissures widened, Emerson's philosophy took on a new urgency as his abolitionist followers zealously condemned what they regarded as a barbarous status quo. These intuitions inspired not only the transcendentalism Emerson championed but the massive abolitionist movement that pressed, with ever greater fervor, for freedom for the four million people held in slavery in the American South.

To Emerson, the truth of these intuitions was beyond doubt, and the law that required helping runaway slave-catchers was the quintessential evil. "If our resistance to this [the fugitive slave law] is not right," he said, "there is no right."[2] In blistering terms he denounced Massachusetts senator Daniel Webster for supporting the "filthy" fugitive slave law, part of the Compromise of 1850. "The word *liberty* in the mouth of Mr Webster," Emerson wrote, "sounds like *love* in the mouth of a courtesan."[3] The law imposed "penalties of treason on acts of common humanity." It violated a higher law, and he would not obey it: "An immoral law makes it a man's duty to break."[4] He arranged a room in his attic to hide fleeing slaves and readied his carriage to spirit them to the train station.[5]

To Emerson, the U.S. government was a disgrace. "This has ceased to be a representative government," he wrote. "Manifest Destiny, Democracy, Freedom, fine names for an ugly thing." There was little doubt where the fault lay. "In this country for the last few years," he continued, "the government has been the chief obstruction of the common weal."[6] It was time to stop waiting for the government to act. In 1845, speaking in celebration of West Indian emancipation, he promised listeners, "[A] revolution is preparing at no distant day to set these disjointed matters right."[7]

For Emerson, John Brown stood as an ideal, in marked contrast to the spineless Webster.[8] Brown "did not believe in moral suasion, he believed in putting the thing through."[9] Brown, Emerson avowed, was a true transcendentalist, an "idealist."[10] When Brown visited Concord in 1857, Emerson invited him to his home and raised money for him.[11] Brown's 1859 raid on Harpers Ferry may have failed in sparking a slave rebellion, but Brown made "the gallows glorious like the cross,"[12] Emerson wrote. Brown did not forget Concord's hospitality: he bequeathed his sword to Emerson's equally fervid friend Thoreau.

Holmes's father was a keen admirer and friend of Emerson, though the closeness of their relationship is uncertain. One biographer has written that Emerson frequently visited the Holmeses in Boston; another reported that Holmes Junior "felt closer to Emerson . . . than his own father" and referred to Emerson as "Uncle Waldo."[13] Another dismisses such claims as undocumented. What is clear is that Holmes Senior met regularly with Emerson as part of the Saturday Club, a group of Boston intellectuals of which both were members, and wrote one of the first biographies of Emerson, published in 1884.[14] It's also clear that he transmitted his admiration of Emerson to his son. For the Harvard freshman's seventeenth birthday, his father gave Wendell, as he was known, a five-volume set of Emerson's writings.[15]

Young Holmes was mesmerized. As G. Edward White put it, he "assum[ed] the role of an Emersonian camp follower" and implicitly adopted the perspective of transcendentalism in his undergraduate writings.[16] He wrote prodigiously. In December 1858 Holmes published an essay titled "Books" in *Harvard Magazine*, of which he was an editor,[17] largely repeating an article of the same title published earlier in the same year by Emerson, which had inveighed against religious orthodoxy and urged readers to think independently about religious issues and come to their own conclusions.[18] Another essay Holmes published in *Harvard Magazine* analyzed the art of the engraver Albrecht Dürer (copies of whose works decorated Holmes's sitting room seventy years later).[19] Holmes, enamored with Emerson and convinced of the singularity of truth and beauty, sought to establish how artists such as Dürer might be objectively ranked. A great work of art, like a great idea, "partakes of what is eternal," Emerson wrote; its "ideal tendency" traced to a "conception of the harmonious whole."[20] Holmes agreed. Truth exists out there in the world of art as it does in the world of ideas, he suggested; it can be discovered without resort to divine revelation, and it imposes obligations which are "not less binding had the Bible never been written, or if we were to perish utterly tomorrow." "[A] noble philosophy,"

Holmes believed, "will suffice to teach us our duties to ourselves and our neighbors."[21]

To some, sidestepping the theological foundation of morality in this manner seemed blasphemous. One of his classmates responded that Holmes's Platonic "talk about the 'Eternal Truth,' the 'Absolute Virtue,' the 'ideal Good,' 'Objective and Essential Beauty'" demeaned the teachings of "the divine Nazarene."[22] The free-spirited Holmes soon afterward had his first exposure to the censor's hanging sword of Damocles when his father received a letter from the president of Harvard complaining that the *Magazine* had "assumed the liberty of criticizing the proceedings of the College" and announcing that "printed or oral acts of disrespect" by students would not be permitted. Holmes Senior, he hoped, would bring his "son to see this matter rightly."[23] We have no record of any response by either Holmes or his father, but the *Magazine* did not soften its tone.[24]

Holmes remained in Emerson's thrall throughout his college years. Holmes's transcendentalism reinforced his zealous opposition to slavery. As Stephen Budiansky notes, Holmes "felt no inclinations to temporize":

> Holmes would later recall being "deeply moved by the Abolition cause" in his years at Harvard before the war. In his sophomore year "a Negro minstrel show shocked me with its demeaning representation of blacks." When Wendell Phillips was scheduled to address the Massachusetts Anti-Slavery Society at Tremont Temple on January 24, 1961, Holmes readily volunteered to serve on his bodyguard.[25]

As he left Harvard in his senior year to join his regiment in 1862, Holmes carried with him the autograph of his hero, Ralph Waldo Emerson.[26]

3

The Certain Sage of Concord

Emerson, age sixty-one at the time of Holmes's 1864 visit, was by all accounts a man of genuine warmth and decency. "His usual manner carried with it something penetrating and sweet beyond mere description," Walt Whitman said. "There is in some men an indefinable something which flows out and over you like a flood of light—as if they possessed it illimitably—their whole being suffused with it. . . . Emerson's whole attitude shed forth such an impression."[1] John Muir, who met Emerson in California in 1871, recalled him as "the most serene, majestic, sequoia-like soul I ever met. His smile was as sweet and calm as morning light on the mountains. There was a wonderful charm in his presence; his smile, serene eye, his voice, his manner, were all sensed at once by everybody."[2]

In Concord, Emerson's generosity was legendary. He found work for Thoreau, got his writings published, loaned him money, and lent him the land at Walden Pond where he built his cabin. He helped Nathaniel Hawthorne and his wife return to Concord and enabled them to marry, arranging the rental of the house where they would live. (It was called the Old Manse; through its window, Emerson's grandfather had watched British redcoats run from the musket fire of Minutemen at the North Bridge.) The educator Bronson Alcott and his daughter, Louisa May, author of *Little Women*, were close friends. Emerson paid for Bronson Alcott's ticket to England, paid the Alcotts' rent, and lent them money for setting up their experimental community, Fruitlands. Another beneficiary was the editor of *The Dial*, Margaret Fuller, who lived with Emerson's family. Emerson seemed to know and like everyone in Concord, and his affection was returned. When his house suffered a serious fire, the townspeople of Concord took up a collection to help pay for its repair.[3]

Emerson and transcendentalism were all but synonymous.[4] He saw good in everyone and everything, and transcendentalism developed into a kind of pantheism, a loose set of beliefs that saw the divine everywhere, especially in nature. To see God in the face, Concord transcendentalists believed, take a walk in Walden Woods or paddle down the Assabet River on a kaleidoscopic

Free Speech and Turbulent Freedom. Michael J. Glennon, Oxford University Press. © Oxford University Press 2024.
DOI: 10.1093/oso/9780197636763.003.0003

October afternoon or play the flute on the sandy shore of Walden Pond by moonlight (as did Thoreau). "In the woods," Emerson wrote, "we return to reason and faith."[5] There we think clearly, unencumbered by the din and dirt of cities. There we see most readily our link with the "Over-soul."

The term apparently was first used by Emerson when a divinity student at Harvard and was made famous in his 1841 essay "The Over-Soul." It refers to a higher power of absolute goodness that infuses all forms of life. "The Supreme Critic on the errors of the past and the present," Emerson wrote, "and the only prophet of that which must be, is that great nature in which we rest, as the earth lies in the soft arms of the atmosphere; that Unity, that Over-soul, within which every man's particular being is contained and made one with all other; that common heart."[6] Here lies a world of perfect tranquility, goodness, and absolute beauty, a priori knowledge available directly through personal intuition. For Emerson, the challenge to philosophy is "for all that exists conditionally to find a ground unconditional and absolute."[7] We need not be prisoners of language and logic, Emerson believed. Language and logic can be transcended.

How? By recognizing that communication is superfluous. Communicability is not a prerequisite for knowledge: each of us can know what cannot be expressed. Not surprisingly, Emerson's philosophy was embraced by Friedrich Nietzsche, who called Emerson his "twin soul" and filled his copies of Emerson's books with marginal notations. Nietzsche's Superman personifies in many respects the Emersonian ideal of rising above the petty requirements of language and logic; he lives in a world of his own creation, stepping, to borrow Thoreau's phrase, "to the music which he hears, however measured or far away."[8] After reading Emerson's *Essays*, Nietzsche wrote that he had never "felt so at home in a book; felt so much, indeed, as if the home were my own."[9] Argumentation, debate, and contestation are of no interest. A "foolish consistency is the hobgoblin of little minds."[10] Insight is not logical; it is, in a word, *mystical*. It can be communicated—if at all—not with our traditional tools of language and logic but only dimly, in imagery, in metaphor, in indirection. But its imagery cannot be reduced to syllogisms; it *rises above* syllogistic logic, which is at once its polemical strength and its weakness, captured in Wittgenstein's conversation-stopping verdict on mysticism: "Whereof one cannot speak, thereof one must be silent."[11]

Therein lies the difficulty in Emerson's mystical epistemology. Emerson does not remain silent. His writings on politics, law, and morality are scaffolded with unfalsifiable, often poetic imagery, yet revert to logic and

reason to argue that we ought to, among other things, follow our own intuition, disregard immoral laws, and raze existing social structures inconsistent
with our moral instincts. The inconsistencies and contradictions in his approach abound, rendering it, in the word of a prominent member of the audience at Emerson's "Nature" address, "incoherent."[12] Emerson, Louis Menand
concludes, "used the concept of intuition as an excuse for abandoning sys-
tematic thinking altogether."[13]

If it is fair, then, to subject Emerson to the same requirements of logic and
consistency that constrict non-mystics whose views he challenges, consider
the compatibility of the two principal strands in his thought. On the one
hand, he preached certainty. (*Preached* is the right word; Emerson was formerly a Unitarian minister.) Absolute truth exists. It does not change over
time. It is the same everywhere. It mandates a universal morality, a worldide
higher law that at once condemns lying, stealing, and murder along with
slavery and other malignities. "Fundamental perceptions are intuitive and
inarguable,"[14] his leading biographer, Robert Richardson, puts it. This universality makes it possible to evaluate societies past and present on an objective moral scale. It also makes it possible to assess human progress: some
societies are morally superior to others.

The case in point for Emerson was, again, the United States under the fugitive slave law. It presented, for him, the ultimate teachable moment, "a university to the entire people. It has turned every dinner-table into a debating-club,
and made every citizen a student of natural law."[15] The only citizens who
seemed to be failing as students of this version of natural law were the lawyers
responsible for enforcing that pernicious edict. "I am surprised that lawyers
can be so blind as to suffer the principles of Law to be discredited," Emerson
said. "A few months ago, in my dismay at hearing that the Higher Law was
reckoned a good joke in the courts, I took pains to look into a few law-books.
I had often heard that the Bible constituted a part of every technical law library, and that it was a principle in law that immoral laws are void."[16] Even
a layman, he insisted, could recognize the accessibility and priority of natural law. "I found, accordingly, that the great jurists, Cicero, Grotius, Coke,
Blackstone, Burlamaqui, Montesquieu, Vattel, Burke, Mackintosh, Jefferson,
do all affirm this." Natural law is out there, awaiting discovery, and it prevails
over any incompatible human-made law.

Yet at the same time Emerson preached individualism. He believed that
the purpose of life, as Richardson explains, "is individual self-cultivation,
self-expression, and self-fulfillment."[17] Each individual senses natural law

intuitively, Emerson believed: "A man is the façade of a temple, wherein all wisdom and all good abide." Never doubt your own instincts. "You are the measure of the world, of right, of truth, of beauty."[18] Critics must be ignored. "We know truth when we see it, let the skeptic and scoffer say what they choose."[19] All that is necessary is to be open to the truth, the "universal voice" that speaks to "every heart" that listens.[20] Certainty that you are right is a sign of intelligence: "Believe what is true for you in your own private heart is true for all men—that is genius." That truth forms a common bond among the awakened: a "well awake" man "links himself naturally to his brothers, as bees hook."[21]

How is this truth to be found? By looking inward, with confidence in one's connection to the Over-soul: "Trust thyself every heart vibrates to that iron string."[22] Because this self-evident moral insight can be gleaned directly through intuition, no guidance is needed from "expert" intermediaries in the form of clergy and academics. Books and tradition are unneeded. The wise man, Emerson wrote, "needs no library, for he has not done thinking; no church, for he is a prophet; no statute-book, for he has the lawgiver."[23] "[O]ur spontaneous action is always the best.[24]" Look up to no one, past or present. "Go alone," he urged in his 1838 Divinity School address, "and refuse good models."[25]

The contradiction in Emerson's simultaneous embrace of both individual intuition and absolute truth need hardly be pointed out. Cannot perceptive, well-meaning individuals who act in good faith arrive at reasonable differences of opinion? How can every individual intuition be equally valid if validity lies in only one absolute truth?

In the end, Emerson seemed to resolve the clash by choosing absolute truth over individualism. Traditional notions of personal freedom had to give way in the face of absolutist intuitions. Compromise with falsehood must be rejected. Correct thinking required the "recognition of higher rights than those of personal freedom, or the security of property."[26] Instinctive, spontaneous moral insights must prevail over misguided civil and political liberties. Thus "the Constitution and the law in America must be written on ethical principles, so that the entire power of the spiritual world shall hold the citizen loyal, and repel the enemy as by force of nature."[27] A realization of the Good is possible only when the "well awake" come together to cast off stale social structures. Millennial collectivist projects that Emerson supported, such as Brook Farm and Fruitlands, pointed the way for hopeful transcendentalists through enlightened experiments in socialism. Forging this brighter world required demolishing the old, darker world from the ground up. "We are to revise the whole of our social structure, the state, the school, religion, marriage, trade, science, and explore their foundations in our own nature," he insisted. The task is to ensure that the world "fits for us, and to clear ourselves of every usage which has not its root in our own mind."[28]

It is no accident that Emerson, like Plato before him, appeared to turn away from personal freedom that stood in the way of universal truth. Plato was, in the words of his latter-day nemesis Karl Popper,[29] "the embodiment of an unmitigated authoritarianism," an enemy of democracy who believed people incapable of governing themselves and exalted rule by expert "philosopher kings" whose "noble lies" would help prevent confusion and keep ignorant masses subservient. Plato laid out a "multi-faceted mind-control scheme," as Eric Berkowitz has described. In Plato's ideal Republic, art is a tool of state policy. Poetry that depicts the gods as brutal is strictly forbidden, as is poetry that depicts heroes grieving the deaths of comrades or poetry suggesting that evil pays or that good goes unrewarded. Theater is tightly controlled to prevent any encouragement to those who would disobey rulers or disrespect the gods. The task of Plato's artist is to shore up the state, not to stimulate free thought or creativity.[30]

Nor was it an accident that, in selecting the historic figure who best represents democracy, Emerson chose Napoleon. "The instinct of active, brave, able men, throughout the middle class everywhere has pointed out Napoleon as the incarnate Democrat," Emerson wrote. "He had their virtues and their vices; above all, he had their spirit or aim."[31]

Emerson's Napoleon provides a sobering insight into the implications of Emersonian intuitionism. Napoleon, Emerson acknowledges, was a flawed personality. He was unjust, dishonest, credit-stealing, intriguing, calculating, fame-seeking, friendless, egotistical, unscrupulous, ill-mannered, selfish, and ungentlemanly. But these were *personal* flaws, and they were not Napoleon's fault; he "did all that in him lay."[32] Napoleon's *methods*, reliant only upon his own intuition, were fundamentally sound. They were, indeed, the source of his genius. Napoleon eschewed the advice of counselors, the importuning of the benighted masses who followed him, and the guidance of tradition, process, and institutions. He knew what ends were best and had no scruple as to means. "He had a directness of action never before combined with so much comprehension. . . . He is strong in the right manner, namely, by insight."[33] His principal means were in himself. "He asks counsel of no other."[34] Napoleon was a destroyer of prescription and tradition—naturally the dull and conservative English would hate him. Horrible anecdotes may be collected from his history, but these are the necessary price of his successes. This does not mean that he was cruel, but only that there could be no impediment to his will. In Napoleon, a natural king had become a titular king. There were many working kings before him, but none who accomplished a tenth of what Napoleon achieved. By "transcending the ordinary limits of human ability,"[35] he wonderfully encouraged and liberated us. Never was a leader more endowed. Napoleon "knew better than society; and, moreover, knew that he knew better."[36] He knew that the institutions that people so loudly praised were mere ornaments. He "relied on his own sense, and did not care a bean for other people's."[37] He was, in sum, the perfect transcendentalist.

What Emerson omits is that Napoleon was Europe's censor extraordinaire, as Berkowitz points out. "If I allowed a free press, I would not be in power for another three months," Napoleon said. "Four hostile newspapers are more to be feared than a thousand bayonets." Two months after taking power in 1799 he closed fifty of Paris's sixty-three newspapers. No French military defeat could be reported. He banned the words "usurper," "tyrant," and "social compact" and outlawed the works of Tacitus, fearing that the Roman historian's condemnation of tyrants would cast him in a bad light.[38]

For Emerson, the possibility—indeed, the requirement—of individuated discovery of universal truth eliminated any need for discussion or dialogue. Everyone was equally able to tap into the repository of absolute truth, the Over-soul, and would thus arrive in unison at the same moral conclusions.[39] Though Emerson occasionally referred to the utility of speech, the communication he had in mind was not conversation, deliberation, or dialogue; it was one-way speech, an "imparting" of truth akin to the unveiling of a statue by a sculptor. Consider the notion of self-expression set out in the Divinity School address:

> It is very certain that it is the effect of conversation with the beauty of the soul, to beget a desire and need to impart to others the same knowledge and love. If utterance is denied, the thought lies like a burden on the man. Always the seer is a sayer. Somehow his dream is told: somehow he publishes it with solemn joy: sometimes with pencil on canvas; sometimes with chisel on stone; sometimes in towers and aisles of granite, his soul's worship is builded; sometimes in anthems of indefinite music; but clearest and most permanent, in words.[40]

Emerson's belief is that speech is useful simply to *proclaim* and *assert* truth that is discovered, not to float a hypothesis to be subjected to debate and deliberation; what need is there for collaboration among individuals who have a direct line to truth? One prominent critic of Emerson, Kerry Larson, put it this way:

> Those who fail to understand the dangers of certainty, *On Liberty* warns, also fail to appreciate the social benefits of disagreement and dissent. Emerson confirms the correlation. Taking truth to be that which is self-evident, he does not enshrine disagreement as a public good. Far from upholding the importance of controversy and contention in the marketplace of ideas, Emerson consistently deprecates the notion. Disagreement among clashing parties does not indicate a robust, healthy society but is instead a sign of misdirected energy and misplaced priorities.[41]

Even at an early age, Emerson's certitude did not sit well with his young acolyte Oliver Wendell Holmes Jr. It is commonly believed that Holmes's experience in the Civil War destroyed his belief in absolute truth. In fact, Holmes had begun to question Emerson's beliefs even before he set off to war. Those doubts became evident in a student paper Holmes wrote that criticized Plato, which he showed to Emerson, who disapproved. Holmes was of course aware of Emerson's admiration for Plato; Holmes himself was drawn to Plato, he told Learned Hand in 1924, in the hope that in Plato he would find "the secrets of the life revealed."[42] Holmes did not yet, in his 1860 essay, challenge the central tenets of Emerson's idealism, but he laid out the glimmerings of a commitment to empiricism and science that would later blossom into a rationale for protecting a competition among ideas. Some truths, such as those relating to mathematics and perhaps beauty, Holmes speculated, are "necessary ideas permanently existing in the mind of the Creator."[43] The "immutability" of these ideas Holmes at the time considered beyond challenge. From these seminal truths, other, related truths may be inferred. Beauty is "the most sensible presentation" of the Good, he wrote. His transcendentalist instincts remained intact: "Every being that is mortal desires and earnestly strives to partake of these verities which are alone immortal."[44] Yet Holmes unveiled a budding appreciation of empiricism—and found Plato deficient in his ignorance of "science" and disregard of "data." Plato's reliance upon data-free "logic" is circular, Holmes wrote, a "drawing of conclusions already contained in the premise."[45] This "unhappy fallacy . . . runs all through

Plato."[46] The result is a "confused and doubtful" system, "loose and unscientific" in its methods and in need of "a complete remodeling before it would suffice as a sufficient cosmology."[47]

Holmes should hardly have been surprised at Emerson's cool reaction to his essay. "When you strike at a king, you must kill him," Emerson advised.[48] Holmes, who later said he "felt damn bad" at Emerson's response,[49] never seemed to wonder whether Emerson might have been referring to himself.

4

Holmes's Excursion into Doubt

We have no detailed record of the conversation that occurred between Holmes and Emerson that summer evening in 1864, but it seemed to clarify Holmes's thinking on the immediate question before him. Years later, he recollected that the discussion convinced him a career such as Emerson's was too far removed from the roar and battle of life to satisfy him.[1] Law it would be. As to larger issues, Holmes's verdict on Emerson's ideas would be delivered over the course of a lifetime.[2] Emerson's certitude, Holmes would conclude, was unfounded. Holmes never regretted his service in the Civil War, but he did come to realize that there is a safer way to resolve conflict.

Holmes's Plato paper won the prize for best undergraduate essay of the year. For a nineteen-year-old, it is a prepossessing piece of work. It marked the beginning of a deepening skepticism. His thinking ran increasingly opposite Emerson's, whom he came to regard, as noted earlier, as a poet, not a thinker.[3] "[E]poch-making ideas," he said, "have come not from the poets but from the philosophers, the jurists, the mathematicians, the physicists, the doctors—from the men who explain, not from the men who feel."[4] Holmes came to doubt "the Absolute of transcendental idealism," as his friend William James described Emersonian pantheism.[5] "I do not know what is true," Holmes said in 1895. "I do not know the meaning of the universe."[6]

Holmes's doubts were the doubts of an agnostic, not an atheist. He did not believe that it could be proven to a certainty that absolute truth does not exist—he believed *certain* doubt was itself a form of absolute truth—but he came to regard the matter as a question of probability and observed repeatedly that, based on evidence gained from experience, he had never heard a convincing case for absolute truth. Yet he left open the possibility that such a case could be made. When the newly inaugurated President Franklin D. Roosevelt visited Holmes on his ninety-third birthday and asked what he was reading, Holmes said Plato. There was always a chance, Holmes seemed to think, that he might have missed something. Yet there was something that could nonetheless provisionally be *called* truth, and while provisional truth was by definition uncertain, it was likely enough to bet on. This is why, as

Free Speech and Turbulent Freedom. Michael J. Glennon, Oxford University Press. © Oxford University Press 2024.
DOI: 10.1093/oso/9780197636763.003.0004

an iconoclastic legal scholar, dissenting judge, and defender of dissidents, Holmes came increasingly to favor a tentative, experimental individualism over absolute certainty. The irony was that his very skepticism about the certainty of absolutist natural rights philosophies would itself provide a more defensible foundation for freedom of speech: it was doubt itself that drove Holmes's appreciation of variety, and variety that drove his appreciation of a free exchange of ideas.

"Delusory exactness," Holmes wrote in 1921, "is a source of fallacy throughout the law."[7] Illusory precision masked what judges' decisions were actually based on, and it undercut democracy when judges imposed personal ideologies on an unknowing or resistant public. Holmes's lifelong quest as a scholar and jurist was to root delusory exactness out of American law. He started early by debunking myths about the common law and arrived late with the signature constitutional opinions of his career, on freedom of speech. But his effort was constant: to make the law the clearest it can be in the face of intractable epistemic uncertainty.

To Holmes, a chief source of illusion originated, as such problems often do, in the educational system—in the way law was taught in his time. That meant, specifically, the way law schools smugly taught judge-made law, called "common law." Legal education, in those days, consisted entirely of the study of judges' opinions written in appeals from lower court decisions. In these cases, appellate judges looked to earlier cases that presented similar facts, inferred holdings from these cases, pieced together those holdings in a single principle, and applied that principle to the current facts. This had been the legal method in England since 1066, when the victorious Normans applied the same precedents throughout the land (rendering it "common"). Judges applied the common law of England in its North American colonies, using the same technique of inducing a principle from prior cases and then applying that major premise deductively to the facts of subsequent cases. The grand architect of nineteenth-century American legal education, Professor Christopher Langdell of the Harvard Law School, believed that law could be learned exclusively through the study of these cases. His "casebooks," and those of his faculty colleagues, were literally that; they relied entirely on opinions written by appellate judges who purported to spell out a complete account of the reasons they decided cases as they did. Every relevant reason for the decision, the theory was, had been included in the judge's opinion. No other materials were necessary to understand the law. "[A]ll the available materials of [legal] science are contained in printed books," Langdell proclaimed.[8]

Holmes wrote a friend in 1881 that Langdell "represents the powers of darkness."[9] He referred to Langdell as "the greatest living theologian" of American law.[10] Langdell, like many if not most of the judges whose opinions his casebooks contained, believed that those opinions were not products of the judges' own intellects and emotions but rather immutable principles that the judges had discovered, out there, with the guidance of logic. They believed, in effect, that a glimmering, ideal legal regime existed beyond the shifting shadows on the wall of the cave, a regime that consisted of eternal principles ordained by the Creator himself. The common law did not consist of law made by judges; it consisted of "natural" law *found* by judges.

To Holmes, this was of course poppycock, as was the conceit that every reason for a judicial decision was or ever could be included in the judge's opinion. Judicial behavior was no different from any other human behavior; a realistic approach required identifying everything that motivated judges to do what they do and to predict their actions in light of all material, real-world influences. Holmes had no objection to the common law method of reasoning by analogy, induction, and deduction. He was agile at it. But Holmes the judge was no longer the true believer who had rushed to enlist in the Union cause. The image of judges as unerring Platonic guardians who looked solely to timeless morality braided with legal logic was anathema to everything he now believed. The common law was not "a brooding omnipresence in the sky,"[11] he famously wrote. And judges were not guided exclusively by syllogisms. "The life of the law is not logic but experience." These are among the most famous words in American jurisprudence. They denote Holmes's commitment to empiricism, to the belief that, as he explained,

> [t]he felt necessities of the time, the prevalent moral and political theories, intuitions of public policy, avowed or unconscious, even the prejudices which judges share with their fellow-men, have had a good deal more to do than the syllogism in determining the rules by which men should be governed. The law embodies the story of a nation's development through many centuries, and it cannot be dealt with as if it contained only the axioms and corollaries of a book of mathematics. In order to know what it is, we must know what it has been, and what it tends to become. We must alternately consult history and existing theories of legislation. But the most difficult labor will be to understand the combination of the two into new products at every stage.[12]

The common law, Holmes believed, is not eternal or static but constantly evolving as it confronts the need to choose among competing principles that bubble up from lower courts. "It is forever adopting new principles from life at one end, and always retains old ones from history at the other."[13] Sometimes we conclude that even large and important branches of the law are remnants "from more primitive times." In such instances, our earlier, provisional truths are properly modified: "We have a right to reconsider the popular reasons, and . . . to decide anew whether those reasons are satisfactory. . . . If truth were not often suggested by error, if old implements could not be adjusted to new uses, human progress would be slow. But scrutiny and revision are justified."[14] Human progress proceeds haltingly by trial and error. It is a mistake to think we have ever arrived at unchangeable truth. Such a view is *unscientific*. Just as no competent scientist after Darwin could believe that the world had at long last *arrived* at a point of stasis, no competent judge could believe that any judicial opinion settled matters for all time. Holmes, as Vincent Blasi has noted, "associated the rejection of absolutist thinking with the scientific method."[15]

Holmes's commitment to fallibilism and provisionality seems to trace to an early, lifelong interest in Darwin and, more generally, to an appreciation of science, with its emphasis on hypothesis, experimentation, revision, and probabilistic calculation.[16] If, as some believe, the zeitgeist of one's college years has a lifelong impact on one's political and social views, the world's new earth-shattering idea during Holmes's student days was evolution. Darwin's *The Origin of Species* was published in 1859, when Holmes was a junior at Harvard. The book upended thousands of years of religious, scientific, and, ultimately, political and social thought, challenging humanity's fundamental understanding of reality. During his college years, its ideas were "in the air," as he put it.[17] Debate over Darwin's radical, heretical theory raged on the Harvard campus. Few faculty accepted it,[18] but Holmes was persuaded. "Time," Holmes learned, "has upset many scientific laws. . . . [N]o matter how elegant and coherent the explanation and supportive the current data, we might be wrong.[19]" Holmes, writes Blasi, "associated the rejection of absolutist thinking with the scientific method." He wrote in 1919 that "it was the influence of the scientific way of looking at the world" that shaped his view of truth.[20] Provisional truths, like scientific hypotheses, are always subject to reconsideration. "Every original book has the seeds of its own death in it, by provoking further investigation and clearer restatement."[21] His pragmatist friends joined this thinking. John Dewey exalted "the experimental method as the method of getting knowledge"—a method of "making sure it *is* knowledge and not mere opinion."[22] "The development of biology clinches this lesson," Dewey wrote, "with its discovery of evolution."[23] Yet pluralism was undervalued. James faulted traditional philosophers for striving in unison to "clean up the litter" with "pure and definite theories," overlooking the value in the "sensible tangle" that his own "pluralistic empiricism" appreciated.[24] Science, to Holmes and Dewey, was relentlessly tentative.[25]

This tentativeness suffused Holmes's judicial approach. It reflected his recognition of judicial fallibility and his disdain for pretensions of eternal insight on the part of "arrogant" federal judges, as he described them,[26] who believed they could disregard the rules of state law and substitute their own. Holmes believed that it was folly to deny that judges made law and folly to think that in making law the judges "discovered" ultimate truth. There existed, in his view, "no mystic over law to which even the United States must bow."[27] Judges who purported to discover such law thought of themselves as "independent mouthpieces of the infinite."[28] They believed, redolent of Emerson, that there existed "a transcendental body of law outside of any particular state" that constituted a single unit of supreme authority.[29] "But there is no such body of law," he wrote.[30] Federal judges engaged in the common law method were making law up, not discovering it or merely "applying" preexisting precedents. Judge-made rules were policy choices, like other rules. Where did the first precedents come from when the common law was in its infancy? Where did the answer come from when two precedents conflicted, or when no precedent was on point? Of course judges in such cases were *creating* law—no preexisting law was to be found.

What Holmes saw as further judicial arrogance sparked his landmark 1905 dissent in *Lochner v. New York*, a case involving not the application of common law but the interpretation of the Constitution. But here, too, judges seemed to think they had uniquely superior insights into timeless morality. Early in the twentieth century, federal courts consistently struck down regulatory statutes seemingly at odds with principles of natural selection and survival of the fittest that animated economic theories popular within the judiciary. *Lochner* is the most infamous of these cases. In it, the Supreme Court invalidated a New York statute that, for health reasons, limited the number of hours that bakers were permitted to work. The Court ostensibly grounded its decision on the Constitution's contract clause, which prohibits the enactment of any law "impairing the obligation of contracts."[31] Holmes dissented. So broad a construction of the contract clause, he wrote, would place in legal peril a vast range of state regulatory legislation. The real reason for the Court's objection to the New York law, he suggested, lay in the justices' embrace of laissez-faire ideologies such as those promulgated by Herbert Spencer. (One leading Oxford philosopher, G. E. Moore, interpreted Spencer as arguing that the natural phenomena Spencer described were sources of moral obligation.)[32] Spencer may or may not have been correct, Holmes wrote, but a large part of the country did not entertain his views, and it was not for the Court to decide who was right.

The Constitution, wrote Holmes, "does not enact Mr. Herbert Spencer's Social Statics. . . . [A] constitution is not intended to embody a particular economic theory. . . . [I]t is made for people of fundamentally different views."[33] The question, he wrote, is not whether Spencer's views are "natural" but whether a statute rejecting them conflicts with the Constitution. Holmes's answer was no. The Constitution ought not be interpreted as commanding allegiance to some external corpus of economic rights and wrongs supposedly accessible to right-thinking judges but not legislators. If the people's elected representatives believe that some eternal body of truth exists that mandates Spencer's economic theories, they are free to adopt it. They may be wrong. If so, their law can always be changed. But to constitutionalize such a theory would be to etch it into our sacred national writ. This the Framers did not do, and it was not for judges to presume to correct their oversight.

The strands of Holmes's skepticism, as it matured, came together in an approach known as pragmatism, though he himself apparently never used the term to describe his thinking. These strands weave throughout his letters, writings, and judicial opinions and form the basis of his embrace of freedom of speech. The pragmatist approach to law[34] connotes more than the colloquial sense of the term, which implies mere practicality, common sense, and levelheadedness. The juridical concept refers to a multifaceted method of problem-solving rather than a formula for finding a single, correct solution. Pragmatism does not tell us "what we should want to want,"[35] as Holmes put it. It offers no "field theory" of ultimate truth or good. Pragmatists believe that any belief is potentially mistaken, that "correct" outcomes cannot be deduced from foundational principles, and that every belief must be open to scrutiny. Pragmatists recognize that people inevitably have different notions of what is important in life. They therefore accept the need for law that takes the form of tentative, contingent hypotheses that balance competing interests based upon people's changing wants and needs. Pragmatists see these different visions as a product of forces that lie largely beyond the individual's control. They thus believe that many legal problems are actually problems of culture or history or economics or power, that a mix of these forces shapes the socialization of antagonists, and that conflict is largely unavoidable. For these reasons, pragmatists are not utopians. They believe that the best that can be done by the law is often the minimization of consequences of human differences, so that we can muddle through as best we can. To pragmatists, the solutions to difficult legal questions are practical rather than ideological. Ideologues devise solutions by looking only to costs or only to benefits; pragmatists examine both and weigh one against the other. Choice, wrote the pragmatist philosopher Richard Rorty, is "always a matter of compromise between competing goods, rather than a choice between the absolutely right and the absolutely wrong."[36] The crucial question for pragmatists is, therefore, "Compared to what?" Pragmatists find variety essential to assess, comparatively, how preferences can best be fulfilled. Solutions most likely to adapt and survive can be tested only side by side against alternatives. To pragmatists, the value of an idea is thus assessed not by measuring it against other ideas but by assessing the probable future consequences of *applying* the idea, recognizing that every solution's value will vary as the facts to which it applies vary.[37]

These are the themes that recur throughout Holmes's thought and that of other pragmatists. Holmes doubted that universal, *absolute* truth that is out there—or "within," as Emerson would have it—was waiting to be discovered. "Certitude is not the test of certainty," he famously wrote.[38] We may *feel* certain that our beliefs are true—we may have a sense of certitude—but certainty that we are right does not make us right. "I don't believe or know anything about absolute truth."[39] Holmes saw no reason to believe that one person's insights into the meaning of the cosmos or ultimate right and wrong are any more accurate than anyone else's. "Men to a great extent believe what they want to—although I see in that no basis for a philosophy that tells us what we should want to want."[40] Natural law philosophies do not succeed in doing so because the "means do not exist for determinations that shall be good for all time":[41] the "search for criteria of universal validity"[42]is a search that leads in circles.

Holmes's skepticism about accessible criteria anticipated an approach elaborated by Karl Popper in his 1945 magnum opus, *The Open Society and Its Enemies.* One of the twentieth century's leading defenders of liberal democracy, Popper, as noted in Chapter 3, took strong issue with notions of Platonic idealism. It's not possible, he argued, to know absolute truth. To do so would require knowing the criteria by which absolute truth is to be identified—it would require, in other words, a criterion philosophy. But by what criteria might a criterion philosophy be identified? Only by an antecedent, higher-order criterion philosophy, creating an infinite regress that would produce no answer. Absolute certainty, Popper believed, is thus never attainable.

Yet in Holmes's view it was still possible to use the word *truth* meaningfully—not as connoting certainty but as implying degrees of probability. Provisional truth is open to reassessment and revision. It consists of the "felt necessities of the times"[43]—times and necessities that change. "I mean by truth simply what I can't help accepting," he often said.[44] We can't help accepting some things provisionally, not because their recurrence is certain but because it is *likely*—we can bet on it. Holmes called himself a "bettabilitarian," meaning that he settled for truth simply as something likely enough to bet on,[45] something one "can't help" believing: "I believe that we can *bet* on the behavior of the universe in its contact with us. We bet we can know what it will be."[46] At one level it makes no difference whether truth is absolute or provisional, as he believed it was. We can still fight for the world we want to live in—as he had. But at a deeper level, if we disagree or even choose to fight, we may do so with a bit more humility. "When you know that you know persecution comes easy. It is well that some of us don't know that we know anything," he wrote to a friend.[47] We are, in a word, fallible. Law professor John Inazu has suggested that recognition that the "[o]ne unchanged aspect of the human condition is our inability to know with certainty" led Holmes to a stance of "epistemic humility" that promotes a more productive and charitable social discourse.[48] Holmes's recognition of fallibility, as we will see in the next chapter, led directly to his belief in the need to protect freedom of speech, a connection emphasized by John Stuart Mill (with whom Holmes dined while visiting London as a young man). Mill wrote in *On Liberty*, "We can never be sure that the opinion we are endeavoring to stifle is a false opinion. . . . Complete liberty of contradicting and disproving our opinion, is the very condition which justifies us in assuming its truth for purposes of action."[49]

Whatever its origins, Holmes's view of truth as provisional was, again, very close to that later propounded by Popper. Even though there can be no general criterion of truth, we can—without needing a criterion theory—specify the *conditions* under which we choose to regard a statement as true. That is, in fact, what we do throughout the day. We specify the conditions, Popper wrote, under which we regard a person as having tuberculosis, or meat as having gone bad, or one crowd as being larger or smaller than another. Often this is done unthinkingly; life would be impossible without making numerous assumptions that are never questioned as we go about our daily affairs, assumptions that we regard as "true" for purposes of convenience or practicality. Most people implicitly adopt a "correspondence theory" of truth, assuming simply that what's true is what corresponds to the facts as we perceive them, to "what is the case." But that's a bit tautological, and most seemingly basic truths turn out, on analysis, to be conditional. We can therefore, as Popper wrote, "get nearer to the truth"[50] even though we can never know it in any objective or absolute sense. That truth and certainty are not coextensive is significant. "The question is not certainty," law professor Frederick Schauer notes, "but epistemic advance. . . . [B]y characterizing the advance of knowledge as the continual process of exposing error, Popper frees the argument from truth from the problem of certainty."[51]

For Holmes, this difference is critical. We *choose*[52] the conditions by which to identify truth, meaning "that we can always err in our choice—that we can always miss the truth or fall short of the truth; that certainty is not for us. . . ; that we are fallible."[53] What, then, are we to accept? Again, Popper: "The answer is: whatever we accept we should trust only tentatively, remembering that we are in possession, at best, of partial truth (or rightness), and that we are bound to make at least some mistake or misjudgment somewhere—not only with respect to facts but also with respect to the adopted standards."[54] Holmes, surely, would have agreed. Recent commentators have used different vocabularies to describe provisional truth, but the notion of provisionality is much the same. Stephen Smith, for example, refers to "practical certainty" as

> something approximating certainty. Ideas which have been thoroughly investigated and found to be true are at least very likely to be true; ideas which are self-contradictory, or incompatible with experience, evidence or other confirmed beliefs are very likely to be false. "Practical" certainty also suggests certainty which is sufficient for practical purposes—certainty which is strong enough to serve as a basis for personal or public decisions and actions.[55]

For reasons such as these, Holmes thought it improper for judges to substitute their own personal intuitions of morality for the morality of the community as embodied in a statute. Neither judges nor the community tapped into eternal truth in resolving political problems. Each floated hypotheses, tentative solutions to changing social conditions, that could and should be reassessed as conditions changed. To set in stone notions of absolute truth would transform the law into a rigid, partisan set of ethical opinions that blocked social adaptation. Unless the Constitution is violated, therefore, it is the duty of a judge to defer to the public's convictions.[56] The wisdom and morality of a law are the business of the legislature, not the judge. "If my fellow citizens want to go to Hell I will help them," he remarked to Victor Laski. "It's my job."[57]

These were to become the central features of Holmes's thought as it evolved over the course of his career. He could not abide claims of moral certainty. "I detest a man who knows what he knows," he wrote Laski years later.[58] If universal truth is "out there," awaiting discovery by human beings, so far as he could tell it has lain beyond human reach. But he could not and did not rule out the possibility that such truth existed, and he had no objection to continuing the search for it, for "certainty generally is an illusion, and repose is not the destiny of man."[59] As Holmes matured as a judge, the pragmatist cast of his thought became plain: the inevitability of contestation, the inaccessibility of absolute truth, the constancy of change, and the need for continuing experimentation. Fallibilism, probabilism, and contextualism would be his guiding lights. They lit the way to Holmes's most penetrating opinions on the most seminal of issues: freedom of speech.

5

The Pluralist Purposes of the First Amendment

It is ironic that Holmes, the perennial skeptic of certitude, should have become the intellectual architect of the modern First Amendment. The text of the Amendment is, if anything, the constitutional embodiment of "delusory exactness." Its crystalline words shine through law's mist like a ray of sunshine. "The Congress shall make no law," it provides, "abridging the freedom of speech or of the press." On its face it draws the brightest of lines—*no law*. What could be clearer?

Yet the First Amendment plainly doesn't mean exactly what it says, and it's hard to see how it possibly could mean exactly what it says. It does not apply and hasn't been applied to many uses of written and spoken words. Some of the more obvious examples, Schauer has pointed out, are perjury, warnings by robbery lookouts, price-fixing agreements, the mislabeling of prescription drugs, erroneous product instructions, false claims by sellers of securities about prospective investments, and plainly untrue product advertisements.[1] One could add even more: printing a previously undisclosed formula for the hydrogen bomb, standing on the steps of an inadequately guarded jail and urging a mob to lynch a prisoner.[2] Why the exceptions? They stem from historical practice, ad hoc policy judgments, and sheer common sense, as illustrated by Holmes's oft-quoted reference to falsely shouting fire in a crowded theater.[3] The First Amendment simply can't mean exactly what it says.

What was it *intended* to mean? For Holmes, the question had limited significance. Holmes was not an originalist, which is to say he did not give controlling weight to the meaning attached to a constitutional provision by the Framers. He made clear his views on the matter in an important 1920 case, *Missouri v. Holland,* concerning the effect of the Tenth Amendment on the scope of the treaty power.[4] The case raised the question whether the limits imposed by the Tenth Amendment on treaties were the same as the limits it imposed on federal statutes; if so, the United States would be disabled from entering into a growing range of treaties, concerning topics such as human

Free Speech and Turbulent Freedom. Michael J. Glennon, Oxford University Press. © Oxford University Press 2024.
DOI: 10.1093/oso/9780197636763.003.0005

rights and environmental protection, to which other nations increasingly sought U.S. consent.[5] Writing for the Court, Holmes said that in dealing with the words of the Constitution, "we must realize that they have called into life a being the development of which could not have been foreseen completely by the most gifted of its begetters," and that the case therefore had to be "considered in the light of our whole experience and not merely in that of what was said a hundred years ago."[6] Holmes had no greater inclination to delve into the Framers' specific intent concerning the purposes of the First Amendment than he did their intent concerning the purposes of the Tenth Amendment—and, had he done so, he would have found little illumination. Recall that the original Constitution contained no Bill of Rights; the First Amendment was ratified in 1791 with the other nine, four years after the Philadelphia Convention. Constitutional scholars seeking to understand the intent of the Framers of the Amendment[7] have regularly lamented the paltry documentation during its consideration by Congress[8] and the states.[9] Benjamin Franklin probably spoke for many of his contemporaries in commenting on the First Amendment's meaning: "Few of us, I believe, have any distinct Ideas of its Nature and Extent."[10]

Left with this largely blank slate, in the few cases where the issue arose, the Court regarded speech as unprotected under the First Amendment if it had a "bad tendency." Under that test, judges asked whether the speech in question could tend at some indeterminate future point to bring about unlawful conduct.[11] In practice, the test tended, not surprisingly, to reflect judges' intuitive belief that their own moral instincts provided a sure guide in determining what people should be allowed to say. Speech that had a tendency to produce undesirable consequences could therefore be suppressed.

Holmes's own predilection as a judge had been to defer to the popular will as expressed in legislation; this, he believed, was the mandate of a democratic system. He had no desire to "Lochnerize" the First Amendment, i.e., to use it as the due process clause had been used to invalidate legislation based on judges' moral or political philosophy—even his own. He therefore was slow in coming to question legislative curbs on free speech, particularly during the First World War. Indeed, as noted in Chapter 7 of this book, Holmes himself authored opinions for the Court in two controversial wartime cases that found defendants guilty of violating the Espionage Act for comments that by today's standards would be dismissed as insipid.

A fateful, chance meeting on a train with Judge Learned Hand, however, set in motion a series of conversations that led Holmes to change his mind.

Referring later to an earlier, inconsistent opinion he'd written while a justice on the Massachusetts Supreme Judicial Court, Holmes wrote, "I was simply ignorant."[12] The story is well told in Thomas Healy's fine book, *The Great Dissent*. Hand strove to convince Holmes of his error, as did several of Holmes's friends over the coming days, and they succeeded.[13]

Holmes corrected his course in *Abrams v. United States* (1919).[14] The United States had been allied with czarist Russia in the war against Germany, but when the Bolsheviks gained control of the government in 1917, the Russian government signed a peace treaty with Germany. The next year, the United States, claiming the need to maintain an eastern front against Germany, sent a contingent of marines to Vladivostok and Murmansk. The defendants in *Abrams*, poverty-stricken Russian immigrants to the United States, published and circulated two leaflets, one in Yiddish, arguing that the United States was trying to crush the Russian Revolution and calling for a general strike. They were convicted under the Sedition Act of 1918, sentenced to ten to twenty years in prison, and appealed to the U.S. Supreme Court.

The crime, as Holmes described it, was "the surreptitious publishing of a silly leaflet by an unknown man."[15] Joined by Justice Louis Brandeis, Holmes filed what would become the most influential dissent in American law,[16] laying out the conceptual framework of modern First Amendment law by sketching out, for the first time, the image of a marketplace of ideas. Because of its seminal importance, a fuller excerpt is in order:

> Persecution for the expression of opinions seems to me perfectly logical. If you have no doubt of your premises or your power and want a certain result with all your heart you naturally express your wishes in law and sweep away all opposition. To allow opposition by speech seems to indicate that you think the speech impotent, as when a man says that he has squared the circle, or that you do not care whole heartedly for the result, or that you doubt either your power or your premises. But when men have realized that time has upset many fighting faiths, they may come to believe even more than they believe the very foundations of their own conduct that the ultimate good desired is better reached by free trade in ideas—that the best test of truth is the power of the thought to get itself accepted in the competition of the market, and that truth is the only ground upon which their wishes safely can be carried out. That at any rate is the theory of our Constitution. It is an experiment, as all life is an experiment. Every year if not every day

we have to wager our salvation upon some prophecy based upon imperfect knowledge. While that experiment is part of our system I think that we should be eternally vigilant against attempts to check the expression of opinions that we loathe and believe to be fraught with death, unless they so imminently threaten immediate interference with the lawful and pressing purposes of the law that an immediate check is required to save the country. I wholly disagree with the argument of the Government that the First Amendment left the common law as to seditious libel in force. History seems to me against the notion. I had conceived that the United States through many years had shown its repentance for the Sedition Act of 1798 (Act July 14, 1798, c. 73, 1 Stat. 596), by repaying fines that it imposed. Only the emergency that makes it immediately dangerous to leave the correction of evil counsels to time warrants making any exception to the sweeping command, "Congress shall make no law abridging the freedom of speech." Of course I am speaking only of expressions of opinion and exhortations, which were all that were uttered here, but I regret that I cannot put into more impressive words my belief that in their conviction upon this indictment the defendants were deprived of their rights under the Constitution of the United States.

The key word in the opinion is *safely*. It signifies that Holmes is addressing a societal interest, not merely an individual right. We consider the marketplace of ideas the safest bet because our uncertainty as to what is true counsels a need for *variety*, permitting potential alternatives to be considered. The marketplace provides a range of possibilities from which we can more safely forge our own opinions—but not only opinions. Holmes seems to have in mind something more than a trading ground for ideas; he seems to contemplate something in the nature of a public-policy factory, a *safe* consensus-building mechanism carved into the bedrock of our law. The mechanism's aim is not to "find" anything, least of all absolute truth, which, Holmes believed, may or may not exist; if it does exist, it could hardly rest for its existence upon the shifting sands of a market. The aim, rather, is to create a consensus based upon bets about the future that is grounded on experience—the *community's* experience, which is, Holmes suggests, the safest and most stable way to deal with social change. Competition among opinions doesn't *discover*; it *produces*. And what it produces is impermanent, forever giving way to new, provisional truth. Freedom of speech, for Holmes, is a mechanism for attitudinal adaptation, as Vincent Blasi observes, a method of advancing majority

THE PLURALIST PURPOSES OF THE FIRST AMENDMENT

rule by weeding out obsolete ways of thinking and generating new ones. It is a "force for collective adaptation,"[17] a way of facilitating stable social change.

Holmes's key concern is thus safety. The dissent owes its staying power to its focus not on the intent of the Framers but on the social utility of free speech. "We permit free expression because we need the resources of the whole group to get us the ideas we need," as Louis Menand wrote. "Thinking is a social activity. I tolerate your thought because it is part of my thought— even when my thought defines itself in opposition to yours."[18] We ground our action on our wishes and our wishes on truth. Provisional truth is all we have, and we have it because we *make* it together through collective processes, not because we *find* it by ourselves, acting alone. As other provisional truths compete, some are accepted, others are rejected; in that competition, law and policy adapt and evolve.[19] A system that encourages free thought enhances variation, making it easier for society to adopt new ideas that serve common interests and to discard old ones that do not. Those ideas—provisional truths that have stood the test of the marketplace—are the only ones on which society can safely rely. Absolute truths that are imposed on society without the market's test provide a logical rationale for suppression and persecution. It is the greater interests of society, as Stephen Budiansky noted, that are advanced by freedom of speech:

> That Holmes moored freedom of speech not to an individual right of self-expression but to the greater interests of society was precisely the reason his 1919 dissent in *Abrams*, with its soaring invocation of the free trade in ideas, survived even the tempests of cold war politics to be cited more than forty times by the Supreme Court in decisions upholding free speech.[20]

Holmes is thus dismissive of quibbles about the 1791 rationale for the Amendment. He notes, almost in passing, his disagreement with the proposition that the Amendment was intended to permit the punishment of seditious libel—basically, criticism of the government. Rather, the Amendment's purposes are large, noble, and sweeping, having to do with protecting democracy by safeguarding the search for accepted truth and thus keeping open the channels of political change. Holmes's understanding of the Amendment's purpose is that it is one and the same as "the theory of our Constitution."

The reasons for the First Amendment, Holmes suggests, are the reasons animating the entire constitutional framework: the Amendment *encapsulates* the vision that explains the Constitution's entire structure. This is the reason for the dearth of discussion in 1791: that vision didn't need to be re-explained three years later. Many members of the first Congress had also been members of the Philadelphia Convention. The rationale was fresh in everyone's mind in 1791. No one needed to be reminded that the aim was to decentralize power, to prevent the emergence of arbitrary power, to ensure that governing power would be wielded safely by the same people who would be subject to it, and in so doing to respect inevitable differences of opinion. These were the objects of both the First Amendment *and* the Constitution. These are the reasons why power is divided among three branches of the federal government and between the federal government and the fifty states, why checks and balances keep them from encroaching on each other's powers, why we have elections to fill those government offices—and why the *expression* of fundamentally different views is constitutionally protected. *Pluralism* is the premise on which the entire constitutional structure rests.

Consider the arguments made for pluralism in 1787 and 1788 in the *Federalist*—arguments which could with little modification have been made three years later for ratifying the First Amendment. The formation of factions is inevitable, Madison wrote in Federalist 10; the "latent causes of faction are thus sown in the nature of man," resulting in a "zeal for different opinions concerning religion, concerning government, and many other points." These lead people to "vex and oppress each other.... [T]he most frivolous and fanciful distinctions have been sufficient to kindle their unfriendly passions and excite their most violent conflicts." It might be possible to eliminate these differences by suppressing liberty—for "[l]iberty is to faction what air is to fire"—but to do so would be a remedy worse than the disease because liberty "is essential to political life." Differences of opinion are healthy and cannot be eliminated. "It is in vain to say that enlightened statesmen will be able to adjust these clashing interests." The "great security against a gradual concentration" of power, argued Federalist 51, lies in ensuring that power is balanced against power. "Ambition must be made to counteract ambition." The diffusion and decentralization of power animates the entire structure of government. "This policy of supplying, by opposite and rival interests, the defect of better motives, might be traced through the whole system of human affairs, private as well as public."[21]

Protecting plural, competing interests obviously requires protecting individuals' ability to express those interests. "In a free government the security for civil rights must be the same as that for religious rights. It consists in the one case in the multiplicity of interests, and in the other in the multiplicity of sects." These interests might be reflected differently in the different branches of the federal government; hence no one branch, argued Federalist 48, ought to have "an overruling influence" over another. For this reason even the legislature itself is divided. And it is of course a reason for the division of power between the federal government and the states. The "utility and necessity of local administrations, for local purposes," observed Hamilton in Federalist 32, "would be a complete barrier against the oppressive use" of federal power.

Dispersing power into plural sources led inevitably to protecting free speech. William Blackstone, an English judge and scholar, was the foremost authority on the law of free speech at the time of the Constitution's framing;[22] his writing "gripped American thinking."[23] The Framers' scheme of divided authority reflects Blackstone's fear of unchecked, arbitrary power, a concern embodied in his widely quoted belief "Better that ten guilty persons escape than that one innocent suffer." That distrust of power permeated the new constitutional blueprint and led directly to safeguards against censorship, which was antithetical to principles of popular government and civil liberties.[24]

The Supreme Court has often explained the Framers' reasons for structuring the government as they did in terms that also explain why free speech is protected. Those explanations frequently underscore the Framers' deep-seated distrust of concentrated power. Recall, for example, Justice Brandeis's observation that the object of the doctrine of the separation of powers was "to preclude the exercise of arbitrary power" and "to save the people from autocracy,"[25] and Justice Robert Jackson's (and later Justice William Rehnquist's) reminder that the Framers' had no desire to replicate the government of George III.[26] Preventing the rise of autocracy is, of course, one reason for freedom of speech. Such observations of the Framers and the Supreme Court all point to the same conclusion: that the Constitution's decentralized structure and it protection of freedom of speech rest on several identical premises.

The first such premise can be summed up, again, in one word: *pluralism.* "Inevitable friction," as Brandeis put it, is assumed to be part of the struggle for power among the three branches of the federal government and also between the federal government and the states. The Framers believed that conflict within the government, as within the body politic, would be inescapable.

The only way to eliminate that conflict would be to eliminate the oxygen of liberty that fueled it, as Madison recognized.

The second premise is that fractiousness in both government and the body politic is not only inevitable but desirable as a means of avoiding mistakes. The Founders didn't frame their insights in modern terms of cognitive dissonance, pre-deliberation bias, and so forth, but they were familiar with what we now refer to as groupthink. They understood that orthodoxy can be suffocating, in insular government groups as elsewhere. They knew that iconoclasts, naysayers, dissenters, and boat-rockers were necessary to keep the nation's political and intellectual life vibrant. Crackling disagreement within each sphere, they believed, would be invigorating.

The third, related premise is that pluralism promotes legitimacy. The system of divided power in the United States obviously involves Congress; there would be no point in establishing a legislature without giving citizens the means to influence its decisions as to what laws it should make. This requires that citizens of all persuasions be free to exchange views and information, to speak and write and associate freely without fear of retribution. And the converse is true: members of Congress maintain legitimacy through their electoral connection, which would be severed without free and open communication with the electorate. This is a crucial point, to which I return in Chapter 12.

The fourth premise underpinning both freedom of speech and self-government is that the people as a whole are better able than some subgroup to identify and act upon their own best interests. Absent that capacity, there would be no point in having either a marketplace of ideas, which would yield only dross, or a democratic assembly, which would forge that dross into policy.

The fifth and final premise is tolerance. We accept not only speech that we hate but also majoritarian action in governance that we detest because we are accorded the same right to speak and hear, and the same right to form a majority, as those we oppose. Reciprocity is the golden rule of social life. But we also tolerate out of humility. "The spirit of liberty," Judge Hand said, "is the spirit that is not too sure that it is right."[27] We tolerate opposing views because they may turn out to be right.

Holmes was therefore insightful in taking a broad view of the purposes of the First Amendment's protection of free speech. The theory of the constitutional structure of divided powers is also, at bottom, the theory of the

First Amendment. Both rest on the same premises. Both look to plural, decentralized sources of power to provide conflicting information and clashing opinions. Both are directed at preventing the rise of autocracy. Neither can exist without the other: when one is imperiled, both are imperiled.[28] Just as arguments for free speech dovetail with arguments for democracy, as the next chapter suggests, arguments against free speech become, in the end, arguments against democracy.

6

Assessing the Pragmatists' Marketplace of Ideas

This, then, is the nub of Holmes's case for free speech. It is an act of juris-prudential jiu jitsu: Holmes takes the natural law that some claim to be the only route to freedom of speech and, in doubting it, establishes a safer route to that same destination. Freedom of speech, for Holmes, does not rest on absolute truth. The decision to privilege speech is a threshold policy choice, but a policy choice nonetheless; policy choices can be wrong, but they can be changed. The brilliance of Holmes's approach is captured in Menand's apt observation that Holmes was able to write these opinions not because he was suddenly convinced of the inalienability of the right to freedom of expression, but because he saw in these cases a corollary to his principled aversion to faith in principles. He managed to articulate a rationale that had the effect of making free speech a basic right without ever invoking the idea of natural law.[1]

Critiques of Holmes's rationale are grounded in both philosophical and empirical objections. I suggest in this chapter that the philosophical critiques are unpersuasive and that the case for Holmes's marketplace of ideas is not undercut but bolstered by empirical evidence. We turn first to philosophical objections.

Philosophical Critiques

Much philosophical back-and-forth over the value of free speech is a labyrinthine excursion into metaphysics, which Holmes sidestepped. Such arguments, he believed, were dog-chasing-its-tail regressions that led nowhere. His justification for protecting speech was empirical: based on our experience, the weight of the evidence indicates that protecting free speech is more likely than the alternatives to lead to stable social change. He suspected that "logical" arguments for and against protecting speech would be adopted

Free Speech and Turbulent Freedom. Michael J. Glennon, Oxford University Press. © Oxford University Press 2024.
DOI: 10.1093/oso/9780197636763.003.0006

or rejected for reasons having more to do with political, social, and psychological influences than the merits of the arguments themselves. The life of the law, here as elsewhere, was not logic but experience; perhaps for that reason, Holmes largely declined to engage those critics, except to the extent that they drew upon natural law theories to which he had broader objections. Nonetheless, it should not be thought that silence on his part suggests that those critiques are convincing; they are not, as the following brief review indicates.

"Self-canceling" is one philosophical objection to the notion of the marketplace of ideas generally and against Holmes's pragmatist justification in particular. In its more general form, the argument is that, if one really believes in the marketplace of ideas, one must accept that it must be closed to the idea that the marketplace of ideas should be closed. Because this idea, if adopted, would be irreversible, believers in the marketplace cannot allow its adoption; thus, the argument goes, they do not really believe in the marketplace of ideas. Suffice it to note here that the argument is a variation of the so-called tolerance dilemma—must tolerance tolerate intolerance?—which is dealt with concretely in the next chapter in connection with speech advocating overthrow of the government. Without a long digression, it is enough at this point simply to recall that the business of the law is drawing lines. Many goods become bads when carried to excess; here as elsewhere, prudence is not an argument for authoritarianism.

A second, more particular argument, directed at Holmes specifically, is that in rejecting objective truth, Holmes relies on it. This argument takes two forms. The first variation is that Holmes tacitly privileges knowledge and truth above all other values, which are, it is assumed, the ultimate objects of the marketplace of ideas. Why, critics ask, should we assume that knowledge and truth are objectively superior to competing values, such as happiness? Some people find ecstasy belief they are Napoleon; who is to say they would be better off knowing the truth? Holmes's answer, implied in his *Abrams* dissent, might be that he has no basis for judging such people's value choice; his point is merely that, *if* one selects truth and knowledge as values to be maximized, *then* one would want access to the range of information needed to come to a reliable judgment. People, he writes in *Abrams*, "*may* come to believe" that "truth is the only ground on which their wishes can safely be carried out." Nothing compels that choice. People may find that autocracy more safely carries out their wishes. Again, if his fellow citizens chose to go to hell in a handbasket, Holmes said, it was his job as a judge to help them get there.

Holmes's response does not resolve the paradox of tolerance, it is argued. It shows that the protection of free speech leads to absolutism whichever way one turns. On the one hand, to contend that free speech may not be curtailed even to prevent its complete curtailment by a totalitarian dictatorship[2] would be to privilege the idea of free speech absolutely above all conflicting ideas. On the other hand, to contend that speech *may* be curtailed to prevent adoption of the idea of totalitarianism—for the purpose of keeping open the marketplace of ideas in the face of totalitarianism's wish to close it—would *also* privilege the idea of the marketplace of ideas above all others. What is the source of this absolute truth—and Holmes's strenuous objections to natural law if, in the end, his defense of free speech rests on that same foundation? Is Holmes, in the end, a closet naturalist after all?

I think not. The supposed paradox flows from the fallacious assumption that the two "truths" involved—the truth of the totalitarian idea calling for the destruction of the marketplace of ideas, and the truth of the idea of the marketplace of ideas—are both necessarily *absolute* truths. The paradox dissolves if we regard both as *provisional* truths. This is the whole point, again, of Holmesian pragmatism: we might be wrong. Whether an intolerant idea presents a clear and imminent danger to the marketplace of ideas is a bet-able proposition the probability of which will vary from one society to the next and one day to the next. That Holmes might never be willing to make that bet, or that he might be willing to lose that bet as the price to be paid to live in the society he preferred, was his choice to make. Different people and different societies tolerate different levels of risk. But this first variation is an argument about universalism, not about Holmes's conception of the marketplace of ideas.

The second variation of the argument has it that because Holmes necessarily believes that we *ought* to believe his argument, he thereby acknowledges the existence of a world of oughts that exists out there, not of his own creation. Holmes, it is pointed out, wrote the following sentence: "Men to a great extent believe what they want to—although I see in that no basis for a philosophy that tells us what we should want to want."[3] This view also is self-refuting, it is contended, for Holmes presents a philosophy that, in effect, tells us we ought *not* to want a philosophy that tells us what to want; as a matter of absolute truth, such a philosophy does not exist. Holmes thus supposedly refutes himself, the argument goes.

THE PRAGMATISTS' MARKETPLACE OF IDEAS   41

But this argument misreads Holmes. His position is that he has *not yet seen* a persuasive case for absolute truth, not that as a matter of principle it cannot exist. Holmes does not rule out the possibility that such an argument might exist;[4] how could he? He has not heard them all. Holmes simply finds *this particular argument* unconvincing. To him, some other argument for absolute truth could conceivably add up. In the same paragraph, he writes that "one's attitude on these matters is closely connected with one's general attitude toward the universe." He reports the forces that shape our attitudes descriptively; his and others' attitudes are *contingent facts*, not absolute *oughts*. If you want to believe in oughts that exist out there, fine, he suggests, believe in absolute truth and natural law if you like. But be aware that the naturalist road is rutted, muddy, and circular.

Holmes's naturalist critics turn a blind eye to such problems. They should not. "There are reasons that the idea of natural law is a discredited one in our society," John Hart Ely pointed out. Natural law does have an enduring appeal. "The advantage, one gathers, is that you can invoke natural law to support anything you want. The disadvantage is that everyone understands that. Thus natural law has been summoned in support of all manner of causes in this country—some worthy, some nefarious—and often on both sides of the same issue." It has been invoked to deny women admission to the bar, in defense of theocracy, to support revolutionary rights in 1776, to advocate universal adult suffrage, to both oppose and support birth control and abortion and gay sex, to advance both laissez-faire economics and governmental paternalism, and for and against slavery and racial supremacy. We can reason about such issues, Ely wrote, "but reasoning about ethical issues is not the same as discovering absolute ethical truth. . . . [O]ur society does not, rightly does not, accept the notion of a discoverable and objectively valid set of moral principles."[5]

To some, Holmes's skepticism about the existence of such principles is horrific. To accept his view is to place Mother Teresa and Adolf Hitler on the same moral plane. Holmes's marketplace is an exercise in moral equivalence. This, it is contended, is the nihilistic, dystopian world that awaits us unless we commit ourselves to one dogma or another that claims certain truth. If there is no truth out there, how can human dignity—let alone free speech—be defended?[6]

Holmes was no stranger to the specter of nihilism. He bore three scars fighting against a slave-owning dystopia. From his experience, he drew a different lesson than that preached by the absolutists who led him into the war: that certainty begets intolerance; intolerance, animosity; and ani-mosity, bloodshed. Holmes made a prophecy based upon his own imperfect knowledge: that whatever truth emerges from the free exchange of ideas is the ground upon which our wishes can most *safely* be carried out. It was a prophesy based on human history, but we need not go back to discoverers of absolute truth during Christianity's Crusades to recover the Holy Land from Islam, Europe's religious wars, the Inquisition, Savonarola's bonfire of books in Florence, Islam's jihads against the West, or myriad other acts of barbarism perpetrated by certain and unquestioning true believers. Even in the face of that history, the leaders of the great *ism*'s of the twentieth cen-tury sought to carry out truths that were, to them, too certain to be subjected to the competition of other ideas. *They* would not fall victim to the fallacy of moral equivalence; skepticism, questioning, and argumentation were for lesser truths, not *their* truths. The results of that experiment are in. They are available to everyone who believes that absolute truth is the safer way to carry out our wishes. Those absolute truths have left us names: Dachau, the Gulag, the Cultural Revolution. More than one road leads to hell on earth. Holmes understood that we need to consider all those roads, not just one, before de-ciding which is safest. The safest can be identified from experience, not logic. And our experience reveals that an open, robust marketplace of ideas is vital to self-government, and that self-government is the surest route to societal stability and the avoidance of violence.

Let us turn, then, to experiential evidence for and against the notion of the marketplace of ideas.

Empirical Critiques

Many of the empirical objections to the marketplace of ideas are fa-miliar critiques of markets in general. Like other markets, for example, it is argued that the marketplace of ideas can fail.[7] It is distorted by differences in wealth that create unequal access to information and unequal opportunities to express them. Power within the marketplace becomes con-centrated, undermining competition. Media favor some ideas over others. Confirmation bias, pre-deliberation bias, projection bias, groupthink, and other cognitive distortions lead to mistakes and undermine the reliability of the market's outputs. New digital technologies amplify error. Doesn't the ev-idence show that the marketplace of ideas produces as much error as truth?

A law professor friend suggests to his first-year students that the three most important words in legal analysis are *Compared to what?* The words might usefully be recalled by those who reject the marketplace of ideas model in the abstract, who tend to see idealized regulators (too often themselves) as detached from the marketplace and above its distortions and pressures. The tendency is to view society's marketplace as a kind of societal Petri dish in which phenomena occur apart from the lives of observers. Those within the dish are "ordinary people"; the observers are select, extraordinary people who are not subject to the same distortive forces that misshape the concerns of those under their microscope. The critics' temptation is to believe they can create idea regulators in their image—wise, dispassionate, nonpartisan censors who are above the Sturm und Drang of a market peopled with cognitively biased participants. And, they imagine, those censors will act selflessly to advance ideas that are in the public interest, not ideas that advance the censors' self-interest.

This conceit is of course fanciful, as NYU law professor Burt Neuborne points out. If we vest government with discretionary tools to regulate speech, he asks, why should we think "that those tools would be any less subject to the harmful influences" that supposedly distort the speech market? "There is no reason to believe that the powerful private forces" supposedly responsible for such distortions "will not control government decisions about who gets to say what."[8] Those to whom power to regulate speech is delegated will unavoidably be a subset of the public at large, subject to the same pressures that inevitably beset "ordinary" people[9]—*and* to additional pressures flowing from their organizations' structure, history, and missions.[10] In the end, the argument of some of the critics, in Neuborne's words, often comes down to "an exercise in state-imposed self-improvement"—a plea to allow their "social class to use the government to elevate its speech preferences over everyone else's."[11] Deference to these experts might be justified if we had reason to consider them infallible, but we do not.[12] It is, once again, realistic doubts about our ability to make and maintain principled distinctions that counsel against attempting to regulate speech[13]—and when it comes to error correction, governments' track records leave little to commend them.[14] This is the fundamental difficulty with censorship, as numerous scholars over the years have observed. *It's not that no speech is harmless or without value; it's that institutions entrusted with sorting out harmful from beneficial speech inevitably slip into overkill.*[15]

It's true that the modern research in behavioral economics has given us new insights into varieties of cognitive distortion. That human judgment is predictably faulty, however, is not a twenty-first-century discovery.[16] Few of the Framers would have been surprised by the insights of contemporary behavioral economists. Authors of the First Amendment understood, with David Hume, that reason is the slave of the passions, yet they were still inspired by John Milton's *Areopagitica*. Indeed, the Framers' pluralistic constitutional design was intended to counteract many of the same psychological tendencies that have been newly named and documented. In some ways the impact of cognitive distortions may have been even more pronounced when the First Amendment was drafted 230 years ago, for the ideas marketplace known to the Framers was in some ways far less inclusive than that created by the internet. A small handful of wealthy publishers exercised disproportionate influence over what was read and discussed—a vastly different environment from one in which virtually anyone can "publish" a YouTube video or social media post that goes to tens of thousands of users. Informational bubbles are not a new phenomenon.

Such critiques point to a deeper weakness in objections to the marketplace of ideas that conceive of the very *idea* of the marketplace of ideas as somehow separate or apart from other ideas. It is not. The marketplace of ideas is self-inclusive. Like other ideas, the *idea* of the marketplace of ideas can itself be discredited or discounted. When its instrumentalities—newspapers, radio and television stations, social media, etc.—are not seen as reliable, the ideas that they produce are devalued. The public's lessened willingness to believe what it hears and reads in traditional media can of course have dramatic effects on social cohesion, but that is not a sign that the marketplace of ideas has failed; it is a sign that the marketplace is working: it has conveyed the message that instrumentalities within it are not trustworthy.[17] We are *aware* of our cognitive limitations and market failures—thanks to the ideas marketplace. Daniel Kahneman, referring to such cognitive errors, has said that "we are blind to our blindness." We are not, in fact, blind to our blindness. Kahneman himself wrote a best-selling book about it, and thanks to him, those who have read his book are no longer blind. The work of Kahneman and his associates on behavioral economics and prospect theory have entered popular discourse and are topics of incessant commentary in mainstream as well as social media.[18] As a result we are now skeptical of decisions—made by ourselves and others—that we might earlier have accepted uncritically. Similar treatment is accorded other market distortions, such as press bias. Many of the supposed deficiencies of the marketplace of ideas thus turn out, on analysis, to be examples of how effectively the marketplace actually works, not that it is failing.

The Unintended Consequences of Speech Suppression

To the extent that cognitive distortion remains, moreover, it cannot be forgotten that efforts to eliminate it through speech control *themselves* create cognitive distortion. This is an important point, and it goes directly to Holmes's belief that speech suppression is socially and politically destabilizing. Suppression may work in the short term, but ultimately the truth generally gets out, at which point the censors' plans for enforced harmony backfire. The question is not, therefore, whether certain speech is harmful; the question is whether suppressing it is *more* harmful.[19] In fact, censoring information has three dangerous unintended consequences: it makes censored information and speakers more attractive, it discredits the censors and their own messages, and it drives censored speech underground, where it can circulate unchallenged. Consider each in turn.

Empowering Suppressed Speech and Speakers

Censoring information creates a cognitive bias in favor of what is suppressed, a forbidden-fruit phenomenon that artificially values what is off limits.[20] Efforts to suppress hate speech, for example, can increase its visibility and its ultimate societal impact.[21] Similarly, while censorship can stigmatize the speaker in some quarters, public suppression can enhance the speaker's status within other groups. The speaker then becomes a martyr or a hero and the suppressed message more attractive.[22] The related tactic of flooding the marketplace with propaganda may work in the short term, but in the long term it generates resentment against its authors, whose messaging is recognized as indoctrination aimed at populations they consider too dim to sort things out for themselves.

Such phenomena are well known to psychologists who study reactance theory,[23] which explains why people often do the opposite of what they are told. Much of it is common sense. People who believe they are free to engage in certain behavior react negatively when they sense a threat to or loss of that freedom. That reaction may be hostile, angry, or aggressive. The threat need not be obvious or direct—even subliminal or vicarious nudges can arouse reactance. When people feel incapable of changing the situation, their response may be "learned helplessness," a state of withdrawal in which the threat is passively endured—but when they believe they can do something about it, and when they believe their values are affected by the deprivation, people may strive to restore their freedom. "This is a cognitive-reflective process," as several experts summarize it, "leading to negative attitudes toward the message and finally results in lower behavioral intention to follow the message."[24] In the short term, these costs can be mitigated by suppressing speech surreptitiously, as is done with growing sophistication by social media "content moderators." As I point out in Chapter 12, however, this tactic exchanges one set of costs for another, given the ease with which internet censorship can be circumvented by sophisticated users.[25] The long-term consequence is that those who "dig out" the truth come to live in an informational bubble entirely different from those who remain passively uninformed, leading to an ever more polarized society.

A vivid example of the forbidden-fruit phenomenon occurred during World War II, when the BBC broadcast some of Churchill's speeches into Nazi Germany. The German government lacked the technology to block the speeches, so it prohibited German citizens from listening and imposed severe penalties on those caught tuning in to hear Churchill. The British government, naturally curious as to how many Germans were actually listening, had its interrogators pose the question to captured Luftwaffe pilots. It turned out that Churchill was a big hit among the German pilots. The fact that Churchill was banned apparently made them *more* eager to hear the broadcasts, not less.[26] And it also caused the pilots to distrust Germany's leadership, which obviously didn't trust them.

Efforts to suppress speech elsewhere have, similarly, stimulated only wider appeal and suspicion. China's block of Instagram, for example, has inspired millions of social media users to acquire virtual private networks and to join censored websites like Facebook and Twitter.[27] Shares of the *New York Post* article about Hunter Biden nearly doubled after social media started to suppress it.[28] The South African government announced it intended to ban a book describing corruption in the country; the book promptly sold out.[29] One of the most tragic examples of speech controls that boomeranged occurred in Weimar Germany, as reported by Bob Mankoff. "[C]ontrary to what most people think," he writes, "Weimar Germany did have hate-speech laws, and they were applied quite frequently." But in the long term they helped bring about the very evil they were intended to prevent:

Leading Nazis such as Joseph Goebbels, Theodor Fritsch, and Julius Streicher were all prosecuted for anti-Semitic speech. Streicher served two prison sentences. Rather than deterring the Nazis and countering anti-Semitism, the many court cases served as effective public-relations machinery, affording Streicher the kind of attention he would never have found in a climate of a free and open debate. In the years from 1923 to 1933, *Der Stürmer* [Streicher's newspaper] was either confiscated or [its] editors taken to court on no fewer than thirty-six occasions. The more charges Streicher faced, the greater became the admiration of his supporters.[30]

Discrediting the Censors

A second consequence of efforts to squelch speech is to discredit the authorities behind the suppression, who are seen as what they are: censors.[31] Censorship creates a bias against the censoring institutions and their messages. Saudi Arabia's imprisonment of activists for online dissent, for example, not only did not suppress dissent overall but spurred more on-line dissent, including criticizing the ruling family and calling for regime change.[32] A government is respected by its people in part because it respects them, believing them capable of dealing with information that is erroneous, exaggerated, and insulting. A government is not respected by the people if it believes it knows better than they what is good for them to read or write or hear, or if it is seen as unable to withstand their criticism, or if it is capricious or secretive in controlling what they should know. Citizens in a democracy expect that their opinions are worth hearing, that they have something to contribute in making wise policy, that their views should count. A government that tells them otherwise often finds that *its own* views stop counting when it matters most: when it tells them to obey its laws. Jonathan Turley has pointed out that "with the rise of speech controls, the faith of the people in both the government and the media has declined."[33] The public's loss of faith in social media bears him out: according to the Cato Institute, 75% of the American public don't trust social media to make fair content moderation decisions.[34] Given the public's heavy reliance upon social media, discussed in Chapter 11, this distrust dangerously destabilizes American democracy. The need for the "safety valve" of free speech in modern-day America ought not be underestimated: in a highly polarized society often on the cusp of vi-olence, defusing frustration with the satisfaction of "being heard" can mean the difference between, as President John F. Kennedy said, peaceful evolution and violent revolution.[35]

Driving Suppressed Speech Underground

A third effect of efforts to suppress hate speech lies in its tendency to drive it underground.[36] Speech was more easily suppressed when the marketplace of ideas was controlled by relatively few mainstream newspapers and radio and television stations. As noted earlier, however, thanks to the internet, everyone can now be a publisher. Newly devised efforts to control the publication of unwanted ideas and information are discussed in Chapter 12, but it should simply be noted here that, because of modern technology, the notion that ideas can be effectively banned forever is complete fiction. Even before the digital era, the most repressive governments were unable to keep their propaganda safe from questioning and contradiction.[37] *Samizdat*—dissident material disapproved by the Soviet Union's censors, circulated underground and often individually copied and self-published—became widely available, notwithstanding earlier, brutal efforts to stamp it out. The gradual loosening of Soviet repression demonstrated the boomerang effect of porous censorship and hastened the Soviet Union's decline.[38] The best that contemporary censors can do is *temporarily* to deny technologically unsophisticated segments of the population access to information that is shared by those who are technologically more advanced—with a resulting acceleration in societal polarity.

These consequences of suppression have long been evident. For such reasons, Dean Carl Auerbach, who, as noted in the next chapter, defended the constitutionality of legislation banning the Communist Party in the 1950s, nonetheless opposed its enactment. He wrote:

> [S]uppression can drive the entire Communist apparatus underground and deprive the Party of the opportunities which open activities afford to recruit adherents, disseminate propaganda and cloak its conspiratorial activities. This may result in spurring the Party to infiltrate other parties and organizations. Without the Party's open activities, which enable others to read Party literature, identify Party leaders, and attend Party meetings, it will be more difficult to recognize the "Party line" and thereby to expose infiltration. Suppression, too, will encourage the formation of a larger, hard core of Communist fanatics, whereas open activities may lead Party members into paths which induce defection and it may serve us well in the ideological struggle with world Communism to adopt the missionary attitude that every Communist soul is worth saving. . . .

[A]n evaluation of the nature of the danger and the gains to be won by toleration is essential to a wise policy. Communism has suffered its greatest defeats in the field of open political debate. Why should democracy desert a field of battle in which it has been so successful?[39]

This is one of the strongest reasons not to suppress speech: it drives pernicious ideas into hidden sanctuaries where they need fear no rebuttal. Here as elsewhere, sunlight shining through an open marketplace of ideas is the best disinfectant.

~

In sum, the empirical evidence supports a commitment to the marketplace of ideas: if the aim is a society where change occurs *safely*, free speech is the best bet. A society that protects free speech is more stable than one that does not. In the aggregate, repressive efforts generate anger, distrust, and hostility. They rest on a sense of certainty that is recognized as false. They lead to resentment against paternalistic censors who claim the expertise to withhold information that supposedly lesser individuals are unable to handle. They discredit institutions needed for self-correction. They make censored information more attractive. They denigrate people's sense of worth by signaling that they have nothing valuable to say.

The ordinary remedy for bad ideas is therefore not less speech but, as Justice Brandeis (joined by Holmes) famously wrote, more speech.[40] And the safest route to sound public policy and societal stability is not censorship but uninhibited, robust, and wide-open debate.[41] The bet is that the risks entailed in freedom of speech are more safely incurred than the risks entailed by censorship. Broadly protecting freedom of speech inevitably means protecting some speech that has no value and that may in fact be harmful. But the greater risk lies in permitting the state to block speech that it defines as worthless or harmful.[42] In Madison's words, "[S]ome degree of abuse is inseparable from the proper use of every thing; and in no instance is this more true, than in that of the press."[43] The costs and risks of censorship, in the long term, outweigh the costs and risks of freedom of speech.

That is the insight not simply of Holmes, but the insight embodied, largely through his efforts, in the Supreme Court's interpretation of the First Amendment. That interpretation has emerged through a method much like the evolutionary, trial-and-error process contemplated, Holmes thought, by the Amendment itself. His pragmatism does not explain all First Amendment jurisprudence. I suggest, however, that its influence is manifest in the Court's answers to three of the most contentious areas of First Amendment jurisprudence: advocacy of law violation, hate speech, and misinformation. We turn now to Part II of the book, a discussion of these three distinctively American approaches, beginning each discussion with seminal or at least emblematic cases. This will lay the groundwork to turn, in Part III, to the central question posed earlier: whether the scope of the First Amendment's actual coverage is sufficient to protect the contemporary marketplace of ideas. Answering this question will entail comparing the breadth of the Amendment's coverage with the breadth of coverage provided by an encroaching alternative regime, international human rights law, which, through voluntary adoption, has come to govern the regulation of the current marketplace of ideas embodied in social media. As we'll see, the protection accorded the marketplace of ideas by international human rights law falls far short of the protection that would be accorded by First Amendment jurisprudence. Yet if the First Amendment is to be preferred, the question nonetheless arises: Is it up to the task of protecting the free exchange of ideas within the modern digital marketplace? The answer, I will suggest, is yes—yes, that is, if earlier case law is properly deployed to protect the speech freedom of *all* participants within that marketplace, meaning that of not merely the government and social media platforms but also that of social media users and the general public.

PART II

THE PRESENT

7

Incitement to Law Violation or Violence

Western civilization's concept of liberty is grounded on the belief that the state's proper role is marked by the line between thought and action. John Stuart Mill distilled the idea in a sentence: "[O]ver himself, over his own body and mind, the individual is sovereign."[1] Milton,[2] Spinoza,[3] Jefferson,[4] and countless political thinkers over the centuries joined Mill in exalting the inviolability of the individual mind. It is for the individual to think and feel as he or she wishes, they believed, without interference by the state. Whether to like or dislike, accept or doubt, believe or disbelieve, admire or disdain, love or hate—these are decisions for the individual, not the state. It is only when hatred or greed or lust becomes murder or robbery or rape that the state may step in—only when thought is transformed into action.

The principle lies at the heart of American constitutional jurisprudence. "If there is any fixed star in our constitutional constellation, it is that no official, high or petty, can prescribe what shall be orthodox in politics, nationalism, religion, or other matters of opinion or force citizens to confess by word or act their faith therein," Justice Robert Jackson wrote for the Supreme Court in 1943.[5] Thought control—mind control—is the essence of tyranny. It is not for nothing that inmates at some Nazi concentration camps sang "Meine Gedänke Sind Frei" (My Thoughts Are Free), signaling, as Frederick Schauer put it, that "whatever you may do to me, whatever you may compel me to do *or say*, my thoughts are still free because they remain beyond the reach of your powers."[6]

We protect freedom of speech and freedom of the press as necessary corollaries of freedom of thought. To Mill they were "practically inseparable."[7] We could hardly know what we think—we could hardly know *how* to think—without speaking and hearing oral and printed words and images. Yet this presents a dilemma for free states. Words spark not only thoughts; words often spark action—action that the state has a lawful right to prevent. If it can control the *action* that certain words produce, why may it not control the words that produce those actions? And if at some point, sooner or later, it may do so, how soon is too soon?

Free Speech and Turbulent Freedom. Michael J. Glennon, Oxford University Press. © Oxford University Press 2024.
DOI: 10.1093/oso/9780197636763.003.0007

This question weighed on American minds in the 1950s, posed by the struggle against the century's great *ism*'s. The menace of fascism, vanquished recently at the cost of a million combat casualties, seemed to trace in part to a pernicious screed published decades earlier by an obscure oddball, Adolf Hitler; and the menace of communism, still immediate, posed the specter of a putsch, possibly joined by growing numbers of propagandized supporters. Fears instilled by Senator Joseph McCarthy's red-baiting gave the issue new urgency. In either situation, how long must the government wait before moving against *words* that advocate not only law violation but the overthrow of the government?

Alexander Meiklejohn was at the time the nation's leading First Amendment scholar (later to be selected for the Medal of Freedom by President Kennedy). In this charged political environment, Meiklejohn proffered a calm answer in 1955 testimony before the Senate Judiciary Committee, elaborated five years later in his book, *Political Freedom:*

> An incitement, I take it, is an utterance so related to a specific overt act that it may be regarded and treated as a part of doing the act itself, if the act is done. Its control, therefore, falls within the jurisdiction of the legislature. An advocacy, on the other hand, even up to the limit of arguing and planning for the violent overthrow of the existing form of government, is one of those opinion-forming, judgment-making expressions which free men need to utter and to hear as citizens responsible for the governing of the nation. If men are not free to ask and to answer the question, "Shall the present form of our government be maintained or changed?"; if, when the question is asked, the two sides of the issue are not equally open for consideration, for advocacy, and for adoption, then it is impossible to speak of our government as established by the free choice of a self-governing people. It is not enough to say that the people of the United States were free one hundred seventy years ago. The First Amendment requires, simply and without equivocation, that they be free now.[8]

The Supreme Court came to conclude, in *Brandenburg v. Ohio* (1969),[9] that Meiklejohn's answer was right, but it took the Court half a century of fits and starts to get there, regularly saying one thing yet doing another.

The story begins not in the 1950s but in 1919, with *Schenck v. United States.* Holmes, writing for the Court, gave an answer that, on paper at least, was not altogether different from Meiklejohn's. The appropriate test, he said, was "whether the words used are used in such circumstances and are of such a nature as to create a clear and present danger that they will bring about the substantive evils that Congress has a right to prevent."[10] This clear-and-present-danger test, so-called, came to be suspect because it allowed speech suppression that in retrospect seemed clearly ill-advised. In *Schenck,* the test was read as permitting the imprisonment of pamphleteers who had merely argued that military conscription violated the Thirteenth Amendment prohibition against slavery; their pamphlet did not explicitly call upon draftees to resist and created no imminent likelihood that they would resist. Then, in *Debs v. United States* (1919),[11] again writing for a unanimous Court, Holmes applied the clear-and-present-danger test to uphold Eugene Debs's conviction merely for speaking against the war at a Socialist Party convention— after which Debs received nearly a million votes in the next year's presidential election, while running from prison. Two decades later, in *Dennis v. United States* (1951),[12] the Court upheld convictions of leaders of the American Communist Party for advocating the violent overthrow of the government, though they had in fact done little more than teach the texts of four Marxist books. The Court purported to apply the clear-and-present-danger threshold but in reality applied a new,[13] modified version of the test, under which it would look not only at a danger's imminence but also at its gravity and probability. No danger, it concluded, could be graver than the violent overthrow of the government. As the clear-and-present-danger test was regularly applied, then, it looked increasingly like the Court's old, discredited bad-tendency test. The test in effect left advocacy unprotected even if that advocacy presented danger that was neither clear nor present—advocacy could be silenced if it was merely grave and sufficiently probable.

As the country moved out of the political strife of the McCarthy era and into the racial strife of the civil rights era, it became clear that something was amiss in the speech standard the Court had formulated. Was mere advocacy that presented no clear and present danger protected or not? The Court walked back from *Dennis* six years later in *Yates v. United States* (1957),[14] when Justice John Harlan wrote for the Court that, where the issue is preparing a group to engage in violence, speech can be proscribed only "when the group is of sufficient size and cohesiveness, is sufficiently oriented towards action, and other circumstances are such as reasonably to justify apprehension that action will occur." Those to whom advocacy is addressed, he wrote, "must be urged to *do* something, rather than merely to *believe* in something."[15] Still, the question cried out for clarification: How soon was too soon for the government to intervene to suppress speech that could lead to conduct it has a right to prevent?

The Court gave its answer in 1969, when it appeared to rediscover the wisdom of Justice Holmes's *Abrams* dissent (written after his earlier, seemingly conflicting opinions in *Schenck* and *Debs*). As we saw in Chapter 5, Holmes had urged that the proper test was whether the views expressed "so imminently threaten immediate interference with the lawful and pressing purposes of the law that an immediate check is required to save the country."[16] Imminence and immediacy were incorporated into what has become known as a new *incitement* test, the *Brandenburg* test.

Brandenburg v. Ohio arose on appeal from the conviction of an Ohio Ku Klux Klan leader who was charged with violating a state law that prohibited advocating violence to promote political change. At a rally remote from the general public but filmed by a local television station, the defendant spewed a stream of racial epithets and announced that "there might have to be some revengence [*sic*] taken" if authorities continued to suppress Whites. The Supreme Court reversed his conviction, stating the test that has thereafter prevailed. The "constitutional guarantees of free speech and free press," it held, "do not permit a State to forbid or proscribe advocacy of the use of force or of law violation except where such advocacy is directed to inciting or producing imminent lawless action and is likely to incite or produce such action."[17]

More than anything else, it is the high bar of *Brandenburg*'s incitement test that sets the First Amendment apart from other speech-regulating regimes. Note the vast scope of speech it protects. Speech may not be banned unless four strict conditions are met—and the likely gravity of the danger is not one of them. First, the expected consequence of the speech must be violence— "use of force"—or law violation. Second, the speech must be *directed at* that consequence; it must, seemingly, be *intended* to bring about violence or law violation. Third, that consequence must be not merely possible but *probable.* Fourth, that consequence must be *imminent;* even though the speech is highly likely to result in violence or law violation, it cannot be proscribed unless it will occur virtually immediately. As construed in *Brandenburg,* the First Amendment therefore permits the government to punish only *incitement,* not mere advocacy—however probable and however grave its effect. Neither *Abrams* nor *Schenck* nor *Debs* nor *Dennis* would have come out the same way had the facts of those cases been decided under *Brandenburg*'s incitement test.

It's been suggested that *Brandenburg*'s standard is now completely accepted and uncontroversial. That may have been true a few years ago. Recent events, however, including the January 6, 2021, turmoil at the Capitol, have given rise to new doubts of whether *Brandenburg* goes too far in protecting dangerous speech. One reason, perhaps, is that *Brandenburg* did not—and could not—resolve an underlying paradox that lies beyond resolution in any neat legalist formula.

The *Brandenburg* Paradox

The speech paradox that plagues all free governments resembles the paradox that confronts national security policymakers who ponder the use of force to prevent an adversary state from acquiring weapons of mass destruction. The paradox is this: if preemptive force is used early, the capabilities and intentions of an adversary are less certain and the dangers of mistake are greater, but the use of force is more likely to be effective; if preemptive force is used later, while the dangers of a mistake are lessened, preemptive force is less likely to succeed. In the realm of freedom of speech, the paradox is similar: violence is more effectively controlled by suppressing speech before it incites to violence, but if suppression of speech occurs earlier, the likelihood the speech will lead to violence is less certain, and the dangers of a mistake are greater. Coups, genocide, insurrection, subversion, and related security threats typically raise this dilemma; it has arisen notably in the history of genocide in Germany and Rwanda. Consider the problem in the light of logic and experience.

As a matter of pure logic, it would be hard to disagree with *Dennis*'s premise: the Constitution cannot mean that the government "must wait until the putsch is about to be executed, the plans have been laid and the signal is awaited."[18] Justice Robert Jackson, concurring, argued that the clear-and-present-danger test as formulated by Holmes and Brandeis was never intended to apply to a case such as *Dennis*. "If applied as it is proposed here, it means that the Communist plotting is protected during its period of incubation; its preliminary stages of organization and preparation are immune from the law; the government can move only after imminent action is manifest, when it would, of course, be too late."[19] At one point in his dissenting opinion, even Justice William O. Douglas, the Court's leading civil libertarian, wrote that "[t]here comes a time when even speech loses its constitutional immunity." He continued:

> Speech innocuous one year may at another time fan such destructive flames but it must be halted in the interests of the safety of the Republic. That is the meaning of the clear and present danger test. When conditions are so critical that there will be no time to avoid the evil that the speech threatens, it is time to call a halt. Otherwise, free speech which is the strength of the Nation will be the cause of its destruction.[20]

One prominent commentator mentioned in the previous chapter, Carl Auerbach, put it as follows:

> [T]he "clear and present danger" doctrine, whether as enunciated by Holmes or Brandeis or Hand, is an unsatisfactory test to determine the limits which the First Amendment imposes upon congressional action designed to meet the threat of modern totalitarianism. . . . [N]o principle of the Constitution or of democracy requires that a political movement be permitted to engage in the struggle for power if its objective is to crush democracy itself.[21]

The clear-and-present-danger test, Auerbach wrote, "imposes the risk that it restrains action until it may be too late to prevent a totalitarian victory."[22]

Is this argument valid? Its logic rests on two empirical assumptions: first, that it is possible to identify the "period of incubation" of a pernicious ideology fated to command sufficient popular allegiance to destroy self-government; second, that it is then possible to nip that ideology in the bud with carefully tailored preemptive censorship that does not, as Madison warned, remove the air required for liberty. Neither assumption holds up.

Identifying an Idea's "Period of Incubation"

The notion that we can pinpoint an idea's "period of incubation" rests on implicit, counterfactual premises: that we can know how history will unfold if the idea is left to develop unhindered, and that we can also know how history will unfold if the idea is blocked. That human beings are possessed of such prescience is hubristic fantasy. Random, unpredictable events regularly knock history off its expected course. Pandemics and technological breakthroughs, heart attacks and strokes, lucky coincidences and unlucky breaks block our best efforts to know what terrain lies ahead, let alone which course can be charted through or around it. It's plausible that if *Mein Kampf* had been banned the moment it was published in 1925, Hitler's rise, the tragedy of the Holocaust, and World War II all would have been averted— but who was to know *at that time* what impact it and its author ultimately would have? A thousand other equally silly books were almost certainly published in that period by a thousand other equally silly authors. Were all to be banned?[23] The *Dennis* Court's admonition against acting too late to forestall the acceptance of a pernicious idea is all but useless. Of course it's fatal to act too late, but whether action is too early or too late is rarely possible to know, except in retrospect. Simply put, there is no way to identify an idea's period of incubation, no test for distinguishing present imaginings from future depravity.

Nor does history predict the course of a malignant idea that is *allowed* to be ventilated and openly debated. Justice Douglas wrote in dissent in *Dennis* that the four books at issue in the case were "to Soviet Communism what *Mein Kampf* was to Nazism. If they are understood, the ugliness of Communism is revealed, its deceit and cunning are exposed, the nature of its activities becomes apparent, and the chances of its success less likely."[24] There is, in other words, reason to trust in the operation of the marketplace of ideas when the ideas in question are fundamentally at odds with the values of its participants. And there is all the more reason, when autocracy looms, to reinforce the institutional pluralism that protects against it, rather than centralizing authority in censors who adopt autocrats' methods.

Preemptive Censorship

What should be *dis*trusted is our ability to stop a threatening idea in its tracks through preemptive censorship—beginning with our illusory power to identify dangerous ideas that pose genuine security threats. It's a commonplace in popular literature that fear tends to skew risk analysis.[25] Yet "another Hitler" is regularly spotted emerging from the shadows of our fear, triggering the reaction that his threat is easily forestalled by banning the ideas he stands for.

Not infrequently such fears are fanned and further inflated by the security bureaucracy, as discussed in my past work, *National Security and*

Double Government. Security managers operate under a constant incentive to expand personnel and budgets, as well as an understandable
aim to avoid blame for security failures; the penalties for exaggerating
threats are far less than the penalties for underestimating them. The
external consequences of their repeated overestimation of security
threats—Libya, Iraq, Vietnam, World War I, the Spanish-American War,
etc.—need hardly be recalled. But what should be remembered is that
the domestic consequences have been no less catastrophic, and that those
consequences have been particularly destructive of free speech. Law professor Daniel Farber put it well:

> Rather than limiting itself to genuinely dangerous people, the apparatus of
> speech control has swept up an array of characters ranging from harmless
> cranks to those guilty of little more than an offhand remark, not to mention
> tainting through guilt by association many others whose basic commit-
> ment was to democratic politics.[26]

The question is, given the security managers' well-known track record, why
should they be trusted *more than the public at large* to decide what the public
should write and read and think? Cognitive distortion is not unique to the
general public, as pointed out in the previous chapter: the security managers
simply are subject to different cognitive distortions: incentives to keep
their jobs, please their bosses, advance their careers, avoid organizational
embarrassment, and myriad other biases that plague secretive, detached
bureaucracies.[27] Here, as elsewhere, there is scant reason to believe that this
subset of citizens has a better grasp of the public interest than does the public
itself.

Discounting self-serving threat inflation and inevitable biases, however,
the question arises: Aren't there objectively identifiable, dangerous ideas "out
there" that ought to be rooted out before they take hold, ideas of the sort
spelled out in *Mein Kompf*? Considerable academic research exists on the
topic of risk assessment. Professor Paul Slovic is perhaps the leading scholar
in the field. In his 2000 book *The Perception of Risk*,[28] Slovic argues that
risk perception is inherently subjective; risk "does not exist 'out there,' independent of our minds and cultures, waiting to be measured."[29] One can
debate whether some risks (e.g., airplane safety, smoking, tick bites) are subjective, but Slovic's larger point remains: many risks are unknowable in any
absolute sense. The reason is that the occurrence or nonoccurrence of the

event in question is contingent upon the occurrence or nonoccurrence of other, future events and conditions. When it comes to the risk posed by dangerous ideas, these conditions include the characteristics of the individuals comprising the idea's "target" population. This point was made cogently by Erich Fromm in *Escape from Freedom*:

> Any kind of thought, true or false . . . is motivated by the subjective needs and interests of the person who is thinking. . . . [I]deas which are not rooted in powerful needs of the personality will have little influence on the actions and on the whole life of the person concerned.[30]

The result, Fromm concluded, is that the attractiveness of an idea is a function of the psychological characteristics of the people to whom it is addressed, at the time it is articulated. "The influence of any doctrine or idea depends on the extent to which it appeals to psychic needs of the character structure of those to whom it is addressed," he wrote. "Only if the idea answers powerful psychological needs of certain social groups will it become a potent force in history."[31] One cannot predict the appeal of an idea, therefore, without knowing the future receptivity of the social group to which it will be presented.

That knowledge, of course, is seldom within our grasp. Attitudes change. What is welcomed as a sensible idea in one era can be rejected as detestable in the next. The likely adoption of ideas concerning the abolition of slavery, racial integration, or gay marriage depended not on those ideas' intrinsic "danger" but on the historical, cultural, and social background of the individuals exposed to those ideas. Yet individuals' backgrounds evolve as they are exposed to a continuing mix of new ideas. How the aggregated culture will look decades hence is usually anybody's guess, but one thing is clear: even if it were possible, banning ideas that seem threatening would freeze social growth and empower those with a preexisting interest in preserving the status quo.[32] In this important sense, as Mill wrote, silencing the expression of ideas "is robbing the human race."[33]

What should be distrusted, finally, is not simply our ability to identify inchoate malevolence before it metastasizes but the assumed power to avoid unintended consequences in attempting to suppress it. As discussed earlier in connection with reactance theory, overt speech suppression is notorious in making heroes out of suppressed authors and in making best-sellers out of their suppressed works. It does so because it is porous: word inevitably gets out that censorship is afoot, and the censors and their enablers are discredited. The solution embraced by censors is therefore either to move to complete authoritarianism—to send millions to a Gulag, cutting off the air on which dissent and liberty both live, as Madison understood—or to move to innovative methods of clandestine censorship, in which readers and listeners are not aware that they're hearing only what the censors want them to hear. The former is the course on which China has embarked. The latter is now gaining traction within the United States. But those who adopt these new methods of covert suppression are oblivious to its own unintended consequence—providing tools and precedents, should they fail, for use by less fastidious adversaries if and when they should gain power. Afghanistan is not the only battleground where captured weaponry has fallen into the wrong hands.

A case in point was the Weimar Republic and its shortsighted drive to squelch extremism by banning its expression. The Nazis "used the Weimar Republic's emergency laws to strangle the very democracy the laws were supposed to protect,"[34] Jacob Mchangama writes in his important study, *Free Speech: A History from Socrates to Social Media.* Under a "steady stream of increasingly desperate and draconian laws and emergency decrees," he points out, hundreds of newspapers, communist as well as Nazi, were banned in the three years preceding Hitler's ascension to official power.[35] Afterward, Hitler used these same laws ruthlessly to his own political advantage. When his opponents complained, he responded that they had earlier banned his press, his assemblies, and his speeches—and discovered the benefits of free speech only once they fell from power.[36]

The lesson, Mchangama observes, was unfortunately not learned after the war by some international human rights advocates. Eager to preempt a possible Nazi resurgence, they pushed (over American resistance) to include hate speech restrictions in human rights treaties—which "helped legitimate the crackdown on dissent in the Soviet bloc" and also provided legal cover for Muslim activists pushing for a global ban on blasphemy.[37]

The Contingency of Time and Place

Where, then, is the line to be drawn? Justice Harlan's dictum in *Yates*, quoted above, paralleled Justice Holmes's in *Schenck*: the facts of the case are all-important. As Justice Douglas noted, speech that is innocuous one year may in another year be inflammatory. And, he might have added, speech that is innocuous in one country may be inflammatory in another, a point elaborated in Chapter 11's discussion of international human rights law. What constitutes incitement varies from one culture to another. Different societies present different sensitivities, different boiling points, and different risk assessments. If reasonable Rwandan authorities had concluded in 1994 that shutting down an inflammatory Hutu radio station was the only way to save hundreds of thousands of Tutsis from being hacked to death by machetes, no sensible universalist Free Speech Principle would have stayed their judgment.[38] At some point counterspeech within a given society can prove unavailing; at some point advocacy shades into incitement. That advocacy and incitement often are hard to separate does not, however, mean that they do not differ, as Meiklejohn recognized .

Brandenburg's incitement test does not, therefore, preclude halting a real and unmistakable coup in its rhetorical tracks. "It is, of course, understood," Meiklejohn testified, "that if such persons or groups proceed to forceful or violent action, or even to overt preparation for such action, against the government, the First Amendment, in that respect, offers them little protection."[39] *Brandenburg* merely moves forward the line at which government may intervene to the point of emergency, the point at which no further speech can prevent a harm that government clearly has the power to prevent: its overthrow by unconstitutional means. Identifying where that line is to be drawn would in many circumstances be difficult, but the alternative to drawing the line at incitement is, for all intents and purposes, to have no line it all—to revert to a bad-tendency test with some other name. The consequence would be to let those "with the most to lose from those activities they are regulating,"[40] as Schauer put it, to draw that line wherever they wish. Under that standard, freedom of speech would quickly become a historical artifact.

8

Offensive and Hate Speech

Holmes wrote in *Schenck* that the requirement of a clear and present danger is "the question in every case."[1] The implication, as Geoffrey Stone points out, is that the clear-and-present-danger test "is the test for *all* free speech problems."[2] There is indeed every indication that its more principled successor, *Brandenburg*'s incitement test, is intended to be equally comprehensive. As we will now see, the Court's treatment of offensive and hate speech largely reflects the same pragmatist approach. The framework it forged in response to specious claims of subversion during the McCarthy era, it turned out, also gave it a way to think about very real claims of race- and gender-based hatred. The "idea of racial inequality and the idea of revolution," Daniel Farber observes, are "treated equivalently."[3]

We have already addressed arguments for banning hate speech—which are arguments for banning the advocacy of viewpoints, for hatred is a viewpoint. We've also described how efforts to ban speech bring about unintended consequences: they inflate the attractiveness of the censored message and the censored speaker, they discredit the censoring institutions, and they drive the censored messages underground, where they thrive unanswered. We needn't revisit that discussion beyond noting that bans on hate speech, in all those ways, provide a textbook example of how good intentions backfire.

Along with the inevitability of viewpoint discrimination, we'll now examine two additional reasons that argue against trying to squelch hate speech. First, efforts to do so unavoidably rely upon vague definitions. And second, rather than empowering subordinated groups, they effectively isolate and weaken them by taking away the means most useful in fighting subordination: freedom of speech.

Elaborating these three points requires a deeper examination of how the Supreme Court has dealt with these issues. The Court's answers at first blush seem deeply counterintuitive, so understanding how it gets there will entail a closer look at its case law. But fear not: its jurisprudence, deciphered, reduces largely to commonsensical insights that require no legal background to appreciate. The Court's reasoning, indeed, will resonate with the everyday

Free Speech and Turbulent Freedom. Michael J. Glennon, Oxford University Press. © Oxford University Press 2024.
DOI: 10.1093/oso/9780197636763.003.0008

experience of most Americans who have confronted these issues personally. Let's begin by considering some of the headline-provoking cases in which the Court has found the First Amendment to protect speech that many would find not only worthless but hurtful.

No shortage of candidates compete for a spot on a short list of the Supreme Court's most incendiary "hate" cases. In the previous chapter we examined one, *Brandenburg v. Ohio*,[4] in which twelve hooded figures gathered around a large burning cross and uttered words derogatory toward blacks and Jews. The following five cases would probably join it on that list.

- In *Collin v. Smith* (1978),[5] a Nazi organization proposed to march with swastikas and military uniforms in Skokie, Illinois, a city with a large Jewish population and many Holocaust survivors. The village did not expect physical violence but tried to ban the march to prevent "the in-fliction of psychic trauma on resident holocaust survivors and other Jewish residents."[6]
- In *R.A.V. v. City of St. Paul* (1992),[7] several teenagers burned a cross in the predawn hours inside the fenced yard of a Black family. They were prosecuted under a city ordinance that listed race as a protected cate-gory but did not protect other categories, such as homosexuality, union membership, or political affiliation.
- In *Snyder v. Phelps* (2011),[8] protesters on public land picketed the fu-neral of a marine who had been killed in Iraq, bearing signs hostile to the Catholic Church, the United States, and the military's tolerance of homosexuality. The father of the deceased, who later learned of the messages on the signs, sued for intentional infliction of emotional distress.
- In *Texas v. Johnson* (1989),[9] a demonstrator burned an American flag to protest the presence of the Republican National Convention and was prosecuted under the state's flag desecration law.
- In *Cohen v. California* (1971),[10] the defendant was prosecuted for dis-turbing the peace after wearing, in a state courtroom, a jacket bearing the words "Fuck the Draft."

In each of these cases, the courts found the defendants' speech to fall within the protection of the First Amendment. The Nazi march in Skokie was so obviously protected that the Supreme Court didn't even write a full opinion affirming the lower court's decision. How could that be? Each of these decisions was met with outrage by a considerable segment of the public. To many Americans, and to even more citizens of other countries, this broad interpretation of the First Amendment protects too much. Hate has no value to society, they argue, or to individuals within it. It is corrosive and destructive of social harmony and individual flourishing. Why should hurtful words hurled at the innocent be treated any differently than injurious rocks?

It is good to make this clear at the outset: *the First Amendment does not protect hate speech as such*. It protects *some* speech that is hateful. It does not, however, protect *other* speech that is hateful. The misunderstanding stems from the deeper misunderstanding, noted earlier, that the First Amendment is "absolute." It is not. And the types of expression that it does not protect can and sometimes do convey hate. We have already encountered the most obvious exception: hateful speech that incites to immediate violence or law violation. Under *Brandenburg,* speech that crosses the line separating advocacy from incitement is not constitutionally protected. The speech in that case did not constitute incitement. Nor did the speech at issue in any of the five cases just listed. These and similar cases, as Nadine Strossen has pointed out,[11] presented *nonemergency* situations. Time existed for speech to be answered with counterspeech. No need was presented for the government to intervene to stop or punish speech that presented an immediate danger to anyone.

Other situations involving hate present different issues, however—factual issues that the First Amendment resolves differently. Hateful speech that constitutes "fighting words," for example—words "which by their very utterance inflict injury or tend to incite an immediate breach of the peace"— is not protected.[12] Nor is hateful speech protected if it constitutes "true threats," namely, "statements where the speaker means to communicate a serious expression of an intent to commit an act of unlawful violence to a particular individual or group of individuals."[13] Similarly, hate speech that is defamatory—i.e., false statements of fact that injure another's reputation—is not protected.[14]

Still, there is no getting around the fact that racial, ethnic, and gender-related slurs, Nazi memorabilia and symbols of religious animosity, and odious expressions of group-based hostility are protected under the First Amendment. Hate speech *as a category* is not outside the First Amendment's protection. Why not? For three reasons that tie into long-standing principles of First Amendment jurisprudence: banning hate speech as such would constitute viewpoint discrimination, violate due process prohibitions against vagueness, and disarm discreet and insular minorities. Consider each in turn.

Viewpoint Discrimination

The requirement of viewpoint neutrality traces to the wellsprings of Holmesian pragmatism: based on our experience, we bet that it is safer to leave the choice of what to believe to the people at large rather than to some subset of the people. The "people," of course, consist of *individuals*; as pointed out in the previous chapter, our political tradition is founded on the distinction between thought and action, on the premise that it is for the individual to decide what to believe and for the state to intervene only when the individual crosses the line separating belief from conduct. Permitting the state to favor or disfavor a given viewpoint would put a thumb on the scale and distort the operation of the marketplace of ideas, rendering its outcome unreliable. It would represent a return to the old bad-tendency test, under which speech is suppressed because, sometime in the distant future, it could lead to illegal action. It would permit censoring viewpoints that do not incite to violence. It would advantage the ideas of the powerful over those of the weak and the beliefs of the government over those of its critics. To suppress viewpoints would be to subordinate citizens' deliberation to the values and interests of others.[15] Hence the First Amendment requires content or viewpoint neutrality.

The neutrality doctrine was first articulated as such in the 1972 case of *Police Dept. of City of Chicago v. Mosley*.[16] In it, a federal postal employee, Earl Mosley, regularly and peacefully picketed outside a Chicago high school carrying a sign that read, "Jones High School practices black discrimination. Jones High School has a black quota." The Chicago City Council adopted an ordinance that prohibited picketing within 150 feet of any primary or secondary school except for peaceful picketing of any school involved in a labor dispute. Before the ordinance became effective, the Chicago Police Department told Mosley that the ordinance would apply to his picketing, so he stopped picketing and challenged its constitutionality. The Supreme Court unanimously agreed with Mosley: the ordinance was invalid.

The central problem with Chicago's ordinance, wrote Justice Thurgood Marshall for the Court, was that it limited permissible picketing by subject matter. The ordinance permitted picketing on the subject of a school's labor-management dispute but prohibited picketing on other subjects. This the First Amendment did not allow. The First Amendment, the Court said, "means that government has no power to restrict expression because of its message, its ideas, its subject matter, or its content." The Court underscored the impermissibility of government "content control" over the nation's politics and culture, which is the essence of censorship.[17]Debate would not be wide open if the government favored its own ideas, the Court said; differing viewpoints must be treated neutrally.[18]

Viewpoint discrimination was the problem in each of the five cases listed above. This was explicitly noted by the Court; *Texas v. Johnson*,[19] *Collin v. Smith*,[20] *Snyder v. Phelps*,[21] *Cohen v. California*,[22] and *R.A.V. v. St. Paul*[23] all involved attempts by the government to promote viewpoints it liked by penalizing the expression of viewpoints it did not like. Perhaps the country would be better off if pernicious viewpoints such as hatred could be stripped completely from our emotions and the language of hatred extirpated from our vocabularies. But people in a free society have different views as to what views are pernicious, and the government is not a schoolmarm empowered to substitute its morality for theirs. An effort to expunge hate speech from our discourse easily becomes, again, "an exercise in state-imposed self-improvement," to recall Burt Neuborne's words.[24] Improvement is often in the eye of the beholder; is hatred always, necessarily a social evil? Frederick Douglass, among many others, had little hesitancy in voicing his hatred of slavery and those who perpetrated it.[25] Viewers of the ghastly film footage in *Judgment at Nuremberg* may have hated the Nazi executioners. Images of a policeman's deadly knee on a defenseless Black man's neck, of the terrorists' destruction of the Twin Towers, of the carnage from Russian missile attacks on Ukrainian civilians—all generate intense emotions that drive productive public policy reform. Because we recognize that we are not infallible, we do not permit the state to categorize those viewpoints as good or bad, true or false, moral or immoral. We leave that judgment to the individual. Misguided and mistaken though individual viewpoints may often be, we think it unsafe to permit the state to punish or reward individual thought and emotion. Hate speech conveys a viewpoint, a viewpoint integral to advocacy. Arguments concerning racial superiority, gender-based subordination, opinions on LGBTQ+ issues, and so on are all viewpoints—opinions of the sort that are imbedded in advocacy that is constitutionally protected under *Brandenburg*.

Suppose, however, for all our humility and for all our appreciation of the value of pluralism, we were to conclude that some viewpoints are nonetheless utterly indefensible, too dangerous or divisive even to be considered— slavery, say, or genocide, or white supremacy. Why not place the defense of such viewpoints beyond First Amendment protection?

The question poses a preliminary issue: Can those viewpoints be defined with sufficient clarity to prevent abusive or pretextual overenforcement? The law, it turns out, has given a good deal of thought to this problem and has developed a considered answer. It is called the vagueness doctrine, and it is exemplified in the Court's seminal 1972 decision in *Papachristou v. City of Jacksonville.*[26]

Vagueness

In *Papachristou,* eight defendants were convicted in a Florida municipal court of violating a Jacksonville, Florida, vagrancy ordinance in several cases that were consolidated for consideration by the U.S. Supreme Court. In one of the cases, four of the individuals—two Black men and two Black women— were riding in a car on the main thoroughfare in Jacksonville. The four were charged under the ordinance with "prowling by auto." In another case, two individuals were arrested for "loitering" for little more than walking down a street. In another, an individual merely leaving a hotel was charged with "disorderly conduct." The ordinance defined vagrants to include "rogues and vagabonds," "dissolute persons who go about begging," "persons who use juggling," "common drunkards," "common night walkers," "lewd, wanton and lascivious persons," "common railers and brawlers," "persons wandering or strolling around from place to place without any lawful purpose or object," "habitual loafers," "disorderly persons," and various others.

In a 7–0 decision written by Justice William O. Douglas, the Court struck down the ordinance as plainly at odds with constitutional standards.[27] The ordinance, it held, was void for vagueness. It failed to give a person of ordinary intelligence fair notice as to what conduct is forbidden, and it permitted arbitrary and erratic arrests and convictions. Living under a rule of law requires that all persons "are entitled to be informed as to what the State commands or forbids."[28] Vague laws "allow the net to be cast at large, to enable men to be caught who are vaguely undesirable in the eyes of police and prosecution, although not chargeable with any particular offense." The Court emphasized that it is marginalized groups who are subjected to selective enforcement that bear the brunt of such laws.[29]

Papachristou well illustrates the need for precision in the law.[30] In the United States, this requirement is mandated by the Constitution's prohibition against any deprivation of life, liberty, or property without due process of law. The Constitution's Framers were explicit in their rejection of vague legal standards. James Madison asked how a rule can even be regarded as a rule if it is "little known and less fixed."[31] The guesswork rules Madison condemned are in modern times said to suffer from invalidating vagueness.[32] When people "of common intelligence must necessarily guess at its meaning," the Supreme Court has said, a law is unconstitutionally vague.[33] As early as 1875, the Supreme Court forcefully stated the rationale for the vagueness doctrine: "A citizen should not unnecessarily be placed where, by an honest error in the construction of a penal statute, he may be subjected to a prosecution."[34]

The vagueness doctrine is thus directed at preventing the unfairness of punishing a person who was not given prior notice as to what conduct was prohibited. To meet constitutional due process requirements, a law must provide "sufficiently definite warning as to the proscribed conduct when measured by common understanding and practices."[35] A statute is vague "if it authorizes or even encourages arbitrary and discriminatory enforcement."[36]

As these cases suggest, a vague law has two pernicious effects. First, it makes possible selective enforcement, conferring veiled discretion that is often abused in favor of the powerful, giving their views an advantage in the marketplace of ideas. As the Supreme Court put it, when a law fails to provide minimal guidelines, "a criminal statute may permit a standardless sweep that allows policemen, prosecutors and juries to pursue their personal predilections."[37] Second, such a law may chill constitutionally protected speech, creating a fear of punishment where none lawfully can be imposed. Vague laws cause citizens to self-censor, to "steer far wider of the unlawful zone" than do statutes that clearly mark forbidden areas.[38] Hence the Court struck down a statute that prohibited the state from hiring a "subversive person" or a person who refused to swear that he or she was not subversive, on the ground that the law's wording was "unduly vague, uncertain, and broad."[39]

All this bears directly, of course, on efforts to distinguish and define hate speech and protected groups. No one has delved more deeply into such efforts than Nadine Strossen, the former president of the ACLU. Her conclusion is unequivocal: "I have done my best to track down and read every 'hate speech' law that has been enacted or proposed, and have yet to encounter one that avoids the serious flaws that I have identified." Those flaws are woven into the project of suppressing hate speech. "[T]he very concept of 'hate speech' is irreducibly riddled with ambiguity, conflicts, and confusion," she writes. "Therefore, even if we were willing to depart from the fundamental viewpoint neutrality and emergency principles, any 'hate speech' law would still run afoul of fundamental free speech principles because it would be unacceptably vague or overbroad."[40] Strossen notes the concurrence of Eleanor Holmes Norton, the first woman to head the Equal Opportunity Employment Commission, who wrote, "It is technically impossible to write an anti-speech code that cannot be twisted against speech nobody means to bar. It has been tried and tried and tried."[41] The codes lead inevitably to the bottom of a slippery slope, where tools created with the best of intentions are used to shatter the cherished values of their authors.[42] It takes little familiarity with history to recognize that the sweeping latitude conveyed by vague authority to squelch noxious ideas has consistently been abused. Prosecutorial discretion inevitably broadens during wartime, when minorities have faced consistent suppression.[43] But peacetime drives to quash unwanted viewpoints have also been broadly facilitated by hate speech laws.[44]

The research of Strossen and others illustrates these difficulties. One need search no further than the statutes struck down by the Supreme Court to discover the inevitable elasticity and indeterminacy that pervade legislative efforts to outlaw signs of hate or related emotions. The Court has, for example, rejected a "dignity" standard and an "outrageous" standard as "inherently subjective" and violative of its long-standing refusal to permit the suppression of speech that "has an adverse emotional impact on the audience."[45] Intractable definitional difficulties are inherent even in seemingly narrowly drawn laws that proscribe only slurs and epithets. The "line-drawing problem," writes Farber, "seems irresolvable."[46]

In short, absent clear, principled lines that limit censors' power, victims of hate speech risk finding themselves victims of something far worse: a marketplace of ideas at the mercy of guardians of public morality who, exercising unbridled discretion, fill in the blanks of vague laws to make *their* views the views of the public.

Disarming and Isolating Minorities

A final constitutional rationale for declining the temptation to suppress hate speech is not doctrinal, like concerns about viewpoint discrimination and vagueness, but more in the nature of an underlying, overall purpose or motivation— the Constitution's aim "to keep the machinery of democratic government running as it should, to make sure the channels of political participation and communication are open."[47] Those are the words of John Hart Ely, interpreting the Court's famous "Footnote Four" in *United States v. Carolene Products* (1938). In the footnote (to an obscure opinion on the valisity of a "filled milk" law), the Court emphasized its heightened concern about safeguarding from prejudice "the operation of those political processes ordinarily to be relied upon to protect minorities."[48] The need to protect popular government and the need to protect minorities, Ely points out, both arise from the same concern:[49] that meaningful redress cannot be expected from representative institutions that have been rendered dysfunctional by a breakdown in political processes. As discussed in Chapter 12, at the heart of those political processes are channels of communication—namely, freedom of speech. The first "fix" for minorities that long have gotten the short end of the stick, as well as for legislative bodies that have become detached from public sentiment, is to ensure that the marketplace of ideas is up and running smoothly. Protecting minorities requires protecting free speech.

David Cole, legal director of the ACLU, put this constitutional theory concretely:

> Here is the ultimate contradiction in the argument for state suppression of speech in the name of equality: it demands protection of disadvantaged minorities' interests, but in a democracy, the state acts in the name of the majority, not the minority. Why would disadvantaged minorities trust representatives of the majority to decide whose speech should be censored?[50]

The danger of abusive majorities has long been recognized, but the phenomenon has of late become especially notable in countries where speech is not protected as rigorously as it is in the United States. As Stanford law professor Michael McConnell wrote in 2012, "[I]t is hard to find a case anywhere in the world where speech in support of dominant ideologies is punished for the protection of the weak. The opposite is frequently the case."[51] He cites real-world examples of abusive hate speech laws:

> In 2009, a member of the Belgian Parliament was convicted of distributing leaflets with the slogans: "Stand up against the Islamification of Belgium," "Stop the sham integration policy" and "Send non-European job-seekers home."

In 2006, protesters were convicted of distributing leaflets to Swedish high school students saying homosexuality was a "deviant sexual proclivity," had "a morally destructive effect on the substance of society" and was responsible for the development of H.I.V. and AIDS.

In 2008, a French cartoonist was convicted of publishing a drawing of the attack on the World Trade Center in a Basque newspaper with the words: "We have all dreamed about it. . . . Hamas did it." The European Court of Human Rights affirmed all three convictions, rejecting defenses based on freedom of speech.

In Poland, a Catholic magazine was fined $11,000 for inciting "contempt, hostility and malice" by comparing a woman's abortion to the medical experiments at Auschwitz. The Dutch politician Geert Wilders was temporarily barred from entering Britain as a "threat to public policy, public security or public health" because he made a movie that called the Koran a "fascist" book and described Islam as a violent religion. In France, Brigitte Bardot was convicted of publishing a letter to the interior minister stating that Muslims were ruining France. And Canada's human rights tribunal, which has harassed magazines for anti-Muslim statements and for republishing the famous Danish Muhammad cartoons, has been so hostile to freedom of the press that efforts are under way to repeal that nation's hate speech laws.

The patchy protection accorded free speech by international human rights law is discussed in Chapter 11, but note here that its rules, such as they are, fall far short of the safeguards of the First Amendment. It is not, as McConnell notes, that we doubt that hate speech inflicts real harm on vulnerable minorities—"we simply fear censorship more." Holmesian pragmatism counsels *comparative* risk analysis, in which the probability of one set of dangers is weighed against the probability of another set of dangers. In choosing worse over worst, the "point is not, of course, that such expression is harmless," Stone acknowledges. "It is, rather, that there are better ways to address that harm than by giving government the power to decide which ideas the citizens of a free and self-governing nation may and may not express."[52] Odious opinions will be expressed; useless and hurtful information will be published. Opening the marketplace to ideas we hate means, as Farber observes, that "even Nazis are entitled to compete in the marketplace of ideas."[53] An unpalatable result—except for all the alternatives.

This, then, is one consequence of vague and viewpoint-discriminatory speech bans: their availability as a weapon for use against minorities that need free speech to bring their plight to the majority's attention and to press for reform—to seek a "redress of grievances," in the words of the First Amendment. "Without freedom of speech and the right to dissent," said Martin Luther King's colleague John Lewis, "the Civil Rights movement would have been a bird without wings."[54] On the eve of the Civil War, Douglass decried the slaveholders' censorship of calls for emancipation and predicted the end of slavery if speech were left free.[55] It was the ability of advocates such as Lewis and Douglass to speak and be heard that brought about a rejection of notions of white supremacy. Free speech throughout history has been the ally of other oppressed groups as well. A group's "escape from subordinate status is accomplished primarily through persuasion," as UCLA law professor Kenneth Karst observed.[56] To disable despised oppositional groups from conveying their message is to take from them the tool that they have used so effectively to free themselves: convincing argument in a competition of ideas.

Finally, note the breadth of categories potentially eligible for potential protection, ranging from age to veteran status, polygamy, and those already on the list. Even if it were possible to justify the exclusion of given groups from protected categories without regard to their political power, and even if it were possible to draw meaningful lines around such groups to preclude pretended membership, the official designation of such groups can nonetheless have the perverse effects of entrenching separateness,[57] reinforcing hostility and conflict,[58] sparking conflict between protected and unprotected groups,[59] and creating a false sense of distinctness where identity is complex and ambiguous.[60] Public acceptance of a group is not advanced when its "protection" from unwanted speech is based not on principled criteria but on sheer power. Instead of empowering minority groups, formally singling out protected groups from hate speech can weaken their protection by entrenching their identity.[61]

In contrast, the equal participation of all groups in an "uninhibited, robust, and wide-open" public debate can lead to a broader sense of community in which conflict is resolved through discussion and deliberation. Those are the words of the Court in the most famous free speech case of era, *New York Times v. Sullivan*,[62] in which it overturned a libel judgment and an exorbitant damages award brought by a public official against the newspaper. Its errors were protected unless made with "actual malice," the Court held—the statement had to be made with knowledge of its falsity or with reckless disregard of whether it was true or false. The successful, in that debate as in the nation in which it occurs, are those able to withstand opposition, criticism, and even hatred because they know that the greater dignity derives from living in a pluralistic society comprised of individuals with widely differing views—individuals who are strong enough, in Douglass's words, to "tolerate free speech."[63] This resistance to concentrated power and its pragmatist respect for pluralism and fallibilism shaped the Court's approach in curbing governmental efforts to silence "false ideas," to which we now turn.

9

Disinformation

Roughly half of U.S. adults (48%), the Pew Research Center reported in August 2021, believe the government should "take steps to restrict false information online, even if it means losing some freedom to access and publish content."[1] Why not do so—indeed, why restrict only *online* falsehoods? False information, one might think, has no social or political value, regardless of its source or mode of transmission. It leads only to erroneous decisions. It wrecks lives and undermines democracy. Why not allow the government to punish someone who, for example, falsely claims to have received the Medal of Honor?

That question was in fact addressed by the Supreme Court. Xavier Alvarez, an elected member of his local water board, had an uneasy relationship with the truth. The Court put it more bluntly. "Lying was his habit," it said in *United States v. Alvarez*.[2] Alvarez lied in claiming that he had played hockey for the Detroit Red Wings and lied in claiming he had been married to a Mexican movie star. When Alvarez lied in announcing he received the Congressional Medal of Honor, the Court's plurality said, he ventured into new ground, "for that lie violate[d] a federal criminal statute,"[3] the Stolen Valor Act.

Yet the Court found that Alvarez's speech was protected by the First Amendment. The reason false information is constitutionally protected should at this point be unsurprising: each of the three rationales for protection discussed earlier, in connection with the incitement, viewpoint neutrality, and vagueness doctrines, point to the error of allowing the government to censor what it labels false. Consider each in turn.

Incitement and the Marketplace of Ideas

In holding Alvarez's speech to be protected, six members of the Court reaffirmed its commitment to the marketplace of ideas. The plurality cited Holmes, writing that the "theory of our Constitution is 'that the best test of truth is the power of the thought to get itself accepted in the competition of

Free Speech and Turbulent Freedom. Michael J. Glennon, Oxford University Press. © Oxford University Press 2024.
DOI: 10.1093/oso/9780197636763.003.0009

the market,"[4] and Brandeis: " 'If there be time to expose through discussion the falsehood and fallacies, to avert the evil by the processes of education, the remedy to be applied is more speech, not enforced silence.' "[5] No emergency existed; Alvarez's lie did not incite to imminent violence or law violation. Plenty of time was available to expose his falsehood. The remedy therefore was not enforced silence, the Court held. "The remedy for speech that is false is speech that is true."[6] It continued:

> The First Amendment itself ensures the right to respond to speech we do not like, and for good reason. Freedom of speech and thought flows not from the beneficence of the state but from the inalienable rights of the person. And suppression of speech by the government can make exposure of falsity more difficult, not less so. Society has the right and civic duty to engage in open, dynamic, rational discourse.[7]

The nation well knows, the Court recognized, that it incurs costs in permitting people to speak freely and sometimes falsely. But the alternative is worse. Authoritatively identifying false information requires identifying *true* information. Some official source would have to be established against which the truth or falsehood of information is to be assessed. Inevitably, this would require establishing a Ministry of Truth, the Court noted. It would endorse governmental authority to compile an endless list of subjects about which false statements are punishable; "it would give government a broad censorial power unprecedented in this Court's cases or in our constitutional tradition."[8] Our entire constitutional tradition, the Court concluded, stands against such ideas.

But, it might be answered, again, that false speech has no worth. Democracy suffers if people spread falsehoods, particularly about public officials and institutions. False statements impede our ability to think well about who should lead us.[9] People lose faith in their leaders and even in government itself.

In assessing this argument it's useful to examine a concrete example. Consider, therefore, President Trump's claim that the size of the crowd attending his inauguration was larger than that attending President Obama's.[10] Trump's claim was indisputably false; in the oft-quoted words of his counselor, it was an "alternative fact."[11] All that was necessary to reveal its falsity was to compare overhead photographic evidence. Was the effect of Trump's claim, as he may have intended, to diminish public respect for Obama and enhance public respect for himself? Quite the contrary: the falsehood more likely had the effect of calling into question not only Trump's veracity but his mental soundness as he maintained his claim in the face of clear, disconfirming evidence. That people might lose faith in a leader because of false claims is not a sign of the failure of the marketplace of ideas—it is a sign of its success. Allowing Trump freely to express that falsehood and not suppressing it afterward advanced the efficient operation of democracy rather than undermining it. It helped people to think accurately about those who seek their votes.

That is how the marketplace also operated with respect to Alvarez. After his lie was discovered, the press reported it, and Alvarez was publicly ridiculed and resigned in disgrace. People lost faith in him because he did not deserve their trust—which the marketplace revealed. "Free speech does not cure stupidity," Jonathan Turley observed; "it merely exposes it."[12]

The second problem with the argument that the government should weed out falsehood is one that the Court hints at when it points out the inevitable need for a Ministry of Truth. The problem is that such a body can be wrong. Neither the government nor any other participant in the marketplace is infallible. "In a survey of 1,406 journalists conducted by the International Centre for Journalists, a non-profit organization in Washington," the *Economist* reported, "46% said that elected officials were the source of misinformation relating to covid-19 that they had encountered."[13] As is discussed in Chapter 12, sometimes the government itself is actually the source of *dis*information—information that it in fact knows to be false. The realization that government lies was shocking in 1971, when the Pentagon Papers revealed it had repeatedly lied about progress on the war in Vietnam; it generated barely a yawn in 2019 when, five decades later, the *Washington Post* published evidence of similar deceit concerning progress on the war in Afghanistan.[14]

Sometimes, of course, the government is the source of false information that it may not know to be false—*mis*information. Many examples exist; Chapter 12 recounts a number of them. Whether the statements in question were known or not known at the time to be untrue—whether the government was mistaken or flat-out lying—would not alter the central point: that it would still be short-sighted to allow the government to authoritatively determine "the truth" and to suppress information that challenges it. The truth emerged gradually that these assurances were incorrect, although it might not have emerged at all but for the operation of the marketplace of ideas.

Censoring COVID "misinformation" on social media that challenged the government's false statements did no one any service—it merely prolonged a national tragedy and prevented the public from addressing risks that could have been recognized earlier in a fully open and robust marketplace of ideas. This is why, as the *Alvarez* plurality put it, the "suppression of speech by the government can make exposure of falsity more difficult, not less so."[15]

Viewpoint Neutrality

The second reason to protect false information is that its suppression frequently would lead to content or viewpoint discrimination. This was a prime concern in *Alvarez*. The Stolen Valor Act, the plurality said, illustrated, "in a fundamental way, the reasons for the Law's distrust of content-based speech prohibitions."[16] A claim of having won the French Open or an academy award or a Pulitzer Prize would not have been prosecutable; only content falsely claiming a military award broke the law. The Act also seemed to discriminate based on viewpoint. Congress permitted the punishment of someone who falsely claimed to have *won* military honors, but not someone who falsely *denied* having won military honors. It's not hard to imagine situations in which a job applicant or political candidate might seek to bury any record of military service in a conflict that has since become unpopular, such as the Vietnam War. During his 2004 presidential campaign, a heated controversy arose over whether John Kerry, who became a leader of the antiwar movement, had publicly thrown away medals or ribbons he had earned during his deployment in Vietnam.[17] Like the flag desecration statute invalidated in *Texas v. Johnson*,[18] the Stolen Valor Act operated "in only one direction,"[19] penalizing false claims but not false denials.

The evil in content and viewpoint discrimination, here as elsewhere, is that it subordinates the values of the censored for the values of the censor. It officially labels one set of values correct and conflicting values incorrect. It takes from the individual the right to choose freely among conflicting values. The foundational premise is that value choices are left to the individual, to "the person most interested in his own well-being," as John Stuart Mill put it.[20] Through deliberation and a free exchange of ideas, values are sifted and aggregated, and society arrives at its own composite values. Truth-seeking, as Robert Post has written, requires an important set of shared social practices: the "capacity to listen and to engage in self evaluation, as well as a commitment to the conventions of reason, which in turn entail aspirations toward objectivity, disinterest, civility, and mutual respect."[21] That may be why the *Alvarez* plurality forcefully affirmed that "[s]ociety has the right and civic duty to engage in open, dynamic, rational discourse. These ends are not well served when the government seeks to orchestrate public discussion through content-based mandates."[22]

Vagueness

At a surface level, no problem of vagueness inhered in the Stolen Valor Act, which in effect traded vagueness for very specific content and viewpoint discrimination. At a deeper level, however, the Court appeared concerned about pervasive vagueness problems. What is the underlying, intelligible criterion under which falsehoods can be identified and extirpated from the marketplace of ideas? There is none, the Court concluded. No "limiting principle" would restrict the government from arbitrarily deciding which falsehoods are officially disapproved:

> Permitting the government to decree this speech to be a criminal offense, whether shouted from the rooftops or made in a barely audible whisper, would endorse government authority to compile a list of subjects about which false statements are punishable. That governmental power has no clear limiting principle. . . . Were this law to be sustained, there could be an endless list of subjects the National Government or the States could single out.[23]

A moment's reflection reveals why this skepticism is well founded. Intuition tells us that falsehood is not hard to spot. The sun revolves around the earth, whales can fly, France is in Africa—those statements are false. Cows eat grass, cancer can kill, Lincoln was assassinated—those statements are true. Truth and falsehood are discrete categories, it seems; although considerable investigation is often required, statements can reliably be placed in those two categories. To knowingly repeat a falsehood is to intentionally deceive or mislead.

The problem, of course, is that not all statements can be filed in two neat categories. "Donald Trump should be prosecuted" and "Hillary Clinton belongs in jail"; "COVID vaccines work" and "Masks are ineffective";

"America is an exceptional country" and "The United States is systemically racist"—one can think of countless examples of statements that are not readily categorizable as either true or false. If white and black categories of truth and falsehood exist, there is also an enormous gray zone, and which statements go where is often anything but self-evident.

It's not simply that the line between fact and opinion is hazy. At the most mundane level, how would one classify jokes, satire, or garden-variety puffery or flattery? The truth of many ostensibly empirical claims is not actually "established" but falls somewhere on a continuum between probability and improbability; what if that degree of probability is uncertain or unknowable? Different people have different levels of skepticism, gullibility, and sophistication in seeing through propaganda, fakery, and spin; whose level is the proper reference point—who do we protect from "misleading" information? "Deep fakes" created by artificial intelligence manipulate us by distorting our perception of reality; is use of a modern teleprompter part of a deep fake that tricks us into thinking that a tongue-tied politician is actually coherent? The president sometimes appears in front of what look like actual windows and a digital view of the Rose Garden, styled to look like the White House interior—but the scene is entirely fake, shot not in the Oval Office but next door in the Eisenhower Executive Office Building. Is that disinformation? Or worse yet, is it "mal-information," as the Department of Homeland Security calls information that "is based on fact, but used out of context to mislead, harm, or manipulate"?[24]

Why should a conscientious censor not think big—why focus on simple, single statements or images that often are only a small part of a larger myth system that integrates the speakers' values and aspirations and animates mass political movements and challenges to benevolent social institutions? Yuval Harari has argued that such myth systems shore up an "imagined order" that is necessary for large-scale cooperation.[25] The myths have no material reality; they exist only in the minds of those who embrace them. If the object of censorship is to nip in the bud large-scale cooperation that may be sparked by falsehood, shouldn't the farsighted censor go to the heart of the danger and root out the entire narrative in which the offending information is embedded? The propriety of expunging falsehood from top to bottom seems implicit in the view of one respected scholar in averring that "freedom of speech should not be taken as forbidding efforts to protect reality."[26]

One can easily see how quickly the power to police the marketplace of ideas for falsehood could become, as the Court said, the power to orchestrate public discussion. The beneficiary of that power, as always, would be the orchestra's conductor: the government. One can rest assured that it will be the government's opponents and not its friends and supporters who are found to be the purveyors of misinformation, disinformation, or mal-information. This has been the story in country after country that has justified censorship in the name of eliminating "fake news." Some of the most well-intentioned efforts of the most committed democracies have ended up as prototypes for the crudest suppression, as the *Economist* reported in describing the effects of Germany's fake-news regulations:

> Germany's Network Enforcement Law (Netzdg), passed in 2017, is meant to protect readers from fake news and hate speech by requiring social-media platforms to remove material deemed incendiary. More than a dozen countries, from Russia to Turkey, have copied this legislation as a way to suppress dissent online. Many of these countries expressly referred to the German law as justification for their repressive legislation.[27]

The reasons for fearing the vagueness in disinformation controls is familiar. The threat of being penalized for making a false statement inhibits a speaker from making a true statement, the *Alvarez* plurality reminded us.[28] It concluded:

> Were the Court to hold that the interest in truthful discourse alone is sufficient to sustain a ban on speech . . . it would give government a broad censorial power unprecedented in this Court's cases or in our constitutional tradition. The mere potential for the exercise of that power casts a chill, a chill the First Amendment cannot permit if free speech, thought, and discourse are to remain a foundation of our freedom.[29]

It is true that free speech, thought, and discourse may lead people to imagine a reality different from the government's. As Holmes and others have realized, sometimes through no small sacrifice, people simply have fundamentally different views of reality. In the U.S. constitutional tradition, it is not for the government to determine which of those views is correct. It is a choice left to the individual, a choice that includes the right to be wrong.

PART III
THE FUTURE

10

Is the First Amendment Outdated?

Why do these strictures of a pre-internet First Amendment have any relevance to communications in a twenty-first-century United States where information and opinions are distributed and restricted by private social media companies, which the Supreme Court has acknowledged are the "modern public square"?[1] Private companies, it is widely understood, are not subject to First Amendment limits. The Constitution prohibits abridgment of speech only by the government; "state action" is required to trigger constitutional limits, and the government long ago got out of the business of jailing seditious newspaper editors and rounding up curmudgeonly pamphleteers. Whatever else may threaten free speech today, the reader may well think, it's not the government.

This has been, in fact, social media's answer when confronted with First Amendment questions. In response to state legislation limiting social media companies' power to remove certain content or to attach labels to users' posts, the companies have responded simply that the First Amendment invalidates all such regulations.[2] Facebook is like a private newspaper, it contends, enabling it to publish or refuse to publish whatever it pleases. As the next chapter discusses, Facebook made the same argument when it blocked President Trump from using his account following the January 6, 2021 riots at the Capitol. His speech was not protected by the First Amendment, Facebook asserted, because the First Amendment "does not govern the conduct of private companies." Other social media platforms have taken the same view: it's *their* marketplace of ideas, and their marketplace need be open only to whatever ideas they choose to let in.

The state action doctrine is not the only source of tension for free speech. The so-called government speech doctrine dovetails with it. Its effect is so ubiquitous that its importance is not widely appreciated. Like private actors, the government acts not only by *doing*—it also acts by *saying*, through speech as well as conduct. Government officials speak constantly, opining on myriad topics related and unrelated to official law and policy. The government could hardly function otherwise; broad protection of its speech is essential to carry

Free Speech and Turbulent Freedom. Michael J. Glennon, Oxford University Press. © Oxford University Press 2024.
DOI: 10.1093/oso/9780197636763.003.0010

out its purposes. Hence the government speech doctrine, which has it that neither the First Amendment nor anything else in the Constitution limits what government actors can say.[3]

As a result, the government can use its *own* speech to abridge private speech—which it cannot constitutionally abridge through its conduct. By encouraging and "recommending" private conduct or speech with its *words*, the government can work hand in hand with private parties to curtail constitutionally protected private speech. When the state action and government speech doctrines come together, however, the consequences for the marketplace of ideas can be devastating. Examples are discussed in Chapter 12; in one such instance, governmental health officials plotted and executed "a quick and devastating published take down" to discredit the writing of Oxford, Harvard, and Stanford scientists who questioned the official government line on COVID vaccine efficacy—speech that social media promptly banned—but the health officials of course faced no constraints because theirs was government speech. The officials were simply expressing their opinions, they claimed, and there was, after all, no state action in the platforms' view since social media are private companies.[4]

The question is: Can it be right that a technological innovation not more than two decades in the making may for all intents and purposes eviscerate the most fundamental of Americans' constitutional rights, a right that has its roots in centuries of Western thought? Can it be right that government now has unlimited power to quash free speech and stigmatize speakers—to abridge freedom of speech—so long as it does so through its speech rather than conduct, or through private intermediaries rather than direct action?

If maintaining a robust marketplace of ideas is the justification for free speech, I suggest in this part of the book the answer must be no—the answer must be that the safeguards of the First Amendment cannot have *no* application to the modern marketplace of ideas. The enduring rationale for free speech, outlined in earlier pages, continues to pertain even in the face of technological breakthroughs that would have been unimaginable to the Amendment's Framers. No modern technology has eliminated the effects of censorship that have been recognized for centuries: it demeans would-be listeners, discredits the censors, valorizes the suppressed communication, undermines our search for knowledge, impedes peaceful social change, and generates political instability. It's not my purpose in this Part to spell out how the First Amendment principles reviewed in Part II should resolve the myriad individual "content moderation" cases that arise, or even what specific rules the Amendment's application should require in such contexts. It is good and sufficient, it seems to me, to establish a single cornerstone principle: that the First Amendment has not become functionally irrelevant in the digitized twenty-first century. *Some* corollaries follow from that, but there is no point in debating which yet-to-be-devised precepts should follow unless that starting point is clear. It cannot be right that the Constitution's protection of free speech no longer has any real-world meaning. The threshold question is: What body of law applies? The answer must be: the First Amendment. Judges, as Holmes wrote, have failed adequately to recognize the societal consequences of their decisions.[5] Unless they begin to do so in applying the First Amendment to social media, there will soon be little left to apply.

The point, then, which is developed in Chapter 12, is not that First Amendment limits should be applied in toto, across the board to all government speech or to all social media activity. There *is* a place for government jawboning to advance constitutionally formulated public policy. There *is* a danger of undermining the free speech rights of private publishers if the speech of would-be writers is forced into their pages—which is why newspapers cannot, for example, be forced to publish letters to the editor or op-eds they dislike. But a well-run democracy must be able to reconcile competing values, to give maximum possible effect to one value without discarding altogether other, equally strong values. That is the task, to recall Holmes's words once again, of a constitution written for people with fundamentally different views. The alternative to reconciliation is conflict. At some point conflict may be inevitable; at some point values may not be reconcilable; at some point unbridled discretion and primordial intuition may prevail. But a well-run democracy avoids reaching that point as long as possible. Ours can do that by giving broader effect to the values and purposes underpinning the First Amendment than a cramped and formalistic reading would allow.

How a broader application of First Amendment principles will play out in particular cases in which parties have differing, competing interests is, for these reasons, beyond the scope of this book. What is fair to ask is how these doctrines which impede that application might be overcome. If under the state-action doctrine constitutional restraints apply only to the government, not to private parties, and if under the government-speech doctrine government actors are free to say anything they like, how can the First Amendment's vision of the marketplace of ideas realistically be saved?

The answer, elaborated at length in Chapter 12, is that neither the state-action doctrine nor the government-speech doctrine is a constitutional straitjacket. Contrary to popular impression, the courts have not been blind to the reality that the government sometimes works indirectly through private actors. The Supreme Court has recognized in a number of cases that the line between the government and private actors is not well defined. Private actors sometimes act—officially or unofficially, consciously, or inadvertently—as arms of the state. They do so, for example, when they are coerced by the government or engage in a joint enterprise with the government or enter into a symbiotic relationship with a governmental actor. When they do so, they are subject to the same constitutional restraints that limit the government itself. The government cannot contract out its work to escape constitutional limitations and restrictions on its power. The court has in recent years been less willing to find state action where public and private conduct is intertwined—but earlier cases remain good law, and those cases can provide the seeds of a new jurisprudence to revivify the marketplace of ideas. Similarly, the Court has found that the government's power to jawbone is not unlimited; where a constitutional limit is at issue, earlier cases outlined in Chapter 12 suggest that the government can go only so far in coercing private conduct without stepping over the line. And let there be no doubt about what the government has been up to of late: as that chapter details, the security state has been working hand in glove with private parties to curtail free speech, and it has been using its own speech or encouraging the speech of others to constrict the marketplace of ideas. It's crucial to realize, as Chapter 12 details, that considerable evidence of this collusion was available in the public record long before it was confirmed beyond doubt in *Missouri v. Biden* and by the "Twitter Files," for that public record is a damning commentary on the fecklessness of legislative oversight and the futility of recourse to misguided legislators who have pushed for more censorship, not less. The system will not self-correct so long as the channels of political change are blocked. Judicial intervention is required, and unless the courts have much more to say about government speech and "private" conduct than they have in the past, free speech in the United States faces extinction.

Before turning to these issues in Chapter 12, though, a more immediate question arises: What's the alternative to retaining and applying the First Amendment? It's not, after all, as though social media companies have been operating under no rules. They've applied their own rules that, they proudly proclaim, incorporate international human rights law. Why not look to it to protect their users? Might international human rights law be better suited to regulating the U.S. marketplace of ideas than the First Amendment?

In addressing that question, it is useful to consider, first, why social media companies might find international human rights law more appealing than the First Amendment. We can then compare how international human rights law would deal with cases arising in the three subject areas we've discussed in Chapters 7, 8, and 9—incitement to violence, hate speech, and the publication of falsehoods—contrasting its treatment of those issues with the First Amendment's. And we can, in the process, assess whether international human rights law as applied in such cases passes its own most basic test—whether it lays out rules that are clear and accessible.

The answer, outlined in the next chapter, is that it does not.

11

International Human Rights Law

A president of the United States, speaking from the White House, makes a statement to Americans on a communications platform operated by a U.S. corporation, and because of the content of his speech, the platform blocks further speech and suspends his account—guided not by the principles of the First Amendment but by international human rights law.

Set aside, for a moment, the identity of the actors—they were Donald Trump and Facebook[1]—and consider the question without regard to the party or politics of the president. Set aside the scope of Facebook's legal right to prescribe its own posting rules. And set aside also, for the time being, *who* ought to apply the rules—Facebook or the government. Consider one question: Which set of rules should apply—those of the First Amendment or international law?

The stakes that turn on this choice could hardly be more momentous.[2] Facebook has nearly three billion active monthly users worldwide. By 2017, Facebook's advertising was larger than the entire global commercial radio business.[3] At the time the Trump case arose, roughly three-fourths of American adults had Facebook accounts.[4] Two-thirds relied upon social media as their prime source for news.[5] In the twenty-first-century United States, as Suzanne Nossel observed, a "small handful of giant companies have more or less complete control of what has become one of our central marketplaces of ideas."[6] For millions of Americans and billions of people worldwide, the marketplace of ideas has become the internet, and the internet has become Facebook.[7]

Facebook's rationale for preferring international law was suggested in 2019 by the company's head of policy management. "The borderless and dynamic nature of social media communications requires standards that are globally applied," she wrote, "and [national] speech laws are ill suited for global application." In 2017, YouTube was available in more than eighty-five countries, Facebook in more than one hundred languages. Over 85% of Facebook users and 79% of Twitter users were from outside the United States. They engage in a web of interactions, she argued: someone in Norway can post a photo taken

Free Speech and Turbulent Freedom. Michael J. Glennon, Oxford University Press. © Oxford University Press 2024.
DOI: 10.1093/oso/9780197636763.003.0011

in India and send it to an Australian for comments, sparking a lively online discussion. "To preserve this sort of dialogue, people need to be seeing the same content, and they need to be able to engage in real time. And for that, they need one set of global content standards." It would be impractical and inefficient, she argued, for Facebook to "evaluate content against multiple, subjective, evolving laws" of different nations, which "cannot substitute for a set of standards specifically crafted for a large, global community."[8]

Trump, with 35 million followers on Facebook,[9] used social media extensively to communicate with the public. He did so twice on January 6, 2021, the day a mob overran the U.S. Capitol. Because of those posts, Facebook blocked Trump's access to his account (as did YouTube and Twitter). Facebook then announced that it had referred its decision to its Oversight Board, Facebook's internal Supreme Court. It comprised, at the time of the Trump case, twenty individuals appointed by the company. Some were internationally prominent; only five were Americans. Facebook asked the Board whether the decision to suspend Trump's account complied with Facebook's own "community standards," values, and corporate policies that govern the posting of materials on its website. On May 4, the Oversight Board announced its decision. Applying Facebook's community standards and international human rights law, the Oversight Board did not reach the question whether Trump had incited violence. It found instead that blocking Trump's posts and suspending his account was appropriate because he had praised and supported violence (though the length of the suspension could not be undefined, the Board said; Facebook later set it at two years). The Board added that the penalty was necessary for national security reasons, to safeguard domestic constitutional processes: "The riot directly interfered with Congress's ability to discharge its constitutional responsibility." The Board did not, however, address the implications of the Constitution for Facebook's action. It did "not apply the First Amendment of the U.S. Constitution," it said, "which does not govern the conduct of private companies."[10]

What specific international human rights standards had Facebook, at the time of the Trump case, committed itself to honor? (Twitter and Google[11] also have claimed allegiance to human rights law.)[12] Facebook's human rights director, asked directly what specific international human rights rules Facebook applied, dodged the question and provided no useful answer.[13] Sift through Facebook's various corporate policies, community standards, stated values, bylaws, tweets, press releases, blog posts, and other online materials in looking for an answer, and one is struck that, if anything, the Oversight Board understated matters when it reiterated in its Trump opinion that the "patch-work of applicable rules makes it difficult for users to understand why and when Facebook restricts accounts, and raises legality concerns." References to international human rights law are now sprinkled throughout Facebook's web pages. At the time of Trump's posts, the Charter of Facebook's Oversight Board provided simply that "[w]hen reviewing decisions, the board will pay particular attention to the impact of removing content in light of human rights norms protecting free expression."[14] On March 16, 2021, however—over two months after Trump's speech occurred—Facebook elaborated that guidance and announced a new corporate policy that would include vol-untary "respect" for international human rights law, including the United Nations Guiding Principles on Business and Human Rights (UNGPs); the Universal Declaration of Human Rights; the International Covenant on Economic, Social and Cultural Rights; the International Covenant on Economic, Social and Cultural Rights; and various other international human rights instruments, "depending on the circumstances."[15] The com-pany thus retained discretion to determine which rules, and which interpre-tation of those rules, would be applied in any given context.

In reaching its judgment in the Trump case, the Board applied the bedrock standard of international human rights law, the so-called legality doctrine. The Board summarized the doctrine as follows:

> In international law on freedom of expression, the principle of legality requires that any rule used to limit expression is clear and accessible. People must be able to understand what is allowed and what is not allowed. Equally important, rules must be sufficiently clear to provide guidance to those who make decisions on limiting expression, so that these rules do not confer unfettered discretion, which can result in selective application of the rules.[16]

I suggest that this fundamental requirement that rules limiting freedom of expression be clear and accessible is not met by reliance upon generic inter-national human rights law to decide social media content disputes such as the Trump case. Those rules do not pass muster under their own requirement of clarity and accessibility. I focus on their application in the Trump case be-cause that case is in many respects emblematic of content moderation gen-erally, and because what happened to a sitting president of the United States can happen to any social media user. But it should be recognized that the companies have blocked, buried, or banned innumerable messages and provided no actual notice to the user as to what rule has been violated—leaving users to speculate as to how they might have failed to comply and whether the companies' actions have been arbitrary or invidious.[17]

I emphasize that this is not an argument that the First Amendment, or any other uniquely American rules, for that matter, should govern the resolution of such disputes in other countries. It is for those nations to assess whether importing American values and practices concerning freedom of speech and other constitutionally guaranteed liberties would serve their people's needs. Many of the unintended costs of suppression outlined in Chapter 6 would seem to be incurred by other societies as well, but that is, again, for them to judge, as is the relative weight of suppression's benefits; this chapter is about the law within the United States, not abroad.

Nor is this an argument, I need hardly point out, against international human rights law. I testified as a witness for Nicaragua in its case against the United States before the International Court of Justice concerning human rights abuses by the Contras, who were supported by the United States. I have elsewhere urged repeatedly not only that the United States comply with applicable human rights rules[18] but that, subject to potential congressional disapproval, the interstices of U.S. domestic law should be filled in provisionally, case by case, with clearly defined and widely accepted international human rights norms.[19] Following World War II, the United States has played a leading role in promoting international human rights, and for all its occasional hypocrisy and double standards, there seems little doubt that those efforts have on balance made for a more tolerant and humane world. Human rights advocates within and outside of the United States have nobly advanced a worthy cause.

The appeal of international human rights law for Facebook is thus understandable. For Facebook, global standards, as Facebook's head of policy management put it, are preferable to country-specific standards.[20] Voluntary adoption of human rights norms implies a commitment to values of decency, morality, and human dignity redolent of Google's "Don't Be Evil" slogan (long since scrapped).[21] It distracts attention from human rights embarrassments, such as Facebook's use by genocidal oppressors of the Rohingya in Myanmar[22] and compliance with data or censorship requests from autocratic governments in Turkey[23] and elsewhere. It staves off rigorous regulation if a plausible claim can be made that existing international human rights constraints are tight enough. With only a single, centralized regulatory regime to understand and target, lobbying public officials is easier.

It makes for friendships with administrators and activists in international organizations and NGOs. It deflects blame if controversial decisions can be explained as nondiscretionary compliance with unyielding legal rules. And above all, it allows social media companies to reap the benefits of a commitment to free speech by lowering the risk that they will have to comply with the most speech-protective legal regime in the world, the First Amendment of the U.S. Constitution. It makes perfect sense, therefore, for Facebook and its defenders to exalt international human rights law as a single, universal, pertinent, consistent, and determinate body of law, rules that are fundamentally like those of domestic law and that can be applied out of the box, as it were, to decide what Facebook can or should keep off its website.

The problem is that the international human rights regime governing freedom of expression is none of those things. It is fundamentally different from domestic law. It was written to protect individuals' rights from interference by states, not from interference by other individuals or businesses. Adherence to it by private companies is voluntary and nonbinding. It is not a single, monolithic body of law. It is incomplete, fragmented, and inconsistent. Some of its elements—including, as will be seen, the treaty provisions Facebook relied upon in the Trump case—allow speech suppression that is flatly incompatible with that permitted by the U.S. Constitution. The principal provisions of those treaties are vague and loophole-ridden. They have spawned state practice and customary international law that are confusing and contradictory. The net effect is a false universalism, a façade of consensus that masks indeterminacy and enables the arbitrariness and cherry-picking that Chief Justice John Roberts cautioned about in his confirmation hearings: "looking out over a crowd and picking out your friends."[24] To repeat the point of this chapter: *the fundamental requirement of international human rights law that rules limiting freedom of expression be clear and accessible is not met by reliance upon a generic international human rights law regime to decide social media content disputes.*

This becomes clear upon considering each of those features, beginning with pretensions to completeness.

Incompleteness

The idea is prevalent in much human rights advocacy, particularly in the realm of social media content moderation, that international human rights law constitutes a single, comprehensive, complete system.[25] The assumption is that the rules are comprehensive, comprising categories like squares in a huge juridical quilt that covers every possible fact situation, leaving no legal question unanswered. The implication is that only one correct answer exists for every such question,[26] since *universal* human rights can by definition leave no room for multiple, equally correct, conflicting answers to the same question. Finding the correct answer is merely a matter of accurate classification: identify the characteristics of the speech in question, and then place it neatly within the appropriate legal category. That there exist gray areas on the margins of each category makes classification more difficult but does not defeat it. The right answer is out there, waiting to be discovered, embedded in "community values,"[27] earlier rules,[28] their overarching purposes, or some other juridically endogenous source that transcends humanity's fleeting differences. Righteous enforcers everywhere ultimately will come to the same correct conclusion as to how ambiguities should be resolved and which category is the right one.

This view has obvious attractions. It eliminates the specter of a "legal vacuum" from which, it is supposed, believers in the rule of law ought naturally recoil. It promises a Holy Grail of universality, the glimmering possibility that good intentions and assiduous effort will yield unanimity. It eradicates analytic confusion by giving every question a crystalline answer. It provides emotional succor to those who seek refuge from the bewildering tangle of conflicting human wants, needs, and emotions that spring from cultural, political, and philosophical differences. It removes the perilous possibility that a nonexistent gap in the law might be exploited by the likes of Antifa or QAnon and their ilk as a pretext for violation. It counters the growing fragmentation of the international system. And it eliminates the frustrating need to come to consensus on new rules: if no gaps need be filled, no new rules need be devised. For those puzzling over the rules that govern social media, this view of law is beguiling. It has but one drawback.

The idea of completeness is fanciful.

It's the wrong way to think about international law generally and the wrong way to think about international human rights law in particular. The approach has been rejected by the International Court of Justice[29] and dismissed by legal scholars for over a hundred years as arid formalism, legal fundamentalism, noble dreams, mechanical jurisprudence, myth making, and various other pejoratives[30]—for understandable reasons.

Think back to the earliest years, the years in which international human rights law was young and its rules few. Did these pioneering, stand-alone rules leave no gaps? The few early rules were isolated patches; the "quilt" of international human rights law, such as it is, emerged only gradually, over many years. In the initial years of the law's development, numerous matters that were later to be addressed by the rules remained obscure.[31] At what point in the law's evolution did it become all-encompassing, leaving no question unanswered, like the rules of chess? At what point did human imagination freeze, losing all capacity to exploit ambiguities in the existing rules? When, precisely, did the law's development end? With the Universal Declaration of Human Rights in 1948? With the International Covenant on Civil and Political Rights in 1976? When did the system become complete? *How would we even know if it were complete?*

Unless one takes some form of natural law as transforming itself into legal rules,[32] no evidence exists to suggest that international human rights law has arrived—or ever will arrive—at some millennial zenith beyond which no further refinement need be contemplated. Evolving human wants, needs, and emotions will continue to produce the ever-changing mishmash of clashing, culturally variant preferences from which international human rights law flows.[33]

Consider closely the analogical process involved in comparing social media platforms with states, and it quickly becomes apparent that categorization involves inevitable subjectivity. The circumstances that led to an old rule's creation can be similar in some respects to current circumstances but different in others; which elements take priority? There exists no objective standard by which to identify the characteristics of an act or thing that are salient for classification purposes, or how much weight one characteristic is to be given relative to another, or the level of generality or particularity with which they are to be stated, or whether instrumentalities or effects are dispositive. One often can pull the accordion of analogy wide or push it tightly together without risk of being proven wrong.[34] Much the same can be said of efforts to establish the law's completeness and continuousness through reliance upon supposed community values and underlying purposes. The assertion that community values concerning freedom of speech are "shared" is belied by state practice, outlined below. To the extent that consensus does exist, it must be formulated at so high a level of generality and embrace so many different values, policies, and political preferences as to support multiple, equally compelling and sometimes conflicting conclusions, animated, at times, by equally compelling but conflicting rationales. These can be over-come only by presupposing an international consensus that does not now exist and never did exist.[35] Thus formalist analysis easily becomes outcome-oriented, producing, in the words of Hersch Lauterpacht, a "deceptive clarity":

> [A]pparent indecision [by the International Court of Justice] . . . may—both as a matter of development of the law and as a guide to action—be preferable to a deceptive clarity which fails to give an indication of the in-herent complexities of the issue.
>
> In so far as the decisions of the Court are an expression of existing inter-national law—whether customary or conventional—they cannot but reflect the occasional obscurity or inconclusiveness of a defective legal system.[36]

False claims of clarity aimed at concealing the obscurity and inconclusive-ness of legal rules that may or may not apply to hard cases generate only in-coherence. What makes hard cases hard is their incommensurability and our inability to devise objective criteria that render them commensurable.[37] In fact, as H. L. A. Hart wrote, "[s]uch cases are not merely 'hard cases'"; the problem is that "the law in such cases is fundamentally *incomplete*: it provides *no* answer to the questions at issue in such cases."[38]

Some insist that, because its various categories at least have a clear *core*, the ostensible gaps in international human rights law disappear. Even as-suming that the category in question does have a clear core, however, it is ambiguity *at the margins* that produces gaps—gaps that disappear only if it's assumed that every ambiguity is in the end spurious and has a single, correct resolution, or that nothing but law goes into the making and interpretation of law, or that a relevant, preexisting rule always twinkles like some far-off star exerting emanations from a penumbra that lights up the sole correct answer. Yet how, again, do we know this? To some, the galaxy seems empty; to others, the galaxy seems to contain equally radiant stars. The intuitionists present no standard to assess which star is brighter, insisting only that one *must* be brighter and that reasonable people *must* come to the same, unfalsifiable out-come. But legal rules are not like stars; they don't emit luminosity that can be measured;[39] we have only the naked eye to judge their proximity. Rules are made up, created by human beings. Sometimes, but not always, they're given a specified priority as against other rules, as in the case of constitu-tional rules and statutes. But even then, the nearest rules can be so remote in

time, subject, or specificity as to generate honest doubt about their applica-
bility.[40] Conflicts can arise among rules of the same priority, efforts to reconcile the rules can fail, reasonable disagreement can arise as to which prevails,
and a court can fairly resolve the controversy either way[41]—or can decline to
resolve the controversy at all in the belief that its writ does not extend to rule-
making. The word that describes such a situation is *gap*.

None of this is to suggest that the international human rights regime is a
blank slate. Clichéd but true, precepts of international law that have taken
shape over centuries are the received wisdom of the ages, to be ignored by
the digitally distracted at their peril. New technologies do not defeat ancient
truths. That international human rights law does not unequivocally either
permit or proscribe the suspension of Trump's Facebook account does not
mean that its rules are irretrievably vague about torturing prisoners or poi-
soning political opponents.

Nor do I proffer any new answer to the dilemma of when law-interpreting
begins and law-making ends, about how the needs of the present ought be
reconciled with the commands of the past, about when the impulses of the
living ought to defer to the designs of the dead. I do suggest that the old
lawyers' saying—*Le mort saisit le vif,* The dead grip the living—has it backward: the living grip the dead, in my view, not because they must but because
holding fast to settled solutions is the best way to invest law with the predictability and stability it requires, to nail down what we regard as progress, and
simply to save ourselves work. The urge to loosen that grip grows stronger
with every "next big thing" in communications technology, however. "[I]t is
never enough to claim a country; it must be held. It must be held and made
secure, every generation,"[42] as Hilary Mantel wrote. The claim that the law
doesn't reach *their* conduct will forever be made by scofflaws seeking to
evade its reach. That claim is no less repugnant in the realm of social media—
but in content moderation, as elsewhere, that claim must be considered, for
in no realm can either law-givers or law-interpreters evade the command of
the law to decide what the rules cover and what they do not. The response to
a spurious assertion of a gap, therefore, is not to profess that gaps do not exist;
the response is to assess whether a particular gap *does* exist and, if not, to enforce the law.

Realistic choices, in international law as elsewhere, entail more than mechanical, on/off, light-switch classification. Realistic lawyers are skeptical of
essentialist and foundationalist value claims.[43] Realistic lawyering reflects
the genealogy of legal rules, the consequences of one interpretation versus

another, the structure of incentives and disincentives that a given interpretation would yield, the political and historical context in which a legal
issue arises, the expectations of the parties, the level of compliance that
rules actually generate, and a variety of other matters, none of which can
be captured in neat interpretive algorithms as part of a robotic exercise of
categorization. A broader approach, redolent of Holmes's pragmatism,[44]
doesn't purport to be certain, universalist, or complete. It acknowledges
the law's inevitable indeterminacy and inability to foresee, let alone resolve,
every possible future case. It recognizes the inconvenient truth "that existing
legal rules themselves can be understood only in the light of ideas and information drawn from outside law."[45] It accepts the risk of phony assertions of
gaps in the law as the price of keeping the law honest, alive, and understandable. It counsels against reliance upon past choices that are wrongly claimed
to have eliminated the need for future choices.[46] But it does identify, or at
least tries to identify, what's really at stake in free speech disputes, whether
old categories are up to the task of resolving those disputes, and where new
categories might be needed. And it doesn't stifle reform with specious claims
of systemic completeness.

False Universalism

In addition to contending that international human rights law is complete,
many activists advance the related claim that human rights are universal.
"Put simply," Henry Steiner and Philip Alston observe, "the partisans of universality claim that international human rights, like rights to equal protection, physical security, free speech, freedom of religion and free association,
are and must be the same everywhere."[47] This notion of universality has animated human rights discourse since the earliest days. No local differences,
it is claimed, affect human rights' application. "The doctrine of human rights
has aspired from the outset to be universal," Antonio Cassese writes, "to
be a doctrine that applies everywhere to everyone, irrespective of nation-
ality, culture, tradition, ideology, or social conditions."[48] This idea, Anthea
Roberts notes, inspires "international lawyers' romantic understanding of
themselves and their field as universal and cosmopolitan."[49] It traces from
at least the Magna Carta through the writings of John Locke and into the
American Declaration of Independence and the French Declaration of the
Rights of Man and Citizen. But in France, Louis Henkin wrote, the Reign

of Terror destroyed the ideology of rights, and it was not resurrected under Napoleon and his successors. Nor did it resurface in England, which fought the French Revolution and rejected its ideology. Nineteenth-century English philosophers such as Jeremy Bentham dismissed natural rights as anarchical fallacies and nonsense on stilts.

In the United States, however galvanizing its rhetorical impact in 1776 as a revolutionary call to arms, the philosophy of natural rights made no reappearance eleven years later when the new Constitution was drafted in Philadelphia. Nor did it revive three years thereafter when the Constitution was amended to include a Bill of Rights. The philosophy's utility has been polemical, not juridical—as it was when deployed as a political ideology during the Civil War by abolitionists such as Emerson. It found a muted resonance when President Franklin Roosevelt articulated his "Four Freedoms" in 1941, and then full-throated expression in the United Nations General Assembly's most famous resolution, the 1948 Universal Declaration of Human Rights, which incorporated the Four Freedoms into its preamble. The Declaration lays out a broad panoply of rights. While not intended to be binding,[50] it has served as the template for later treaties, internationalizing rights that had previously been respected, if at all, only within domestic legal systems. Its real importance, however, lies in "[e]schewing—in its quest for universality—explicit reliance on divine inspiration or natural rights." As Henkin put it, "It helped convert a discredited philosophical idea (natural rights) into a dominant political ideology."[51]

Some of the reasons that philosophy was discredited were discussed in Chapter 6. It need hardly be pointed out that there are, in Cassese's words, "no generally accepted principles for distinguishing good from evil in the world community."[52] How could there be? Even at a national level, as John Mearsheimer notes, where a population shares relatively similar cultural, historical, and religious reference points, "[w]ell-informed, well-meaning citizens disagree profoundly over whether there is a right to abortion or to affirmative action. These are matters that deal with the good life, and they show that we should not expect reason to provide collective truths."[53] The belief that it can do so leads to what Mearsheimer calls "false universalism."

Absent common philosophical ground, international human rights lawyers have been forced to butress claims of universalism on empirical data—on common human needs and wants, for example, or on what governments and people actually say and do. Rosalyn Higgins, for example, the former president of the International Court of Justice, writes as follows:

I believe, profoundly, in the universality of the human spirit. Individuals everywhere want the same essential things: to have sufficient food and shelter; to be able to speak freely; to practice their own religion or to abstain from religious belief; to feel that their person is not threatened by the state; to know that they will not be tortured, or detained without charge, and that, if charged, they will have a fair trial. I believe there is nothing in these aspirations that is dependent upon culture, or religion, or stage of development.[54]

Higgins is no doubt correct that some human wants and aspirations are universal, but it hardly follows that every want or aspiration implies a corresponding right. Aside from the need to hurdle the yawning gulf separating *is* from *ought*, there is the slight matter of separating human wants from needs; that an annual two-week paid vacation is universally wanted does not seem a persuasive basis to regard it as a universal human right. Different societies, moreover, have different values. Given continuing differences among peoples on everything from head scarves and female genital mutilation to laws on Holocaust denial and blasphemous cartoons, the effort to achieve universality in the regulation of such practices turns into a constant battle between generality and concreteness: norms must be stated at a level of abstraction broad enough to provide an all-encompassing common denominator but narrow enough to prevent scofflaws from relying upon the norm to escape its application. The battle is often lost, of course, because the divisions are too great. Hence the emergence of *grundnorms* such as "dignity" or "no superfluous cruelty"—values that no one opposes and that are, in the end, too general to rule in or out virtually any practice, however benign or malign. Meanwhile, the most cursory observers of state behavior come to realize that the system pretends to a universality of which it obviously is not possessed; internationalists try to force universalist, monocultural solutions on societies where those solutions don't fit; and the range of malevolent international behavior broadens, as it has in the realm of freedom of expression.[55]

Inapplicability to Private Persons and Businesses

The most notable feature of the treaties relied upon by Facebook's Oversight Board to resolve the Trump dispute is that, as with other treaties, they were drafted to restrain governments, not individuals or businesses. The

International Covenant on Civil and Political Rights (ICCPR), for example, begins by imposing on states the duty to respect the rights recognized in the Covenant and, in 105 references to "states," repeatedly elaborates that obligation in varying contexts. Even when the text makes no reference to states, it is clear that it is not intended to apply to the conduct of individuals. Article 6, for example, provides that "[e]very human being has the inherent right to life" and that "[n]o one shall be arbitrarily deprived of his life."[56] That prohibition is not violated by a private person who engages in murder. Article 9 provides that "[e]veryone has the right to liberty and security of person. No one shall be subjected to arbitrary arrest or detention."[57] That prohibition is not violated by a private person who engages in a kidnapping. Article 17 provides that "[n]o one shall be subjected to arbitrary or unlawful interference with his privacy, family, home or correspondence, nor to unlawful attacks on his honour and reputation. . . . Everyone has the right to the protection of the law against such interference or attacks."[58] That provision is not violated by a private person who engages in burglary. The treaty is violated by a *government* that does not comply, not by individual murderers, kidnappers, and burglars.

That the ICCPR applies to states but not private parties is reaffirmed by the understandings formulated by the United States when it ratified the treaty. They provided that the treaty "shall be implemented by the Federal Government to the extent that it exercises legislative and judicial jurisdiction over the matters covered" by the treaty, "and otherwise by the state and local governments" to the extent of their jurisdiction. No one at the time of ratification suggested that private persons or businesses within the United States had an obligation to implement the treaty. It imposed obligations on the federal government and state governments, not individuals.

Article 19, applied by the Oversight Board in the Trump-Facebook dispute, illustrates the awkwardness in taking a limitation written to restrict states and trying to repurpose it to restrict persons:

1. Everyone shall have the right to hold opinions without interference.
2. Everyone shall have the right to freedom of expression; this right shall include freedom to seek, receive and impart information and ideas of all kinds, regardless of frontiers, either orally, in writing or in print, in the form of art, or through any other media of his choice.
3. The exercise of the rights provided for in paragraph 2 of this article carries with it special duties and responsibilities. It may therefore be

subject to certain restrictions, but these shall only be such as are provided by law and are necessary:

(a) For respect of the rights or reputations of others;

(b) For the protection of national security or of public order (ordre public), or of public health or morals.

These words were clearly written to limit states, not people. The right of an individual to impart information through the "media of his choice" does not mean that any book publisher or newspaper that an individual happens to choose has an obligation to publish the individual's submission; it means that the individual and the medium in question have the right to proceed to publication without governmental interference. The exceptions set forth in paragraph 3 confirm that the article was intended to protect individuals' free expression right from interference by the government, not by private persons or businesses. In the United States as elsewhere, the protections of national security and public order, health, and morals have traditionally been regarded as core obligations of government, not private individuals or businesses.

These and other public interests are relegated by sovereignty to the protection of governments for obvious reasons. Governments balance, reinforce, and trade off such interests with other governments when they negotiate treaties. Internationally recognized human rights are one result. Governments with a stake in that give and take have a subsequent stake in compliance or noncompliance with human rights treaties. Another party's violation of a treaty may affect its own willingness to continue to comply, a decision that requires weighing and reconciling often competing national interests.

A private business, in contrast, has limited responsibilities that give it no such stake in larger calculations of the public interest. Its primary obligations are to its owners or shareholders: its fiduciary responsibility is to maximize profits on their investments. Facebook is not responsible for protecting the national security, public order, health, or morals of any of the states in which it operates. The company's owners or shareholders may choose to pursue additional social or humanitarian interests, but when they do so, it is reasonable to expect that this is done for the purpose of profit maximization. "The profit motive dictates that media companies act in their own self-interest,"[59] as Nossel succinctly put it. It therefore makes little sense to expect private businesses, left to themselves, to take on public responsibilities that traditionally have been entrusted to governments. Mark Zuckerberg famously remarked, "In a lot of ways Facebook is more like a government than a traditional company."[60] But in the most fundamental respect, Facebook is not like a government: its object is to advance a private interest, not the public interest.

Private businesses not only lack the incentive to advance the public interest; they lack the capacity. A private business may of course find it profitable to *appear* to take on responsibility for certain aspects of the public interest. But it is seldom likely that a private company will have the resources, incentive, knowledge, or expertise to do so with the expertise of a government. In the Trump case (as in other disputes), for example, the Oversight Board undertook the task of applying a community standard that required assessing who is a "dangerous individual" or what is a "dangerous organization." This assessment normally cannot be made reliably, however, absent the sources and methods available to the intelligence and law enforcement agencies that exercise the investigatory and coercive powers of a government. As I point out below in discussing governments as stakeholders, and in the next chapter as well, this provides an incentive for a close, mutually beneficial relationship between the government's national security apparatus and big tech, which is of course possessed of users' personal data that is highly useful to government snoopers. Acting on their own, however, companies like Facebook are hardly in a position to enforce rules that embrace a robust, thoroughgoing commitment to the public interest. Nor are they normally subject to the constitutional accountability of government officials who break those rules. The rules were written to restrain governments, not private businesses.

It was, indeed, the inapplicability of international human rights law that permitted private companies like Nike and Shell[61] at the turn of the twenty-first century to operate with virtual impunity in the abusive treatment of workers in developing companies. In the face of such depredations, human rights activists proposed legally binding instruments to impose on businesses essentially the same human rights obligations that are imposed on states by treaties. To the surprise of no one, the effort failed. Businesses everywhere rejected it. Governments offered no support. The project remains alive in the bowels of the United Nations,[62] but attention turned to the possibility of developing nonbinding principles that businesses might voluntarily adopt as a matter of corporate social responsibility.

Whence came the UN's Guiding Principles on Business and Human Rights.[63] Endorsed by the UN Human Rights Council in 2011—but never approved by the UN General Assembly or ratified by any state—businesses are therein called upon to "respect" human rights as set out in thirty-one principles. "As a global corporation committed to the UNGPs," the Oversight Board stated in the Trump case, "Facebook must respect international human rights standards wherever it operates."[64] In fact, the term *must* is misleading; as the Board notes elsewhere, compliance is entirely voluntary. The principles impose no binding duties on Facebook. As the UNGPs' precatory text states, "Nothing in these Guiding Principles should be read as creating new international law obligations."[65]

Indeed, it is hard to see how they could be read as creating new obligations. The UNGPs appear to be addressed not to questions of the sort posed by social media content moderation (an issue that did not arise until after the UNGPs were issued), but, as Evelyn Douek noted, seem intended to deal with traditional corporate concerns such as "physical business operations, supply chain issues, or labour rights."[66] One such principle cited by the Facebook Oversight Board (number 11) provides, for example, that "[b]usiness enterprises should respect human rights. This means that they should avoid infringing on the human rights of others and should address adverse human rights impacts with which they are involved."[67] Of the principles that could apply to disputes such as the Trump case, most are platitudes that could be cited by parties on either side of a dispute; it is hard to see how any but the most gruesome corporate behavior would have to be changed to avoid violation. In the Trump case, the Board notes the existence of a half-dozen such principles (11, 13, 15, 18, 19, and 22) but makes no effort to apply them, nor does it even suggest that they indicate Trump's culpability. The principles seem to provide, at best, legal-sounding window dressing used to shore up a decision reached for other reasons.

John Ruggie, the author of the UNGPs, rejected the idea of a single, binding treaty on the subject with the argument that "a general business and human rights treaty would have to be pitched at so high a level of abstraction that it would be of little if any use to real people in real places."[68] But the UNGPs are subject to the same objection. They have become, in the hands of Facebook, what (in Ruggie's words) much of the human rights community feared "corporate social responsibility" would become: "little more than self-interested self-regulation, designed to burnish the reputation of companies, limit external pressure, and thereby diminish the prospect of 'hard' regulatory measures without providing adequate accountability and remedy."[69]

One of the great difficulties in addressing such problems within an international legal framework, Ruggie rued, was the "fragmentation of global policy- and law-making" that was becoming clear by the late 1990s.[70] The international legal order was, in a word, fragmenting; it was fragmenting because of conflicts within the different sources of international law and also because of conflicts among different countries and regions of the world. A closer look at international human rights law's evolution reveals that these concerns were prescient.

Fragmentation

The Charter of the Oversight Board, as noted above, set out Facebook's commitment to international human rights law. It provides simply as follows: "When reviewing decisions, the board will pay particular attention to the impact of removing content in light of human rights norms protecting free expression."[71] Where might one look to find those norms?

At its most fundamental level, international law consists of treaties and customary international law. These are, again, the two ways that states express their consent to rules: by word, through treaties, and by custom, through practice they accept as legally binding. The problem is not, as a member of the Oversight Board put it, "simply . . . [that] there are different systems that interpret different treaties and come out differently in their interpretations."[72] The problem is that, together, they form more a collage than a single, coherent whole, as close examination of each reveals.

Treaties

Begin with the treaty on which the Oversight Board places greatest weight in the Trump case, the ICCPR. The Board treats the ICCPR as a single treaty. But it is not. It is a mélange of different treaties, created by reservations added by various parties, and by differing responses to those reservations by other parties. Together, these reservations and responses create a web of multiple treaties, with different rights and obligations for different parties, as is often true with multilateral treaties that are ratified by many parties.

A quick word of background will explain how this occurs.[73] When a state expresses its consent to be bound by a treaty, the state may formulate a reservation, if the treaty permits. A reservation is like a counteroffer—it does not bind another party unless that party explicitly or implicitly accepts it. If one party accepts a state's reservation but another rejects it, two different treaties in effect result. Neither of those parties is bound by the other's action. The process can get more complicated, but that's essentially the way the law of treaties deals with reservations. The upshot is that one can't assess a state's legal rights and obligations under a large multilateral treaty unless one knows what reservations it has formulated and whether the other party in question has rejected or accepted those reservations.

The U.S. ratification of the ICCPR is an example. In ratifying the ICCPR the United States formulated a series of reservations. The most controversial of those reservations concerned the status of the ICCPR in U.S. domestic law. It declared that "the provisions of Articles 1 through 27 of the Covenant are not self-executing"[74] (which is to say that they would not become effective within U.S. law until the enactment of implementing legislation). Eleven states objected to this declaration, mainly on grounds that the declaration undermines the ICCPR's object and purpose.[75] No party appears to have said that the U.S. declaration precludes the treaty from coming into force between it and the United States, although all had that option—which conceivably might also have been exercised in response to reservations entered by other states as well—with the result, again, that one can assess the ICCPR's rights and obligations of one party as against another only by identifying all the reservations that have been formulated and responses by the other state in question. In state practice, then, there is no *single* ICCPR in force that binds all parties to the same obligations.

In addition to this non-self-executing declaration, the United States formulated additional reservations applicable to the two ICCPR articles that bear directly upon freedom of expression. These were explicitly relied upon by the Oversight Board in the Trump case, *without noting either reservation*. They are Articles 19 and 20.

Article 19 ICCPR

The text of Article 19 is set out above. Note the broad, vague exceptions in paragraph (3): a government is permitted to suppress speech if its object is "respect of the rights or reputations of others," "protection of national security," "public order," or "public health or morals." Of course, protecting the rights or reputations of others can justify restricting speech in a wide variety of circumstances, particularly when "rights" are, as in Article 19, undefined and where reputations are, as in many countries (other than the United States), protected by libel laws that permit deep-pockets plaintiffs to quell all criticism. The next exception, for national security, is also broad and undefined; U.S. national security adviser Jake Sullivan, as discussed in the next chapter, announced upon his appointment that national security would henceforth include combating "inequality in all forms."[76] The maintenance of "public order" has, similarly, been a rationale of tyrants everywhere for silencing opponents. And one need only scan the pretzeled excuses offered by social media companies for silencing debate on COVID treatment (also discussed in the next chapter) to appreciate the breadth of the loophole for public health and morals. Article 19 does limit restrictions to those necessary and required by law, and human rights organizations regularly decry violations, but these limitations provide scant safeguards against autocrats or despotic majorities intent upon limiting free expression; "law" has been interpreted to include "norms,"[77] and what's "necessary" often lies in the eye of the autocratic beholder. An unbiased, impartial tribunal is seldom available to adjudicate whether these exceptions have been validly invoked. Little wonder that the U.S. Senate found it necessary in approving the ICCPR to add the following: "The United States declares that it will continue to adhere to the requirements and constraints of its Constitution in respect to all such restrictions and limitations."[78]

Article 20 ICCPR
Article 20 of the ICCPR provides as follows:

1. Any propaganda for war shall be prohibited by law.
2. Any advocacy of national, racial or religious hatred that constitutes incitement to discrimination, hostility or violence shall be prohibited by law.

This provision has its roots in persistent efforts in the late 1940s by the Soviet Union and its allies to generate support for international restrictions on propaganda for war and racial, national, and religious hatred of the sort propagated by Nazi propagandists. It was opposed by the United States and other Western powers. Eleanor Roosevelt, heading the U.S. delegation, argued that "any criticism of public or religious authorities might all too easily be described as incitement to hatred and consequently prohibited."[79] The United Nations General Assembly nonetheless ignored her caution and approved it in 1961 by a vote of 52 to 19, with the United States abstaining.[80]

To Americans schooled in the jurisprudence of *Brandenburg*, the provision is malign. Some civil rights activists may conceivably have advocated the hatred of southern sheriffs who turned loose dogs on the Freedom Riders of the early 1960s, and that advocacy may have generated hostility, but as discussed in Chapter 7, advocacy of ideas, however heinous, is constitutionally protected in the United States. It is only when speech is intended to persuade people to commit a crime and likely to have that imminent result that speech constitutionally can be prohibited. This is what is meant, in U.S. constitutional jurisprudence, by "incitement." One incites to *action*. To speak of incitement to "hostility" or "hatred" or some other mental state makes no sense.

Moreover, the term *war* covers wide ground. The word is not used in the operative provisions of the UN Charter, which recognizes the permissibility of defensive use of force. Paragraph (1) would seem clearly to require states to suppress peaceful advocacy of use of force to curtail intrastate genocide or ethnic cleansing, as occurred during the run-up to NATO's intervention in Kosovo.[81] It is unimaginable that the Senate could have remained silent in the face of this plain incompatibility with the First Amendment, and of course it did not. It formulated the reservation "[t]hat Article 20 does not authorize or require legislation or other action by the United States that would restrict the right of free speech and association protected by the Constitution and laws of the United States."[82]

Nonetheless, Article 20 was explicitly relied upon by the Oversight Board to uphold the restrictions on Trump's access to Facebook for praising violence—without, again, any reference to American objections to Article 20. The Facebook rule prohibited praise of violence (until that prohibition cramped supporters' praise of Ukraine in its war with Russia, as discussed in the next chapter) even if the speech in question was not intended to incite to violence and even if it was not likely to result in imminent violence. Such speech is of course constitutionally protected under the First Amendment from governmental abridgement.

Other Speech-Regulating Treaties

The ICCPR is not the only treaty that regulates speech. Many states are a party to more than one such treaty. This creates uncertainty as to which takes priority in application to the same pattern of facts, giving social media content moderators a smorgasbord of agreements from which they can pick and choose to select the rule most favorable to a desired outcome. Unfettered discretion is the inevitable consequence of a process that self-consciously aims to apply international human rights standards in a "holistic and comprehensive"[83] way, as Facebook's Nick Clegg put it. A "holistic" approach is fine if rules are selected *before* the conduct occurs—that's one way the rule of law remains vibrant—but not if the conduct occurs afterward. The fundamental requirements of clarity and accessibility to which Facebook committed itself do not permit outcome-oriented, after-the-fact rule-making.

To illustrate the challenge created by an à la carte menu of available rules, consider options presented by the range of treaties ratified by the United States. In addition to the ICCPR, the United States is also a party to the Convention on the Elimination of Racial Discrimination (CERD), which Facebook has committed itself to "respect" as a matter of corporate policy.[84] Article 4 of CERD overlaps with Articles 19 and 20 of the ICCPR but goes far beyond even Article 20 in permitting speech suppression.[85] Article 4 requires parties not simply to outlaw but to criminalize "all dissemination of ideas" concerning racial superiority or hatred or "incitement to racial discrimination." The United States ratified the CERD in 1994, but it did so subject to both a reservation[86] and a proviso[87] indicating that the United States is obliged to do nothing under CERD inconsistent with the Constitution.

In addition, the United States is a signatory to the American Convention on Human Rights, which, in Articles 13 and 14,[88] tracks some of the text of the ICCPR. And like the ICCPR, the American Convention presents constitutional problems. The Carter administration, when it was signed, recommended that these be the subject of reservations.[89] The Convention has not been approved by the Senate, although most nations in the Western Hemisphere have ratified it. Facebook's Oversight Board made no reference to it in the Trump case—why, it did not say.

Other states are parties to additional regional human rights treaties that also overlap with the ICCPR and CERD. None of these treaties is as speech-protective as the First Amendment. Most European states, for example, are parties to the European Convention on Human Rights, Article 10 of which regulates speech. It guarantees the right of freedom of expression—except for restrictions prescribed by law that are necessary "in the interests of national security, territorial integrity or public safety, for the prevention of disorder or crime, for the protection of health or morals, for the protection of the reputation or rights of others, for preventing the disclosure of information received in confidence, or for maintaining the authority and impartiality of the judiciary."[90] The African Charter on Human and Peoples' Rights also guarantees the right of "every individual to access and disseminate opinions," but only "within the law."[91] The law may restrict that right in the name of "the rights of others, collective security, morality and common interest."[92] Such broad exceptions often swallow the rule.

An assortment of reports, interpretations, findings, and sundry other pronouncements is regularly churned out by the UN "machinery," as Evelyn Aswad referred to it.[93] Little if any of it is binding on states, which are not asked to approve it, so it drifts about like juridical flotsam and jetsam, waiting to be picked up by assorted advisory committees, commissions, NGOs, and social media content moderators, "depending on the circumstances," as Facebook would have it.

One such document is the Rabat Plan of Action, relied upon by Facebook's Oversight Board in its Trump opinion. The Rabat Plan is a series of six tests devised to make more concrete the notion of incitement in Article 20 of the ICCPR, the provision rejected by the United States. As noted earlier, the Oversight Board declined to address the question whether Trump had *incited* to violence, choosing instead to find him guilty of *praising* violence. Nonetheless, for reasons that are baffling, the Board found it appropriate to shoehorn the criteria from the Rabat Plan into its opinion in the portion relating to whether Facebook's remedy was proportional to Trump's offense, which is presented as nonarbitrary. (Frederick Schauer views proportionality as more "open-ended and discretionary" than rules-based approaches.)[94] The Board seemed neither to notice nor to care that the Rabat standards were relevant to an entirely different question: incitement, not proportionality.

It is understandable that norms applicable to states in the emerging body of international human rights law would necessarily be ill-formed and inchoate. That is the nature of emerging norms in any young legal system. Many people alive today were born at a time when virtually no international human rights law existed. But it must not be forgotten that we are dealing here with norms that were intended to limit states, not individuals. When individual rights are at stake, much greater specificity and clarity are required. States inhabit a world of diplomatic ambiguity where vagueness often is useful. A system intended to protect individual rights and political freedoms, however, requires specificity, concreteness, and notice that is understandable to persons of reasonable intelligence. And it must be clear and accessible to them before they act, not afterward. That is the fundamental requirement of the principle of legality, the foundational precept[95] of international human rights law and one that the Facebook Oversight Board, as noted below, has committed itself to upholding.

These, then, are the principal relevant treaty obligations of international human rights law. But the words of treaties, in international law, are not the whole story. How those words are interpreted *in practice* is also relevant, the matter to which we now turn.

State Practice and Judicial Rulings

Efforts to dismiss state practice as irrelevant to states' obligations under international law are ubiquitous but mistaken. As noted earlier, international law is a consent-based system, and states sometimes indicate their consent to or rejection of international norms through their actions. For this reason, practice is relevant in two respects. First, as also indicated earlier, state practice is an integral component of custom,[96] and customary norms are an integral component of international human rights law.[97] Second, under established principles of treaty law, the subsequent practice of the parties in the application of the treaty is evidence of their interpretation of it. What states actually *do* day to day in the real world thus bears directly on the scope of their legal obligations. In assessing the extent to which international human rights law is universal and consistent, therefore, state practice and judicial rulings are an essential reference point. They provide a reality test; they sort out paper rules from working rules.

How effective are its free speech rules? Two prominent international barristers, Amal Clooney and Philippa Webb, have concluded in an important study that "the tide around the world is turning against free speech."[98] A member of the Facebook Oversight Board, Evelyn Aswad, has sought to rebut their conclusions. "[T]he state of international law on the ability of individuals to insult or otherwise engage in offensive speech is not bleak, as portrayed in their article," she argues, "but rather this body of law contains robust and principled speech protections."[99] On-the-ground experience helps assess these conflicting claims; let's take a look at it. Begin with the actual practice of the United States' most important power competitor: China.

China

Few nations in the world are more influential than the People's Republic of China. Its population of 1.45 billion—18% of the world's population—is four times larger than that of the United States. Its territory is larger than that of the United States. The value of its annual exports exceeds that of the United States. Its GDP is expected to surpass that of the United States in 2026. Through its Belt-and-Road Initiative it has invested over $100 billion in infrastructure improvements in over seventy countries around the globe. And it has, on paper at least, joined the major international human rights treaties. It signed the ICCPR in 1998 and has promised to ratify it, and it ratified the CERD in 1981. How does its government interpret these commitments?

An illuminating answer was given in 2013 in its "Communiqué on the Current State of the Ideological Sphere," known informally as Document No. 9. Document No. 9 was issued secretly, at the time, by leaders of the Chinese Communist Party. It urges the eradication of subversive currents within Chinese society.[100] Leaked copies were viewed by the Western press, the authenticity of which have been confirmed by China scholars.[101] In its scope and importance, Document No. 9 is similar to white papers used by Western democracies to outline fundamental strategic policy, such as the National Security Strategy Statement in the United States. Document No. 9 provides an extraordinary if sobering insight into how Chinese leaders plan to honor international human rights commitments concerning freedom of speech.

Document No. 9 announces that the Party is "putting forth new measures to benefit the people" aimed at, among other things, "promoting unification of thought." One of the "false ideological trends" that must be combated is the idea that "Western freedom, democracy, and human rights are universal and eternal," for there are "essential differences between the West's value system and the value system we advocate." One of these lies in "the West's idea" of freedom of the press. "The ultimate goal of advocating the West's view of the media is to hawk the principle of abstract and absolute freedom of press, oppose the Party's leadership in the media, and gouge an opening through which to infiltrate our ideology." This lie has led to "slandering our country's efforts to improve Internet management by calling them a crackdown on the Internet." Foreign media must be restricted. "[M]istaken views and ideas exist in great numbers in overseas media," and "[i]f we allow any of these ideas to spread, they will disturb people's existing consensus on important issues." These incorrect ideas are propagated by private organizations "filming documentaries on sensitive subject matter, disseminating political rumors, and defaming the party and the national leadership." " 'Dissidents' and people identified with 'rights protection' are active."

What is to be done? "Party members and governments of all levels" must take the lead. "They must clearly recognize the essence of false ideas and viewpoints . . . [f]orcefully resist influential and harmful false tides of thoughts, help people distinguish between truth and falsehood, and solidify their understanding." "We must not permit the dissemination of opinions that oppose the Party's theory or political line, the publication of views contrary to decisions that represent the central leadership's views, or the spread of political rumors that defame the image of the Party or the nation."

In 2020, seven years after issuing Document No. 9 and after initiating its implementation through its infamous social credit system,[102] China was elected to the UN Human Rights Council, the UN organ "responsible for the promotion and protection of all human rights around the globe."[103]

Other Nations

It might be assumed that China is unique in interpreting its international human rights commitments as permitting the flat-out censorship outlined in Document No. 9. Other states that have signed on to those instruments, however, also see themselves as free to pursue a wide variety of divergent and often conflicting speech control practices, apparently regarded by them as fully consonant with their international obligations. Michael McConnell, as noted above, provided a small sampling in 2012 of a few of the more egregious speech-suppressive actions taken by states that have committed themselves to the international human rights treaties. (McConnell has been a co-chair of the Facebook Oversight Board.) Clooney, Webb, and Strossen are among those who have added examples to that list. Together, they demonstrate, again, the wide breadth of discretion to stifle speech that many parties to these treaties believe they continue to enjoy notwithstanding their ratification. Consider some of the laws that parties have adopted:

- India has enacted a law that criminalizes a speaker who "brings or attempts to bring into hatred or contempt, or excites or attempts to excite disaffection towards the government."[104]
- Cyprus has enacted a law that makes it a crime to insult the army or a foreign head of state.[105]

- Denmark has enacted a law that criminalizes attacking a public official "with insults, abusive language or other offensive words or gestures."[106]
- Germany has enacted a law that criminalizes defaming the president.[107]
- Qatar has enacted a law that criminalizes the creation of a website that jeopardizes the "general order" of the state by spreading false news.[108]

Prosecutions under these and other laws have been numerous in recent years:

- In Turkey over a two-year period, more than two thousand people have been prosecuted for insulting President Recep Tayyip Erdoğan, and a former minister and member of Parliament were convicted of "incitement to hatred and hostility" for criticizing the government's human rights policies.[109] Earlier, the owner of a publishing company was prosecuted for publishing a newsletter that accused the "fascist Turkish army" of atrocities.[110]
- In the Netherlands, a political official was convicted of hate speech for calling for fewer Moroccans in the country.[111]
- In Egypt, the senior staff of Al Jazeera television was prosecuted for broadcasting "false news abroad regarding the internal situation in the country."[112]
- In Russia, the band Pussy Riot was prosecuted for singing a punk song with the lyrics "Virgin Mary, Mother of God, banish Putin, banish Putin, banish Putin!"[113]
- In China, a well-known free speech activist who called on public officials to disclose their assets and urged China to ratify the ICCPR was prosecuted for "picking quarrels and provoking trouble."[114]
- In Myanmar, a café owner from New Zealand who posted an image on Facebook of Buddha wearing headphones was prosecuted for insulting Buddhism.[115]
- In Singapore, a teenager who posted a Facebook video containing "remarks against Christianity" was convicted of "wounding religious feelings."[116]
- In Greece, a man who satirized a deceased orthodox monk on Facebook was prosecuted for "malicious blasphemy and insulting religion."[117]
- In Denmark, a man who said that "Islam wants to abuse democracy in order to get rid of democracy" was prosecuted for criticizing the "ideology of Islam."[118]
- In France, twelve pro-Palestinian activists were prosecuted for wearing T-shirts in a supermarket with the message "Long live Palestine, boycott

Israel" and for handing out flyers that said "Buying Israeli products means legitimizing crimes in Gaza."[119]

- In Denmark, a historian was prosecuted for saying that there was a high crime rate in areas with high Muslim populations.[120]
- In France, the newspaper *Le Monde* was prosecuted for inciting hatred against Jews in an editorial that criticized Israeli policies and referred to Israel as "a nation of refugees."[121]
- In Germany, a historian was prosecuted for statements he made about Nazi history in a private letter addressed and sent to another historian.[122]

Such laws and prosecutions represent a tiny fraction of abusive state practice that occurs in the regulation of free speech. Other scholars and NGOs provide long lists of additional examples of how states interpret their obligations under international human rights law. And that is the point: the states that have engaged in this suppressive conduct *are almost all parties to the main international human rights agreements*. Out of 195 nations worldwide, 173 are parties to the ICCPR. That includes all of the states referred to above other than Myanmar and Singapore. The CERD is even more widely accepted, with 182 parties. There is no getting around the bleak reality: either states view international human rights law as granting them wide latitude to suppress free speech, or they are, through a pattern of knowing violations, forging supervening customary norms at odds with the obligations imposed by the treaties. Either way, state practice hardly commends the treaties as models for emulation by social media content moderators.

What, one might ask, has been the response of the international "machinery" established to ensure enforcement and compliance with the treaties? Surely international judicial and administrative mechanisms have not been indifferent to divergent interpretations of states' duties under their international commitments. And that is true; some state disagreements have been addressed.

The international machinery's treatment of so-called Holocaust denial laws has been instructive. A number of European countries, such as Switzerland, Austria, and Germany, make it a crime to deny that the Holocaust occurred. Whether such laws are permissible under international human rights law has been a major point of contention. The European Court of Human Rights appears to regard such laws as permissible under the European Convention on Human Rights.[123] While the UN's Human Rights Committee, interpreting the ICCPR, has found that laws that "penalize the expression of historical facts" are incompatible with states' obligations under the ICCPR,[124] the Committee nonetheless upheld France's law penalizing Holocaust denial.[125] Yet another position appears to have been staked out by the committee responsible for overseeing the CERD: the CERD, it has opined, permits laws that criminalize the denial of genocide so long as the denials "clearly constitute incitement to racial . . . hatred."[126] The cacophony is hard to summarize, but Clooney and Webb make a valiant effort at distillation:

> [T]he Human Rights Committee and the European Court have in some cases insisted that, in order to be criminal, speech has to be intended to incite violence. But at other times a lower level of intent or no specific intent is required. Similarly, in some cases, the speech must foreseeably lead to imminent harm in the form of discrimination, hostility or violence; in others, only imminent violence will suffice; and in others still no showing of likely harm is required at all.[127]

Little wonder that Facebook's Zuckerberg might initially mandate that posts denying the Holocaust were permissible,[128] and then engage in a complete about-face and direct Facebook to take them down—all the while, of course, "respecting" Facebook's commitment to honor international human rights law. He may well have respected it—but that would have been possible only because international human rights law permits equally valid but opposite answers.[129]

Indeterminacy

If this à la carte legal system sounds familiar, it should. It was very much the indeterminacy of federal common law and the ability of federal judges arbitrarily to pick and choose rules within it that Holmes bridled against before the Supreme Court put a stop to the practice in 1938.[130] International human rights law today gives social media censors essentially the same broad discretion. If they don't like one treaty, they can look to another; if they don't like one precedent, they can look to another; if they don't like one strand of state practice or customary norm, they can look to another. The system of course provides reams of legal verbiage to mask that discretion, but speech regulation by international human rights law has produced very much the same result in the international legal order that prevailed in the United States prior to the rigorous enforcement of the First Amendment in the latter half of the twentieth century: a system in which a select few are able to silence speech because under *their* values, worldviews, and political attitudes,[131] the speech has a "bad tendency." It's not Spencer's *Social Statics,* but the result is the same: wide leeway for censors to impose their own intuitive notion of what's best for users to read and write.

Defenders of deploying international human rights law to regulate speech argue that its conflicting regional regimes are not really part of the "international" system, and that in any event its contradictions can be explained away as the inevitable "evolution" experienced by every growing legal system.[132] These two assertions illustrate how, as Anthea Roberts observed, international lawyers "often resist emphasizing national or regional approaches because they are seen as potentially threatening to the field's universalist aspirations."[133] The first claim is simply incorrect: regional treaties and customary norms are an integral part of international law[134] and are relied upon regularly by judicial and arbitral tribunals charged with applying pertinent international standards in resolving disputes. And rightly so—the Statute of the International Court of Justice, in defining the sources of international law,[135] makes no distinction between international and regional norms (on which it, too, occasionally opines).[136]

As to the second claim, it surely is true that real and potential inconsistencies are endemic in young legal systems, which sometimes become more coherent as they evolve. But whether inconsistencies represent merely early phase growing pains or fatal, insurmountable incompatibilities can be assessed only retrospectively, after a system has evolved (or withered). At this earliest stage the future of international human rights rules governing speech, particularly online speech, is still very much in doubt. Many experts openly question such rules' viability. Jack Goldsmith and Tim Wu have written, "[T]here is very little to say in favor of a single global rule for Internet speech." The problem is not simply to find the right way to word such a rule; the problem lies in how to take account of clashing views as to what speech should be permitted. "These dramatically different attitudes toward proper speech among the mature democracies reflect important differences—differences in cultures, histories, and taste."[137] There is little reason to expect those differences to evaporate, particularly with globalism in apparent retreat. "[G]lobal consensus not only does not exist," Douek writes, "but likely never will."[138]

Meanwhile, the specious precision—the "delusory exactness"—of international human rights law's rules allows companies like Facebook to pull the wool over the eyes of naïve publics grateful for any nod to what they assume to be enlightened humanitarian norms. The rhetorical embrace of those rules by the companies gives them, Sejal Parmar observed, "a sense of global legitimacy, credibility, and appeal especially outside the United States."[139] But it takes only a cursory familiarity with those norms—and the record of state conduct—to recognize those companies' "commitment" as shallow. They have in fact committed themselves to do virtually nothing. Douek presents this specter starkly, explaining that the risk is

> companies are embracing the terminology so readily because they know that it will not act as much of a constraint at all. As non-binding norms, there is no mechanism to coerce a company into compliance. A variant of 'blue washing,' companies are prepared to wrap themselves in the language of human rights, co-opting its legitimacy at little cost.

With the companies facing no need to adjust their operations or business models, international human rights law "becomes a kind of 'signaling' and mere cheap talk."[140]

Round Pegs, Square Holes: Three Cases

This, then, is international human rights law: incomplete, inapposite, in-consistent, and indeterminate on freedom of speech. It comes nowhere close to meeting the Facebook Oversight Board's requirements of clarity and accessibility—which, the Board indicates, international human rights law itself requires. Users of Facebook are not "able to understand what is allowed and what is not allowed" by looking to international human rights law. Its rules are not "sufficiently clear to provide guidance to those who make decisions on limiting expression," but instead give Facebook virtually "unfettered discretion, which can result in selective application of the rules." And notwithstanding the Oversight Board's effort to suggest otherwise in its Trump opinion, international human rights law does not square with the First Amendment. International human rights law is not founded on the precept that "the best test of truth is the power of the thought to get itself accepted in the competition of the market." To the contrary, international human rights law and practice, as Schauer observes, is at odds with "virtually the entire range of freedom of speech and freedom of the press topics"[141] addressed by the U.S. Constitution. It is barely accurate to describe the United States as merely an "outlier." Schauer sums up that clash succinctly:

> If Paul Cohen is protected by the First Amendment when he articulates his objection to military conscription by publicly wearing a jacket emblazoned with the words "Fuck the Draft," if people who use words like "mother-fucker" are protected when they talk back to police officers, and if all forms of vituperation against one's opponents are permitted in political debate, then the American constitutional prohibition on viewpoint discrimination prevents treating people who call others "niggers" differently from those who call others "motherfuckers" and prevents treating people who carry Nazi flags differently from people who burn American ones. That even in 1978 the United States Supreme Court deemed the march of the Nazis in Skokie so plainly protected as not even to warrant a full opinion speaks volumes about the First Amendment's unwillingness to treat Nazis differ-ently from Socialists, to treat Klansmen differently from Republicans, or to treat intimidation on grounds of race, religion, or ethnicity differently from any other form of intimidation. In much of the developed world one uses racial epithets at one's legal peril, one displays Nazi regalia and the other trappings of ethnic hatred at significant legal risk, and one urges discrimination against religious minorities under threat of fine or impris-onment, but in the United States all such speech remains constitutionally protected.[142]

The reality is that the United States grounds the protection of speech on a foundational value that is not shared with most of the rest of the world. "[T]he consensus outside the United States," William Marshall writes, "is that the position that truth is the foundational value for freedom of speech is essentially misguided."[143]

To reiterate, I do not suggest that freedom of speech standards devel-oped in the United States for American society can or should be applied to other societies with different histories, cultures, and values. Neither, however, would it be appropriate for standards that have emerged from those societies to supplant standards that have been grown organically in American society, developed through thousands of volumes of scholar-ship and hundreds of cases handed down over the decades by dozens of Supreme Court justices and which give the United States, all told, the most subtle and profound corpus of commentary on freedom of speech that the world has ever produced. Yet this jurisprudence is ignored by social media's resort to lowest-common-denominator "community standards" patched together from communities other than the United States. Consider what this has meant in the three areas we have examined, concerning incitement, falsehoods, and hate speech. And consider, again, whether Facebook's content moderation rules, promulgated to "respect" international human rights norms, pass muster under the international law's legality test that Facebook sees as its lodestar.

Incitement: The Trump Case (2021)

The basic contours of the Trump case were laid out earlier. Before Facebook suspended his account, Trump, with 35 million followers on Facebook,[144] used social media extensively to communicate with the public. As noted, he did so twice on January 6, 2021, the day a mob overran the Capitol. The first was a one-minute video posted to his Facebook page at 4:21 p.m., after the riot was underway. In it he said the following:

> I know your pain. I know you're hurt. We had an election that was stolen from us. It was a landslide election, and everyone knows it, especially the other side, but you have to go home now. We have to have peace. We have to have law and order. We have to respect our great people in law and order. We don't want anybody hurt. It's a very tough period of time. There's never been a time like this where such a thing happened, where they could take it away from all of us, from me, from you, from our country. This was a fraudulent election, but we can't play into the hands of these people. We have to have peace. So go home. We love you. You're very special. You've seen what happens. You see the way others are treated that are so bad and so evil. I know how you feel. But go home and go home in peace.

At 5:41 p.m., Facebook removed the post. At 6:07 p.m., Trump posted a written statement:

> These are the things and events that happen when a sacred landslide election victory is so unceremoniously viciously stripped away from great patriots who have been badly unfairly treated for so long. Go home with love in peace. Remember this day forever!

Facebook removed this post at 6:15 p.m. and imposed a twenty-four-hour block on his ability to post any further material.

On the next day, January 7, 2021, Facebook announced that the block would be extended indefinitely, and on January 21 that it had referred its decision to the Oversight Board, asking whether the decision to suspend Trump's account complied with Facebook's community standards and corporate policies that govern the posting of materials on its website, including international human rights law.

On May 5, the Board announced its decision. It agreed with Facebook that President Trump's two January 6 posts violated Facebook's community standards. Specifically, it said, Trump had violated the standard on dangerous individuals and organizations, which prohibits users from posting content that "praises" or "supports" what are termed "violating events," or that expresses support or praise for individuals involved in violating events. "Facebook designated the storming of the Capitol as a 'violating event,'" the Board found, "and noted that it interprets violating events to include designated 'violent' events." The Board's opinion does not indicate whether that designation was made before or after Trump's materials were posted. The key point for the Board, however, appears to have been that "[b]oth posts praised or supported people who were engaged in violence."

Significantly, the Board on May 5 did not find that Trump had incited violence. But on January 7, CEO Zuckerberg, in announcing the suspension of Trump's account, had accused him of "use of our platform to incite violent insurrection against a democratically elected government."[145] Incitement to violence is prohibited in another community standard; the standard on which the Board relied, concerning dangerous individuals and organizations, prohibited praise or support for individuals involved in violence, not incitement to violence.

Having concluded that Facebook's actions were permissible under its community standards, the Board then turned to international human rights law. "The Board analyzes Facebook's human rights responsibilities through international standards on freedom of expression and the rights to life, security, and political participation," it said. Applying international law standards,[146] the Board found that it was not permissible for Facebook to keep Trump off the platform for an undefined period. But blocking his posts and suspending his account were appropriate, it concluded, because he had praised and supported violence—and, indeed, these actions against Trump were necessary for national security reasons, to safeguard domestic constitutional processes: "The riot directly interfered with Congress's ability to discharge its constitutional responsibility."

The Board did not, however, address a more basic question: In the event of a conflict between Facebook's community standards and international human rights rules, which prevails? A Facebook user cannot understand what posts are allowed or not allowed without knowing the answer. The community standards do not resolve the question. Indeed, as Oversight Board member Nossel has acknowledged, Facebook's "published standards represent only a small portion of guidelines that dictate content removal decisions."[147] Its content rules change constantly:

> A February 2019 investigative report by technology website The Verge detailed "near-daily changes and clarifications" to the site's content rules, moderators who misconstrued posts due to a lack of cultural or political context, and "frequent disagreements among moderators about whether the rules should apply in individual cases."[148]

Like Facebook's commitment to international human rights law, its standards can, indeed, be revoked, expanded, or modified at any time by Facebook's corporate management, without approval or consultation with the Oversight Board. While Facebook may have a "Supreme Court" in its Oversight Board, it has no legislature. Its rules, such as they are—presumably, for Facebook's decision-making process is a black box— are Zuckerberg's rules. If Facebook is like a government, as he has said it is, it is a kind of duchy, with Zuckerberg its grand duke. Facebook's public "commitment" to international human rights law was announced not through a change in its community standards (which could itself have been affected by Zuckerberg alone) but by decree, through a simple announcement of corporate policy made on March 16, 2021. Like the community standards, that announcement said nothing about its priority as against potentially conflicting community standards. It could hardly have been "clear and accessible" to a user such as Trump, whose conduct occurred before the announcement was made. Other users can, similarly, be restricted or suspended based on rules made applicable—or made up—after their conduct has occurred. Facebook's rules confer precisely the "unfettered discretion" that the Board says international law prohibits. Its content rules permit both Facebook and the Oversight Board itself to pick and choose arbitrarily among rules after material is posted, leaving users unable "to understand what is allowed and what is not allowed."

Whether Trump's speech would have been impermissible under the incitement standard of the First Amendment is a close question. But it is not a close question whether glorification of violence can be suppressed under the First Amendment. It cannot. If it could be, commemorations of the Boston Tea Party, the battles of Lexington and Bunker Hill, and the Shaw Memorial on the Boston Common celebrating African American soldiers in the Union Army's 54th Regiment all would be unprotected expression.

Culture matters—sometimes. It didn't matter to the Oversight Board in the Trump case. But it did matter in two other cases, both involving hate speech and misinformation. Note, in each case, that the Board defers to local cultural context while seeking to apply the same rule worldwide, ignoring whatever local norm that particular culture may have generated. Note also that the outcome in each precedent—which apparently applies within the United States—would never have occurred under the principles of the First Amendment.

Hate Speech: The South Africa Case (2021)

In May 2021 a Facebook user posted content in English in a public group. The post targeted a group of Black South Africans. It discussed "multi racialism" in South Africa and argued that poverty had increased among Black people and that White people came to hold most of the nation's wealth. It closed by indicating that anyone who thought otherwise is, among other things, a "kaffir."

The Oversight Board upheld Facebook's decision to remove the post under its hate speech community standard.[149] "Kaffir," the Board found, was on Facebook's confidential list of prohibited slurs "for the Sub-Saharan market" and historically was used by white people in South Africa as a derogatory term to refer to Black people. The word, the Board found, is a "particularly hateful and harmful word in the South African context." Considering Facebook's values of dignity and safety, the Board found that use of the word "in the context of South Africa can be degrading, excluding and harmful to the people targeted by the slur." Applying Article 19 of the ICCPR, the Board found that the restriction was legitimate because it sought to protect people's rights to equality and nondiscrimination, and that it was proportionate because it was "the least intrusive instrument among those which might achieve their protective function." The Board asked Facebook whether a slur's appearance on any market list means it cannot be used globally; Facebook answered unresponsively

> that its "prohibition against slurs is global, but the designation of slurs is market-specific, as Facebook recognizes that cultural and linguistic varia-tions mean that words [that] are slurs in some places may not be in others." The Board reiterated its initial question. Facebook then responded "[i]f a term appears on a market slur list, the hate speech policy prohibits its use in that market. The term could be used elsewhere with a different meaning; therefore Facebook would independently evaluate whether to add it to the other markets slur list." It remains unclear to the Board how Facebook enforces the slur prohibition in practice and at scale. The Board does not know how Facebook's enforcement processes to identify and remove violating content operate globally for market-specific terms, how markets are defined, or when and how this independent evaluation occurs.

Whatever the answer, note that banning slurs would never have been per-missible under the First Amendment principles described in Chapter 8.

Misinformation: The Brazil Case (2021)

In March 2021, a state-level medical council (part of the government) in Brazil posted on its Facebook page material relating to measures to re-duce the spread of COVID-19. The material contained inaccurate infor-mation, misquoting a medical authority and stating that the World Health Organization (WHO) had condemned lockdowns; it had not. It would not have been permissible under these rules[150] to take down the material, the Oversight Board found, because the content did not create a risk of immi-nent harm.

Under international law, however, the Board advised that it *would* be per-missible for Facebook to consider less intrusive measures than removing the materials, the reason being that the governmental entity in question, the medical council, had violated its "duty" under Article 19 of the ICCPR "to ensure that it disseminates reliable and trustworthy information about matters of public interest." "This duty is particularly strong when the infor-mation is related to the right of health, especially during a global pandemic." Thus it would be permissible for Facebook to consider "disrupting economic incentives for people, pages, and domains that propagate misinformation" or "reducing the distribution of content rated false by independent fact checkers." The Board did not indicate how the exercise of these options would square with what it said is the requirement of Article 19, that "people should have enough information to determine if and how their access to information may be limited."[151]

While the material in question would be available globally as a consequence of the Board's action, it advised that Facebook should "take into consideration local context and consider the current situation in Brazil when assessing the risk of imminent physical harm." The risk of imminent physical harm potentially resulting from the publication of misinformation was a function, the Board found, of "the local context" as well as the advice of the WHO, the U.S. Centers for Disease Control and Prevention, "the national public health authority in Brazil," and "other leading public health authorities" which Facebook and the Board consulted.

Why should Facebook be concerned about the spread of misinformation? Misinformation, the Board said, "can endanger people's trust in public information about appropriate measures to counter the pandemic." It emphasized the need to "prevent the dissemination of misinformation on public health [that] can affect trust in public information and the effectiveness of certain measures that, in the words of the World Health Organization, may be essential in certain contexts." Promoting trust in government-provided information, the Board underscored, is an important part of Facebook's mission. Needless to say, in the United States the First Amendment would not permit the suppression of speech on the theory that it undermines trust in the government.

The Misguided Culture/Law Distinction

The question for our purposes is not whether the Oversight Board correctly applied the principles of international law that it selected.[152] The question here is whether international law rather than national law is the proper reference point for social media in drawing speech boundaries within the United States. Monika Bickert, Facebook's head of policy management, put the problem succinctly: "Different cultures have very different levels of tolerance for speech."[153] It was recognition of this cultural variance that presumably led Facebook's Oversight Board to emphasize *context*, to recognize that a term such as *kaffir* that is a "particularly hateful and harmful word in the South African context" might not be hateful or harmful in another culture—such as that of the United States, where virtually no one knows what it means—and to recognize that the publication of inaccurate information about public health that creates a risk of imminent harm in one culture could be ignored or laughed at in another culture. It is, the Board recognized, important to pay heed to cultural variation. "[C]ommunities themselves traditionally set speech boundaries in the form of social norms,"[154] Bickert wrote, drawing the obviously correct conclusion: "The laws are therefore likely to reflect, at least in democracies, the social values of the local population."[155]

But Facebook does not follow that logic through to the next step: *If norms on free speech are culturally variant, and if social media need to respect cultural variation in setting speech boundaries, why not respect a society's highest, concretized reification of its cultural norms-its laws?* If Facebook is willing to defer to the social values of the local population as to what slurs are locally hateful and what misinformation is locally harmful, why not defer to the social values of the local population on the *rules* it has put in place to *govern* which slurs and what misinformation it is willing to tolerate? Why should the population of the United States—or Denmark or Thailand or Nepal or Germany—be governed by speech rules tailored to the local cultural norms of Brazil or South Africa?

It is not, after all, as though these are new questions for the population of the United States. As noted earlier, the question of proper speech boundaries has been addressed by more scholars in more books and by more judges in more cases—and at a deeper level—in the United States than in any other nation in history. Hundreds of cases decided by the U.S. Supreme Court alone grapple with virtually every aspect of free speech.[156] That body of learning and law was already at an advanced stage before most nations in the world even came into existence. If those nations now wish to develop their own jurisprudence and draw speech boundaries differently on issues such as hate speech or misinformation, they have a sovereign right to do so. Different cultures balance competing values differently; that is why cultures differ. But as Michael Ignatieff has observed, "America . . . has articulated its identity in terms of its rights,"[157] and no right is more central to American culture and the Constitution it has created than the right of free speech. So again: If local cultural norms are to be respected, why not defer as well to the local *legal* norms that those cultural norms generate?

Social media's answer is, in a word, *balkanization*. "Legislation that imposes particular content standards" in different countries, Bickert argues, will force companies to "balkanize their standards." Enormous volumes of content would be subjected to differing national standards, making it "all but impossible for companies to function in those jurisdictions."[158] Massive teams of lawyers would be required to measure such content against "multiple, subjective, evolving laws."[159] Relying on "each nation's laws as the basis for governing social media content in individual countries," she concludes, would simply be "impractical."[160] Global standards such as those set forth in international human rights law are required to simplify the process.

Given that Facebook's more than three billion users are spread about the planet, there are, no doubt, advantages of scale to be had in applying worldwide content rules that do not derive from any one national or regional legal system. But concerns about the impracticality of regionalized rules are easily overstated and often conflate profitability with technological feasibility. The two are very different: tailoring rules to specific groups of users is not technologically infeasible. It is simply more expensive.

It's thus puzzling why, in the South Africa case, Facebook was unwilling to give its Oversight Board a straight answer concerning the company's capability of enforcing slur prohibitions within specific national markets. Obviously Facebook had the technological capability to do so; that had existed for years.[161] This is Bickert's summary of that capability:

> Major social media companies have built tools that allow them to block content in one country but leave it visible elsewhere. This means they have the technical ability to apply different content standards in different countries. And, in fact, social media companies implement this sort of "geoblocking" solution with some regularity, as shown in their transparency reports.[162]

These geoblocking tools "permit the company to block only the precise post or photo or other piece of content that is illegal and block it in only the country where it is illegal."[163] The impediment to relinquishing control through the interpretation of international human rights norms is therefore not technological. A more significant reason for social media companies' resistance to national legal norms is the financial cost. Bickert writes that the companies' effort to "survive financially" could be imperiled by assigning greater value to home countries' "external inputs."[164] No doubt more national lawyers would need to be hired, more nationally individuated education for content moderators would need to be provided; costs would increase. But the costs of business operations are seldom absorbed by managers and shareholders; they are passed on to customers. The business model of the social media world as it currently exists is based on advertising. "Customers"—users—do not pay directly; data derived from their use is sold to third parties, and sometimes they themselves pay social media such as Facebook to, in effect, advertise their content by giving it wider circulation, which is accomplished by calling it more directly to the attention of other Facebook users. As it is, the cost of indifference to national content norms (such as the First Amendment in the Trump case) is externalized and is borne by unwilling and often unknowing citizens of those nations, whether or not they use Facebook. But much of that cost could be internalized, for example by increasing advertising fees to cover the cost of respecting local laws, or by moving in whole or in part to a different business model, based on user subscription fees. Other creative possibilities exist for meeting added costs of respecting traditional cultural and legal norms more fully. The companies may not choose to incur those costs without being required to do so by national legal authorities. But the point is that expenses can be met—if the company or the nation in which it operates decides that the value to be derived is worth it. In short, the alternative to international human rights law is not "multiple, subjective, evolving laws"—that, as demonstrated in detail above, is an apt description of international human rights law. The alternative is deference to the cultures of people who speak on social media and the laws their cultures have generated.

In the case of nations such as China, that conclusion provides no solution for companies intent on promoting free speech; some weight need be accorded the character of the lawmaking processes by which domestic rules are generated, recognizing the legitimacy problem posed by speech-suppressive rules that are formulated within speech-suppressed lawmaking processes. That, however, is a topic for another day. The inquiry here is, again, what body of rules should apply within the United States, not China. It is not self-evident that the internal free speech regulations of each deserve equal deference by social media.

Outlier—or International Scofflaw?

If deference is owed to nations' cultural differences, and if deference to a nation's culture counsels greater deference to a nation's laws, where does that leave charges of American exceptionalism in light of the country's status as a self-acknowledged outlier on free speech? The question highlights important differences between the international and domestic legal systems. It also invites inquiry into law's purposes and the sources of its legitimacy. These are monumental issues, but a few brief words may be useful.

The machinery of international law and the human rights norms contained within it differs fundamentally from that of domestic law. To take the U.S. constitutional system as an example, its default premise is that government can do nothing that is not explicitly or implicitly *authorized* by law. Absence of legal authorization prohibits the government from acting. In the international legal order, the reverse is true: a nation is assumed to be authorized to act unless international law prohibits the state from acting. States do not need "permission" to act. This is international law's famous "freedom principle." The international order is consent-based, voluntaristic: states are bound only to those rules that they freely accept. Domestic legal systems, in contrast, are largely coercion-based. Actors within a domestic legal system— people, businesses, government officials—cannot opt out of its rules; they are compelled to obey, whether they accept the rules or not.

Violation of the law is therefore treated differently by the two systems. Noncompliant conduct by actors within a domestic legal system does not reshape the rules. Violation of domestic law has no effect in modifying the law. But that is not true in the international system. Because no higher authority than states exists in the international order, whatever law exists is made by states, through their consent. They express consent either by word (treaties) or by deed (custom). The actors within the international system *are* its lawmakers; their rules are the rules they honor. If they don't honor a rule, that matters.[165]

This sketch obviously is done with a broad brush, but the two systems' structural differences are nonetheless profound. Those differences pervade the operation of both systems and make it difficult to import rules from one into the other. Try as we might to make them work, therefore, imported rules often just don't fit. They are jarring to the population on which they are imposed.

This creates problems for the rule of law. One of law's prime functions is to enhance predictability—to prevent people from being surprised.[166] The law aims to enable people to realize reasonable expectations. Those expectations are primarily a product of their own cultures, not other nations' cultures. When the law's enforcement leaves people feeling jolted, the law's integrity erodes. That doesn't mean that homegrown rules are always perfectly tailored to a society's needs; of course they are not—intractable disagreement over what constitutes "the good life" is endemic to the human condition and sparks divisions within even the best-run democracies, let alone between and among nations. But on balance, rules which a self-governing people make for themselves are less likely to be as jarring as rules made by others. Efforts by outsiders to impose "taxation without representation" and other rules did not fare well in North America.

The law's capacity to prevent people from being surprised by its application goes to its legitimacy, as former Supreme Court justice Stephen Breyer has recognized. "In the United States, it is the people, not a central authority," he writes, "who are the source of legitimate federal power."[167] "We the people of the United States" give government its power, the Constitution affirms. We are able to trace every exercise of governmental power back to the people's consent. In contrast, Justice Breyer asks, who are the people who give substance to international law? His answer is "international courts, foreign courts, and scholars." And what, he asks, "is their connection to the 'people of the United States'?" The law's legitimacy is not a serious impediment when courts resolve technical issues. But, he rightly suggests, "basic human rights—rights that our own Constitution protects"[168]—fall into a different category.

This is a compelling reason to look to the jurisprudence of the First Amendment rather than to imported rules of international human rights law, as the body of law governing the digital marketplace of ideas within the United States. *Rights that our own Constitution protects*—freedom of speech and freedom of the press protected by the First Amendment—are far more familiar to the American people than Article 19 of the International Covenant on Civil and Political Rights or General Comment 34 of the Human Rights Committee or the Rabat Plan of Action. Those First Amendment freedoms have been tailored to American society in hundreds of cases decided over a century by eminent American jurists steeped in the culture of the American people. The United States has no reason to look elsewhere to manage the free exchange of ideas in Americans' digital marketplace. Whatever the moral implications, that differing societies have differing ways of meeting differing expectations is an empirical fact, and nations' continuing power to meet those expectations in differing ways is a feature of the prevailing state system.

Is this an example of American hypocrisy and exceptionalism, pushing other nations to accept international rules while it flouts those rules itself?

I think not. The international legal system is, to repeat, voluntarist: states are bound only by those rules to which they consent. The United States has repeatedly made clear that it does not consent to international restrictions on freedom of speech that conflict with the First Amendment. As indicated earlier, in ratifying treaties that would do so, it has made clear that it accepts no international obligations inconsistent with the First Amendment. U.S. practice has made abundantly clear, during the period in which restrictive, inchoate customary international law norms have been in the process of formation, that it does not accept their application to the United States—which customary international law allows.[169] While the United States may be an *outlier* in holding fast to its own speech-protective rules, therefore, it is not a *violator*. To the contrary: from the beginning of the human rights movement, it has underscored its commitment to the most rigorous protection of free speech, which is vastly different from opting out of norms that permit the stifling of speech. The United States' objection has not been that emerging international rules protect too much speech; it has been that they protect too little. Nations that protect speech more rigorously than others have no reason to water down that protection, let alone apologize for it.

Government as Stakeholder

It is easy to suspect, as have various commentators, that social media companies embrace international human rights law merely as a ruse. The companies, critics suggest, have discovered the PR value of the beguiling vocabulary of *international human rights law*. Its words have a strong visceral appeal, particularly to those who understand little about how international law is made, interpreted, or enforced. Its galvanizing prose taps into genuine and deeply felt feelings of empathy and victimization. The rhetorical pull tugs the heartstrings of all who oppose *hate, discrimination, misinformation, violence*, and *war*.

But the vocabulary's elasticity allows it to be stretched to cover very different aims. It allows the companies to commit publicly to respect rights while privately exercising arbitrary power to promote or impede whatever their own ideologies or their balance sheets might suggest—to "move fast and break things." And moving and breaking can be accomplished most readily by depriving the weak of their defenses, the most potent defense being freedom of speech.

Social media companies' embrace of international human rights parallels in many ways businesses' general embrace of environmental, social, and government (ESG) policies and commitment to "stakeholder capitalism." Indeed, social media companies themselves frequently draw upon the language of ESG and stakeholder capitalism in fashioning human rights pronouncements. Stakeholder capitalism has been a reaction against the long prevalent view, argued in the writings of Milton Friedman and others, that the purpose of business is financial profit—maximizing shareholder value. Companies intent on maximizing profits in a free market, the argument went, best serve the interests of everyone affected by their operations; a company that spends its money to meet "social responsibilities" in effect spends the money of its stockholders, customers, or employees, who should be free to choose for themselves how to spend that money.[170] Nothing prevents them from moving to other companies if they believe that a given company is failing to meet its social obligations; that's how a free market works.

Stakeholder capitalism contends that this view denies companies' social responsibilities. Stakeholder capitalism's most prominent advocates have been Klaus Schwab and the World Economic Forum that he heads. Schwab argues that in making business decisions, a company ought to take into account not simply shareholders' profits but stakeholders' interests. A "Great Reset" is required. It's mistaken, he writes, to "focus on the more granular and exclusive objectives of profits or prosperity in a particular company or country rather than the well-being of all people and the planet as a whole." Companies should seek instead to advance the well-being of all these stakeholders. Schwab spells out who these are:

> They are: governments (of countries, states, and local communities); civil society (from unions to NGOs, from schools and universities to action groups); companies (constituting the private sector, whether freelancers or large multinational companies); and the international community (consisting of international organizations such as the UN as well as regional organizations such as the European Union or [the Association of Southeast Asian Nations]).[171]

This broader focus, Schwab suggests, will better advance the interests of the planet and its people, as it should: "The planet is the center of the global economic system, and . . . it is incumbent on all of us as global citizens to optimize the well-being of all."

It's not my purpose here to assess the merits of shareholder capitalism versus stakeholder capitalism. In many respects the two are poles on a spectrum rather than oppositional categories. Smart business practices sometimes entails considering the social and political preferences of employees, customers, and others *for the purpose of* maximizing shareholder profits. Visibly avaricious businesses often shortsightedly sacrifice profits by ignoring the social and political consequences of their actions. Facebook may be a case in point; it's hard to see how the self-interestedness and seeming indifference to health and safety revealed by the *Wall Street Journal* redounded to its shareholders' financial benefit.[172]

Nor is it my purpose here to suggest that social media's professed affection for international human rights law is motivated exclusively by a strategy of masking profit-enhancement in globalist, altruistic rhetoric that has little effect on real-world corporate decision-making. Organizations, like the people they comprise, act for mixed motives that are hard to disentangle. I merely point out, with other skeptics, that international human rights law presents an easy deflective mechanism, and that social media companies have not been oblivious to the benefits of pretended benevolence.

What I do want to address is something that has received far too little attention: the pernicious consequence of regarding *governments* as stakeholders in companies that manage modern societies' marketplace of ideas. Let there be no doubt: that is how social media now see government—as a constituency with a stake in their operations, as a power whose interests they need to satisfy. In the Brazil case, noted earlier, the Facebook Oversight Board explicitly identified part of the company's mission as promoting public trust in government-provided information. In the Trump case, the Board assumed that it is Facebook's job to assess Congress's proper role in the presidential selection process and to suppress information that, in Facebook's exclusive judgment, threatened the legislative role. Scan their websites and one finds that, like the rhetoric of international human rights, the rhetoric of stakeholder capitalism pervades the public relations of Facebook and other social media. Social media behemoths make no effort to hide their attempts to ingratiate themselves with government regulators. The companies' messaging brims with concern for stakeholders—including the government. Facebook proclaims that its human rights "policy is founded on meaningful engagement with rights holders and other stakeholders," including governments.[173]

As the next chapter points out, government is not merely a Facebook stakeholder. As Zuckerberg said, Facebook is like a government: it and other social media in many respects have become surrogates of the government. In critical respects, social media censors have come to act as arms of the state. Yet American freedom of expression is grounded on the bedrock principle that government has *no role* in determining what ideas people read and write about. Thinking of government as a stakeholder in decisions about what content appears on social media inevitably gives government a direct role in those decisions. It encourages social media companies to do government's bidding—to decide as the government would wish them to decide, to seek the government's views in making content decisions. And it encourages the government to intervene actively in those decisions, sometimes by invitation, often with threats, usually covertly—but always with the effect of shaping a marketplace of ideas that the First Amendment intended to remove from governmental control. Freedom of speech, in this new marketplace, will mean freedom to express any idea—any idea that government and social media don't hate.

12

Symbiotic Security and Free Speech

The previous chapter concluded with the observation that the major social media platforms have become surrogates of the government, effectively arms of the state. This chapter elaborates, unfolding in four sections.
In the first section, I trace the origins and evolution of the security-media
complex—I call it a cartel because of the level of conscious parallelism and
outright coordination—through the emergence of the nation's double government, describing its recent appearance and suppression of speech during
two prominent series of events: the COVID-19 pandemic and news reports
concerning Hunter Biden. The second section suggests that, throughout
these efforts, the security apparatus has been entwined symbiotically with
the dominant social media platforms to the degree that separating state action from private action and government speech from private speech in any
principled manner is not possible. In the third section, I outline a variety
of existing constitutional approaches that, invigorated and amplified, could
provide starting points for protecting the modern, digitized public square
from the cartel. I conclude that the First Amendment's vitality depends upon
a deepened commitment by the courts to ensure this protection.

From Double Government to Freestanding Power

A recent book by Bob Woodward and Robert Costa alleged that General
Mark Milley, chairman of the Joint Chiefs of Staff, promised Speaker of the
House Nancy Pelosi that he would thwart any presidential order to take military action, lawful or unlawful, that he considered immoral, unethical, or
crazy, and that he ordered subordinates to call him if they received such orders, "no matter where they're from."[1] Whether General Milley actually
positioned himself to foil presidential orders is disputed. The more important question is how the nation arrived at the point where many Americans
appeared to agree with the Senate majority whip Dick Durbin, who, in
responding to those allegations, said, "It is a shame we reached that point in

Free Speech and Turbulent Freedom. Michael J. Glennon, Oxford University Press. © Oxford University Press 2024.
DOI: 10.1093/oso/9780197636763.003.0012

America's history that's necessary, and I think he did the responsible thing to keep America out of war."[2] How did it come about that a general with no command authority could now be seen as properly inserting himself into the constitutional chain of command above the president of the United States? More important, why should we care? Aren't other political rights and civil liberties, such as freedom of speech, independent of structural safeguards such as civilian control of the military and separation of powers?

The answer to the latter question is an emphatic no. Justice Brandeis's familiar summary of the object of the separation of powers doctrine is worth recalling:

> The doctrine of the separation of powers was adopted by the convention of 1787, not to promote efficiency but to preclude the exercise of arbitrary power. The purpose was not to avoid friction, but, by means of the inevitable friction incident to the distribution of the governmental powers among three departments, to save the people from autocracy.[3]

Saving the people from autocracy is, of course, also the purpose of the Bill of Rights. Prohibitions against abridgments on free speech, denials of due process, unreasonable searches and seizures, cruel and unusual punishment, and the like also are directed at precluding the exercise of arbitrary power. When structural safeguards such as civilian control of the military or the checking authority of Congress are weakened, so is the protection of civil liberties from arbitrary power. Separation of powers and political freedom are *inter*dependent. They are the warp and weft of the fabric of constitutional democracy. They share the same ends, the same means, and rest on the same premises of pluralism, decentralization, and equilibrating political disputation.[4] Both are oxygenated by the same vascular system with streams of fresh information and opinions. Neither can exist without the other. This was the enduring insight of one of America's greatest First Amendment scholars, Alexander Meiklejohn, who wrote that in a self-governing society, "the governors and the governed are not two distinct groups of persons. There is only one group—the self-governing people. Ruled and rulers are the same individuals."[5] And he added this crucial point: "Unless we can make clear that distinction, discussion of freedom of speech or of any other freedom is meaningless and futile."[6]

The vitality of civil and political liberties such as freedom of speech thus depends upon the vitality of structural checks that curb authorities' exercise of undelegated power. The health of self-government is a function of the health of those checks. If authorities break free of those checks, self-government and individual freedom both are threatened.

Let us turn, then, to the question posed by General Milley and Senator Durbin: How healthy are those structural checks—how healthy is self-government—in the United States today? The answer, alas, is that in the realm of national security, the rulers and the ruled are no longer the same individuals.

The Rise of Postwar Double Government

The erosion of the separation of powers in the security realm opened the door for what I earlier referred to as a system of double government.[7] The late Dean Acheson, archdeacon of the national security priesthood, spoke for many associates when he articulated its animating premise early in the Cold War. "If you truly had a democracy and did what the people wanted," Acheson said, "you'd go wrong every time."[8] To avoid this misfortune, the people were taught that critical decisions concerning national security are made by the nation's "Madisonian institutions": the presidency, Congress, and the courts. But the Madisonian institutions evolved into mostly window-dressing. In reality, most consequential national security decisions since the Truman administration were made by a largely concealed directorate consisting of several hundred leaders of the military, law enforcement, and intelligence departments and agencies of the executive government. They did so not as part of any vast conspiracy to subvert the constitutional order but in response to deep-seated structural incentives, long recognized principles of organizational behavior, and political imperatives arising from the perceived security needs of the world's strongest superpower. Yet these managers, I suggest, operated increasingly free from constitutional restraints, moving the nation steadily toward autocracy.

Over decades of confronting both real and inflated threats, the courts, Congress, and even presidents have deferred to the expertise and experience of these security managers. More and more topics went into the ever-expanding security portfolio. No judge, senator, or president wanted to risk responsibility for a devastating national security mistake. The courts, for their part, wove together an elaborate jurisprudence of ripeness, mootness, the state secrets doctrine, the political question doctrine, and lack of standing to avoid reaching the merits of national security disputes.[9] By the early 2000s, congressional oversight became increasingly "dysfunctional," to quote the 9/11 Commission[10]—more hindsight than oversight. Congress knew little and cared less about a vast array of constitutionally questionable activities ranging from black site prisons and torture to mass domestic surveillance. Blame-avoiding, credit-seeking members of Congress were more than happy to steer clear of potentially career-imperiling positions on issues that the "true professionals" in the security bureaucracy would eagerly handle. Even the Executive had every incentive to defer to the security managers' judgment, resulting in remarkable policy continuity from one administration to the next on drone strikes, troop deployments, telephone and internet surveillance, covert action, whistleblower and leak prosecutions, claims of state secrets, and numerous other security matters. Barack Obama—who campaigned on the promise of "change we can believe in"—might just as well have been referring to the entire national security "community" when he explained to his staff that "[t]he CIA gets what it wants."[11] The beauty of this deferential arrangement was that whatever went wrong, responsibility and accountability were easily diffused among myriad agencies and leaders in a faceless national security apparatus.[12]

The resulting interdependence between the security managers and the Madisonian officials, and the massive transfer of power that it brought about, occurred almost entirely behind closed doors—where it necessarily needed to stay. For the system of double government to survive, both the security managers and the Madisonian institutions needed to appear publicly to be on the same page. It was necessary always to project a persuasive public image of harmony; if the impression of a single, unified edifice was shattered, public confidence would falter.

The arrangement's stability relied upon each participant's source of legitimacy. When a president claimed the need to act immediately in response to a national security emergency, say, to blockade Cuba in response to a Soviet missile buildup, people respected the president's decision because of the electoral connection—the president had been chosen in an election by the people. The president's judgment was also accepted because he relied upon, and was known to rely upon, bona fide experts in assessing that threat. If a president publicly demeans the only available experts or replaces them with sycophants or bases his decisions on his own gut feelings or ideology, why should people believe that he is making the right decisions?

As with the president, the security managers' power also depended upon their constitutional legitimacy. But unlike the president, they have no direct electoral connection; their legitimacy flows from the president's. No one voted for intelligence chiefs like Richard Helms, Avril Haines, or Bill Burns. Their institutional authority is derivative: it is tied to and justified by the president's legitimacy. Should that link be broken, the source of their legitimacy would vanish. To retain that authority, extraconstitutional scaffolding would therefore be necessary to shore up that legitimacy—scaffolding that might be provided in the form of direct support from the public.

The Breakup of Double Government

But the link was broken during the Trump administration. Barely a week went by in which a salvo was not exchanged between the president and managers of the security bureaucracy.[13] The president tweeted that the former FBI director was an "untruthful slime ball,"[14] compared the CIA to Nazis,[15] and described its former leaders as hacks;[16] the security managers and their alumni colleagues responded with a counterbarrage of name-calling and leaks. The *Washington Post*[17] cited nine senior intelligence sources for one critical story, the *New York Times*[18] cited four for another. The forging of new alliances between the security managers and influential domestic constituencies then proceeded in full swing. As the battle lines hardened to the shock of an astounded public, the security managers found ready support within mainstream and social media that were still reeling from the 2020 election results and not eager to witness, let alone enable, Trump's political reemergence.

The frequent appearances of former intelligence and law enforcement officials as commentators and analysts on major television networks[19] helped elevate the security apparatus into a friendly, autonomous institution. Completely forgotten was the historical record of these agencies when they were left unchecked.[20] Constituencies that earlier had been wary of unaccountable power became its keenest admirers, oblivious to reversions to form.[21] Senate Majority Leader Charles Schumer warned Trump in 2017 to heed the security managers' wishes. The president, Schumer said, was "being really dumb" in taking on the intelligence community.[22] "Let me tell you," Schumer said, "you take on the intelligence community, they have six ways from Sunday at getting back at you."[23] The next year, a former top official in both the CIA and FBI, Philip Mudd, reiterated Schumer's warning on CNN:

So, the FBI people—I'm going to tell you—are ticked, and they're going to be saying, I guarantee it, you think you could push us off this because you can try to intimidate the director, you'd better think again, Mr. President. You've been around for 13 months; we've been around since 1908. I know how this game is going to be played, and we're going to win.[24]

Bill Kristol, a prominent political commentator, said that he would prefer the deep state to the Trump state.[25] The *New Yorker* predicted that the intelligence community's managers would challenge Trump before Congress. "This is just the sort of thing we want to see happening" as part of "the fabled 'checks and balances' in the U.S. system."[26] "God bless the 'deep state,'" wrote *Washington Post* columnist Eugene Robinson.[27] Its existence should be celebrated, he urged: "The deep state stands between us and the abyss."[28] If the "president does not serve the best interests of the nation," Robinson said, the "loyal and honorable deep state" has the higher duty to step in and stop him.[29]

It is hard to overstate the significance of the unprecedented, seismic split between the Oval Office and the nation's security directors. No longer would the security agencies depend upon elected politicians for their legitimacy—now they would generate their own legitimacy with support directly from the body politic. No longer was the so-called deep state deep—it was entirely out in the open, soon taken as a fact by nearly three-fourths of the public.[30] No longer would the security managers operate behind the scenes—now they were openly competitors for power. The final freeing of the security managers from Madisonian control was made possible by the validation of their independence by influential elements of the public.

Constitutionally, the security managers' new, stand-alone power marked an epic break from the nation's structure of governance. The Constitution sets up only three branches of government, and the security bureaucracy is not one of them. The security bureaucracy is not empowered to check the other three branches; it is expected to be checked *by* them. Under the Constitution, power is delegated *to* the security bureaucracy, not *by* it. Inverting that constitutional hierarchy of power in the security realm represents an entirely different form of government, a system in which the governed and the governors are not the same.

It was not only constitutional principles that mandated a nonpartisan security apparatus. At least as important as the constitutional subordination of the security apparatus was its traditional political subordination. The origins and history of the political dimensions of the norm are explained in Samuel Huntington's classic 1957 study, *The Soldier and the State.* Huntington focuses on civilian control of the military, but much of his analysis applies equally to the military's partners the within intelligence and law enforcement bureaucracy, which shares in its power and influence and which now performs frequently overlapping functions. The essence of civilian control, Huntington wrote, "is a clear distinction between political and military responsibilities and the institutional subordination of the latter to the former."[31] The "exclusion of the military from political power . . . has been so effective that Americans have called it a fundamental principle of their system of government."[32] Integrally tied to this political norm are underlying constitutional precepts, as the Supreme Court has pointed out. Keeping the military "insulated from both the reality and the appearance of acting as a handmaiden for partisan political cause or candidates," the Court said in *Greer v. Spock,* ". . . is wholly consistent with the American constitutional tradition of a politically neutral military establishment under civilian control."[33]

With their link to that constitutional tradition threadbare and their electoral connection frayed as a result of the punch-up with Trump, the security leaders faced a continuing risk of becoming too detached from the wellsprings of public support. Yet the benefits of freestanding authority could be momentous. Drawing on their own independent legitimacy could now buttress them from assaults by the political branches of the sort launched in the mid-1970s by the Church and Pike committees; they could be not merely a fourth, coequal branch of government but guardians of the guardians, the *superior* branch of the government, entitled to check misguided efforts of the other branches and to resist their encroachments. Alliances with friendly domestic constituencies could cement that power. All the more beneficial could be ties to groups experienced in information control and appreciative of its utility.

It was thus no surprise that the national security mission should expand as it has. No longer would its aim be merely to protect the physical safety of the American people; now it would be to combat mis-, dis-, and mal-information[34] and (as the new national security adviser Jake Sullivan proclaimed) "inequality in all forms,"[35] at home and abroad. Milley articulated the scope of this broader mission in a telling justification of a (mistargeted) military strike, which he characterized as "righteous"[36]—what is moral, good, virtuous. These themes would later resonate within quarters that had hitherto been critical.

Yet a security apparatus immersed in the political fray risks alienating other segments of the public that have a different view on what is righteous. One solution is to eliminate the fracas by eliminating its cause: conflicting ideas. This is tricky to carry out by law, given the traditional restrictions of the First Amendment. "Eliminating such ideas [was the] very purpose"[37] of a state statute struck down in 2021 by the Tenth Circuit Court of Appeals. Workarounds are therefore required. One is to operate through private partners whose speech is protected by the First Amendment. Applicants are not in short supply. Corporate media and regulation-averse social media, for example, are ever-eager to ingratiate themselves with an appreciative security bureaucracy. Another is to rely upon the government's own speech to recommend ways its partners can counter misinformation, disinformation, and mal-information called "MDM" by the Department of Homeland Security.[38] Because the government's speech is deemed exempt from First Amendment restriction,[39] it can flood media with approved messaging, stigmatizing dissidents and neutralizing their speech. Isolating out-of-the-mainstream cranks not only keeps "unacceptable views"[40] (in Canadian prime minister Justin Trudeau's memorable words) out of the marketplace but solidifies support among friendly domestic groups that can forestall any assault on the information managers' power.[41] Compiling and disseminating dissidents' "social credit scores" could, hypothetically, easily be accomplished within the limits and protections of state action and government speech.[42] Skillful information control manufactures *acceptable* views.

Ham-handed information control, on the other hand, can easily backfire. Overt censorship—jailing dissidents, closing presses, jamming broadcasts, etc.—is very twentieth century. Its unintended consequences make the costs of open censorship far greater than its benefits. Publicly visible censorship creates martyrs or heroes out of suppressed authors, as described earlier. It gives their squelched messaging a "forbidden fruit" quality, making it more attractive and credible than it otherwise would be. It drives those messages underground, where they are less open to rational rebuttal. It alienates the public and generates distrust.[43] Not only for legal reasons but for practical reasons, observable censorship is passé.

What's more effective is *self*-censorship. Self-censorship keeps unacceptable views from ever reaching the marketplace of ideas; no words need be suppressed because no words are written or spoken. It therefore leads to no noisy objections or lawsuits. Potential listeners and readers are unaware of what was never said or written. Nothing finds refuge underground, and nothing requires rebutting. To censors, the silence of self-censorship is golden.

Better still, self-censorship is not hard to induce. Dissenting speakers and disliked news outlets can be stigmatized so that they are not read or listened to. Potential dissidents can be made to feel they will stand isolated and embarrassed for speaking up. Rather than being persecuted for their views, they can be given the option of comfortable silence that leaves them bereft and exasperated, perhaps, but not alone.

The skillful censor, therefore, must know how to suppress speech covertly, without even the speaker able to detect a censorial hand on the mute button. Effective modern-day censorship is thus clandestine. As Senator Daniel Patrick Moynihan put it, "[S]ecrecy is the ultimate form of regulation because people do not even know they're being regulated."[44] Undetectable "friction" can be applied: disliked social media content can be hidden and users can experience unexplained posting or searching problems. As Joan Donavan has observed, "Over the years, crude mechanisms like blocking content and banning accounts have morphed into a more complex set of tools, including quarantining topics, removing posts from search, barring recommendations, and down-ranking posts in priority."[45] Silencing critics without their knowing it minimizes the likelihood of backlash, and if backlash does occur, the bureaucracy has no difficulty masking accountability. Moreover, the airwaves and social media can be deluged with approved messaging, making it hard to find unapproved speech. The net result is a public that is, to borrow a phrase from Pink Floyd, "comfortably numb." Its thinking and behavior will have been modified without its consent or even its knowledge. Mark Zuckerberg gave an example of this more sophisticated form of censorship in an interview with podcast host Joe Rogan, pointing to Facebook's superior methods as compared with Twitter's. Twitter, Zuckerberg pointed out, had banned President Trump outright, whereas Facebook deftly applied friction, leaving Trump's posts online but limiting their distribution to make them harder to find.[46]

Concealed censorship does not always remain concealed, however, which leads modern information warriors to appreciate the utility of one last weapon: the threat of direct, coordinated sanctions. Censors are not yet able to deploy the entire range of economic weapons governments use against foreign enemies, but enough weapons are now available to the private sector to lessen the need for explicit government directives. Tom Friedman has written that as "the world is now so wired, superempowered individuals, companies and social activist groups can pile on their own sanctions and boycotts, without any government orders, amplifying the isolation and economic strangulation."[47] The public or private character of digitized economic sanctions directed at commentators normally does not matter because the effect is the same;[48] a social media "influencer" or an aspiring public intellectual will likely think twice if an impetuous tweet means not only no social media accounts[49] but also dried up Amazon book sales,[50] frozen bank accounts,[51] demonetization of a YouTube business,[52] or a fine by PayPal for promoting "intolerance that is discriminatory."[53]

Why might those who wield these weapons use them to curb free speech? The answer is complex. The story does not begin, as one might expect it to, with the deadly domestic security crisis posed by COVID; unlike the use of passenger jets as missiles, the pandemic was neither novel nor unanticipated. Rather, the story begins two decades earlier, when the government's security managers encountered a pressing need to control public discussion of sensitive bioweapons research.

The Utility of Deflection: COVID-19

In 2001, the United States was subject to a terrifying bioweapons attack with anthrax, which killed five people and sickened seventeen others.[54] By that point, it was widely understood to be all but impossible to distinguish an artificially engineered pathogen introduced by a hostile power from one occurring in nature without human intervention; "the epidemiological techniques needed to investigate deliberate and natural outbreaks are the same,"[55] and the devastating consequences can be the same. Security planners knew what was required to meet such a threat, and the requirements were the same as in 2020 when COVID-19 hit: a national early warning system was needed to sound the alarm before disease hit and adequate public health infrastructure was needed to deal with the aftershocks. The most recent National Security Strategy Statement issued before the emergence of COVID-19, from 2017, explicitly recognized the "threats on national security" posed by biological agents and the urgent needs those threats generated:

> Biological incidents have the potential to cause catastrophic loss of life. Biological threats to the U.S. homeland—whether as the result of deliberate attack, accident, or a natural outbreak—are growing and require actions to

address them at their source. Naturally emerging outbreaks of viruses such as Ebola and SARS, as well as the deliberate 2001 anthrax attacks in the United States, demonstrated the impact of biological threats on national security by taking lives, generating economic losses, and contributing to a loss of confidence in government institutions.[56]

The security managers therefore committed to "detect and contain biothreats at their source."[57] This was a "priority action":

> We will work with other countries to detect and mitigate outbreaks early to prevent the spread of disease. We will encourage other countries to invest in basic health care systems and to strengthen global health security across the intersection of human and animal health to prevent infectious disease outbreaks. And we will work with partners to ensure that laboratories that handle dangerous pathogens have in place safety and security measures.[58]

Given the strength and clarity of this commitment, when COVID began crippling healthcare systems overseas, one would have expected security officials to have been standing on the rooftops shouting at the tops of their lungs "Emergency!" and to have arranged for hospital capacity, personal protective equipment, respirators, trained doctors and staff, contact tracing, a testing regime, dignified treatment of the dead, and all the rest. But they had not. The security planners failed abysmally to fulfill the commitments they had laid out in 2017.[59]

The importance of this breakdown in detection and containment ought not be misunderstood as merely a public health collapse. If the security managers had earlier been correct that health security is a component of national security, COVID was a *security* failure—as monumental as any the nation had ever experienced. *Over a million Americans died.* The ensuing public trauma of course generated insistent questions: Where had the pathogen originated? How could it best be remedied? What had gone wrong? With a broader security portfolio comes broader accountability—who was responsible?

Rather than addressing such concerns in an open and robust marketplace of ideas, however, government officials and private actors, joining together to fight COVID, settled upon a new enemy: speech—specifically, speech labeled "mis-, dis-, and mal-information."[60] The COVID warriors appeared to believe they could exclude that speech from that marketplace with the same tactics of information warfare that the security apparatus had perfected for use abroad. Now, however, those techniques could also be directed internally, at the American people.[61]

The improvisation and confusion surrounding COVID's arrival and the security managers' immediate concerns about information control were distressingly familiar to the few who lived through their scrambled reaction and awkward silences during the 2001 anthrax attack. The origins of that threat and the response to it are worth recalling. The story begins with a sensitive matter that came to light a week before September 11 and two weeks before the anthrax attack.

On September 4, 2001, the *New York Times* published an extraordinary (and now all but forgotten) account of secret U.S. research on biological weapons.[62] Among other things, the authors reported that the CIA and Pentagon drew up plans to engineer a new, genetically altered, more potent variant of anthrax.[63] President Bill Clinton, they reported, was intensely interested in germ weapons but had never been briefed on this or various other programs that were underway or contemplated.[64] Moreover, some administration officials reportedly believed that some of those programs violated the Biological Weapons Convention.[65] In addition to unawareness by the White House of the full scope of the research, the authors highlighted three indelicate aspects of the programs that, then as now, the security managers did not regard as productive topics for public debate.[66]

First, lab leaks and accidents occur with alarming frequency.[67] In all, the *Times* reporters noted that leading up to 2001, "the scientists made enough mistakes to become victims of their own pathogens 456 times."[68] The record afterward improved little. From 2002 to 2007 more than seventy accidents occurred relating to work with dangerous pathogens, according to Lyn Klotz and Edward Sylvester in their study, *Breeding Bio Insecurity*.[69] "Three plague-infested rats were unaccounted for in a big BSL-3 laboratory in the heart of a Newark, New Jersey, residential area," they recounted.[70] "A leaky foolproof aerosol chamber infected three lab workers with tuberculosis. Tularemia sickened three researchers who thought they were working with a benign strain of the rabbit fever agent."[71]

Second, the research was highly dangerous. Gene splicing—bioengineering—that began in the 1970s held the promise of saving lives, curing illness, and improving human health. But it also could produce deadly new diseases for which there were no known cures. Some of the scientists who had pioneered the research warned of its destructive potential. Joshua Lederberg, for example, the Nobel Prize winner whose discoveries were central to the new science, understood the risk. "To be enhancing that technology," he wrote, "I thought was in the long run suicidal."[72] Research on synthetic genes constituted "the most perilous genocidal experimentation."[73] Breakthroughs in germ warfare were "akin to our arranging to make hydrogen bombs available at the supermarket."[74] Advances in the field "could well become the most efficient means for removing man from the planet."[75] Lederberg was far from alone in his fears. Donald Henderson, for example, who spearheaded smallpox eradication efforts for the World Health Organization, warned that the "potential implications of an infected lab worker—and [of] spread beyond the lab—are terrifying."[76]

Third, the *Times*'s investigation confirmed that the Biological Weapons Convention is feckless. The 1972 treaty is the international instrument that purports to ban biological weapons. But it prohibits the development of biological agents only if those agents have "no justification for prophylactic, protective or other peaceful purposes,"[77] and it prohibits the development of weapons designed to use such agents only "for hostile purposes or in armed conflict."[78] If a genetically modified superbug is developed for "peaceful" or protective purposes—for the supposed purpose of developing an antidote or vaccine, for example—that development is permitted. Similarly, if a bioweapon is developed for the purpose of developing a defense to that weapon rather than for a hostile purpose or for use in armed conflict, development of that weapon is permitted. The "purpose," of course, lies in the mind of the developer, so that merely by labeling the purpose peaceful, a nation can easily claim not to be engaged in prohibited research and to possess no bioweapons. One authority summed up what all government experts likely knew: that "permitted uses and undefined limits offer clear opportunities to circumvent the prohibitions, so the convention is widely seen as porous, at best."[79] The result is that the Convention's looseness can legitimate the most malign programs. The Soviet Union, for example, having ratified the Convention, went on to employ tens of thousands of people to turn anthrax, smallpox, and bubonic plague into "weapons of war"—all while claiming that the programs were for purely defensive purposes.[80]

The *Times*'s 2001 reporting and the threat of public disclosure of the full scope of U.S. bioresearch thus risked not only worldwide condemnation of the activities themselves; it also risked underscoring that the Convention was toothless, which could energize efforts at regulation that security officials opposed. The experiments and programs underway in the United States, officials told the *Times*, "would draw vociferous protests from Washington if conducted by a country the United States viewed as suspect."[81] A draft protocol (later abandoned) was then being considered that would have strengthened enforcement of the Convention, but it was opposed by the George W. Bush administration largely because of the perceived need to maintain the secrecy of projects that involved gene-splicing or germs likely to be used in weapons.[82] Even accounts of experimentation by other countries created a danger of emulation or the release of information that could aid in the creation of more deadly bioweapons. Pentagon officials were alarmed when a scientific journal in late 1997 published an article describing Russian scientists' preparation of a new strain of anthrax.[83] The question arose whether the new strain could defeat the vaccine that the Pentagon had decided to require for U.S. soldiers; when efforts to obtain a sample of the new strain failed, the CIA and Pentagon secretly drew up plans to replicate it.[84] From the security managers' perspective, it was easy to conclude that public discussion of even the general topic of bioweapons research could serve no useful purpose; it could lead only to awkward and partial explanations, further questions, tighter regulation of bioresearch, and less authority for those directly overseeing it.

That belief could only have been reinforced when the source of the anthrax used in the 2001 attacks was finally identified: the U.S. "government's own laboratories, most likely those at Ft. Detrick, Maryland."[85] The victims who were infected had been exposed to the so-called Ames strain of anthrax, isolated two decades earlier and sent out to nearly a dozen other laboratories, most of them military.[86] Who, precisely, was responsible in 2001 for mailing anthrax to news organizations and two Senators, killing five people? It was impossible to say, given that hundreds[87] if not thousands[88] of people eventually had access to the Ames strain at the time of the attack. "That is why the mystery is not likely to be solved," write Klotz and Sylvester. "What it clearly does show is that, *even ordinarily*, hundreds of lab workers do have access to potential bioweapons agents, such as the Ames strain of anthrax. We clearly are not safe from our own laboratories."[89] One lesson that "emerges with crystal clarity," they conclude, is that "the proliferation of high-level BSL-3 and BSL-4 laboratories radically increases our risk of a deadly bioweapons attack."[90]

Perhaps the most disturbing realization, the *Times* reporters revealed, was that the scale of the anthrax attacks was remarkably small compared with the cataclysmic outbreaks experts had discussed only three years earlier with President Clinton.[91] In 1998, a group of experts convened by the White

House had warned that "a recombinant virus that would express itself in distinct phases" would wreak havoc on the nation, as revealed by a role-playing simulation:

> [S]tate and local officials were overwhelmed by the demands of thousands of hypothetically sick and dying people. Local medical offices rapidly exhausted their stocks of antibiotics and vaccines. Federal quarantine laws turned out to be too antiquated to deal with the rapidly spreading epidemic, and no state had adequate plans to take care of the people it had isolated. Officials did not know where to store and bury the still-contaminated dead. . . . [O]fficials began quarreling among themselves and with Washington over how to stem the epidemic. No one seemed to be in charge.[92]

Those who were ostensibly in charge managed a "maze of federal agencies that handle public health, security, intelligence, and scientific research."[93] That maze was the subject of Klotz and Sylvester's study.[94] After the anthrax attack, they reported, elements within that maze became increasingly militarized and secretive.[95] The National Institute of Allergy and Infectious Diseases (NIAID), for example, took on new responsibilities in treating and preventing diseases that emerge naturally or are deliberately introduced as an act of bioterrorism. NIAID does so by, among other things, supporting and conducting research aimed at developing vaccines for specific pathogens.[96] Public health authorities, long under the control of the medical profession, came "'under the thumb of public safety,' whose military-like organization often demanded secrecy."[97] In 2004 and 2005, after the Centers for Disease Control and Prevention (CDC) were reorganized[98] to make fighting terrorism a primary mission,[99] one of its two "overarching goals" was to protect "people in all communities" from terrorist threats (recognizing the difficulty of "distinguishing deliberate use from a naturally occurring threat").[100] Scientists chafed under "the catastrophic reorganization" and bridled at leadership's new conviction that "there are things that are too important or dangerous to tell people about." Many professionals "tramp[led] each other at the exits to get out."[101]

In 2020, that tangle of agencies, depleted and repurposed though some were, was activated when COVID turned much of the 1998 simulation into reality. Attention within the CDC, as within the public generally, turned immediately to the source of the virus: Had it originated in an open-air wildlife market in Wuhan, China, or from a nearby bioresearch facility?

In one way the answer made little difference, for again, the *effects* of the virus would have been the same had it come from nature or a lab, or had it been intentionally released. Each such event would create the chaos and devastation that the Clinton administration's simulation had predicted, and each would represent a colossal breach of security on the security managers' part. "Many of the very worst-case characteristics of an intentional event are also being seen in this naturally occurring pandemic," said Dr. Robert Kadlec, the assistant secretary for preparedness and response at the U.S. Department of Health and Human Services, in May 2020.[102] Bill Gates had warned in 2017 that it made little sense to distinguish between the two. "Whether it occurs by a quirk of nature or at the hand of a terrorist," he told the Munich Security Conference, the number of deaths from a fast-moving airborne pathogen would still be catastrophic; the defensive measures would be the same.[103] "Most of the things we need to do to protect against a naturally occurring pandemic," he said, "are the same things we must prepare for an intentional biological attack."[104] Security planners knew this—and regarded both as a security threat. That conviction was not limited to career security officials. One of the "major threats to our national security," wrote Senators Barack Obama and Richard Lugar in 2005, comes "from nature, not humans—an avian flu pandemic."[105]

Yet when the crisis suddenly hit in March 2020, the nation was unprepared. Masks and tests were in short supply. Retirement homes were decimated. Exhausted healthcare workers collapsed. Intubated patients died alone. COVID victims in New York were buried in mass graves. Schools closed. All the warnings, all the simulations, all the strategy statements had been for naught.

In another way, however, COVID's origin mattered a great deal: it could underscore the porosity of the legal regime that supposedly regulated that research,[106] potentially creating pressures for meaningful regulation and greater transparency, and the mere *inquiry into the question* could call attention to the dangerous bioresearch the United States was conducting or supporting and the risk of leaks. Whether or not the virus had actually escaped accidentally from the Wuhan lab, *it could have* escaped from a lab.[107] This was the September 2022 finding of the *Lancet* COVID-19 Commission, a panel of independent experts convened by the respected British medical journal that drew on two years' work by more than 170 other experts.[108] The Commission concluded that "the infection of a researcher in the laboratory while studying viruses that have been genetically manipulated" was one possible pathway of COVID's emergence.[109] According to the Commission, the risks of such research are plain: "Advances in biotechnology in the past two decades have made it possible to create new and highly dangerous pathogens through genetic manipulation."[110] Experts, as noted above,[111] earlier warned that leaks of equally or even more dangerous pathogens could escape from such labs. Yet no independent investigation has thus far been carried out regarding the bioengineering of such viruses; according to the Commission, this is because the American laboratories engaged in such research have refused to give access to relevant materials and the "National Institutes of Health (NIH) has resisted disclosing details of the research on SARS-CoV-related viruses that it had been supporting."[112]

There were therefore obvious reasons for an investigation *at the outset*— but also, as various commentators have pointed out, obvious reasons for a cover-up, including

> the odd coincidence of a pandemic originating in the same city where a Chinese lab was conducting high-end experiments on bat viruses; the troubling report that some of the original Covid patients had no contact with the food markets where the pandemic supposedly originated; the fact that the Chinese government lied and stonewalled its way through the crisis.[113]

Nicholas Wade, writing in the *Bulletin of the Atomic Scientists*, highlighted the issue's clear importance:

> One might think that any plausible origin of a virus that has killed three million people would merit a serious investigation. Or that the wisdom of continuing gain-of-function research, regardless of the virus's origin, would be worth some probing. Or that the funding of gain-of-function research by the NIH and NIAID during a moratorium on such funding would bear investigation.[114]

In fact, in response to a request by President Joe Biden, the intelligence community reported on May 26, 2021, that it could not rule out the possibility that the virus had originated in a lab.[115] A year later, a team of scientists convened by the World Health Organization also acknowledged that the possibility that the virus escaped from a lab needs "'further investigations.'"[116]

Yet as the virus spread across the United States in 2020, the immediate and continuing reaction of the security managers and their allies within social and corporate media was to try to quash the story.[117] The lab-leak possibility was characterized as a conspiracy theory, not a more probable national security failure. One who pooh-poohed the possibility was Dr. Anthony Fauci, director of the National Institute of Allergy and Infectious Diseases. Fauci, a *New York Times* opinion piece observed, "aggressively cast the lab leak theory as fringe."[118] *Vanity Fair* reported that State Department officials discouraged investigation of the possibility of a lab leakage.[119] The magazine reported in June 2021 that State Department officials had been studying the Wuhan Institute of Virology for months and had recently become aware that "three WIV researchers conducting gain-of-function experiments on coronavirus samples had fallen ill in the autumn of 2019, before the COVID-19 outbreak was known to have started."[120] When they discussed whether to share this with the public, their superior apparently told them "not to say anything that would point to the U.S. government's own role in gain-of-function research."[121] They were, in fact, "repeatedly advised not to open a 'Pandora's box,'" according to former State Department officials.[122] Some officials even stated that they were "'absolutely floored'" afterward and that it "'smelled like a cover-up.'"[123] The *Washington Post* also referred to the lab leak possibility as a "fringe theory."[124] "[N]umerous experts," the *Post* told its readers, have "dismissed the possibility the coronavirus may be man-made."[125] Other media sources were equally dismissive, the *New York Times* also referring to it as a "'fringe theory'" and NPR reporting that scientists had "'debunk[ed]'" the lab accident theory.[126] Facebook banned discussion of the lab escape theory from its platform[127]—until Biden's announcement that the lab leak theory could not be ruled out,[128] whereupon Facebook, acting "in lockstep with the government," promptly unbanned it.[129] Prominent outlets such as PolitiFact[130] and FactCheck.org[131] debunked the idea. Widely relied upon[132] was a letter published in *The Lancet* by twenty-seven scientists proclaiming that they "stand together to strongly condemn conspiracy theories suggesting that COVID-19 does not have a natural origin. . . . Conspiracy theories do nothing but create fear, rumours, and prejudice that jeopardise our global collaboration in the fight against this virus."[133]

Had the press looked into it—and it would have taken scant investigation, since this was a matter of public record—it could quickly have been discovered that the letter's lead author had direct ties to the Wuhan lab,[134] where researchers were led by Shi Zheng-li, China's principal expert on bat viruses.[135] Indeed, a minimally curious press would have found, as did

Nicholas Wade of *Bulletin of the Atomic Scientists*, that U.S. and Chinese government officials shared "a strange common interest":

> Neither is keen on drawing attention to the fact that Shi's coronavirus work was funded by the US National Institutes of Health. One can imagine the behind-the-scenes conversation in which the Chinese government says, "If this research was so dangerous, why did you fund it, and on our territory too?" To which the US side might reply, "Looks like it was you who let it escape. But do we really need to have this discussion in public?"[136]

Instead, the press went mute. It erected, in Wade's phrase, "serried walls of silence"[137]—and then, when Biden on May 26, 2021, finally gave the intelligence community the effective go-ahead to get to the bottom of the matter, the press did an about-face. *Vox*, which Facebook used for fact-checking to identify misinformation, reportedly stealth-edited earlier stories to align them with the government's current agnosticism on the issue,[138] while Facebook announced that it would cease to remove content that suggested the virus came from a lab rather than through human-animal transmission.[139] But a formidable new alliance had emerged of public and private partners intent on keeping the wrong information and opinions out of the marketplace of ideas. Despite the urging of prominent, nonpartisan investigators,[140] as of this date no independent inquiry has been undertaken to determine the origin of COVID-19.

By the time of the 2020 presidential election, techniques of information control had become so effective that the security managers seemingly had little awareness of when a dangerous line was crossed. With the aid of friendly social and corporate media, they helped keep the lid on news reports that could have led to the reelection of their great antagonist, Donald Trump.

The Power of Authoritative Opinion: Hunter Biden

The information in question was potentially devastating. Beginning on October 14, 2020, the *New York Post* reported in a series of articles that, among other things, Joe Biden's son Hunter had discussed using his connection with his father, who was vice president at the time, to boost his pay from a Ukrainian natural gas company[141] and that he had introduced his father to an executive in the firm before his father pressured government officials in Ukraine into firing a prosecutor who was investigating the company.[142] The *Post* said its reporting was based on emails contained in a laptop and hard drive (eventually seized by the FBI)[143] that had been left for repair in a Delaware computer repair shop but never picked up.[144]

The emails were genuine. On March 16, 2022, the *New York Times* reported that it had "authenticated" emails that appeared to come from Hunter Biden's abandoned laptop, which federal prosecutors were in the process of examining[145]—though *Politico* reporter Ben Schreckinger's 2021 book, *The Bidens: Inside the First Family's Fifty-Year Rise to Power* had already established the authenticity of the emails on which the *New York Post* relied.[146]

Five days after the initial *New York Post* story appeared, however, on October 19, fifty-one former intelligence officials, the vast majority from the CIA, signed an open letter responding to the report.[147] These included Jim Clapper, Mike Hayden, Leon Panetta, John Brennan, and Michael Morell. They noted that "nine additional former [intelligence community] officers who cannot be named publicly also support the arguments in this letter."[148] They emphasized their ties to the intelligence community. They were known to have held high-level security clearances. They identified the governmental positions they had held and emphasized their understanding of "overt and covert activities that undermine United States national security."[149] Based on their expertise, the signers assured readers that the unveiling of the emails "purportedly belonging to" Hunter Biden "has all the classic earmarks of a Russian information operation"[150]—though the letter provided no evidence of any Russian involvement. "We want to emphasize that we do not know if the emails . . . are genuine or not and that we do not have evidence of Russian involvement,"[151] they wrote. "[But] our experience makes us deeply suspicious that the Russian government played a significant role in this case."[152] Such an operation "would be consistent with Russian objectives" and methods.[153] There were press reports that Russia had been involved in influence operations. "We do not know whether these press reports are accurate," they wrote. "[But] it is high time that Russia stops interfering in our democracy."[154] The same day it appeared, Joe Biden's spokesperson Jen Psaki tweeted that the "Hunter Biden story is Russian disinfo, dozens of former intel officials say."[155] She did not, however, deny the authenticity of the emails.[156]

The letter did the trick. Press coverage of the matter all but disappeared. The mainstream corporate press instituted a de facto blackout. "[V]irtually every media outlet," Glen Greenwald wrote, ". . . began completely ignoring the substance of the reporting and instead spread the lie over and over that these documents were the by-product of Russian disinformation."[157] Explaining NPR's silence, its managing editor wrote on October 22, "We don't want to waste our time on stories that are not really stories, and we don't want to waste the listeners' and readers' time on stories that are just pure distractions."[158] Social media companies followed suit. In response to an FBI communication,[159] Facebook announced that it was "reducing its distribution" pending a fact-check that apparently never materialized.[160] Twitter locked the *New York Post*'s account for nearly two weeks,[161] labeled the link to the story "potentially unsafe,"[162] and blocked references to it in communications among users.[163] Over two years after the original *New York Post* report appeared, Matt Taibbi reported, YouTube continued to post materials—unmarked as disinformation or misinformation—falsely indicating that the laptop story is untrue or the work of Russian intelligence.[164]

The letter proved to be critical in the October 23, 2020 presidential debate. Biden neglected to include the intelligence officials' disclaimer that they had no evidence of Russian involvement when he flatly claimed that fifty former intelligence officials and CIA heads had said the emails were "a bunch of garbage."[165] "Look, there are 50 former National Intelligence folks who said that what this, he's accusing me of is a Russian plan," he said.[166] "They have said that this has all the characteristics—four—five former heads of the CIA, both parties, say what he's saying is a bunch of garbage."[167] The moderators of the debate did not point out what the intelligence officials had actually said: that they had no evidence of actual Russian involvement. The impression stuck; using all the esoteric tools of their trade, the objective experts in the intelligence community had examined the story, weighed all the evidence, and found it fake. No further discussion was needed; case closed.

It is impossible to know for certain whether this tactic swayed the 2020 presidential election. A week before the election, however, and a week after the letter appeared, 51% of likely voters believed the discovery of Hunter Biden's laptop was Russian disinformation.[168] Had forty-four thousand votes in three swing states—Georgia, Arizona, and Wisconsin—been cast for Trump rather than Biden, the two would have tied in the Electoral College.[169] Nearly a third of Americans viewed the results of the election as illegitimate.[170]

Yet there can be little doubt that the American people were deprived of information on which to make an informed choice in a presidential election. The security managers had achieved the power to shutter the marketplace of ideas, even in the heat of a presidential election campaign, by trading upon their privileged positions of trust to express supposedly neutral professional assessments that were accepted by the media as actual fact. The media then carried the approved narrative, uninvestigated and uncontradicted, as it engulfed additional informational channels. Whether the narrative was true or false was beside the point: it was authoritative.

The Symbiotic Snarl

How had this level of information control become possible? How, indeed, had it suddenly become so easy? The answer lies in good part in the rapid digitization of the marketplace of ideas—specifically, in social media. For millions of Americans as well as for billions of people worldwide, the marketplace of ideas has become the internet, and the internet has become social media.[171] Two-thirds of Americans rely upon social media as their prime source for news.[172] The internet companies often proclaim that they are private businesses, but the reality is that in the world of social media, it is all but impossible to separate government actors from private actors in any nonarbitrary way. The categories demarking clear public and private spheres do not work.[173] Where it counts, voices of the government and social media platforms have become indistinguishable; their interlocking words and actions have become so entangled as to create, in Daphne Keller's word, a "snarl."[174]

The intimacy of that partnership came to light most vividly for the public in 2013 with documents leaked from the National Security Agency by Edward Snowden, which revealed, among other things, that the social media platforms were feeding the NSA information about their users.[175] Nearly a decade later, the collaboration continues; Facebook reportedly has "a formalized process for government officials to directly flag content on Facebook or Instagram and request that it be throttled or suppressed through a special Facebook portal that requires a government or law enforcement email to use."[176] The partnership between big tech and the security apparatus is not new, however. They have, in fact, been enmeshed from the beginning. Two decades ago, the intelligence community worked closely with Silicon Valley to shape research and development efforts on search engines.[177] "The original research by Larry Page and Sergey Brin which led to their founding of Google," according to the *Washington Post*, "was funded by grants from the NSA, CIA, the Pentagon's DARPA program and the National

Science Foundation."[178] The companies have since profited from lucrative contracts for their services.[179] Since their inception, social media companies have been given a bulletproof shield against the slings and arrows suffered by all other publishers (which they claim not to be).[180] Section 230 of the 1996 Communications Decency Act immunizes companies from liability for content posted by their users[181] and has financially advantaged the companies over competing media not sheltered from lawsuits by their users and readers. "I don't think any of the social media companies would exist in their current forms without Section 230," one authority asserted.[182] Many agreed, including the social media companies. "Section 230 made it possible for every major internet service to be built,"[183] said Facebook CEO Zuckerberg. "If every Facebook post or tweet had to undergo libel vetting," wrote a member of Facebook's Oversight Board, Suzanne Nossel, "the Internet as we know it would not exist."[184] Google (which bought YouTube in 2006) has acknowledged that without Section 230 protection, it would "not be able to filter content at all."[185] High-ranking Washington officials often remind the tech companies of their reliance on government largesse in the form of Section 230 immunity. House Speaker Nancy Pelosi told them that Section 230 is a "gift" to tech companies—a gift "that could be removed."[186]

The giving and threatened retraction of governmental gifts proved to be continually useful carrots and sticks. In April 2022, seven former national security officials openly lobbied against tighter regulation of internet companies that would have prohibited discrimination against business users.[187] In September 2021, twelve former and current security officials—all with major ties to the tech companies—warned against enforcing antitrust laws against them on national security grounds[188] (a claim also advanced by Apple's CEO, Tim Cook).[189] The argument is sometimes made that those who do not like big tech's social media platforms can simply go elsewhere, but comparable alternatives rarely exist[190]—and the lessons of Parler loom large for those who might try to create them.[191] The same applies to the argument that the censored can simply post on another platform, as the Fifth Circuit Court of Appeals observed in September 2022 in *NetChoice v. Paxton*: "As Justice Thomas has aptly pointed out, that's like telling a man kicked off the train that he can still 'hike the Oregon Trail.' "[192]

Today the internet companies and the government are woven together in a web of interlocking relationships that make it impossible to tell where one ends and the other begins.[193] Groups and individuals who are partly in and partly out of government[194] coordinate and cooperate to ensure that unwelcome information and ideas are not expressed.[195] This is not done by legal fiat, such as statutory enactments that close presses, silence television stations, or ban speeches, but through government "recommendations" and "guidance."[196] Explicit quid pro quos are rare, but conscious parallelism is evident: government actors make their wishes known, and private actors align their conduct accordingly. In this way, speech is silenced with what Keller has called "laundered" state action.[197]

Often the government's wishes do not need to be spelled out. Social media companies know how broadly the government now defines its security mission. For generations, protecting the nation's security was thought to mean safeguarding its people's physical safety, defending the population against real or threatened violence. The new security apparatus has taken on responsibility for far more. Combating infectious diseases[198] is one expanded mission. Another is to "advance gender equality, LBGTQI+ [sic] rights, and women's empowerment as part of our broader commitment to inclusive economic growth and social cohesion," aims set out in the most recent National Security Strategy.[199] Perhaps its most far-reaching new mission involves it in domestic information warfare and an extraordinary objective: combating information that is true but, in its view, harmful.

Fighting misinformation, disinformation, and mal-information that is "introduced and/or amplified by foreign and domestic threat actors" is a paramount goal, the Department of Homeland Security (DHS) said in a national terrorism advisory bulletin on February 7, 2022.[200] The Cybersecurity and Infrastructure Security Agency, the agency within DHS responsible for federal cybersecurity, defines "mal-information" as based on fact but used out of context to mislead, harm, or manipulate.[201] The term *context* is not defined. Presumably, it falls to the government, as each case arises, to determine whether its "context" permits the speech in question. "Threat actors," the bulletin says, use mis-, dis- and mal-information "to exacerbate societal friction to sow discord and undermine public trust in government institutions to encourage unrest."[202] DHS's announced solution to the problem of mal-information is to stop its "proliferation," i.e., its publication.[203] It will do this, DHS announced, by working with public and private sector partners, as well as foreign counterparts, to identify and evaluate mis-, dis-, and mal-information, including false and misleading narratives.[204] Who these partners will be, what they will do, and whether they will be trained, paid, or rewarded by the government for joining it in preventing the publication of speech is not specified; their aim will be to help the government slow the "introduc[tion] and amplifi[cation]" of mal-information and to prevent its authors from "undermin[ing] public trust in U.S. government institutions."[205]

DHS doubled down on the war against unwanted speech on April 27, 2022, when its head announced to Congress that it would be setting up the Disinformation Governance Board;[206] its functions were largely unspecified, but the White House press secretary said the next day that "the objective of the board is to prevent disinformation and misinformation from traveling around the country in a range of communities."[207] Scholars pointed out that the new board brought to mind President Woodrow Wilson's Committee on Public Information. That board was announced without congressional approval in a vague, three-sentence executive order, was headed by a pyrotechnic muckraker, and "grew willy-nilly into a ministry of propaganda."[208] Following an avalanche of public criticism, the launch of the new board was "paused"[209] and then suspended.[210] Nowhere did DHS indicate concerns about disinformation[211] originating from the government itself.[212] DHS's interest lay in curtailing *corrections* to the government's disinformation.

The regulatory sword of Damocles thus hangs constantly over social media companies, which adjust their content policies accordingly. "Platforms' anticipatory obedience spares governments the need to enact actual laws,"[213] Keller explains; the subtlest hint from government often gets quick results. Examples abound, many of which are familiar.[214] Taken together, they reveal a public-private tapestry that is too tightly knit to unweave, government actors who offer guidance that is hard to refuse, and private actors whose conduct aligns with that guidance. "If members of the public were more aware of all the ways that the U.S. government works with and makes 'requests' of these companies," David Pozen has written, "I suspect findings of state action would be more forthcoming."[215]

"Yep, on It!"

Members of the public were given an unusual window into the ways the government colludes with social media in August 2022 with the release of hundreds of pages of documents turned over in discovery in *Missouri v. Biden.*[216] The case stemmed from a lawsuit brought by the attorneys general of Missouri and Louisiana, who alleged that the Biden administration breached the First Amendment by encouraging social media platforms to suppress viewpoints at odds with the government's messaging on COVID-19 and other subjects. The documents, mostly emails, revealed a network of forty-five federal officials in eleven federal departments and agencies, including the White House, who communicated regularly with five major social media companies about disfavored information and its suppression.[217] These efforts, the plaintiffs said, went beyond what they "could ever have anticipated."[218]

The companies' collegial relationship with the government—their "oozing solicitousness,"[219] as the *Wall Street Journal* Editorial Board described it—is reflected in a July 20, 2021, email exchange between the White House and Facebook.[220] A White House official asks Facebook to deactivate a parody of Anthony Fauci that appeared on Instagram, which Facebook owns. "Hi there," the official says, "any way we can get this pulled down. It is not actually one of ours." "Yep, on it!" comes the chipper Facebook reply.[221] In another email, written the same day President Biden accused Facebook of "killing people,"[222] a senior Facebook official writes the surgeon general, stating, "I know our teams met today to better understand the scope of what the White House expects from us on misinformation going forward."[223] Another describes a meeting between Twitter and White House officials intended to allow the White House to "partner" with Twitter in suppressing COVID misinformation.[224] In another, the head of the Cybersecurity and Infrastructure Security Agency texts another CISA official about "trying to get us in a place where Fed can work with platforms to better understand the mis/dis trends so relevant agencies can try to prebunk/debunk as useful."[225] The platforms, the email rues, are hesitant to work with the government: "Platforms have got to get more comfortable with gov't. It's really interesting how hesitant they remain."[226]

The companies apparently managed to overcome that hesitancy. Officials at CISA, the documents show, routinely received reports of perceived disinformation and forwarded them to social media companies; the Department of Health and Human Services provided lists of examples of disfavored posts, fact-checked for the platforms, and organized weekly meetings to flag disfavored content.[227] Meanwhile, the companies gave government officials special confidential communication channels to convey what they wanted the companies to suppress. Facebook trained CDC and Census Bureau officials to use a "Facebook misinfo reporting channel."[228] Twitter provided federal officials a privileged channel for flagging misinformation through its Partner Support Portal.[229] YouTube gave "trusted flagger" status to Census Bureau officials.[230]

DHS secretary Alejandro Mayorkas described these efforts to police speech on social media as occurring "across the federal enterprise."[231] The enterprise is indeed, as the plaintiffs' summary of the documents indicates, a "massive, sprawling federal"[232] effort to suppress private speech that federal officials disfavor. But no one should have been surprised. The broad contours of the program were visible before formal confirmation occurred, as even the public record suggests.

Government "Recommendations"

Multiple government officials have publicly pressured social media heads to suppress misinformation and other disliked information. Examples are numerous; in a comprehensive study, Will Duffield identified sixty-two occasions on which government officials have made demands on social media platforms.[233] Senator Dianne Feinstein set the tone at a Senate hearing in 2017 when she told tech company executives, "You've created these platforms and now they are being misused, and you have to be the ones to do something about it, or we will."[234] Such demands did not, however, come only from legislators. "[T]he tech companies have to stop allowing specific individuals over and over again to spread disinformation," said White House climate adviser Gina McCarthy, who also praised Congress for "trying to hold companies accountable."[235] Biden's surgeon general condemned the companies' publication of misinformation. "Misinformation poses an imminent and insidious threat to our nation's health," he said during remarks at the White House.[236] "We must confront misinformation as a nation. . . . Lives are depending on it."[237] He asked the social media companies to step up, arguing, "[W]e can't wait longer for them to take aggressive action."[238] Suppressing what the government regarded as disinformation was later discussed directly with the head of DHS, who described what he said were "robust" discussions with Silicon Valley leaders who were committed to curbing it:[239] "I think that false narratives present a threat to our security."[240] One false narrative Press Secretary Psaki spotted had been presented by Joe Rogan; asked about some of Rogan's comments, she responded that major tech platforms needed to ensure access to accurate information, "and that certainly includes Spotify," where Rogan's podcasts appeared.[241] "[W]e want every platform to continue doing more to call out mis- and disinformation while also uplifting accurate information."[242] The administration and leading Democrats in Congress continued to point out these "false narratives" and pushed social media to take action.[243]

The possible repeal or narrowing of the platforms' immunity under Section 230 has been a continuing source of leverage. On July 16, 2021, for example, after earlier proposing to revoke Facebook's immunity under Section 230 on the grounds that it is "propagating falsehoods they know to be false,"[244] President Biden went further and asserted that platforms like Facebook were "killing people"[245] by allowing disinformation about the coronavirus vaccine to spread online. Psaki had said the previous day, "We're flagging problematic posts for Facebook that spread disinformation. . . . So we're helping get trusted content out there."[246] Asked about the possible revision of Section 230 immunity, the White House responded, "We're reviewing that, and certainly they should be held accountable."[247]

Social media targets have not remained passive in the face of such "recommendations." Facebook responded to the White House accusations with a statement that they were already doing a lot to combat misinformation, pointing to their implementation of all eight of the surgeon general's earlier recommendations on the matter. Facebook's policy was to "[a]mplify communications from trusted messengers and subject matter experts,"[248] it said. In a retweet of a post that accused the new conservative social media company Parler of illegal behavior and violating the rules of the Apple App Store and Google Play for content surrounding the January 6 attack on Congress, Representative Alexandria Ocasio-Cortez asked what Apple and Google were doing about the offending content.[249] Later that same day, she pressed Google on what they would do in response to Apple indicating they would take action with respect to Parler.[250] It was fair to question whether these were merely informational requests.[251] The day after Ocasio-Cortez's tweets, Apple's App Store, Google, and Amazon removed the Parler application from their services, without which it could not operate.[252] Twitter banned Trump (after his defeat was confirmed).[253] By the time of the reversal of the de facto ban on the lab-leak story, Facebook had removed 18 million posts on COVID-19.[254] YouTube, the *New York Times* reported, was also vigilant:

> YouTube said that in the past year it had removed over 130,000 videos for violating its Covid-19 vaccine policies. But this did not include what the video platform called "borderline videos" that discussed vaccine skepticism on the site. In the past, the company simply removed such videos from

search results and recommendations, while promoting videos from experts and public health institutions.[255]

It was not enough to remove unwanted substantive content. Facebook flagged at least one article on the dangers of COVID censorship as "missing context" and marked it with a link to a separate article fact-checking claims of vaccine ineffectiveness.[256]

Identifying Truthful Information

Once the propriety of censoring misinformation or disinformation is accepted, some authoritative source of *correct* information is needed as a metric. The government knows instinctively where correct information can be found: the government. Inevitably, the censor and the source become identical. Social media companies have fallen quickly in line, looking to fact-checkers that rely heavily on government sources to ascertain what can be trusted.[257] Unfortunately, these sources themselves, not surprisingly, often turn out to be unreliable.

Sometimes government misrepresentations are intentional, as exemplified by the rosy news the government regularly reported with respect to progress in the war in Afghanistan. The security managers flooded the marketplace of ideas with information about Afghanistan that was false and sometimes known to be false, as the *Washington Post* reported in a December 9, 2012, comprehensive investigative review of the U.S. government's performance in combating the Taliban and "nation building" in Afghanistan. The paper's exposé left little doubt whether trust in government and media accounts of progress in the war would have been well-placed. Despite U.S. officials' constant assertions that they were making progress, the report concluded, "[t]hey were not, and they knew it."[258] The "American people have constantly been lied to," said the head of the federal agency that conducted an after-action report. "Every data point was altered to present the best possible picture," one senior military adviser stated.[259] But it was "impossible to create good metrics," a senior National Security Council official said. "We tried using troop numbers trained, violence levels, control of territory and none of it painted an accurate picture. . . . The metrics were always manipulated for the duration of the war."[260] This, he said, "went on and on for two reasons, to make everyone involved look good, and to make it look like the troops and resources were having the kind of effect where removing them would cause the country to deteriorate."[261] In August 2021, Biden himself "bluntly affirmed" to the *New York Times* that Americans had been lied to over the course of the war.[262] "Yes. Yeah," he told the paper's Editorial Board.[263]

Intentional or not,[264] misstatements occur too often to view government-related sources as reliable arbiters of truth, let alone of scientific certainty. The government's record on COVID vaccines is illustrative. By August 2022, most coronavirus deaths were of people who had been vaccinated or boosted.[265] Yet as vaccines became available, government officials regularly issued assurances that vaccination would prevent infection.[266] Biden and virtually every major public health official in the United States have claimed that COVID shots stop the virus, as Jordan Schachtel has reported.[267] Biden said, "You're not going to get Covid if you have these vaccinations."[268] Fauci said:

> When you get vaccinated, you not only protect your own health, that of the family, but also you contribute to the community health by preventing the spread of the virus throughout the community. And in other words, you become a dead end to the virus. And when there are a lot of dead ends around, the virus is not going to go anywhere.[269]

CDC director Rochelle Walensky affirmed Fauci's statement: "Our data from the C.D.C. suggests that vaccinated people don't carry the virus, don't get sick. . . . And that it's not just in clinical trials, but it's also in real-world data."[270] YouTube did not remove these statements,[271] although the CDC later acknowledged that "vaccinated people can still become infected and have the potential to spread the virus to others."[272] Twitter blocked the *critics* of the government's misinformation—sometimes after the White House asked questions about why Twitter had yet to take action against specific individuals.[273]

Official pronouncements regarding masks were similarly uncertain, confused, and contradictory. Trump's surgeon general Jerome Adams initially implored Americans to wear masks. In February 2020, in a widely reported statement, he inveighed against them: "Seriously people—STOP BUYING MASKS!" He warned the public that masks did not work. "They are NOT effective in preventing general public from catching #Coronavirus."[274] Four months later, however, the same surgeon general urged the public to wear a face covering in public. "Wear a face covering when you go out in public," he said in June 2020. "It is not an inconvenience."[275] His earlier tweet was not removed, nor were references to the later message that contradicted it.[276]

These were not the only times the CDC reversed itself or acknowledged errors in the data on which its conclusions have been based. In October 2021, the CDC released a study indicating that vaccination offers higher protection than previous COVID-19 infection.[277] Three months later, it released a study indicating that "persons who survived a previous infection had lower case rates than persons who were vaccinated alone."[278] In March 2022, the CDC admitted that it had overcounted COVID-related deaths by 72,277 across twenty-six states, or about 7.5% of all supposed COVID deaths, resulting in the inflation of pediatric deaths by 24%.[279] The massive statistical change was attributed to a "coding logic error."[280] Whether the CDC possesses data that would contradict its published data is unknown; in February 2022, the CDC admitted that it had collected data on hospitalizations for COVID-19 in the United States and broken it down by age, race, and vaccination status, but that it had not made most of that information public.[281]

The point is not to fault the CDC or any other public health authority for reversing itself or acknowledging error. Science is relentlessly provisional. Its truths, such as they are, are not fixed; scientific theories and hypotheses are in a state of constant flux, through formulation and revision, validation and invalidation. Science's fitful movement toward likelier explanations rests upon allowing, indeed encouraging orthodox explanations to be challenged, sometimes by what are little more than hunches. Stifling criticism drains science of its lifeblood. Nowhere is an open and robust marketplace of ideas more vital than in the realm of science.

Stifling criticism was, however, often the very object of government officials who were intent upon squelching "misinformation" concerning COVID. Indeed, the mission was not simply to discredit what they dubbed misinformation but to freeze the very process of disputation. A case in point involved the so-called Great Barrington Declaration, issued by several dozen prominent doctors and scientists on October 4, 2020.[282] The statement expressed grave concerns about the damaging physical and mental health impacts of the prevailing COVID-19 policies, particularly lockdowns.[283] The three lead authors were experts in epidemiology, biostatistics, immunology, vaccine development, and public health from Harvard, Stanford, and Oxford. Four days after the Declaration was issued, the head of the NIH, a federal government agency, emailed Fauci, the head of another government agency, the NIAID. "There needs to be a quick and devastating public take down of its premises," the email advised.[284] A massive campaign ensued against the Declaration and its signers. The Oxford signer described the "onslaught of insults, personal criticism, intimidation and threats" directed at their proposal.[285] Another signatory, Dr. Jay Bhattacharya of Stanford University, participated in an April 2021 panel discussion with Florida's governor, Ron DeSantis, at the state's capitol.[286] The panel discussion was covered by a local television station and the video was posted on YouTube—until YouTube removed it as violative of its standards.[287] The panel, Bhattacharya said, "was a policy forum, in which it is appropriate to consider both the benefits and costs of a policy (child masking) when making judgments and recommendations"; blocking the video was "a violation of basic standards of scientific conduct, which stand in opposition to unreasoned silencing of contrary views and require the free exchange of ideas."[288]

Why would health scientists, of all people, circle the wagons to defend an approved policy orthodoxy? Censorship is, after all, harmful not only to science but to the public; it leads to "important views, information and scientific evidence being disregarded."[289] Government support for scientific research is critical. "The NIH invests most of its $45 billion budget in medical research for the American people,"[290] its website proclaims. Like other researchers and analysts funded by the government, however, NIH scientists are subject to the same incentives to defend rather than criticize the source of their funding and to resist restrictions on their work. "Virologists are worried that fingering a lab leak will affect their flow of grant money," Matt Ridley and Alina Chan observe, "or result in more oversight and regulation of virology research."[291] Intentionally or not, funders can shape the research they fund and the attitudinal patterns of researchers.[292] The distortive effect on the marketplace of ideas can be invidious when the government promotes rigid policies while entwining itself with organizations and individuals that are expected to exercise independent judgment.

Redefining Dangerous Groups and Individuals

Public health is not the only realm in which social media companies have coordinated content control to align it with evolving governmental policies. Glorifying violence has long been a ground for barring content; Facebook suspended Trump for violating that prohibition in its community standards. With the February 22, 2022, Russian invasion of Ukraine, however, the government and social media corporations confronted a dilemma: How should posts glorifying Ukrainian violence in response to the Russian invasion be handled? "Social media can be used as an 'instrument' for governments to achieve wartime aims," noted Ukraine's minister for digital transformation.[293] On March 12, Psaki met with about thirty social media "influencers"[294] to ensure, a White House official said, that they had "the latest information from an authoritative source."[295] The aim, it seemed, was to align social media content moderation practices with the government's policy on the war in Ukraine. As the war progressed, Facebook proceeded to modify the application of its content standards to posts from users in Russia, Ukraine, and other Eastern European nations because its rules were changing too quickly to be enforced.[296] Facebook's workers, the *New York Times* reported, "could not keep up with shifting rules about what kinds of posts were allowed about the war in Ukraine."[297] Sometimes it changed its rules daily, causing "internal confusion" and "whiplash," the paper reported.[298] Facebook revised its content policies more than six times in little more than a month to sometimes permit posts that earlier would have been removed, including some calling for the death of Putin and violence against Russian soldiers.[299]

Which groups and individuals qualify as extremist, supremacist, and terrorist is constantly changing in both government and social media usage; the concepts are notoriously malleable, varying widely from country to country.[300] Companies such as Facebook accede to U.S. government "terrorist" designations and remove such users from their platforms,[301] sometimes acknowledging as much in their community standards.[302] Not all such collaboration in this regard is transparent. In September 2019, for example, representatives of Facebook, Google, Microsoft, and Twitter met with U.S. law enforcement and intelligence officials to discuss election security. According to Facebook's head of cybersecurity policy, the goal was to "further strengthen strategic collaboration," and they discussed ways to "improve how we share information and coordinate our response to better detect and deter threats."[303]

The impulse to coordinate is understandable. Ferreting out unwanted information platform by platform involves duplicative efforts; it is far more efficient to centralize the process. Some of the unwanted content comes from, in Facebook's words, "dangerous individuals and organizations";[304] it is far preferable to look to authorities possessed of the intelligence and law enforcement resources that are necessary to reliably identify them. Moreover, a platform can be open to criticism for taking down the same content that another leaves up, or for de-platforming a user that another platform still hosts; it is far better to coordinate. Hence the emergence of cooperative arrangements among governments and private companies such as the Global Internet Forum to Counter Terrorism, GIFCT.

GIFCT oversees a shared hash database of material taken down by member companies. A member can add material that violates its rules, and then another company, confronted with certain material, can access the database to match that material and apply its own rules to leave it up or take it down.[305] GIFCT is governed by an operating board made up of personnel from Facebook, Microsoft, Twitter, and YouTube, as well as at least one rotating company from GIFCT's broader membership.[306] Its inaugural executive director formerly served as the director of the U.S. National Counterterrorism Center, held senior posts in the intelligence community, and recently returned to government service.[307] Its advisory committee members consist of representatives of the NSC and of six other countries.[308] This "voluntary" organization was formed in response to pressure from European governments,[309] which maintain legal regimes far less speech-protective than that of the United States. Smaller platforms continue to face pressure to adopt its tools.[310] "Little is publicly known about the database,"[311] Keller writes, nor do we know how heavily members rely on it in content moderation, as Evelyn Douek points out: "[B]ecause we do not know which platforms are responsible for adding the content or how they use the database to police their individual services, we do not know the power or effectiveness of the individual platforms' participation in the project."[312]

A group of leading NGOs, including ARTICLE 19, Human Rights Watch, and the Electronic Frontier Foundation, have expressed concern that "[t]here is little visibility to anyone outside of the GIFCT member companies as to what content is represented in the hash database."[313] What is clear, they warned, is that the "existence of a centralized resource focused on content removal across platforms" raised the possibility that "protected speech is being censored."[314] That concern was accentuated by the fact that "governments have been directly involved in the negotiations about the future of the GIFCT" by "increasing reference by governments to GIFCT as a quasi-official body," and by the possibility that GIFCT "would ultimately be vested with some kind of governmental authority or otherwise entangled with state actors."[315] GIFCT's members have done little to assuage these apprehensions. "[O]ne of the things we've done over time is to expand the mandate of the

[GIFCT]," said Facebook's head of global policy management, Monica Bickert.[316] Facebook's security chief has also called for the tech companies to join in establishing a "much more ambitious coordinating body"[317]— echoing the belief of Senator Kamala Harris that "you can't have one set of standards for Facebook and another for Twitter."[318] The social media are now moving on from coordinated content control and are "agreeing to cooperate on the enforcement of more uniform norms of what should be available on-line,"[319] Douek writes.

In short, old ways of thinking about the marketplace of ideas—specifically, the notion that it can be preserved merely by protecting speakers from government interference—are outdated. "Those who claim that censorship can only be imposed by the state," Andrew Doyle observed, "are making arguments that are over twenty years out of date."[320]

The First Amendment

This, then, is today's public-private cartel—a massive, amorphous security-media complex in which government recommendations shade into directives, in which voluntary private conduct melts into coerced compliance, and in which benefits are continually exchanged between a public and a private sector that have become indistinguishable. It is a new phenomenon in the American experience, unprecedented in the power of the forces behind it, in its capacity to shape public opinion, and in its resistance to categorization within our existing jurisprudence. While its participants clearly collaborate in monitoring and suppressing speech, its existence, again, is not the product of a conspiracy; like the earlier structure of double government, it has emerged organically in response to incentives baked into the U.S. political and financial order. Yet the cartel is now subverting the core purposes of the First Amendment, the "linchpin of the American constitutional regime."[321]

How, if at all, can that be prevented? The answer could hardly be more consequential for the survival of the marketplace of ideas in the United States. On it depends the scope of legislative power in both the states and Congress to limit these activities, as well as the authority of the courts to address them absent statutory regulation. The dilemma is not made simpler by the reliance of both the government and social media companies upon free speech claims.

It is thus useful to begin with the case for the government and the companies. Both look to the First Amendment to justify suppressing the speech of social media users. The government begins with the argument that its speech is immunized from judicial review under the government speech doctrine, the companies with the argument that they are private businesses, not state actors, engaged in their own protected speech. After outlining the government's and companies' First Amendment arguments that only their speech interests count, I turn to the opposing argument. As indicated at the outset, I present no recommendation as to how specific controversies should be resolved. I suggest merely a simple, initial premise: that the First Amendment cannot mean that only the speech of the government and the companies is entitled to protection, without regard to the free speech interests of social media users and the general public.

The Case for the Government and the Companies

In several early cases on the subject, the Supreme Court affirmed seemingly unlimited governmental speech rights. "The Government's own speech . . . is exempt from First Amendment scrutiny," the Court said in 2005.[322] In 2015, Justice Breyer wrote that " 'government speech' escapes First Amendment strictures."[323] In that same year, the Court reiterated, "When government speaks, it is not barred by the Free Speech Clause from determining the content of what it says."[324] The logic of these rulings was further developed in 2017, when the Court explained that the government could not function subject to a viewpoint-neutrality requirement imposed on its speech: "When a government entity embarks on a course of action, it necessarily takes a particular viewpoint and rejects others."[325] The First Amendment hardly demanded, for example, that the millions of posters the government produced and distributed to promote the war effort during World War II be balanced with posters rebutting that view.[326] What constitutes misinformation concerning public health, the war effort in Ukraine, racialized vigilantism, or other national security concerns is also, it might be argued, a question on which government officials must be free to express their views without confronting First Amendment limits. How private citizens and businesses, such as social media companies, choose to respond to the government's views is up to them, the argument would go; they have their own free speech rights and can accept, reject, or ignore the government's views as they see fit.

The courts thus should not seek to monitor the government's words, for "it is the democratic electoral process that first and foremost provides a check on government speech."[327]

The case for the social media businesses begins with the proposition that they are not state actors. Their own First Amendment free speech rights, they argue, shield their efforts to control content on their websites. Since 1976, the Supreme Court has found that the First Amendment protects the free speech rights of corporations as it does individual citizens.[328] A "corporation is simply a form of organization used by human beings to achieve desired ends," the Court said in 2014, and the rights extended to corporations "protect the rights of these people."[329] When social media companies determine what content to place on their websites, they have argued, they are exercising editorial discretion which the First Amendment immunizes from regulation. The U.S. District Court of the Western District of Texas, in a case featuring the social media companies' assertion of the First Amendment rights, held that "[s]ocial media platforms have a first amendment right to moderate content disseminated on their platforms."[330] Social media companies contend they have a "constitutional right not to be compelled to include unwanted content on their platforms" and "a right to engage in their own direct expression,"[331] and are thus permitted to "prohibit all sorts of speech that they deem harmful or objectionable or against their policies, including medical misinformation, hate speech and slurs (spanning the spectrum from race and religion to veteran status), glorification of violence and animal abuse, and impersonation, lies, and misinformation more broadly."[332]

The decision not to carry such content, they claim, is therefore protected by the First Amendment—a point that is often misunderstood. President Obama, for example, said, "The First Amendment is a check on the power of the state. It doesn't apply to private companies like Facebook and Twitter."[333] That is not the companies' position; their position has been that the protection of the First Amendment very much *applies* to them—to the point of trumping the conflicting free speech interests of any of their users. The companies embrace a single-actor approach, under which only their own speech freedom is entitled to constitutional protection. In controlling online content, they are on the same constitutional footing as newspapers making editorial decisions about what to publish. Other actors' speech freedoms, however weighty, are in this view entitled to no constitutional consideration;[334] the only issue is whether the defendant is a state actor.[335]

The courts have generally agreed. A classic example of this approach is the federal district court's dismissal of Trump's action against Twitter following Twitter's suspension of his account. In it, the court based its decision entirely on Twitter's status, concluding that it is a private actor, and it accorded no weight to the speech interests of Trump, other users, or the general public.[336] The First Amendment, so construed, would empower the companies to suppress any content by any user for any reason. As the Fifth Circuit Court of Appeals observed in upholding Texas's regulation of large social media platforms in *NetChoice LLC v. Paxton*, "On the platforms' view, email providers, mobile phone companies, and banks could cancel the accounts of anyone who sends an email, makes a phone call, or spends money in support of a disfavored political party, candidate, or business."[337]

The Case against the Government and the Companies

Before considering countervailing constitutional principles, two preliminary points. First, I accept, for purposes of argument, the companies' claim that the editorial discretion involved in curating material and deciding what to post constitutes a form of speech. There are powerful reasons to reject that argument, as did the Fifth Circuit in *NetChoice*—pointing out, among other things, that the platforms themselves have repeatedly denied engaging in editorial judgment,[338] and that Congress, in granting them immunity, explicitly rejected the proposition that they are publishers or speakers.[339] Nonetheless, it is useful to accept their argument merely to see that it is not dispositive: even if the companies are engaged in a kind of speech, other participants in the marketplace of ideas also have speech interests that warrant protection.

Second, as the Fifth Circuit suggested, it is important to note the practical consequences of the companies' argument.[340] As numerous scholars have observed, the identity of the censor often does not matter; censorship's effects are equally pernicious whether the delete key is pushed by a government bureaucrat or a social media content moderator.[341] Multiple parties have free speech interests in "content moderation" disputes, not simply the social media companies. The user whose content is blocked or degraded has a free speech interest. The listener who cannot hear or read that content has a free speech interest. Others in society at large who look to those speakers and listeners to create and maintain a vibrant exchange of ideas—third parties who sometimes have little to do with social media—also have a free speech interest.[342] The government itself needs to hear its citizens' views.

These interests are neither speculative nor hypothetical. The Supreme Court has recognized the public's need for access to the free flow of information. The public has, in fact, a right to hear or listen separate from the First Amendment right to speak. In 1965, the Court confronted a statute that required persons who received "communist political propaganda" sent through the mail by foreign governments to explicitly request delivery by placing their names on a post office registry.[343] The Court struck down the law even though, as Burt Neuborne has pointed out, it found that the "speaker"—the foreign government—had no First Amendment rights whatsoever.[344] The Court ruled that the recipient had an independent right to receive the literature.[345] "[W]here a speaker exists," the Court later elaborated, ". . . the protection afforded is to the communication, to its source and to its recipients both."[346] The right to hear or read that communication is "an inherent corollary of the rights to free speech and press that are explicitly guaranteed by the Constitution."[347] The Court added that "the right to receive ideas follows ineluctably from the *sender's* First Amendment right to send them."[348]

If the Amendment's purpose is to foster what the Supreme Court has famously described as an "uninhibited, robust, and wide-open" debate,[349] recognizing *only* the free speech interests of one set of participants in that marketplace—the internet company "speakers"—falls short of that objective by abridging other participants' freedom of speech. This is not to suggest that others' free speech interests necessarily would or should prevail against the speaker's. As is true in all constitutional litigation, rights will sometimes conflict with other rights (such as a putative interest in associating freely in an online community free from abusive speech); different contexts will counsel different accommodations.[350] Trade-offs will be unavoidable. Yet it remains true that modern First Amendment doctrine, as Neuborne has written, "has become increasingly speaker centered to the virtual exclusion of everyone else" and needs to be reformulated to respect both speakers and hearers.[351] "The full First Amendment," he writes, "is a story about the interaction between free speakers and free hearers in a democracy."[352] Speech without hearers is the sound of one hand clapping. Protecting the interest of speakers, hearers, and the public in a vibrant marketplace of ideas is essential to keeping the machinery of deliberative democracy up and running.

If the objective is protecting democracy's marketplace of ideas, it should not matter whether large-scale deprivation of free speech interests comes from the government or from outside the government. The marketplace of ideas can wither in response to threats from either source. Moreover, when the modern marketplace has in so many respects become the town hall of modern social media, as the Supreme Court indicated in *Packingham v. North Carolina*,[353] those deprivations and denials can mean its collapse. A blinkered reading of the First Amendment that would protect only the social media companies' freedom of speech would not fulfill its broader purpose of sustaining the marketplace of ideas. The Amendment's reach must be broadened, and that will require, in Neuborne's words, "thinking about when an otherwise unprotected speaker should be allowed to borrow the rights of others in the first place."[354]

Over the decades, the Supreme Court has developed a set of doctrines that, in effect, do exactly that—doctrines tailored to shielding essential speech freedoms in circumstances where an exclusive focus on governmental infringement would not be adequate. Each of those theories suggests that *some* protection must be available for the speech of persons outside the government and social media companies. The doctrines call for respecting all competing speech freedoms rather than embracing one while repudiating all others.[355] A brief sketch of these theories follows. Read together, they affirm the courts' historic responsibility famously set out in Footnote Four of *Carolene Products*,[356] in John Hart Ely's words, "to keep the machinery of democratic government running as it should, to make sure the channels of political participation and communication are kept open."[357] Read together, they counsel the application of a constitutional precautionary principle: given the fundamentality of freedom of speech as "the matrix, the indispensable condition, of nearly every other form of freedom,"[358] when the threat of serious, irreversible damage to that freedom arises, lack of proof of certain governmental responsibility should not be used as a reason for ignoring First Amendment constraints.[359]

Government Speech

The government's free speech rights, contrary to intimations in some early judicial opinions, are not in fact unlimited. The Supreme Court warned in 2017 that "while the government-speech doctrine is important—indeed, essential—it is a doctrine that is susceptible to dangerous misuse."[360] One specific danger of misuse lies in the government's power to evade constitutional

limits through verbal coercion—to threaten action that would invade constitutionally protected rights. This verbal coercion, the Court has held, is prohibited. The protection of First Amendment rights from government threats
has been a particular concern: "[A] government's ability to express itself is
[not] without restriction. . . .[361] [T]he Free Speech Clause itself may constrain
the government's speech."[362]

Moreover, the courts have held that the government cannot deputize
intermediaries to do its censoring. The seminal case is *Bantam Books, Inc.
v. Sullivan*,[363] decided in 1963. In it, the free speech clause itself was held
to constrain the government's speech.[364] A Rhode Island commission sent
notices to wholesale book distributors that certain books they were selling
contained objectionable content.[365] The notices thanked the distributors in
advance for their "cooperation" and informed them that the notices had also
been circulated to local police departments.[366] Police officers then visited
the distributors to learn what action had been taken; the distributors usually responded that copies had been returned to the publishers.[367] "People
do not lightly disregard public officers' thinly veiled threats to institute criminal proceedings against them if they do not come around," the Supreme
Court observed.[368] It held that the threats had subjected the distribution of
constitutionally protected publications to "a system of prior administrative
restraints," a "system of informal censorship," "a scheme of state censorship
effectuated by extralegal sanctions."[369] The commission had used "informal
sanctions—the threat of invoking legal sanctions and other means of coercion, persuasion, and intimidation"[370]—deliberately to suppress the circulation of protected materials. The authors of these materials were not parties
to the case. The government did not threaten the authors, at least not directly. The government went after intermediaries—wholesale distributors—
with presumably less direct interest in defending authors' free speech rights
than the authors would have had themselves. But the thinly veiled system
of informal censorship carried out by distributors was of course directed at
preventing the authors' works from being read. It was the authors' and their
readers' interests in free speech that were impinged by the sanctions. That the
government's "speech" vivified those sanctions made the scheme more, not
less, constitutionally infirm.

In 2015, the Seventh Circuit Court of Appeals addressed a similar scheme
in *Backpage.com v. Dart*.[371] In that case, Sheriff Tom Dart of Cook County,
Illinois, set out to, in the court's words, "crush" Backpage,[372] an online
forum carrying "adult" and other content, including some constitutionally

protected content.[373] To "crush" the website, Dart went to intermediaries—credit card companies—and requested that they prohibit use of their cards for ad purchases on Backpage.[374] His aim was "to proceed against Backpage not by litigation but instead by suffocation, depriving the company of ad revenues by scaring off its payments-service providers."[375] The credit card companies "knuckle[d] under," as the court put it, as their cost in potential civil liabilities and negative press far exceeded the small part of their income they received from dealing with Backpage and its advertisers.[376] However, Dart's clever scheme was constitutionally defective. "The First Amendment," the court held, citing *Bantam Books*, "forbids a public official to attempt to suppress the protected speech of private persons by threatening that legal sanctions will at his urging be imposed unless there is compliance with his demands."[377] The court found, therefore, Dart's claim that his own First Amendment rights permitted such speech unavailing.[378] Had his speech "stop[ped] short of threats," he could legally have publicly criticized the credit card companies.[379] But Dart did not stop short of threats; he used his office to intimidate, and the court found that there is a difference "between government expression and intimidation—the first permitted by the First Amendment, the latter forbidden by it."[380]

The *Dart* court then looked to a Second Circuit opinion, *Okwedy v. Molinari*, in which the government devised another scheme using intermediaries to carry out its censorship—and again confronted the prohibitory wall of the First Amendment.[381] At issue in *Okwedy* were objections conveyed by the Staten Island borough president to a billboard company that had displayed messages offensive to gay and lesbian residents, and the company's response—to take down the signs.[382] Here again, the court rejected the claim that the borough president was merely exercising his own First Amendment free speech rights, holding that "[w]hat matters is the distinction between attempts to convince and attempts to coerce."[383] The court also stated that "[a] public-official defendant who threatens to employ coercive state power to stifle protected speech violates a plaintiff's First Amendment rights even if the public-official defendant lacks direct regulatory or decision-making authority over the plaintiff or a third party that facilitates the plaintiff's speech."[384] The *Okwedy* court noted that in a prior case, a court had found for plaintiffs even when the threats in question came from an individual member of the U.S. House of Representatives.[385]

The democratic electoral process is therefore far from the only check on government speech. The courts protect actors from government speech that threatens to suppress their speech through government coercion.[386] When the government squelches the speech of specific individuals through government threats or enticements, it violates the First Amendment.[387] That the intermediary is a private actor is of no constitutional consequence. In 2022, the Supreme Court reiterated its intent to police the line separating government speech from private expression. In *Shurtleff v. City of Boston*, the Court stated that, when the boundary between the two blurs, it will conduct a holistic inquiry to determine "the extent to which the government has actively shaped or controlled the expression."[388] At that point, as suggested below, government speech considerations shade into state action concerns, and state action claims become unavailing.

State Action

The First Amendment, to reiterate, limits only action by the government. The Constitution provides no protection against private conduct, however wrongful.[389] A murderer or kidnapper or robber does not violate the Constitution. Their actions may interfere with our life, liberty, and property *interests*, but they do not deny or deprive us of our *rights*. According to the state action doctrine, the Constitution protects rights only from government interference.

It's noteworthy that neither *Bantam Books* nor *Dart* nor *Okwedy* was decided on state action grounds. In fact, the issue of state action was not explicitly addressed in any of the three opinions. Each of the three courts refused to be distracted by the existence of private intermediaries, as has the Supreme Court. A state normally can be held responsible for a private decision, the Court said in *Blum v. Yaretsky*, "only when it has exercised coercive power or has provided such significant encouragement, either overt or covert, that the choice must in law be deemed to be that of the State."[390] In *Bantam Books*, *Dart*, and *Okwedy*, government coercion and encouragement were obvious: the choice in each case was unmistakably the state's.[391] But in many cases, where, when, and by whom the "choice" is made is anything but obvious. At that point, the government speech and state action doctrines dovetail, triggering the question posed in *Shurtleff*, whether the speaker is the government or a private actor. Coercive power or significant encouragement by the government, it will be seen, pervade many environments—such as the snarl of interrelationships between the governmental and internet companies—and many cases stand ready to be deployed by a court that is willing to give weight to speech interests beyond those of only the companies. What follows is a summary outline of those cases.

In some such cases, as the Court noted in *Blum*, government coercion or encouragement can be covert or more subtle than it was in *Bantam Books*, *Dart*, and *Okwedy*. Subtlety may make the coercion harder to detect, but it is not constitutionally immunizing. It is "axiomatic that a state may not induce, encourage or promote private persons to accomplish what it is constitutionally forbidden to accomplish," the Court said in 1973 in *Norwood v. Harrison*, finding state action in the government's provision of free textbooks to a private school with racially discriminatory practices. The program violated the Fourteenth Amendment, as it had "a significant tendency to facilitate, reinforce, and support private discrimination."[392]

Sometimes the benefits the government derives from facilitating, reinforcing, or supporting private activity and the correlative benefits private actors derive from government involvement are so great that a symbiotic relationship results. Such a dynamic occurred in *Burton v. Wilmington Parking Authority*, decided in 1961. In that famous case, the Court found state action in the discriminatory practices of a private restaurant that rented space in a public parking garage. Both benefited from the arrangement. Upkeep of the building was paid for out of public funds, and guests in the restaurant were afforded a convenient place to park their cars, while the government took in additional revenues from the restaurant and additional demand for its parking facilities. As Erwin Chemerinsky has observed, "the government was so entangled with the restaurant that there was a 'symbiotic relationship' sufficient to create state action."[393] The Court found it irrelevant that the government acted through omission rather than by commission. "By its inaction," the Court found, the government not only made itself a party to the refusal of service to Black restaurant customers, "but has elected to place its power, property and prestige behind the admitted discrimination. The State has so far insinuated itself into a position of interdependence with [the restaurant] that it must be recognized as a joint participant in the challenged activity."[394]

Burton is sometimes said to represent the jurisprudence of an earlier era, but even justices disinclined to find state action recognize that state action is created when private organizations act in a symbiotic relationship with the government. In 2001 the Supreme Court reaffirmed that excessive entanglement indicates state action, holding in *Brentwood Academy v. Tennessee*

Secondary School Athletic Association that the government's "pervasive en-twinement" in the structure and operations of a private organization that oversaw high school sports in public and private high schools constituted state action.[395] The breadth of the Court's holding was not lost on Justice Thomas, who, joined by three other dissenters, wrote, "We have never found state action based upon mere 'entwinement.' Until today, we have found a private organization's acts to constitute state action only when the organiza-tion performed a public function; was created, coerced, or encouraged by the government; or acted in a symbiotic relationship with the government."[396] State action can be found with respect to organizations that do not perform a public function but that are encouraged by the government and act in a sym-biotic relationship with it—organizations like major social media companies.

Another concept sometimes dismissed as outdated is the notion of the public square—until it was revived by the Supreme Court in 2017, when the Court relied upon the notion to invalidate a North Carolina law that made it a felony for a registered sex offender to access social media websites like Facebook and Twitter. The Court found in *Packingham v. North Carolina* that the law barred access to what it called the "modern public square":

> By prohibiting sex offenders from using those websites, North Carolina
> with one broad stroke bars access to what for many are the principal sources
> for knowing current events, checking ads for employment, speaking and
> listening in the modern public square, and otherwise exploring the vast
> realms of human thought and knowledge. These websites can provide per-
> haps the most powerful mechanisms available to a private citizen to make
> his or her voice heard. They allow a person with an Internet connection to
> "become a town crier with a voice that resonates farther than it could from
> any soapbox."[397]

The concept of the public square thus is not only alive and well in existing case law; the Court has explicitly recognized that the major social media platforms are "perhaps the most powerful mechanisms" within it.

The seminal public square case is, ironically, one in which the Supreme Court did not use the term: *Marsh v. Alabama*.[398] *Marsh* posed the ques-tion whether a company-owned town could prohibit the distribution of lit-erature by Seventh Day Adventists that would be constitutionally protected had the streets and sidewalks not been privately owned. The Court answered no, finding state action. "[T]he town and its shopping district are accessible to and freely used by the public in general," the Court found, "and there is nothing to distinguish them from any other town and shopping center except the fact that the title to the property belongs to a private corporation."[399] It did not matter whether speech was stifled by the government or by a private company—the effect was the same: "Whether a corporation or a municipality owns or possesses the town the public in either case has an identical interest in the functioning of the community in such manner that the channels of communication remain free."[400] Residents in both public and private towns had the same need for access to those channels of communication to fulfill the responsibilities of citizenship. "Just as all other citizens," the Court said, "they must make decisions which affect the welfare of community and nation. To act as good citizens, they must be informed. In order to enable them to be properly informed, their information must be uncensored."[401] The Court reemphasized the need to be informed in *Packingham*: "A fundamental principle of the First Amendment is that all persons have access to places where they can speak and listen, and then, after reflection, speak and listen once more."[402] It is entirely plausible, Geoffrey Stone has observed, that cases such as *Marsh* could be deployed against what the Court "might perceive as profound private threats to our system of free expression."[403] He continues:

> For example, one could imagine the Court holding that extraordinary powerful internet sites, like Facebook, Twitter, and Google, are so powerful that they are in effect government actors and must therefore be deemed the equivalent of public forums. *Marsh*, which dealt with company towns, might be a good jumping-off point for such an analysis.[404]

The owners of the company town, the *Marsh* Court opined, had no more right to censor information than did "the owners of privately held bridges, ferries, turnpikes and railroads," which are "built and operated primarily to benefit the public" and perform "essentially a public function."[405] None of these private concerns operated "as freely as a farmer does his farm" and thus, the Court reasoned, none was able to ban the distribution of objectionable literature.[406]

Though he did not mention *Marsh*, the passage quoted above presaged the much-discussed concurring opinion of Justice Thomas in *Biden v. Knight First Amendment Institute*. Historically, Justice Thomas wrote, businesses known as common carriers, such as railroad companies, insurers, and telegraph companies, have long been subject to special regulations, including a general requirement to serve all comers.[407] "In many ways," Thomas wrote, "digital platforms that hold themselves out to the public resemble traditional common carriers."[408] Digital platforms also, he suggested, resemble public utilities and places of public accommodation—places that provide lodging, food, entertainment, or other services to the public—where companies' right to exclude has similarly been limited.[409] The idea has generated considerable support among free speech scholars. The Fifth Circuit in *NetChoice* found that the common carrier doctrine supports the constitutionality of imposing nondiscrimination obligations on the platforms[410] and, importantly, observed that courts have imposed common carrier duties absent statutes requiring or authorizing them to do so.[411]

The point to be emphasized, made implicitly by Justice Thomas and the courts in the earlier cases outlined above, is—again—that focusing exclusively on the status and interests of only one actor is too limited. It makes more sense to examine all interests at issue, identify the precise rights that are potentially impinged, and protect those rights directly, rather than safeguarding only those that happen adventitiously to be represented by a single particular litigant.[412] The Court has recognized a "profound national commitment to the principle that debate on public issues should be uninhibited, robust, and wide-open."[413] The interests of the listener or reader and of the general public to know and be informed are crucial in upholding that commitment. It should not matter whether information is withheld from intended recipients by an officious Federal Express or an officious U.S. Postal Service. *Lamont* (1965), described earlier,[414] underscores the independent right to read and hear. The *Lamont* Court might well have been referring to the internet when it quoted Justice Holmes, who wrote that the post office "is almost as much a part of free speech as the right to use our tongues,"[415] or when it quoted the D.C. Circuit:

> Whatever may have been the voluntary nature of the postal system in the period of its establishment, it is now the main artery through which the business, social, and personal affairs of the people are conducted and upon which depends in a greater degree than upon any other activity of government the promotion of the general welfare.[416]

The "main artery through which the business, social, and personal affairs of the people are conducted" is now social media. These are the channels through which the people now receive information, and the right to receive publications, Justice William Brennan argued in his concurrence in *Lamont*, is a fundamental right. "The dissemination of ideas can accomplish nothing if otherwise willing addressees are not free to receive and consider them," he wrote. "It would be a barren marketplace of ideas that had only sellers and no buyers."[417] And, we might add today, it would be a barren digital marketplace that protected only the speech interests of the government and the social media platforms but not their users or the general public.

Summary

Freedom of speech is neither liberal nor conservative; it is the operating system of our political order on which the smooth and safe functioning of all else depends. In the digital era, it is possible to freeze that operating system by inducing widespread public deference to authoritatively defined truths. A sprawling, unelected security-media cartel now does so. It employs new tools of soft censorship to keep unwanted ideas and information out of the marketplace of ideas. That cartel defies constitutional categorization as either public or private. Yet its interwoven components seek immunity in established constitutional doctrines concerning state action and government speech. The marketplace of ideas will not likely survive if the First Amendment, cramped by those doctrines, is construed as protecting only the speech freedom of the government and its big tech partners but not the speech freedom of social media users or the general public. If ever a threat to freedom of speech counseled the application of a constitutional precautionary principle, described above,[418] it is the menace posed by the security-media cartel.

For those trained in the law, who have honed skills in placing established facts into fixed categories, the analytic challenge is formidable. Multiple actors move in and out of a constantly shifting mix of technocrats, managers, political operators, lobbyists, alumni, content moderators, internet moguls, intelligence and law enforcement officials, and allied groups. The cartel is diffuse; at its core are networks within networks,[419] adapting continually to changing political currents with ever-improving technologies. In its structure as in its "unwarranted influence," it resembles the amorphous military-industrial complex memorably identified by President Dwight Eisenhower.[420] Yet its very shapelessness and its resistance to classification within traditional categories allow it to elude legal limits—and indicate the urgent need to address its malign effect: the cartel chokes the traditional channels of information and political change on which legislative reform depends,[421] with the result that legislative inaction can no longer stand in the way of judicial redress.

The courts' jurisprudential challenge will be particularly daunting. The pervasive presence of state actors within the cartel requires assessing second- and third-order effects that courts normally avoid. The questions before them concern nothing less than the system-wide impact on democracy of efforts to stopper the channels of political communication. It will be tempting for judges to vacillate in the face of recognized cultural constraints on judicial capacity.[422] It will be tempting to look to earlier decisions that, in a simpler era, turned upon straightforward, immediate questions of *who* was speaking and *whether* that person was with the government. But times have changed. With those changes have come corresponding changes in the meaning of the constitutional predicate for judicial intervention.[423] If individual cases can still be abstracted so reductively, the larger controversy—the larger *crisis*—cannot. To place the survival of free speech on the resolution of those narrow *who* and *whether* questions will hasten its disappearance.

Some members of the public will neither rue nor even notice its absence. They will have been convinced that only hate speech or medical disinformation or foreign propaganda has disappeared. They will not see what never reaches their eyes. They will be gratified to read no challenges to their worldview in inoffensive search results or in deeply buried social media posts or in politically tailored news feeds. But the free exchange of ideas in America will be a relic of an earlier era. A diligent few will still dig out dissent, but their views will increasingly be shunted aside as extremist, and free speech itself will increasingly be dismissed as dispensable.

The security-media cartel and its allies already consider free speech dispensable. They believe that they, not the people, are better able to decide how to advance the people's well-being. They do so by excluding information and ideas from the marketplace. Sometimes they are right. The people do not always distinguish fact from fiction; pernicious ideas sometimes prevail. But the American republic is premised on the belief that choices made by the people at large are more trustworthy than choices made for them by a select, unaccountable subset of the people.

There is no reason to believe that recent technological breakthroughs have suddenly made the noble lies of modern-day philosopher-kings more compatible with democracy. Nor is there any reason to suppose that the cult-ishness and mobthink to which the public is sometimes vulnerable cannot also infect decision-making at "senior" levels. The censors assume that they are immune from the familiar frenzies, biases, and cognitive distortions that beset the public. Their assumption engenders a sense of infallibility, an un-awareness that they are subject to their own distinctive array of cognitive biases, a conceit that they are possessed of unique expertise and an exclu-sive capacity to ferret out error. To acknowledge that the security agencies are themselves susceptible to error is hardly to suggest their expendability. One need look no further than daily news reports to know that safeguarding national security requires an infrastructure of the trained and prepared, led by the honest and the able. Nor is it to imply invidious intent; unaccount-ability, insularity, and banality plagued bureaucracy long before Hanna Arendt's incisiveness.[424] But the impulse is ever-present to mistake personal preference for universal truth. It is the highest object of free speech to keep both the governed and the governors from succumbing to that temptation. And it is the highest duty of the judiciary to protect free speech when it is imperiled. "If we would guide by the light of reason," Brandeis wrote, "we must let our minds be bold."[425] The courts have met this duty boldly in the past, bequeathing the United States the most speech-protective legal regime the world has ever known. Its survival now depends upon renewed judicial boldness.

13

Conclusion

Over the span of scarcely a century, the United States has come full circle in protecting free speech. It has gone from jailing a popular presidential candidate who criticized the government's war-making,[1] to broadly protecting advocacy of even violence and law violation,[2] to a "coordinated campaign . . . orchestrated by federal officials that . . . likely 'had the intended result of suppressing millions of protected free speech postings by American citizens.'"[3] Many Americans who are indifferent to today's censorship seem to believe that the free exchange of information and ideas is unnecessary—that what is true for them in their private hearts is true for everyone else—that unexamined impulse and naked preference are a sound basis for public policy.

Given that state of mind, it makes perfect sense, as Holmes said, to persecute the expression of opinion—in modern parlance, to do "whatever it takes" to gain or retain political power. We need look no further than Holmes's experience to see where their certitude can lead. Its consequences are foreseeable. Three years before the Civil War began, New York senator William Seward warned of the incompatibility of the two sides' political aims, which would lead to "an irrepressible conflict between opposing and enduring forces."[4]

The alternative to civil strife is a reinvigorated marketplace of ideas—a full, free, and unfettered societal discussion in a stable public square that respects the free speech interests not only of speakers but also of listeners and bystanders—a square that protects society's *safety* by seeking its *ultimate good* through a *free trade in ideas*. These words—Holmes's own words—are social terms, recognizing the interests of more than a lone speaker. They refer to a societal process aimed at societal adaptation and societal security. A revitalized, democratized societal marketplace of ideas could provide a new legitimating principle—it could truly be, and could be seen to be, the matrix of all other freedoms, revitalizing the stabilizing institutions that have in recent years demeaned themselves by choosing to stifle speech rather than protect it.

Free Speech and Turbulent Freedom. Michael J. Glennon, Oxford University Press. © Oxford University Press 2024.
DOI: 10.1093/oso/9780197636763.003.0013

Reversing the withered state of free speech in the United States and enshrining it as a legitimating principle will require underscoring its heightened level of protection—and dropping erroneous assumptions. One such assumption is that only censorship by the government need be a concern. The great enemy of free speech today is a powerful symbiotic public-private regime that defies traditional constitutional categories and quashes speech with impunity. Another mistaken assumption is that only individual speakers need be protected under the First Amendment. Speakers do need protection, but so too do listeners and bystanders, who also have an interest in the stable interchange of ideas. The censorship cartel threatens everyone's safety—society's safety —not only speakers' safety. "The harms that radiate from such conduct," the Fifth Circuit said in *Missouri v. Biden*, "extend far beyond just the Plaintiffs; it impacts every social media user."[5]

Because this censorship has choked the channels of political communication upon which legislative reform relies, the task I have outlined is primarily one for the courts. The system will not correct itself if the courts sit on the sidelines. Even if the courts are successful in protecting freedom of speech, however, they cannot by themselves establish a new legitimating principle. Judicial intervention is necessary but will not be sufficient. The state alone cannot create a public sphere where communication is unburdened and unchilled, where differences are resolved cooperatively, where positions are justified by reasoned argument, where conflicting values are accepted as a feature of the human condition rather than a defect to be corrected. The creation of such a sphere will depend upon habits of mind, inculcated over time. Those habits spring from individuals' commitment to pre-agreed processes over preferred outcomes; from the iternalized acceptance of lawful policies we disagree with; from the recognition that others forge their own provisional truths; from the awareness that we are not always right; from the conviction that an informed, deliberative, self-governing people will meld those truths in policies worthy of our respect; from the realization that the only alternative is chaos. For freedom of speech is not, in the end, solely about societal truth. It is about societal safety. In a pluralistic society intent upon ensuring its safety, there is no other way.

Acknowledgments

Trite but true, this book would not exist without the generosity of many people. It was written mostly over a sabbatical during which research support was provided by the Fletcher School of Law and Diplomacy at Tufts University, where I teach. I benefited from the comments of family, friends, and colleagues who looked over earlier portions of the manuscript, including John Cerone, Mark Glennon, Bernice Hamilton, Hurst Hannum, Robert Hillman, Nadia Morales, John Shattuck, Robert Sloane, Nadine Strossen, and Charles Tiefer. Conversations with Klaus Scharioth sharpened my thinking about many questions addressed in this book. The indefatigable research assistance of excellent students helped considerably. Danielle Bertaux, Alex Betley, Fiona Davis, Joe Jamison, and Arthur Lo ably assembled pertinent materials in the early stages of the project. The Hitachi Foundation provided valuable support for their research. Later, the editorial assistance of Constantinos Angelakis, Andre Gellerman, and Dillon Kim went far beyond fastidious footnote fixing. Ann Cullen and Ellen McDonald of Fletcher's Ginn Library staff were, as always, prompt, professional, and patient. Oxford's David McBride, Alexcee Bechthold, and Hemalatha Arumugam gave expert, unstinting assistance from the outset. The final chapter in the book, "Symbiotic Security and Free Speech," first appeared as an article published in the *Harvard National Security Journal* 14 (2022): 1–114. Its editors and staff were in every respect superb. Portions of the book also draw upon three earlier articles, "Populism, Elites, and National Security," published in *Humanitas* XXXI, nos. 1 and 2 (2018): 35–45; "Security Breach: Trump's Tussle with the Bureaucratic State," published in *Harper's Magazine* in June 2017; and "The Road Ahead: Gaps, Leaks and Drips," published in *International Law Studies* 89 (2013): 362–386.

No words can express the depth of my gratitude to my wife, Joanna. Finally, I thank my students, whose questions keep the adrenaline flowing. To them I dedicate this book.

Notes

Preface

1. I draw here on my article, "Security Breach," *Harper's*, June 2017, 41, https://harpers.org/archive/2017/06/security-breach/.
2. The Twitter Files consisted of a series of communications among Twitter employees and with government officials revealing that the FBI and other security agencies were enmeshed in decisions concerning what materials and accounts Twitter would suppress. The Files were made available by Elon Musk, Twitter's new owner, to journalists Lee Fang, Michael Shellenberger, Matt Taibbi, and Bari Weiss and published on Twitter and elsewhere from December 2022 to March 2023. See generally Aimee Picchi, "Twitter Files: What They Are and Why They Matter," cbs *News*, December 14, 2022, https://www.cbsnews.com/news/twitter-files-matt-taibbi-bari-weiss-michael-shellenberger-elon-musk/. As Chapter 12 indicates, considerable evidence of the symbiotic relationship between social media platforms and the national security state was on the public record before publication of the Twitter Files.
3. *Missouri v. Biden*, No. 3:22-01213, memorandum ruling on request for preliminary injunction (Western District of Louisiana, Monroe Division), July 4, 2023.
4. *Missouri*, 154.
5. *Missouri*, 154.
6. *Missouri*, 94.
7. *Missouri,* 2. As this book went to press, the district court's judgment was affirmed by the United States Court of Appeals for the Fifth Circuit with respect to the White House, the Surgeon General, the CDC, and the FBI. The appeals court ordered their officials to "take no actions, formal or informal, directly or indirectly, to coerce or significantly encourage social-media companies to remove, delete, suppress, or reduce, including through altering their algorithms, posted social-media content containing protected free speech." *Missouri v. Biden*, No. 23-30445 at 70 (5th Cir.), September 8, 2023, chrome-extension://efaidnbmnnnibpcajpcglclefindmkaj/https://www.ca5.uscourts.gov/opinions/pub/23/23-30445-CV0.pdf.
8. I described that domination in *National Security and Double Government* (New York: Oxford University Press, 2015).

Chapter 1

1. Francis Biddle, *Mr. Justice Holmes* (New York: Scribner, 1942), 35–36.
2. Louis Einstein, introduction to *The Holmes-Einstein Letters: The Correspondence of Mr. Justice Holmes and Louis Einstein, 1903–1935*, ed. James Bishop Peabody (New York: St. Martin's, 1964), xvi.

3. William F. Fox, *Regimental Losses in the American Civil War, 1861–1865* (Albany, NY: Albany Publishing, 1889), 3.

4. Oliver Wendell Holmes Jr. to Dr. and Mrs. O. W. Holmes, May 16, 1864, quoted in G. Edward White, *Justice Oliver Wendell Holmes: Law and the Inner Self* (New York: Oxford University Press, 1993), 65.

5. Louis Menand, *The Metaphysical Club: A Story of Ideas in America* (New York: Farrar, Straus and Giroux, 2001), 35.

6. Stephen Budiansky, *Oliver Wendell Holmes: A Life in War, Law, and Ideas* (New York: W. W. Norton, 2019), 93.

7. Budiansky, *Oliver Wendell Holmes*, 96.

8. Budiansky, *Oliver Wendell Holmes*, 96.

9. Menand, *The Metaphysical Club*, 55.

10. Quoted in Budiansky, *Oliver Wendell Holmes*, 122.

11. Mark DeWolfe Howe, ed., *Touched with Fire: Civil War Letters and Diary of Oliver Wendell Holmes, Jr. 1861–1864* (Cambridge: Harvard University Press, 1946), 142.

12. Howe, *Touched with Fire*, 142.

13. Howe, *Touched with Fire*, 148–50.

14. Howe, *Touched with Fire*, 148–50.

15. Oliver Wendell Holmes Jr., to Morris Cohen, February 5, 1919, "The Holmes-Cohen Correspondence," ed. Felix S. Cohen, *Journal of the History of Ideas* 9 (1948): 15.

16. Robert D. Richardson, *Emerson: The Mind on Fire* (Berkeley: University of California Press, 1995), 250–51.

17. Ralph Waldo Emerson, "Self-Reliance" (1841), in *The Complete Works of Ralph Waldo Emerson*, vol. 2: *Essays*, University of Michigan Digital Library, 2006, https://quod.lib.umich.edu/e/emerson/4957107.0002.001/1:6?rgn=div1;view=fulltext.

18. Ralph Waldo Emerson, "Speech at the Kansas Relief Meeting in Cambridge Wednesday Evening, September 10, 1856," in *The Complete Works of Ralph Waldo Emerson*, vol. 11: *Miscellanies* (Cambridge: Riverside Press, 1883), 247.

19. Quoted in Liva Baker, *The Justice from Beacon Hill: The Life and Times of Oliver Wendell Holmes* (New York: HarperCollins, 1991), 106.

20. *Mahanoy Area School District v. B. L.*, 141 S. Ct. 2038, 2046 (2021).

21. Leslie Gelb, "The Devil and the Details," *Washington Post*, April 27, 2008, https://www.washingtonpost.com/wp-dyn/content/article/2008/04/24/AR2008042401459.html?tid=a_inl_manual (quoting Richard Cheney).

22. Kyle Kondik, J. Miles Coleman, and Larry J. Sabato, "New Initiative Explores Deep, Persistent Divides between Biden and Trump Voters," UVA Center for Politics, September 30, 2021, https://centerforpolitics.org/crystalball/articles/new-initiative-explores-deep-persistent-divides-between-biden-and-trump-voters/.

Chapter 2

1. G. Edward White, *Justice Oliver Wendell Holmes: Law and the Inner Self* (New York: Oxford University Press, 1993), 40.

2. Ralph Waldo Emerson, "The Fugitive Slave Law," in *The Complete Works of Ralph Waldo Emerson*, ed. E. W. Emerson (Boston: Houghton Mifflin, 1903–4), 187.

3. Quoted in Louis Menand, *The Metaphysical Club: A Story of Ideas in America* (New York: Farrar, Straus and Giroux, 2001), 21.

4. Emerson, "The Fugitive Slave Law," 186.

5. Liva Baker, *The Justice from Beacon Hill: The Life and Times of Oliver Wendell Holmes* (New York: HarperCollins, 1991), 86.

6. Ralph Waldo Emerson, "Speech at the Kansas Relief Meeting in Cambridge Wednesday Evening, September 10, 1856," in *Emerson's Complete Works*, vol. 11: *Miscellanies* (Cambridge: Riverside Press, 1883), 244.

7. Ralph Waldo Emerson, *Emerson's Antislavery Writings*, ed. Len Gougeon and Joel Myerson (New Haven, CT: Yale University Press, 1995), 37.

8. Len Gougeon, "Militant Abolitionism: Douglass, Emerson, and the Rise of the Anti-Slave," *New England Quarterly* 85, no. 4 (2012): 622–57.

9. Ralph Waldo Emerson, "Remarks at a Meeting for the Relief of John Brown at Tremont Temple, Boston, November 18, 1859," in *Emerson's Complete Works*, vol. 11: *Miscellanies* (Cambridge: Riverside Press, 1883), 254.

10. Emerson, "Remarks at a Meeting for the Relief of John Brown," 254.

11. Robert D. Richardson, *Emerson: The Mind on Fire* (Berkeley: University of California Press, 1995), 498.

12. James Elliot Cabot, *A Memoir of Ralph Waldo Emerson* (Boston: Houghton Mifflin, 1888), 597.

13. Frederick C. Fiechter, "The Preparation of an American Aristocrat," *New England Quarterly* 6, no. 1 (1933): 3, https://doi.org/10.2307/359360. Another dismisses such claims as undocumented. See White, *Justice Oliver Wendell Holmes*, 28.

14. White, *Justice Oliver Wendell Holmes*, 35.

15. Baker, *The Justice from Beacon Hill*, 85.

16. White, *Justice Oliver Wendell Holmes*, 38–39.

17. Baker, *The Justice from Beacon Hill*, 164.

18. White, *Justice Oliver Wendell Holmes*, 35.

19. Michael H. Hoffheimer, "The Early Critical and Philosophical Writings of Justice Holmes," *Boston College Law Review* 30, no. 5 (1989): 1221, 1245n75.

20. Ralph Waldo Emerson, "Essay XII," in *The Collected Works of Ralph Waldo Emerson*, vol. 2: *Art Essays*, ed. J. Slater, A. Ferguson, and J. Carr (Cambridge, MA: Belknap Press of Harvard University Press, 1979), 209.

21. Oliver Wendell Holmes, "Notes on Albert Durer," reprinted in Hoffheimer, "The Early Critical and Philosophical Writings," 1255.

22. Baker, *The Justice from Beacon Hill*, 92.

23. Baker, *The Justice from Beacon Hill*, 88.

24. Baker, *The Justice from Beacon Hill*, 89.

25. Stephen Budiansky, *Oliver Wendell Holmes: A Life in War, Law, and Ideas* (New York: W. W. Norton, 2019), 69 (footnotes omitted). His service was unneeded as the event was canceled.

26. Baker, *The Justice from Beacon Hill*, 125.

Chapter 3

1. Robert D. Richardson, *Emerson: The Mind on Fire* (Berkeley: University of California Press, 1995), 530–31.

2. Ralph Waldo Emerson Memorial Association, "Friends Who Came to Visit," n.d., https://www.ralphwaldoemersonhouse.org/friends-who-came-to-visit.

3. Susan Cheever, *American Bloomsbury: Louisa May Alcott, Ralph Waldo Emerson, Margaret Fuller, Nathaniel Hawthorne, and Henry David Thoreau: Their Lives, Their Loves, Their Work* (New York: Simon & Schuster, 2007), 4, 7, 8, 37–38.

4. Ralph Waldo Emerson, *The Transcendentalist* (1842). Emerson summarized the idealist roots of transcendentalism as follows.

   What is popularly called transcendentalism among us is idealism: idealism as it appears in 1842. As thinkers, mankind have ever divided into two sects, materialists and idealists, the first class founding on experience, the second on consciousness; the first class beginning to think from the data of the senses, the second class perceiving that the senses are not final, and saying that the senses give us representations of things, but what are the things themselves, they cannot tell. The materialist insists on facts, on history, on the force of circumstances, and the animal wants of man; the idealist on the power of Thought and of Will, on inspiration, on miracle, on individual culture. These two modes of thinking are both natural, but the idealist contends that his way of thinking is in higher nature. He concedes all that the other affirms, admits the impressions of sense, admits their coherency, their use and beauty, and then asks the materialist for his grounds of assurance that things are as his senses represent them. But I, he says, affirm facts not affected by the illusions of sense, facts which are of the same nature as the faculty which reports them, and not liable to doubt; facts which in their first appearance to us assume a native superiority to material facts, degrading these into a language by which the first are to be spoken; facts which it only needs a retirement from the senses to discern. Every materialist will be an idealist, but an idealist can never go backward to be a materialist.

   Ralph Waldo Emerson, "The Transcendentalist," in *Ralph Waldo Emerson, Essays & Lectures*, ed. Joel Porte (Library of America, 1983), 193.

5. Ralph Waldo Emerson, *Nature Addresses and Lectures* (1849), vol. 1 of *The Complete Works of Ralph Waldo Emerson*, University of Michigan Digital Library, 2006, https://quod.lib.umich.edu/e/emerson/4957107.0001.001/1:9.2?rgn=div2;sort=occur;subview=detail;type=simple;view=fulltext;q1=reason+and+faith.

6. Ralph Waldo Emerson, "The Over-Soul" (1841), in *The Complete Works of Ralph Waldo Emerson*, vol. 2: *Essays*, University of Michigan Digital Library, 2006, https://quod.lib.umich.edu/e/emerson/4957107.0002.001/1:14?rgn=div1;submit=Go;subview=detail;type=simple;view=fulltext;q1=common+heart.

7. Ralph Waldo Emerson, "Idealism" (1836), in *The Complete Works of Ralph Waldo Emerson*, vol. 1: *Nature Addresses and Lectures*, University of Michigan Digital Library, 2006, 55, https://quod.lib.umich.edu/e/emerson/4957107.0001.001/1:9.7?rgn=div2;sort=occur;subview=detail;type=simple;view=fulltext;q1=for+all+that+exists.

8. Henry David Thoreau, *Walden*, ed. J. Lyndon Shanley (Princeton, NJ: Princeton University Press, 2016), 326.

9. Benedetta Zavatta, Daniel Berthold, and Ann Lauterbach, "Nietzsche Reads Emerson," Hannah Arendt Center for Politics and Humanities, November 13, 2019, https://hac.bard.edu/nietzsche-reads-emerson.

10. Ralph Waldo Emerson, "Self-Reliance" (1841), in *The Complete Works of Ralph Waldo Emerson*, vol. 2: *Essays*, University of Michigan Digital Library, 2006, 57, https://quod. lib.umich.edu/e/emerson/4957107.0002.001/1:6?rgn=div1;view=fulltext.

11.   Ludwig Wittgenstein, *Tractatus Logico-Philosophicus*, trans. C. K. Odgen (London: Kegan Paul, Trench, Trubner, 1922), 90.

12. Quoted in Samuel Elliot Morrison, *Three Centuries of Harvard, 1636–1936* (Cambridge, MA: Harvard University Press, 1936), 248–49.

13. Louis Menand, *The Metaphysical Club: A Story of Ideas in America* (New York: Farrar, Straus and Giroux, 2001), 249. Emerson's notion of research, Menand writes, was to "skim works of literature and philosophy . . . with an eye to ideas and phrases he could appropriate for his own use" (58).

14. Richardson, *Emerson: The Mind on Fire*, 538.

15. Ralph Waldo Emerson, "The Fugitive Slave Law" (1851), in *The Complete Works of Ralph Waldo Emerson,* vol. 11: *Miscellanies,* University of Michigan Digital Library, 2006, 199, https://quod.lib.umich.edu/e/emerson/4957107.0011.001/1:11?rgn= div1;sort=occur;subview=detail;type=simple;view=fulltext;q1=debating-club.

16. Emerson. "The Fugitive Slave Law," 186.

17. Richardson, *Emerson: The Mind on Fire*, 538.

18. Ralph Waldo Emerson, "Spiritual Laws" (1847), in *The Complete Works of Ralph Waldo Emerson,* vol. 2: *Essays,* University of Michigan Digital Library, 2006, 139, https://quod.lib.umich.edu/e/emerson/4957107.0002.001/1:8?rgn=div1;view= fulltext.

19. Emerson, "The Over-Soul," 279.

20. Benjamin E. Park, "Transcendental Democracy: Ralph Waldo Emerson's Political Thought, the Legacy of Federalism, and the Ironies of America's Democratic Tradition," *Journal of American Studies* 48, no. 2 (2014): 490.

21. Ralph Waldo Emerson, "Speech at the Kansas Relief Meeting in Cambridge Wednesday Evening, September 10, 1856" (1856), in *The Complete Works of Ralph Waldo Emerson,* vol. 11: *Miscellanies,* University of Michigan Digital Library, 2006, 262, https://quod.lib.umich.edu/e/emerson/4957107.0011.001/1:14?rgn=div1;view= fulltext.

22. Emerson, "Self-Reliance," 47.

23. Ralph Waldo Emerson, "Politics" (1844), in *The Complete Works of Ralph Waldo Emerson,* vol. 3: *Essays,* University of Michigan Digital Library, 2006, 216, https:// quod.lib.umich.edu/e/emerson/4957107.0003.001/1:11?rgn=div1;sort=occur;subv iew=detail;type=simple;view=fulltext;q1=needs+no+library.

24. Ralph Waldo Emerson, "Intellect" (1841), in *The Complete Works of Ralph Waldo Emerson,* vol. 3: *Essays,* University of Michigan Digital Library, 2006, 328, https:// quod.lib.umich.edu/e/emerson/4957107.0002.001/1:16?rgn=div1;sort=occur;subv iew=detail;type=simple;view=fulltext;q1=spontaneous+action.

25. Ralph Waldo Emerson, *The Complete Works of Ralph Waldo Emerson*, vol. 1: *Nature Addresses and Lectures*, ed. E. W. Emerson (Boston: Houghton Mifflin, 1903–4), 145, https://quod.lib.umich.edu/e/emerson/4957107.0001.001/1:11?rgn=div1;sort= occur;subview=detail;type=simple;view=fulltext;q1=go+alone.

26. Emerson, "Politics," 219.

27. Ralph Waldo Emerson, "The Fortune of the Republic" (1878), in *The Complete Works of Ralph Waldo Emerson,* vol. 11: *Essays,* University of Michigan Digital Library, 2006, 540, https://quod.lib.umich.edu/e/emerson/4957107.0011.001/1:36?rgn=div1;sort= occur;subview=detail;type=simple;view=fulltext;q1=law+in+America+must+be+ written+on+ethical+principles.

28. Ralph Waldo Emerson, "Man the Reformer" (1878), in *The Complete Works of Ralph Waldo Emerson,* vol. 1: *Essays,* University of Michigan Digital Library, 2006, 228, https://quod.lib.umich.edu/e/emerson/4957107.0001.001/1:14?rgn=div1;sort= occur;subview=detail;type=simple;view=fulltext;q1=the+school%2C+relig ion%2C+marriage%2C+trade%2C+science%2C.

29. Karl R. Popper, *Conjectures and Refutations: The Growth of Scientific Knowledge*, 3rd ed. revised (London: Routledge & K. Paul, 1969), 131.

30. Eric Berkowitz, *Dangerous Ideas: A Brief History of Censorship in the West, from the Ancients to Fake News* (New York: Beacon Press, 2021), 28–29.

31. Ralph Waldo Emerson, "Napoleon; or, The Man of the World" (1850), in *The Complete Works of Ralph Waldo Emerson,* vol. 4: *Essays,* University of Michigan Digital Library, 2006, 224, https://quod.lib.umich.edu/e/emerson/4957107.0004.001/1:10?rgn= div1;sort=occur;subview=detail;type=simple;view=fulltext;q1=Napoleon+as+the+ incarnate+Democrat.

32. Emerson, "Napoleon," 258.

33. Emerson, "Napoleon," 232.

34. Emerson, "Napoleon," 232.

35. Emerson, "Napoleon," 246.

36. Emerson, "Napoleon," 247.

37. Emerson, "Napoleon," 248.

38. Berkowitz, *Dangerous Ideas*, 119, 138–39.

39. Emerson, "The Over-Soul."

40. Ralph Waldo Emerson, "An Address," in *Ralph Waldo Emerson, Essays & Lectures*, ed. Joel Porte (Library of America, 1983), 83.

41. Kerry Larson, "Illiberal Emerson," *Nineteenth-Century Prose* 33, no. 1 (Spring 2006): 8.

42. G. Edward White, *Justice Oliver Wendell Holmes: Law and the Inner Self* (New York: Oxford University Press, 1993), 500n177.

43. Oliver Wendell Holmes, "Plato," in *The Collected Works of Justice Holmes: Complete Public Writings and Selected Judicial Opinions of Oliver Wendell Holmes*, ed. Sheldon M. Novick (Chicago: University of Chicago Press, 1995), 148.

44. Holmes, "Plato," 149.

45. Holmes, "Plato," 149.

46. Holmes, "Plato," 149.

47. Holmes, "Plato," 149.

48. Stephen Budiansky, *Oliver Wendell Holmes: A Life in War, Law, and Ideas* (New York: W. W. Norton, 2019), 145.

49. Oliver Wendell Holmes Jr. to Patrick Sheehan, October 27, 1912, in *The Essential Holmes: Selections from the Letters, Speeches, Judicial Opinions, and Other Writings of Oliver Wendell Holmes, Jr.*, ed. Richard Posner (Chicago: University of Chicago Press, 1992), 64.

Chapter 4

1. Francis Biddle, *Mr. Justice Holmes* (New York: Scribner, 1942), 35–36. Holmes "yearned to do a real job, and not to delay the doing."

2. One biographer reported that Emerson had spoken "eloquently, passionately, about his beliefs," but "he knew that Emerson had not reached him as once he would have." Catherine Bowen, *Yankee from Olympus: Justice Holmes and His Family* (Boston: Little, Brown, 1944), 201.

3. Oliver Wendell Holmes Jr. to Patrick Sheehan, October 27, 1912, in *The Essential Holmes: Selections from the Letters, Speeches, Judicial Opinions, and Other Writings of Oliver Wendell Holmes, Jr.*, ed. Richard Posner (Chicago: University of Chicago Press, 1992), 64.

4. Remarks at a Tavern Club Dinner, March 4, 1900, in Posner, *The Essential Holmes,* 48.

5. William James, *What Pragmatism Means*, in Louis Menand, ed., *Pragmatism: A Reader* (New York: Vintage Books, 1997), 107.

6. Address to the graduating class at Harvard University, May 30, 1895, in Posner, *The Essential Holmes*, 89.

7. *Truax v. Corrigan*, 257 U.S. 312, 256 (1921) (Holmes, J., dissenting).

8. C. C. Langdell, "Harvard Celebration Speech," *Law Review Quarterly* 9 (1887): 124.

9. Quoted in G. Edward White, *Justice Oliver Wendell Holmes: Law and the Inner Self* (New York: Oxford University Press, 1993), 197.

10. Oliver Wendell Holmes, "Book Review," *American Law Review* 14 (1880): 233.

11. *Southern Pacific Company v. Jensen*, 244 U.S. 205, 222 (1917) (Holmes, J., dissenting).

12. Oliver Wendell Holmes, Jr., "The Common Law," in *The Collected Works of Justice Holmes: Complete Public Writings and Selected Judicial Opinions of Oliver Wendell Holmes*, ed. Sheldon M. Novick (Chicago: University of Chicago Press, 1995), 115.

13. Stephen Budiansky, *Oliver Wendell Holmes: A Life in War, Law, and Ideas* (New York: W. W. Norton, 2019), 172; Oliver Wendell Holmes, *The Common Law* (New York: Dover, 1991), 36.

14. Holmes, *The Common Law*, 133.

15. Vincent Blasi, "Holmes and the Marketplace of Ideas," *Supreme Court Review* 1 (2004): 20.

16. Blasi, "Holmes and the Marketplace of Ideas," 1–46, 19.

17. Oliver Wendell Holmes Jr., to Morris Cohen, February 5, 1919, in *The Essential Holmes: Selections from the Letters, Speeches, Judicial Opinions, and Other Writings of Oliver Wendell Holmes, Jr.*, ed. Richard Posner (Chicago: University of Chicago Press, 1992), 110.

18. Budiansky, *Oliver Wendell Holmes*, 83.
19. Blasi, "Holmes and the Marketplace of Ideas," 19.
20. Blasi, "Holmes and the Marketplace of Ideas," 17.
21. Oliver Wendell Holmes Jr. to Harold Laski, February 1, 1919, in Posner, *The Essential Holmes*, 265.
22. John Dewey, *Democracy and Education* (1916; University Park: Pennsylvania State University Press, 2001) 345.
23. Dewey, *Democracy and Education*, 344.
24. William James, *A Pluralistic Universe* (Cambridge, MA: Harvard University Press, 1977), 26.
25. In Stanley Fish's words, science produces truth that "remains contingent; it can always be upended when researchers, for any number of reasons, many of them unpredictable, go down another path at the end of which they find a new truth." Stanley Fish, *The First: How to Think about Hate Speech, Campus Speech, Religious Speech, Fake News, Post-Truth, and Donald Trump* (New York: Atria/One Signal, 2019), 172.
26. Oliver Wendell Holmes Jr. to Frederick Pollock, February 17, 1928, quoted in White, *Justice Oliver Wendell Holmes*, 389.
27. *The Western Maid*, 257 U.S. 419, 432 (1922).
28. Oliver Wendell Holmes Jr. to Harold Laski, January 29, 1926, quoted in White, *Justice Oliver Wendell Holmes*, 386.
29. *Black & White Taxicab & Transfer Co. v. Brown & Yellow Taxicab & Transfer Co.*, 276 U.S. 518, 533, (1928) (Holmes, J., dissenting).
30. *Black & White Taxicab & Transfer Co.*, 533.
31. U.S. Const. art. I, § 10.
32. James Fieser, "Moore, Spencer, and the Naturalistic Fallacy," *History of Philosophy Quarterly* 10 (1993): 271.
33. *Lochner v. New York*, 198 U.S. 45, 198 (1905) (Holmes, J., dissenting).
34. For elaboration, see Michael J. Glennon, *The Fog of Law: Pragmatism, Security, and International Law* (Stanford, CA: Stanford University Press, 2010), 3.
35. Oliver Wendell Holmes, "Natural Law," *Harvard Law Review* 32, no. 1 (1918): 40, in Posner, *The Essential Holmes*, 181.
36. Richard Rorty, *Philosophy and Social Hope* (London: Penguin, 1999), xxvii.
37. On probable future consequences, see generally Gerald D. Rosenberg, *The Hollow Hope: Can Courts Bring about Social Change?* (Chicago: University of Chicago Press, 1991). Consequences are assessed by weighing costs against benefits, by balancing one set of risks against opposing risks, by focusing more on a knowable present than on a speculative future, by recognizing trade-offs rather than ignoring them. How that will be done depends upon the relative power of pertinent actors. Pragmatists thus focus upon situationality and law's inevitable contingency. "The mark of a master," Holmes wrote, "is that the facts which before lay scattered in an inorganic mass, when he shoots through them the magnetic current of his thought, leap into an organic order, and live and bear fruit." Oliver Wendell Holmes, "Oration before the Harvard Law School Association, at Cambridge, Nov. 5, 1886," in Posner, *The Essential Holmes*, 225.
38. Holmes, "Natural Law," 40, in Posner, *The Essential Holmes*, 181.

39. Oliver Wendell Holmes Jr. to John C. H. Wu, June 16, 1923, in *Justice Oliver Wendell Holmes: His Book Notices and Uncollected Letters and Papers*, ed. Harry C. Shriver (New York: Central Book Company, 1936), 164–65, quoted in Blasi, "Holmes and the Marketplace of Ideas," 14n42.

40. Holmes, "Natural Law," 40, in Posner, *The Essential Holmes,* 181.

41. Oliver Wendell Holmes, "The Path of the Law," *Harvard Law Review* 10 (1897), in Posner, *The Essential Holmes*, 167.

42. Holmes, "Natural Law," 40, in Posner, *The Essential Holmes,* 180.

43. Holmes, *The Common Law*, 5.

44. Budiansky, *Oliver Wendell Holmes*, 149.

45. Baker, *The Justice from Beacon Hill* (New York: Harper Collins, 1981), 76; *see also* Budiansky, *Oliver Wendell Holmes*, 149.

46. Oliver Wendell Holmes Jr. to Frederick Pollock, August 30, 1929, quoted in Louis Menand, *The Metaphysical Club: A Story of Ideas in America* (New York: Farrar, Straus and Giroux, 2001), 217.

47. Holmes to Pollock, August 30, 1929, quoted in Menand, *The Metaphysical Club*, 62.

48. John Inazu, "Holmes, Humility, and How Not to Kill Each Other," *Notre Dame Law Review* 94, no. 4 (2019): 1631–32.

49. John Stuart Mill, *On Liberty* (Kitchener: Batoche Books, 2001), 19–21.

50. Karl R. Popper and E. H. Gombrich, *The Open Society and Its Enemies* (Princeton, NJ: Princeton University Press, 2013), 491.

51. Frederick F. Schauer, *Free Speech: A Philosophical Enquiry* (Cambridge: Cambridge University Press, 1982), 25.

52. I do not agree that "it seems clear that a rejection of determinism is implicit in any intelligible version of liberalism," as Schauer writes in *Free Speech* (212n2). A determinist can still object to being gagged.

53. Popper and Gombrich, *The Open Society and Its Enemies*, 490

54. Popper and Gombrich, *The Open Society and Its Enemies*, 505.

55. Steven Smith, "Skepticism, Tolerance, and Truth in the Theory of Free Expression," *Southern California Law Review* 60 (2012): 684.

56. Budiansky, *Oliver Wendell Holmes*, 272.

57. Budiansky, *Oliver Wendell Holmes*, 397.

58. Oliver Wendell Holmes Jr. to Harold J. Laski, October 24, 1930, in *The Correspondence of Mr. Justice Holmes and Harold Laski, 1916–1935*, vol. 2: *Holmes-Laski Letters*, ed. Mark DeWolfe Howe (Cambridge, MA: Harvard University Press), 1291.

59. Holmes, *The Path of the Law*, 167.

Chapter 5

1. Frederick Schauer, "Every Possible Use of Language?," in *The Free Speech Century*, ed. Lee C. Bollinger and Geoffrey R. Stone, eds. (New York: Oxford University Press, 2019), 13.

2. John Hart Ely, *Democracy and Distrust* (Cambridge, MA: Harvard University Press, 1980), 109.

3. *Schenck v. United States*, 249 U.S. 47, 249 (1919).

4. *Missouri v. Holland,* 252 U.S. 416 (1920).

5. See Michael J. Glennon and Robert D. Sloane, *Foreign Affairs Federalism: The Myth of National Exclusivity* (New York: Oxford University Press, 2016), 185–244.

6. *Missouri v. Holland,* 433.

7. The dispute centers on questions such as whether subsequent punishment of seditious libel was permissible at the time of its ratification. See generally David A. Strauss, "Freedom of Speech and the Common-Law Constitution," in *Eternally Vigilant: Free Speech in the Modern Era*, ed. Lee C. Bollinger and Geoffrey R. Stone (New York: Oxford University Press: 2002). English law at the time of the Amendment's drafting, according to Blackstone, prohibited prior restraints on publication but not subsequent punishment for that same publication. Prior restraints had earlier most often taken the form of licensing requirements that the government imposed on the press. But licensing requirements were by then a thing of the past in England and had never been imposed in its North American colonies. The Amendment's sponsors would not likely have modified the Constitution to address what they knew to be a nonproblem. The historic confusion is highlighted by the fact that the infamous Sedition Act of 1798, under which about two dozen Jeffersonian newspaper editors were prosecuted, was enacted by a Congress that included many supporters of the Amendment, which after all had been approved only seven years earlier. (Madison, its most influential backer, considered the Sedition Act invalid.) Still, the fairest assessment of their specific intent is probably, as Strauss concludes, that "it simply is not clear what the Framers thought" (41).

8. Leonard W. Levy, *Original Intent and the Framers' Constitution* (New York: Macmillan, 1988), 262.

9. Levy, *Original Intent,* 266.

10. Benjamin Franklin, "An Account of the Supremest Court of Judicature," in *The Writings of Benjamin Franklin*, ed. Albert H. Smyth (New York: Macmillan, 1907), 67.

11. Geoffrey R. Stone, "The Origins of the 'Bad Tendency' Test: Free Speech in Wartime," *Supreme Court Review* 2002 (2002): 414.

12. Oliver Wendell Holmes Jr. to Zechariah Chafee, June 12, 1922, quoted in Thomas Healy, *The Great Dissent* (New York: Metropolitan Books, 2013), 243.

13. Thomas Healy, "Anxiety and Influence: Learned Hand and the Making of a Free Speech Dissent. A Decision for the Ages: A Symposium Marking the Centenary of *Masses Publishing Co. v. Patten*," *Arizona State Law Journal* 50 (2018): 805–8.

14. *Abrams v. United States*, 250 U.S. 616, 624–31 (1919) (Holmes, O. W., Dissenting).

15. *Abrams,* 628.

16. "If there was a single, inspired moment at which the central feature of the American system of freedom of expression was decreed," David Strauss writes, "it was not the adoption of the First Amendment; it was Holmes's dissent in *Abrams*" ("Freedom of Speech," 49).

17. Vincent A. Blasi, "Rights Skepticism and Majority Rule at the Birth of the Modern First Amendment," in Bollinger and Stone, *The Free Speech Century*, 24.

18. Louis Menand, *The Metaphysical Club: A Story of Ideas in America* (New York: Farrar, Straus and Giroux, 2001), 431. The key to Holmes's civil liberties opinions is that he thought not in terms of the individual but only in terms of aggregate social forces (65). It is not clear, however, why a focus on society versus the individual would necessarily yield different results, since society comprises aggregated individuals who partake in society's rights.

19. Vincent Blasi, "Holmes and the Marketplace of Ideas," *Supreme Court Review* 2004, no. 1 (2004): 1–46. "A political regime that discourages and punishes free thought reduces the incidence of variation in the realm of ideas," Blasi writes, "variation both in the production of new ideas and in the embrace of politically unpopular ideas."

20. Stephen Budiansky, *Oliver Wendell Holmes: A Life in War, Law, and Ideas* (New York: W. W. Norton, 2019), 460.

21. Federalist 51 (James Madison).

22. Strauss, "Freedom of Speech," 43.

23. Levy, *Original Intent*, 147.

24. Leonard Levy notes Blackstone's belief that "liberty of the press is indeed essential to the nature of a free state." Its essentiality, Levy continues, "derived also from the fact that the press had become the tribune of the people by sitting in judgment on the conduct of public officials. A free press meant the press as the Fourth Estate or, rather, in the American scheme, an informal or extraconstitutional fourth branch that functioned as part of the intricate system of checks and balances that exposed public mismanagement and kept power fragmented, manageable, and accountable. . . . Freedom of the press had become part of the matrix for the functioning of popular government and the protection of civil liberties" (273).

25. *Myers v. United States*, 272 U.S. 52, 293 (1926) (Brandies, J., Dissenting).

26. *Youngstown Sheet & Tube Co. v. Sawyer*, 343 U.S. 579, 641 (1952) (Jackson, J., Concurring): "The example of such unlimited executive power that must have most impressed the forefathers was the prerogative exercised by George III, and the description of its evils in the Declaration of Independence leads me to doubt that they were creating their new Executive in his image."

27. Learned Hand, *The Spirit of Liberty: Papers and Addresses of Learned Hand*, ed. Irving Dilliard, 3d ed. (New York: Alfred A. Knopf, 1974), 190.

28. "Freedom of expression," in Tom Ginsburg's words, "is at the core of liberal constitutional democracy, which presumes a set of meaningful political choices. . . . Without robust freedom of expression, alternative policies cannot be offered. Without the ability to express criticism of policies and leaders, democratic accountability fails. Without the ability to speak, political organization is hampered and elections cannot provide for meaningful choices. And without the ability to call attention to the violations of constitutional rights, their protection becomes unlikely." Tom Ginsburg, "Freedom of Expression Abroad: The State of Play," in Bollinger and Stone, *The Free Speech Century*, 193.

Chapter 6

1. Louis Menand, *American Studies* (New York: Farrar, Straus and Giroux, 2002), 50.

2. Holmes appeared to adopt this view in dissent in *Gitlow v. New York*, 268 U.S. 652 (1925), where he wrote, "If in the long run the beliefs expressed in proletarian dictatorship are destined to be accepted by the dominant forces of the community, the only meaning of free speech is that they should be given their chance and have their way" (673).

3. Oliver Wendell Holmes, *Harvard Law Review* 32, no. 1 (1918): 40, in, *The Essential Holmes: Selections from the Letters, Speeches, Judicial Opinions, and Other Writings of Oliver Wendell Holmes, Jr.*, ed. Richard Posner (Chicago: University of Chicago Press, 1992), 181.

4. Holmes, "Natural Law," 40–44, in Posner, *The Essential Holmes*, 181. In the sentence following the sentence quoted, Holmes refers to "cosmic truth, if there is such a thing." In the sentence quoted above, the crucial words are *in that*. Holmes is saying that *the one specific argument* that he has been considering (that people's "attitudes" are a function of early associations, temperament, and a craving for certainty) provides no basis for believing in objective truth. He is not rejecting all such arguments across the board.

5. John Hart Ely, *Democracy and Distrust* (Cambridge, MA: Harvard University Press, 1980), 54.

6. "Actually," Judge Richard Posner writes, "that is not such a difficult question." He continues: "If there is no truth out there, this should make us particularly wary of people who claim to have found the truth and who argue that further inquiry would be futile or subversive and therefore should be forbidden. If there is no objective truth, moreover, this makes it all the more important to maintain the conditions necessary for the unforced inquiry required to challenge and defeat all those false claims to have found the truth at last." Richard Posner, "A Pragmatist Manifesto," in *Pragmatism: A Reader*, ed. Louis Menand (New York: Vintage Books, 1997), 432.

7. For discussion of these arguments, see Vincent Blasi, "Holmes and the Marketplace of Ideas," *Supreme Court Review* 2004, no. 1 (2004): 6.

8. Burt Neuborne, "Blues for the Left Hand: A Critique of Cass Sunstein's 'Democracy and the Problem of Free Speech,'" *University of Chicago Law Review* 62 (1995): 439.

9. Schauer makes a similar point: "As individuals are fallible, so too are governments fallible and prone to error. Just as we are properly skeptical about our own power always to distinguish truth from falsity, so should we be even more skeptical of the power of any governmental authority to do it for us." Frederick F. Schauer, *Free Speech: A Philosophical Enquiry* (Cambridge: Cambridge University Press, 1982), 34.

10. See generally Michael J. Glennon, *National Security and Double Government* (New York: Oxford University Press, 2015), 81–88.

11. Neuborne, "Blues for the Left Hand," 440.

12. Joel Feinberg put it this way: "There are serious risks involved in granting any mere man or group of men the power to draw the line between those opinions that are known infallibly to be true and those not so known, in order to ban expression of the

former. Surely, if there is one thing that is *not* infallibly known, it is how to draw *that* line." Joel Feinberg, *Limits to the Free Expression of Opinion in Philosophy of Law*, 2nd ed., ed. J. Feinberg and H. Gross (Encino, CA: Dickenson, 1980), 192.

13. Schauer summarizes it well: "Freedom of speech is based in large part on a distrust of the ability of government to make the necessary distinctions, a distrust of governmental determinations of truth and falsity, and appreciation of the fallibility of political leaders, and a somewhat deeper distrust of governmental power in a more general sense" (*Free Speech*, 86).

14. Again, Schauer: "Throughout history the process of regulating speech has been marked with what we now see to be fairly plain errors. Whether it be the condemnation of Galileo, religious persecution in the sixteenth and seventeenth centuries, the extensive history of prosecution for expressing seditious views of those now regarded as patriots, or the banning of numerous admittedly great works of art because someone thought them obscene, acts of suppression that have been proved erroneous seem to represent a disproportionate percentage of the governmental mistakes of the past" (*Free Speech*, 81).

15. Yascha Mounk puts it succinctly: "[T]he problem is that no authority can be trusted with the power of forbidding all noxious statements. Whether out of error or self-interest, any institution with the right to censor will sooner or later start banning statements that do have real value." Yascha Mounk, *The People vs. Democracy: Why Our Freedom Is in Danger and How to Save It* (Cambridge, MA: Harvard University Press, 2018), 205.

16. John Milton, *Areopagitica, with a Commentary by Sir Richard C. Jebb and with Supplementary Material* (Cambridge: Cambridge University Press, 1918). "Though all the winds of doctrine were let loose to play upon the earth, so Truth be in the field, we do injuriously, by licensing and prohibiting, to misdoubt her strength. Let her and Falsehood grapple; who ever knew Truth put to the worse, in a free and open encounter?" (58). "Error of opinion," said Jefferson, "may be tolerated where reason is left free to combat it." Thomas Jefferson, "First Inaugural Address," Avalon Project at Yale Law School, Lillian Goldman Library, accessed August 13, 2022, https://avalon.law.yale.edu/19th_century/jefinau1.asp.

17. For a discussion of the digital marketplace see Chapters 11 and 12. "Deep fakes" and other technological innovations can, for a time, catch viewers unaware—but only for a time, until skepticism catches up; the similar possibility of audio splicing has been around for nearly a century, with few pernicious results.

18. In fact, the empirical basis for some supposed cognitive biases is questionable. It's widely believed, for example, that people gravitate toward echo chambers that reinforce their own views and exclude disconfirming information and opinions. As Timothy Garton Ash has pointed out, however, Oxford University researchers have found that nearly four out of five of those surveyed in a number of developed countries expressed a preference for hearing views other than their own. Subsequent research in Italy, Germany, and France confirmed those results. Timothy Garton Ash, *Free Speech: Ten Principles for a Connected World* (New Haven, CT: Yale University Press, 2016), 197–98. This is not to say that informational bubbles pose no problem

for democracy. As discussed below, they do indeed—but as often as not, they are caused by ham-handed and inevitably ineffectual efforts at speech control—by porous censorship that creates disparate, contending cohorts of informed and uninformed citizens.

19. It is insufficient "to show that hate speech inflicts severe and distinctive harms. In addition, one needs to show that legal regulation of hate speech is an effective means of addressing these harms. It is also unnecessary to show that such regulation is unlikely to have other hidden costs." Alon Harel, "Hate Speech," in *The Oxford Handbook of Freedom of Speech*, ed. Adriene Stone and Frederick Schauer (New York: Oxford University Press, 2021), 291 (summarizing an argument of opponents of hate speech regulation).

20. See Tim Wu, "Is the First Amendment Obsolete?," in *The Free Speech Century*, ed. Lee C. Bollinger and Geoffrey R. Stone (New York: Oxford University Press, 2019), 280 (describing the "Streisand effect," under which the act of trying to suppress something makes many more people choose to see it). See also Garton Ash, *Free Speech*, 296.

21. Harel, "Hate Speech," 467n58.

22. For a classic study, see Stephen Worchel and Susan Arnold, "The Effects of Censorship and Attractiveness of the Censor on Attitude Change," *Journal of Experimental Social Psychology* 9 (1973): 365.

23. For a comprehensive review of the literature, see Christina Steindl, Eva Jonas, Sandra Sittenthaler, Eva Traut-Mattausch, and Jeff Greenberg, "Understanding Psychological Reactance," *Zeitschrift für Psychologie* 223, no. 4 (2015): 205–14, doi:10.1027/2151-2604/a000222.

24. Steindl et al., "Understanding Psychological Reactance," 210.

25. Fearing that the use of culturally specific irony and humor (e.g., "Let's Go Brandon!") might evade censors, a piece published by the World Economic Forum proposes the increased use of artificial intelligence to ferret out such efforts. Inbal Goldberger, "The Solution to Online Abuse? AI Plus Human Intelligence," World Economic Forum, August 10, 2022, https://www.weforum.org/agenda/2022/08/online-abuse-artificial-intelligence-human-input/.

26. See Eric Larson, *The Splendid and the Vile: A Saga of Churchill, Family, and Defiance during the Blitz* (New York: Crown, 2020), 278–79.

27. See William R. Hobbes and Margaret E. Roberts. "How Sudden Censorship Can Increase Access to Information," *American Political Science Review* 112 (2018): 621.

28. Abby Ohlheiser, "Twitter's Ban Almost Doubled Attention for Biden Story," *MIT Technology Review*, October 16, 2020, https://www.technologyreview.com/2020/10/16/1010644/twitter-ban-hunter-biden-emails-backfires/.

29. Amanda Watson, "Pauw's New Book Is in the Public Interest," *The Citizen*, November 6, 2017, https://www.citizen.co.za/news/south-africa/1717182/pauws-new-book-is-in-the-public-interest/.

30. Interview with Bob Mankoff, "Copenhagen, Speech, and Violence," *New Yorker*, February 14, 2015, https://www.newyorker.com/news/news-desk/copenhagen-speech-violence.

31. See generally Jonathan Turley, "Harm and Hegemony: The Decline of Free Speech in the United States," *Harvard Journal of Law & Policy* 45 (2022): 578.

32. Jennifer Pan and Alexandra Siegel, "How Saudi Crackdowns Fail to Silence Online Dissent," *American Political Science Review* 114 (2020): 109.

33. Turley, "Harm and Hegemony," 578.

34. David Kemp and Emily Ekins, "Poll: 75% Don't Trust Social Media to Make Fair Content Moderation Decisions, 60% Want More Control over What They See," Cato Institute, December 15, 2021, https://www.cato.org/survey-reports/poll-75-dont-trust-social-media-make-fair-content-moderation-decisions-60-want-more.

35. "Those who make peaceful revolution impossible will make violent revolution inevitable." John F. Kennedy, speech at the White House, March 13, 1962, in Oxford Essential Quotations, ed. Susan Ratcliffe, 5th ed., online version 2017, https://www.oxfordreference.com/display/10.1093/acref/9780191843730.001.0001/q-oro-ed5-00006245.

36. Toni Massaro, "Equality and Freedom of Expression: The Hate Speech Dilemma," *William & Mary Law Review* 32 (1991): 211, 233.

37. Richard Milne, "Kaja Kallas: 'There Is a Certain Naivety towards Russia,'" *Financial Times*, February 18, 2022, https://www.ft.com/content/098ba985-1284-46c6-9abe-f626fa9e47f0.

38. François Furet points out that, under Stalin, the Soviet Union was able to maintain "an airtight space, which nothing could either leak out of or seep into without the police's prior knowledge." Under Khrushchev, however, the Soviets moved from the totalitarian stage to a more lenient system, in which "strange voices were allowed to be heard, voices thought to have been lost forever. The regime had lost the almost perfect power it had held over the vast buzz of self-celebration that had been issuing from the USSR for more than twenty-five years." The "new visibility of persecution," Furet writes, accelerated the regime's downfall. François Furet, *The Passing of an Illusion: The Idea of Communism in the Twentieth Century* (Chicago: University of Chicago Press, 1999), 481–82.

39. Carl Auerbach, "The Communist Control Act of 1954: A Proposed Legal-Political Theory of Free Speech," *University of Chicago Law Review* 23 (1956): 218–19, 220.

40. *Whitney v. California*, 274 U.S. 357, 377 (1927).

41. *N.Y. Times Co. v. Sullivan*, 376 U.S. 254, 270 (1964).

42. See Nico Perrino, Chris Maltby, and Aaron Reese, dirs., *Mighty Ira*, Philadelphia, PA: Foundation for Individual Rights and Expression, 2020.

43. Johnathan Elliot, *The Debates in the Several State Conventions*, vol. 4 of *The Debates in the Several State Conventions on the Adoption of the Federal Constitution* (Philadelphia, PA: Lippincott, 1876), 571.

Chapter 7

1. John Stuart Mill, *On Liberty* (Kitchener: Batoche Books, 2001), 13.

2. He wrote, "Give *me* the liberty to know, to utter, and to argue freely, according to conscience, above all liberties." John Milton, *Areopagitica, with a Commentary by Sir Richard C. Jebb and with Supplementary Material* (Cambridge: Cambridge University Press, 1918), 57.

3. "[E]veryone is by absolute natural right the master of his own thoughts" and must be permitted to "think what he will and say what he thinks." Benedictus de Spinoza, *The Political Works: The Tractatus Theologico-Politicus, and the Tractatus Politicus in Full* (Oxford: Clarendon Press, 1958), https://books.google.com/books/about/The_Political_Works_the_Tractatus_Theolo.html?id=VHSFAAAAMAAJ.

4. "I have sworn upon the alter of God," he wrote, "eternal hostility against every form of tyranny over the mind of man." Thomas Jefferson to Benjamin Rush, September 23, 1800, American History, http://www.let.rug.nl/usa/presidents/thomas-jefferson/letters-of-thomas-jefferson/jefl134.php.

5. *West Virginia State Board of Education v. Barnette*, 319 U.S. 624, 642 (1943).

6. Frederick Schauer, *Free Speech: A Philosophical Enquiry* (Cambridge: Cambridge University Press, 1982), 53.

7. Mill, *On Liberty*, 16.

8. Alexander Meiklejohn, *Political Freedom* (New York: Harper and Brothers, 1960), 123.

9. *Brandenburg v. Ohio*, 395 U.S. 444 (1969).

10. *Schenck v. United States*, 249 U.S. 47, 52 (1919).

11. *Debs v. United States*, 249 U.S. 211 (1919).

12. *Dennis v. United States*, 341 U.S. 494 (1951).

13. *Brandenburg*. 454 (Douglas, J., concurring), describing the plurality's version of the test in *Dennis* as "twisted and perverted."

14. *Yates v. United States*, 353 U.S. 298 (1957).

15. *Scales v. United States*, 367 U.S. 203, 252 n.27 (1961).

16. *Abrams v. United States*, 250 U.S. 616, 630 (1919).

17. *Brandenburg*, 447.

18. *Dennis*, 509.

19. *Dennis*, 570 (Jackson, J. Concurring).

20. *Dennis*, 585 (Douglass, J. Dissenting).

21. Carl Auerbach, "The Communist Control Act of 1954: A Proposed Legal-Political Theory of Free Speech," *University of Chicago Law Review* 23 (1956): 186.

22. Auerbach, "The Communist Control Act," 197.

23. For a convincing response to such suggestions, see the argument of Greg Lukianoff and Nadine Strossen in Eugene Volokh, "Would Censorship Have Stopped the Rise of the Nazis?," Volokh Conspiracy, April 27, 2022, https://reason.com/volokh/2022/04/27/would-censorship-have-stopped-the-rise-of-the-nazis/.

24. *Dennis*, 582.

25. See, e.g., Mala Szalavitz, "10 Ways We Get the Odds Wrong," *Psychology Today*, June 2016, https://www.psychologytoday.com/us/articles/200801/10-ways-we-get-the-odds-wrong: "Fear hits primitive brain areas to produce reflexive reactions before the situation is even consciously perceived. Because fear strengthens memory, catastrophes such as earthquakes, plane crashes, and terrorist incidents completely capture our attention. As a result, we overestimate the odds of dreadful but infrequent events and underestimate how risky ordinary events are."

26. Daniel A. Farber, *The First Amendment*, 5th ed. (St. Paul, MN: Foundation Press, 2003), 81.

27. For a summary of recent literature on basic principles of organizational behavior, see Michael J. Glennon, *National Security and Double Government* (New York: Oxford University Press, 2015), 81–85.

28. Paul Slovic, *The Perception of Risk* (Abingdon: Routledge, 2000).

29. Slovic, *The Perception of Risk,* 392.

30. Erich Fromm, *Escape from Freedom* (New York: Holt Paperbacks, 1994), 64.

31. Fromm, *Escape from Freedom,* 65.

32. The First Amendment, Stone writes, "places out of bounds any law that attempts to freeze public opinion at a particular moment in time." Geoffrey R. Stone, "Dialogue," in *Eternally Vigilant: Free Speech in the Modern Era*, ed. Lee C. Bollinger and Geoffrey R. Stone (New York: Oxford University Press, 2002), 29.

33. Mill, *On Liberty*, 19.

34. Jacob Mchangama, *Free Speech: A History from Socrates to Social Media* (New York: Basic Books, 2022), 3.

35. Mchangama, *Free Speech,* 274.

36. See also Greg Lukianoff, "The Eternally Radical Idea: Dangerous Ideas," Fire, May 7, 2021, https://www.thefire.org/eric-berkowitzs-new-book-dangerous-ideas-is-a-masterpiece-but-i-have-some-quibbles/.

37. Mchangama, *Free Speech*, 4.

38. See Herbert Marcuse, "Repressive Tolerance," in *A Critique of Pure Tolerance* (Boston: Beacon Press, 1955). Marcuse argues that "if democratic tolerance had been withdrawn . . . mankind would have had a chance of avoiding Auschwitz and a World War" (109).

39. Alexander Meiklejohn, Testimony presented before the Subcommittee on Constitutional Rights, U.S. Senate Committee on the Judiciary, November 14, 1955, in Vincent Blasi, *Freedom of Speech in the History of Ideas* (St. Paul, MN: West, 2016), 526.

40. Schauer, *Free Speech*, 82.

Chapter 8

1. *Schenck v. United States*, 249 U.S. 47, 52 (1919).

2. Geoffrey R. Stone, "Dialogue," in *Eternally Vigilant: Free Speech in the Modern Era*, ed. Lee C. Bollinger and Geoffrey R. Stone (New York: Oxford University Press, 2002), 19.

3. Daniel A. Farber, *The First Amendment,* 5th ed. (St. Paul, MN: Foundation Press, 2003), 17.

4. *Brandenburg v. Ohio*, 395 U.S. 444 (1969).

5. *Collin v. Smith*, 578 F.2d 1197 (7th Cir.), cert. denied 439 U.S. 916 (1978).

6. *Collin v. Smith*, 578 F.2d 1197, 1205 (7th Cir. 1978).

7. *R.A.V. v. City of St. Paul,* 505 U.S. 377 (1992).

8. *Snyder v. Phelps*, 562 U.S. 443 (2011).

9. *Texas v. Johnson,* 491 U.S. 397 (1989).

10. *Cohen v. California,* 403 U.S. 15 (1971).

11. Nadine Strossen, *Hate: Why We Should Resist It with Free Speech, Not Censorship* (New York: Oxford University Press, 2018), 14.

12. *Chaplinsky v. New Hampshire*, 315 U.S. 568, 572 (1942).

13. *Virginia v. Black*, 538 U.S. 343, 347 (2003).

14. *N.Y. Times Co. v. Sullivan*, 376 U.S. 254 (1964).

15. Alon Harel, "Hate Speech," in *The Oxford Handbook of Freedom of Speech*, ed. Adriene Stone and Frederick Schauer (New York: Oxford University Press, 2021), 459.

16. *Police Dept. of City of Chicago v. Mosley,* 408 U.S. 92 (1972).

17. "To permit the continued building of our politics and culture, and to assure self-fulfillment for each individual, our people are guaranteed the right to express any thought, free from government censorship. The essence of this forbidden censorship is content control. Any restriction on expressive activity because of its content would completely undercut the 'profound national commitment to the principle that debate on public issues should be uninhibited, robust, and wide-open'" (*Mosley,* 96).

18. "[G]overnment may not grant the use of a forum to people whose views it finds acceptable, but deny use to those wishing to express less favored or more controversial views. And it may not select which issues are worth discussing or debating in public facilities. There is an 'equality of status in the field of ideas,' and government must afford all points of view an equal opportunity to be heard" (*Mosley,* 96).

19. In *Texas*, the Court struck down the Texas law that prohibited flag desecration because, the Court said, it punished only destroying the flag to convey an unpatriotic message but not, for example, the burning of soiled flags in ceremonial disposals. It permitted use of the flag as a symbol "only in one direction," for patriotic messages, thereby prescribing "what shall be orthodox" (417). "If there is a bedrock principle underlying the First Amendment, it is that the Government may not prohibit the expression of an idea simply because society finds the idea itself offensive or disagreeable. . . . [T]he Government may not prohibit expression simply because it disagrees with its message" (417). In *Texas* the Court relied on an earlier case, *Boos v. Barry*, 485 U.S. 312 (1988), in which it had struck down a law prohibiting "the display of any sign within 50 feet of a foreign embassy if that sign tends to bring that foreign government into 'public odium' or 'public disrepute.'" That the law was justified by international law obligations, the Court said, did not mean that it was content-neutral.

20. In the Skokie case, the court of appeals rejected the city's argument concerning the march's traumatizing impact. Quoting an earlier Supreme Court case, it reiterated, "[A]ny shock effect . . . must be attributed to the content of the ideas expressed. It is firmly settled that under our Constitution the public expression of ideas may not be prohibited merely because the ideas are themselves offensive to some of their hearers." *Street v. New York*, 394 U.S. 576, 592 (1969).

21. In *Snyder*, the Supreme Court disallowed the suit, finding that the hurtfulness of the signs did not alter the fact that they addressed issues of public concern: "Speech is powerful. It can stir people to action, move them to tears of both joy and sorrow, and—as it did here—inflict great pain. On the facts before us, we cannot react to that pain by punishing the speaker. As a Nation we have chosen a different course—to protect even hurtful speech on public issues to ensure that we do not stifle public debate" (461).

22. In *Cohen*, the Court overturned Cohen's conviction for wearing the offensive jacket, emphasizing the difficulty of distinguishing style from viewpoint: "Surely the State has no right to cleanse public debate to the point where it is grammatically palatable to the most squeamish among us. Yet no readily ascertainable general principle exists for stopping short of that result were we to affirm the judgment below. For, while the particular four-letter word being litigated here is perhaps more distasteful than most others of its genre, it is nevertheless often true that one man's vulgarity is another's lyric. Indeed, we think it is largely because governmental officials cannot make principled distinctions in this area that the Constitution leaves matters of taste and style so largely to the individual" (*Cohen*, 25). The issue, the Court said, was whether "the States, acting as guardians of public morality, may properly remove this offensive word from the public vocabulary" (22).

23. In *R.A.V.*, the Court held that the St. Paul ordinance in question violated the prohibition against viewpoint discrimination because, in focusing only on racist speech, it was "based on hostility—or favoritism—towards the underlying message expressed" (386). This the First Amendment forbids. The First Amendment "prevents government from proscribing speech because of its disapproval of the ideas expressed" (382).

24. Burt Neuborne, "Blues for the Left Hand: A Critique of Cass Sunstein's 'Democracy and the Problem of Free Speech,'" *University of Chicago Law Review* 62 (1995): 440.

25. Fredrick Douglass to Hugh Auld, October 4, 1857, Gilder Lehrman Collection, https://www.gilderlehrman.org/history-resources/spotlight-primary-source/i-love-you-hate-slavery-frederick-douglass-his-former.

26. *Papachristou v. City of Jacksonville*, 405 U.S. 156 (1972).

27. *Papachristou*, 171.

28. *Papachristou*, 162.

29. "Those generally implicated by the imprecise terms of the ordinance—poor people, nonconformists, dissenters, idlers—may be required to comport themselves according to the lifestyle deemed appropriate by the Jacksonville police and the courts. Where, as here, there are no standards governing the exercise of the discretion granted by the ordinance, the scheme permits and encourages an arbitrary and discriminatory enforcement of the law. It furnishes a convenient tool for 'harsh and discriminatory enforcement by local prosecuting officials, against particular groups deemed to merit their displeasure.' . . . The implicit presumption in these generalized vagrancy standards—that crime is being nipped in the bud—is too extravagant to deserve extended treatment" (*Papachristou*, 162).

30. See generally Michael J. Glennon, *The Fog of Law: Pragmatism, Security, and International Law* (Chicago: Stanford University Press, 2010), 187–88.

31. "It will be of little avail to the people that the laws are made by men of their own choice if the laws be so voluminous that they cannot be read, or so incoherent that they cannot be understood; if they be repealed or revised before they are promulgated, or undergo such incessant changes that no man, who knows what the law is today, can guess what it will be tomorrow. Law is defined to be a rule of action; but how can that be a rule, which is little known, and less fixed?" James Madison, Federalist 62, https://avalon.law.yale.edu/18th_century/fed62.asp.

32. *Kolender v. Lawson*, 461 U.S. 352 (1983). See generally Andrew E. Goldsmith, "The Void for Vagueness Doctrine in the Supreme Court, Revisited," *American Journal of Criminal Law* 30 (2003): 279.
33. *Connally v. Gen. Constr. Co.*, 269 U.S. 385, 391 (1926).
34. *United States v. Reese*, 92 U.S. 214, 219 (1875). The Court continued, "Every man should be able to know with certainty when he is committing a crime" (220).
35. *Jordan v. DeGeorge*, 341 U.S. 223, 231–32 (1951); see also *Giaccio v. Pennsylvania*, 382 U.S. 399, 402–3 (1966) ("[A] law fails to meet the requirements of the Due Process Clause if it is so vague and standardless that it leaves the public uncertain as to the conduct it prohibits or leaves judges and jurors free to decide, without any legally fixed standards, what is prohibited and what is not in each particular case.").
36. *Hill v. Colorado*, 530 U.S. 703, 732 (2000).
37. *Kolender,* 358 (citations omitted).
38. *Baggett v. Bullitt*, 377 U.S. 360, 366 (1964).
39. *Baggett*, 366.
40. Strossen, *Hate*, 14.
41. Strossen, *Hate*, 14.
42. See Eugene Volokh, "The Mechanics of the Slippery Slope," *Harvard Law Review* 116 (2003): 1026.
43. See generally Geoffrey Stone, *Perilous Times: Free Speech in Wartime: From the Sedition Act of 1798 to the War on Terrorism* (New York: W. W. Norton, 2004).
44. Glen Greenwald, "In Europe, Hate Speech Laws Are Often Used to Suppress and Punish Left-Wing Viewpoints," *The Intercept*, May 30, 2017, https://theintercept.com/2017/08/29/in-europe-hate-speech-laws-are-often-used-to-suppress-and-punish-left-wing-viewpoints/.
45. *Boos,* 322, quoting *Hustler Magazine, Inc. v. Falwell*, 485 U.S. 55, 56 (1988).
46. He continues, "Assuming the state cannot ban all language that even the most squeamish person would object to, there seems to be no principled line between acceptable and unacceptable speech. . . . [L]anguage serves to communicate not only ideas but emotions, and purging the language of offensive words would impair that emotive function. Finally, banning certain words would have the effect of banning associated ideas. Indeed, the government might use the censorship of particular words as a pretext for eliminating certain *ideas*" (Farber, *The First Amendment*, 120–21).
47. John Hart Ely, *Democracy and Distrust: A Theory of Judicial Review* (Cambridge, MA: Harvard University Press, 1980), 76.
48. *United States v. Carolene Products,* 304 U.S. 144, 153–53 n.4 (1938).
49. Ely, *Democracy and Distrust*, 86–87.
50. Quoted in Strossen, *Hate*, 81.
51. Michael W. McConnell, "You Can't Say That," *New York Times*, June 22, 2012, https://www.nytimes.com/2012/06/24/books/review/the-harm-in-hate-speech-by-jeremy-waldron.html?nl=books&emc=booksupdateema4_20120622..
52. Stone, "Dialogue," 11.
53. Farber, *The First Amendment*, 131.
54. John Lewis, "Extended Interview," *Religion & Ethics Newsweekly*, PBS, January 16, 2004, https://www.pbs.org/wnet/religionandethics/2004/01/16/january-16-2004-john-lewis-extended-interview/2897/.

55. He said, "No right was deemed by the fathers of the Government more sacred than the right of speech. It was in their eyes, as in the eyes of all thoughtful men, the great moral renovator of society and government. Daniel Webster called it a homebred right, a fireside privilege. Liberty is meaningless where the right to utter one's thoughts and opinions has ceased to exist. That, of all rights, is the dread of tyrants. It is the right which they first of all strike down. They know its power. Thrones, dominions, principalities, and powers, founded in injustice and wrong, are sure to tremble, if men are allowed to reason of righteousness, temperance, and of a judgment to come in their presence. Slavery cannot tolerate free speech. Five years of its exercise would banish the auction block and break every chain in the *South*." Kurt Lash, "Fredrick Douglass's 'Plea for Freedom of Speech in Boston,'" *Law and Liberty*, August 21, 2019, https://lawliberty.org/frederick-douglass-plea-for-freedom-of-speech-in-boston/.

56. "[P]recisely because an important part of a group's subordination consists in silencing, their emancipation requires a generously defined freedom of expression." Kenneth Karst, "Boundaries and Reasons: Freedom of Expression and the Subordination of Groups," *Illinois Law Review* (1990): 115–16.

57. Harel, "Hate Speech," 472.

58. James Jacobs and Kimberly Potter, *Hate Crimes: Criminal Law and Identity Politics* (New York: Oxford University Press, 1998), 8.

59. See Jen Neller, "The Need for New Tools to Break the Silos: Identity Categories in Hate Speech Legislation," *International Journal of Crime, Justice & Social Democracy* 7 (2018): 75.

60. Leslie Moran and Andrew Sharpe, "Violence, Identity and Policing: The Case of Violence against Transgender People," *Criminal Justice* 4 (2004): 395.

61. Harel, "Hate Speech," 472.

62. *Sullivan*, 254.

63. Lash, "Fredrick Douglass's 'Plea.'"

Chapter 9

1. Amy Mitchell and Mason Walker, "More Americans Now Say Government Should Take Steps to Restrict False Information Online Than in 2018," Pew Research Center, August 18, 2021, https://www.pewresearch.org/fact-tank/2021/08/18/more-americans-now-say-government-should-take-steps-to-restrict-false-information-online-than-in-2018/.

2. *United States v. Alvarez*, 567 U.S. 709, 713 (2012).

3. *Alverez*, 713.

4. *Alvarez*, 728.

5. *Alvarez*, 728.

6. *Alvarez*, 728.

7. *Alvarez*, 728.

8. *Alvarez*, 723.

9. Cass R. Sunstein, *Liars: Falsehoods and Free Speech in an Age of Deception* (New York: Oxford University Press, 2021), 50.

10. Julie Hirschfeld Davis and Matthew Rosenberg, "With False Claims, Trump Attacks Media on Turnout and Intelligence Rift," *New York Times*, January 21, 2017, https://www.nytimes.com/2017/01/21/us/politics/trump-white-house-briefing-inauguration-crowd-size.html.
11. Aaron Blake, "Kellyanne Conway Says Donald Trump's Team Has 'Alternative Facts,' Which Pretty Much Says It All," *Washington Post*, January 22, 2017, https://www.washingtonpost.com/news/the-fix/wp/2017/01/22/kellyanne-conway-says-donald-trumps-team-has-alternate-facts-which-pretty-much-says-it-all/.
12. Jonathan Turley, "Harm and Hegemony: The Decline of Free Speech in the United States," *Harvard Journal of Law & Policy* 45 (2022): 577.
13. "Censorious Governments Are Abusing 'Fake News' Laws," *The Economist*, May 4, 2022, https://www-economist-com.ezproxy.library.tufts.edu/international/2021/02/13/censorious-governments-are-abusing-fake-news-laws.
14. Craig Whitlock, "At War with the Truth," *Washington Post*, December 9, 2019, https://www.washingtonpost.com/graphics/2019/investigations/afghanistan-papers/afghanistan-war-confidential-documents/. This is further discussed in Chapter .
15. *Alvarez*, 728.
16. *Alvarez*, 722.
17. Jim Rutenberg and James Dao, "1971 Tape Adds to Debate over Kerry's Medal Protest," *New York Times*, April 26, 2004, https://www.nytimes.com/2004/04/26/us/1971-tape-adds-to-debate-over-kerry-s-medal-protest.html.
18. *Texas v. Johnson,* 491 U.S. 397 (1989).
19. *Johnson*, 439.
20. John Stuart Mill, *On Liberty* (1859; Kitchener: Batoche Books, 2001), 70.
21. Robert Post, "Reconciling Theory and Doctrine in First Amendment Jurisprudence," in *Eternally Vigilant: Free Speech in the Modern Era*, ed. Lee C. Bollinger and Geoffrey R. Stone (New York: Oxford University Press: 2002), 163.
22. *Alvarez*, 728.
23. *Alvarez*, 723.
24. Cyber & Infrastructure Security Agency, "Mis, Dis, Misinformation," Department of Homeland Security, https://www.cisa.gov/mdm.
25. Yuval Harari, *Sapiens: A Brief History of Humankind* (New York: Harper, 2015).
26. Sunstein, *Liars*, 133.
27. "Censorious Governments Are Abusing 'Fake News' Laws."
28. *Alvarez*, 732.
29. *Alvarez*, 723.

Chapter 10

1. *Packingham v. North Carolina*, 137 S. Ct. 1730, 1737 (2017).
2. Jameel Jaffer and Scott Wilkens, "Social Media Companies Want to Co-opt the First Amendment: Courts Shouldn't Let Them," *New York Times*, December 9, 2021, https://www.nytimes.com/2021/12/09/opinion/social-media-first-amendment.html.

3. For cogent analysis of the combined impact of the state-action doctrine and the government-speech doctrine, see Tim Wu, "Is the First Amendment Obsolete?," in *The Free Speech Century*, ed. Lee C. Bollinger and Geoffrey R. Stone (New York: Oxford University Press, 2019), 272–91.
4. Editorial Board, "How Fauci and Collins Shut Down Covid Debate," *Wall Street Journal*, December 21, 2021, https://www.wsj.com/articles/fauci-collins-emails-great-barrington-declaration-covid-pandemic-lockdown-11640129116.
5. Oliver Wendell Holmes, "The Path of the Law," *Harvard Law Review* 10 (1897): 457.

Chapter 11

1. As noted below and in the next chapter, Facebook and YouTube took similar steps.
2. "There is perhaps no more consequential debate for the future of free expression," Evelyn Douek has written, "than how to legitimate and constrain platforms' content moderation." Evelyn Douek, "The Limits of International Law in Content Moderation," *University of California Irvine Journal of International, Transnational, and Comparative Law* 6 (2021): 41.
3. Emily Bell, "The Unintentional Press: How Technology Companies Fail as Publishers," in *The Free Speech Century*, eds. Lee C. Bollinger & Geoffrey R. Stone (New York: Oxford University Press, 2019), 238.
4. Cato Social Media Survey Report, August 2021, Scribd, accessed January 4, 2022, https://www.scribd.com/document/550813283/Cato-Social-Media-Survey-Report.
5. Suzanne Nossel, *Dare To Speak: Defending Free Speech for All* (New York: HarperCollinsPublishers, 2020), 234.
6. Nossel, *Dare To Speak* 331.
7. Similarly, Google, the owner of YouTube, "has morphed into a quasi-monopoly that now controls over 90 per cent of the US, European and UK search-engine market. Gmail, meanwhile, has 1.5 billion monthly users, or about 75 per cent of the market for web-based email. Like many of its oligarchic counterparts, Google now controls a huge revenue base. . . . Shielded from competition, it benefits increasingly not from innovation but from finding new ways to leverage its dominant market position." Joel Kotkin, *Google: Whatever Happened to 'Don't be Evil'?* Spiked, July 20, 2022, https://www.spiked-online.com/2022/07/20/google-whatever-happened-to-dont-be-evil/.
8. Monica Bickert, "Defining the Boundaries of Free Speech on Social Media," in *The Free Speech Century*, eds. Lee C. Bollinger & Geoffrey R. Stone (New York: Oxford University Press, 2019), 260–361.
9. Oversight Board, "Case decision 2021-001-FB-FBR," Oversight Board Website, May 5, 2021, https://www.oversightboard.com/decision/FB-691QAMHJ.
10. Oversight Board, "Case decision 2021-001-FB-FBR."
11. Google, "Human Rights," About Google, https://about.google/human-rights/#:~:text=We%20are%20committed%20to%20respecting,Initiative%20Princip les%20(GNI%20Principles). ("We are committed to respecting the rights enshrined in the Universal Declaration of Human Rights and its implementing treaties, as well

as upholding the standards established in the United Nations Guiding Principles on Business and Human Rights (UNGPs) and in the Global Network Initiative Principles (GNI Principles).)"

12. Jack Dorsey, (@jack). "Agree w all of this. Our early values informed our rules. We likely over-rotated on one value, & then let the rules react to rapidly changing circumstances (some we helped create). We need to root these values in human rights law. A starting consideration:" Twitter, August 10, 2018. https://twitter.com/jack/sta tus/1027962500438843397.

13. Sam Zarifi, "Facebook's Answers to Questions about its Human Rights Policy," Opinio Juris, November 26, 2021, http://opiniojuris.org/2021/06/11/facebooks-answers-to-questions-about-its-human-rights-policy/.

14. Oversight Board, "Oversight Board Charter," Oversight Board Website, https://about.fb.com/wp-content/uploads/2019/09/oversight_board_charter.pdf.

15. Facebook, "Corporate Human Rights Policy," About Facebook, March 2021, https://about.fb.com/wp-content/uploads/2021/03/Facebooks-Corporate-Human-Rights-Policy.pdf.

16. Facebook Oversight Board, "Former President Trump's Suspension," February 1, 2021, https://www.oversightboard.com/decision/FB-691QAMHJ.

17. See, e.g., Jordan B. Peterson, "Article: Twitter Ban," YouTube, July 1, 2022, https://www.youtube.com/watch?v=UYfKWQqvFac&t=725s.

18. See, e.g., Michael J. Glennon and Donald T. Fox, *Report Concerning Abuses against Civilians by Counter-Revolutionaries Operating in Nicaragua* (Washington, DC: International Human Rights Law Group, 1985).

19. See, e.g., Michael J. Glennon, *Constitutional Diplomacy* (Princeton: Princeton University Press, 1990); Michael J. Glennon, "Raising The Paquete Habana: Is Violation of Customary International Law by the Executive Unconstitutional?" *Northwestern University Law Review* 80 (1985): 321; Michael J. Glennon, "Can the President Do No Wrong?" 80 *American Journal of International Law* 80 (1986): 923.

20. Monica Bickert, "Defining the Boundaries of Free Speech on Social Media," in *The Free Speech Century*, eds. Lee C. Bollinger & Geoffrey R. Stone (New York: Oxford University Press, 2019) 360.

21. *See* Kotkin, *Google*.

22. Alexandra Stevenson, "Facebook Admits It Was Used to Incite Violence in Myanmar," *The New York Times*, November 6, 2018, https://www.nytimes.com/2018/11/06/tec hnology/myanmar-facebook.html.

23. Igor Bonifacic, "Facebook Bowed to Demands from Turkey to Block One of its Military Opponents," Engadget, February 24, 2021, https://www.engadget.com/faceb ook-turkey-emails-200407588.html.

24. Confirmation Hearing on the Nomination of John G. Roberts, Jr. to be Chief Justice of the United States Before the Senate Committee on the Judiciary, 109th Cong. 201 (2005) (statement of Chief Justice John G. Roberts, Jr.).

25. Michael J. Glennon, *The Road Ahead: Gaps, Leaks, and Drips*, International Law Studies 89 (2013): 326.

26. For an argument along these lines, see "Judge Hercules'" ability to identify the one right answer in Ronald Dworkin, *Law's Empire* (1986), 239 ("I must try to exhibit [the] complex structure of legal interpretation, and I shall use for that purpose an imaginary judge of superhuman intellectual power and patience who accepts law as integrity. Call him Hercules.").

27. Community-values adherents typically flesh out the concept with reliance upon notions such as security, human dignity, social progress, quality of life, and self-determination. Compare with John Dickinson, "The Problem of the Unprovided Case," *University of Pennsylvania Law Review* 81 (1932): 128 (referring to "the idea that all the materials which enter into the construction of a new legal rule for an unprovided case must themselves be law").

28. Dickinson, "The Problem of the Unprovided Case," 118 ("The notion that legal rules are so connected rationally that one can be deduced from others leads to the conclusion that in the last analysis there is no such thing as an unprovided case.... [T]he law for new cases is to be found inside the law itself and not by resort to considerations and ideas drawn from outside the field of technical law").

29. See, for example, *Barcelona Traction, Light & Power Co., Ltd.* (Belgum v. Spain) (Second Phase), 1970 I.C.J. 3, 33–34 (Feb. 5), in which the ICJ found that "international law has not established its own rules" concerning "the rights of states with regard to the treatment of companies and shareholders"; *Haya de la Torre* (Colombia v. Peru), 1951 I.C.J. 71, 80 (June 13), in which the Court stated that the applicable law did not "give a complete answer" to the asylum question at issue; and *Military and Paramilitary Activities in and Against Nicaragua* (Nicaragua v. U.S.), 1986 I.C.J. 14, 135 (June 27), in which the Court, addressing the question whether international law placed restrictions on a State's military arsenal, declared that "in international law there are no rules, other than such rules as may be accepted by the State concerned, by treaty or otherwise, whereby the level of armaments of a sovereign State can be limited."

30. In Germany, formalism was critiqued by Philip Heck and other proponents of a "jurisprudence of interests." *See* Philip Heck, "The Jurisprudence of Interests: An Outline," in *The Jurisprudence of Interests* 31 (M. M. Schoch ed. & trans., 1948). In France, François Gény argued that formal legal sources were inadequate to address all legal questions. *See* François Gény, *Méthode d'interprétation et sources en droit privé positif* (La. State Law Institute trans., 1963); Richard Groshut, "The Free Scientific Search of François Gény," American Journal of Jurisprudence 17 (1972): 14. In the United States, legal realists pressed for greater attention to the consequences that categories produced, suggesting the propriety of "rule skepticism" and "fact skepticism" in the classification process. *See* Jerome Frank, *Courts on Trial: Myth and Reality in American Justice* (1949); Hans Kelsen, "The Pure Theory of Law: Its Method and Fundamental Concepts," *Law Quarterly Review* 50 (1934): 474; Roscoe Pound, "The Ideal Element in American Judicial Decision," *Harvard Law Review* 45 (1931): 136.

31. *See* Dickinson, "The Problem of the Unprovided Case," 116 ("In the seventeenth and the early part of the eighteenth century, when many of the lines of our present legal

processes were laid down, it is fair to say that the problem of the unprovided case was taken for granted and not clearly envisaged as a problem at all.").

32. For a comment on Michael Walzer's effort to apply his notion of "practical morality" to war, see Michael J. Glennon, "Preempting Proliferation: International Law, Morality, and Nuclear Weapons," *European Journal of International Law* 24 (2013): 109. Though much of the formalism that pervades international human rights law can be attributed to surviving ghosts of a naturalist worldview, additional forces are at play, including the influence in Europe of a civil law tradition with purportedly comprehensive codes and, in the United States, the continued emphasis on appellate cases in legal education, implying no need to examine exogenous, contextual sources to predict case outcomes. *See* Karl N. Llewellyn, "Some Realism About Realism— Responding to Dean Pound," *Harvard Law Review* 44 (1931): 1222. The upshot is that the oft-repeated claim that "we are all realists now" has yet to embrace all within international law's "invisible college."

33. Prosper Weil put it well: "Regardless of the judicial and scholarly endeavors to affirm the completeness of international law, the truth of the matter is that international law is not complete. No legal order is, because there is not, cannot be, and should not be a rule at hand for every concrete or new situation. . . . More than municipal law, international law is by its very nature riddled with gaps." Prosper Weil, "The Court Cannot Conclude Definitively . . .": Non Liquet *Revisited," Columbia Journal of Transnational Law* 36 (1997): 118.

34. For discussion of the levels-of-generality problem in customary law, see Michael J. Glennon, *Limits of Law, Prerogatives of Power: Interventionism after Kosovo* (London: Palgrave Macmillan, 2001), 50–52. See generally Karl N Llewellyn, *The Bramble Bush: The Classic Lectures on the Law and Law School* (New York: Oxford University Press, 2008).

35. Much the same difficulties arise in formulating international rules governing the use of force, which is the subject of profound differences. *See, e.g.,* Advance Questions for Lieutenant General Keith Alexander, USA Nominee for Commander, United States Cyber Command: Before the Senate Armed Services Committee, 111th Cong. 11 (Apr. 15, 2010), http://armed-services.senate.gov/statemnt/2010/04%20April/ Alexander%2004-15-10.pdf ("There is no international consensus on a precise definition of a use of force, in or out of cyberspace. Consequently, individual nations may assert different definitions, and may apply different thresholds for what constitutes a use of force.").

36. Hersch Lauterpacht, *The Development of International Law by the International Court* (1982), 152.

37. See John Finnis, "On Reason and Authority in Law's Empire," *Law & Philosophy* 6 (1987): 357.

38. H. L. A. Hart, *The Concept of Law*, 2d ed. (New York: Oxford University Press, 1997), 252.

39. For the suggestion that normativity exists in gradations, see Prosper Weil, "Towards Relative Normativity in International Law?," *American Journal International Law* 77 (1983): 413.

40. General, elastic norms are sometimes considered principles rather than rules. Rules are more specific, less malleable, and cover less. Rules were described by Pound as "precepts attaching a definite detailed legal consequence to a definite, detailed state of facts." Roscoe Pound, "Hierarchy of Sources and Forms in Different Systems of Law," *Tulane Law Review* 7 (1933): 482. Principles, in contrast, are more general and constitute "authoritative starting points for legal reasoning, employed continually and legitimately where cases are not covered or are not fully or obviously covered by rules in the narrower sense." Pound, 483. Pound thus regarded principles as "hortatory." Roscoe Pound, "For the 'Minority Report,'" *American Bar Association Journal* 27 (1941): 677. Holmes, too, was skeptical of their utility. When on the Supreme Court, he invited his fellow justices to name any legal principle on which they relied, suggesting that he could show them how it could be used to decide the case under consideration either way. *See* Louis Menand, *The Metaphysical Club: A Story of Ideas in America* (2004), 340.

41. *See generally* Joseph Raz, *Between Authority and Interpretation: On the Theory of Law and Practical Reason* (2009), 11 ("[W]e cannot expect the law of any one country to have a uniform way of demarcating the boundary between what belongs to it and what lies outside of it, let alone expect to find that all legal systems demarcate the boundary in the same way.").

42. Hilary Mantel, *Wolf Hall* (London: Picador 2009), 255.

43. *See* Michael J. Glennon, *The Fog of Law: Pragmatism, Security, and International Law* (Stanford: Stanford University Press, 2010), 4.

44. For a contemporary version in this context, see Glennon, *The Fog of Law*, 4. For an earlier, and prescient, exploration of some of the same themes, see Samuel von Pufendorf, *On The Duty of Man and Citizen According To Natural Law*, James Tully ed., Michael Silverthorne trans., (1682; repr., Cambridge: Cambridge University Press, 1991) 108.

45. Dickinson, "The Problem of the Unprovided Case," 122.

46. Compare with Hart, 129.

47. Henry J. Steiner & Philip Alston, *International Human Rights in Context*, 2nd ed. (New York: Oxford University Press 2000), 366.

48. Antonio Cassese, "A Plea for a Global Community Grounded in a Core of Human Rights," in *Realizing Utopia*, Antonio Cassese ed. (New York: Oxford University Press: 2012), 136.

49. Anthea Roberts, *Is International Law International?* (New York: Oxford University Press, 2017), 6. In fact, "different "communities of international lawyers—often in different states or geopolitical groupings—approach international law in different ways."

50. Antonia Cassese, *International Law*, 2nd ed. (New York, Oxford University Press, 2005) 381.

51. Samantha Powers and Graham Allison, *Realizing Human Rights* (London: Palgrave Macmillian, 2006), 11.

52. Cassese, *International Law*, 382.

53. John J. Mearsheimer, *The Great Delusion: Liberal Dreams and International Realities* (New Haven: Yale University Press: 2018), 109–110.

54. Rosalyn Higgins, *Problems and Process in International Law and How We Use It* (Oxford: Clarendon Press, 1994) 96.

55. See, e.g., Jacob Mchangama, *Free Speech: A History from Socrates to Social Media* (New York: Basic Books, 2022), 319–49 (describing the current "free speech recession"); Jonathan Turley, "Harm and Hegemony: The Decline of Free Speech in the United States," *Harvard Journal of Law & Policy* 45 (2022): 577.

56. UN General Assembly, International Covenant on Civil and Political Rights, 16 December 1966, United Nations, Treaty Series, vol. 999, 174, available at: https://www.refworld.org/docid/3ae6b3aa0.html [accessed 10 July 2022].

57. UN General Assembly, International Covenant on Civil and Political Rights, 175.

58. UN General Assembly, International Covenant on Civil and Political Rights, 177.

59. Nossel, *Dare To Speak,* 228.

60. Henry Farrell, Margaret Levi, and Tim O'Reilly, "Mark Zuckerberg Runs a Nation-State and He's the King," Vox, last modified April 10, 2018, https://www.vox.com/the-big-idea/2018/4/9/17214752/zuckerberg-facebook-power-regulation-data-privacy-control-political-theory-data-breach-king.

61. John Gerard Ruggie, "The Social Construction of the UN Guiding Principles on Business & Human Rights," HKS Working Paper No. RWP17-030, Cambridge, MA (2017), 7–8 or http://dx.doi.org/10.2139/ssrn.2984901; https://ssrn.com/abstract=2984901.

62. See, for example, United Nations Human Rights Council, "Open-ended Intergovernmental Working Group on Transnational Corporations and Other Business Enterprises with Respect to Human Rights," OHCHR, https://www.ohchr.org/en/hr-bodies/hrc/wg-trans-corp/igwg-on-tnc.

63. For background see Hurst Hannum, *Rescuing Human Rights: A Radically Moderate Approach* (Cambridge: Cambridge University Press, 2019), 26–35. ("Following the report's submission, the commission requested the Secretary-General to appoint a special representative on human rights and business, whose work over the next several years eventually resulted in adoption by the UN Human Rights Council (which succeeded the commission in 2006) of the Guiding Principles").

64. Oversight Board, "Case decision 2021-001-FB-FBR."

65. Office of the United Nations High Commissioner for Human Rights, *Guiding Principles on Business and Human Rights* (New York and Geneva: United Nations, 2011), 1, https://www.ohchr.org/documents/publications/guidingprinciplesbusinesshr_en.pdf.

66. Douek, "Limits of International Law," 23.

67. Office of the United Nations High Commissioner for Human Rights, *Guiding Principles on Business and Human Rights*, 13.

68. John Gerard Ruggie, "Life in the Global Public Domain: Response to Commentaries on the UN Guiding Principles and the Proposed Treaty on Business and Human Rights" (2015), 5 or http://dx.doi.org/10.2139/ssrn.2554726; https://ssrn.com/abstract=2554726.

69. Ruggie, The Social Construction of the UN Guiding Principles, 8.

70. Ruggie, The Social Construction of the UN Guiding Principles 5.

71. Oversight Board, "Oversight Board Charter," Oversight Board Website, https://about. fb.com/wp-content/uploads/2019/09/oversight_board_charter.pdf.

72. Aswad, "To Protect Freedom of Expression," 77 *Washington and Lee Law Review*, (2020) 657.

73. For background see, 1155 U.N.T.S. 331 (1969), arts. 19–23.

74. U.S. Reservations, Declarations, and Understandings, International Covenant on Civil and Political Rights, 138 Cong. Rec. S4781-01 (1992).

75. Kristina Ash, "U.S. Reservations to the International Covenant on Civil and Political Rights: Credibility Maximization and Global Influence," *Northwestern Journal of International Human Rights* 3 (2005): ¶20.

76. *See* The White House, *Interim National Security Strategic Guidance* (2021), 7, https:// www.whitehouse.gov/wp-content/uploads/2021/03/NSC-1v2.pdf (comments of Jake Sullivan).

77. General Comment No. 34, of the U.N. Human Rights Comm'n at ¶ 25, U.N. Doc. CCPR/C/GC/34 (Sept. 12, 2011).

78. U.S. Reservations, Declarations, and Understandings, International Covenant on Civil and Political Rights, 138 Cong. Rec. S4781-01 (1992).

79. U.N. Comm. on Human Rts., 6th Sess. 174th mtg. 25, U.N. Doc. E/CN.4/SR. 174 (May 6, 1950).

80. See U.N. GAOR, Third Committee, 16th Sess., 1083rd mtg., U.N. Doc. A/C.3/ SR.1083 (Oct. 25, 1961). For further background see Amal Clooney & Philippa Webb, "The Right to Insult in International Law," *Columbia Human Rights Law Review*, 48 (2017): 17; Sarah H. Cleveland, "Hate Speech at Home and Abroad," in *The Free Speech Century*, eds. Lee C. Bollinger & Geoffrey R. Stone (New York: Oxford University Press, 2019), 221.

81. See Glennon, *Limits of Law, Prerogatives of Power*.

82. U.S. Reservations, Declarations, and Understandings, International Covenant on Civil and Political Rights, 138 Cong. Rec. S4781-01 (1992).

83. Nick Clegg, "Facebook, Elections, and Political Speech," About Facebook, September 24, 2019, https://about.fb.com/news/2019/09/elections-and-political-speech/.

84. Facebook, "Corporate Human Rights Policy," About Facebook, March 2021, https:// about.fb.com/wp-content/uploads/2021/03/Facebooks-Corporate-Human-Rights-Policy.pdf.

85. UN General Assembly, International Covenant on Civil and Political Rights, 999 U.N.T.S., 174, (1969), Article 4:

> States Parties condemn all propaganda and all organizations which are based on ideas or theories of superiority of one race or group of persons of one colour or ethnic origin, or which attempt to justify or promote racial hatred and discrimination in any form, and undertake to adopt immediate and positive measures designed to eradicate all incitement to, or acts of, such discrimination and, to this end, with due regard to the principles embodied in the Universal Declaration of Human Rights and the rights expressly set forth in article 5 of this Convention, inter alia:
>
> (c) Shall declare an offence punishable by law all dissemination of ideas based on racial superiority or hatred, incitement to racial discrimination, as well

as all acts of violence or incitement to such acts against any race or group of persons of another colour or ethnic origin, and also the provision of any assistance to racist activities, including the financing thereof;

(b) Shall declare illegal and prohibit organizations, and also organized and all other propaganda activities, which promote and incite racial discrimination, and shall recognize participation in such organizations or activities as an offence punishable by law;

(c) Shall not permit public authorities or public institutions, national or local, to promote or incite racial discrimination.

86. "That the Constitution and laws of the United States contain extensive protections of individual freedom of speech, expression and association. Accordingly, the United States does not accept any obligation under this Convention, in particular under Articles 4 and 7, to restrict those rights, through the adoption of legislation or any other measures, to the extent that they are protected by the Constitution and laws of the United States."

87. "Nothing in this Convention requires or authorizes legislation, or other action, by the United States of America prohibited by the Constitution of the United States as interpreted by the United States."

88. S. Treaty Doc. No. 95-21; 1144 U.N.T.S.123 (1970). Article 13 on Freedom of Thought and Expression provides that:

1. Everyone has the right to freedom of thought and expression. This right includes freedom to seek, receive, and impart information and ideas of all kinds, regardless of frontiers, either orally, in writing, in print, in the form of art, or through any other medium of one's choice.

2. The exercise of the right provided for in the foregoing paragraph shall not be subject to prior censorship but shall be subject to subsequent imposition of liability, which shall be expressly established by law to the extent necessary to ensure:
   a. respect for the rights or reputations of others; or
   b. the protection of national security, public order, or public health or morals.

3. The right of expression may not be restricted by indirect methods or means, such as the abuse of government or private controls over newsprint, radio broadcasting frequencies, or equipment used in the dissemination of information, or by any other means tending to impede the communication and circulation of ideas and opinions.

4. Notwithstanding the provisions of paragraph 2 above, public entertainments may be subject by law to prior censorship for the sole purpose of regulating access to them for the moral protection of childhood and adolescence.

5. Any propaganda for war and any advocacy of national, racial, or religious hatred that constitute incitements to lawless violence or to any other similar action against any person or group of persons on any grounds including those of race, color, religion, language, or national origin shall be considered as offenses punishable by law.

Article 14. Right of Reply

1. Anyone injured by inaccurate or offensive statements or ideas disseminated to the public in general by a legally regulated medium of communication has the right to reply or to make a correction using the same communications outlet, under such conditions as the law may establish.

2. The correction or reply shall not in any case remit other legal liabilities that may have been incurred.

3. For the effective protection of honor and reputation, every publisher, and every newspaper, motion picture, radio, and television company, shall have a person responsible who is not protected by immunities or special privileges.

89. The White House, Message from the President of the United States Transmitting the International Convention on the Elimination of All Forms of Racial Discrimination, S. Exec. Doc. No. 29-118, 18, https://www.foreign.senate.gov/imo/media/doc/treaty_95-19_95-21.pdf.

90. Council of Europe, *European Convention for the Protection of Human Rights and Fundamental Freedoms, as amended by Protocols Nos. 11 and 14*, 4 November 1950, ETS 11, available at: https://www.refworld.org/docid/3ae6b3b04.html [accessed 10 July 2022].

91. 1520 U.N.T.S. 217, (1982), art. 9.

92. 1520 U.N.T.S. 217, (1982), art. 27.

93. Aswad, *To Protect Freedom of Expression*, 635.

94. Frederick Schauer, "The Exceptional First Amendment" in *American Exceptionalism and Human Rights*. Ed. Michael Ignatieff (Princeton: Princeton University Press, 2005) 55.

95. *See* Glennon, *The Fog of Law*, 84–90.

96. Statute of the International Court of Justice, art. 38.

97. Cassese, *International Law*, 393.

98. Clooney & Webb, "The Right to Insult in International Law," 55.

99. Aswad, *To Protect Freedom of Expression*, 615.

100. Chirs Butler, "China Takes Aim at Western Ideas," *New York Times*, August 19, 2013, https://www.nytimes.com/2013/08/20/world/asia/chinas-new-leadership-takes-hard-line-in-secret-memo.html?mcubz=1.

101. ChinaFile Editors, "Document 9: A ChinaFile Translation," ChinaFile, November 8, 2013, https://www.chinafile.com/document-9-chinafile-translation#start.

102. Maya Wang, "China's Chilling 'Social Credit' Blacklist," *Wall Street Journal*, December 11, 2017, https://www.wsj.com/articles/chinas-chilling-social-credit-blacklist-1513036054. ("This is no anodyne credit score. By rating citizens on a range of behaviors from shopping habits to online speech, the government intends to manufacture a problem-free society. Those with low scores will face obstacles in everything from getting government jobs to placing their children in desired schools. It remains unclear exactly who will run the system, whether or how one could dispute scores, or even whether the system is legal").

103. The United Nations Office of High Commissioner for Human Rights (website), https://www.ohchr.org/en/hrbodies/hrc/pages/home.aspx.

104. Clooney & Webb, "The Right to Insult in International Law," 5.

105. Clooney & Webb, 5.

106. Clooney & Webb, 6.

107. Clooney & Webb, 6.

108. Clooney & Webb, 10.

109. Clooney & Webb, 7–8.

110. Cleveland, "Hate Speech at Home and Abroad," 229.
111. Clooney & Webb, "The Right to Insult in International Law," 8.
112. Clooney & Webb, 10.
113. Clooney & Webb, 10.
114. Clooney & Webb, 10.
115. Clooney & Webb, 12.
116. Clooney & Webb, 12.
117. Clooney & Webb, 12.
118. Strossen, Hate, 27.
119. Strossen, 28.
120. Strossen, 28.
121. Strossen, 29.
122. Strossen, 112.
123. In 2019 the European Court of Human Rights upheld the conviction of a German politician for holocaust denial. *See Pastörs v. Germany* (ECHR application no. 55225/14) (2019). *See also* Clooney & Webb, "The Right to Insult in International Law," 39–40; Jeroen Temperman, *Religious Hatred and International Law: The Prohibition of Incitement to Violence or Discrimination* (2015), 253.
124. Human Rights Committee, General Comment No. 34, U.N. Doc. CCPR/C/GC/34 (Sept. 12, 2011) ¶ 49.
125. Faurisson v. France, Comm. No. 550/1993 (Nov. 8, 1986, UNHCR).
126. Clooney & Webb, "The Right to Insult in International Law," 46 n212.
127. Clooney & Webb, 47 (footnotes omitted).
128. Ezra Klein, "The Controversy over Mark Zuckerberg's Comments on Holocaust Denial, Explained," Vox, July 20, 2018, https://www.vox.com/explainers/2018/7/20/17590694/markzuckerberg-facebook-holocaust-denial-recode.
129. As Clooney and Webb conclude, "international standards have proved to be confusing and ultimately inadequate in reining in national laws that restrict free speech." Clooney & Webb, "The Right to Insult in International Law," 37.
130. As discussed in Chapter 4. See *Erie R.R. v. Tompkins*, 304 U.S. 64 (1938).
131. Suzanne Nossel reports that "several former company insiders have confessed, anecdotally, that they have seen employees' values, worldviews, and political attitudes color discretionary decisions." Nossel, *Dare To Speak*, 224.
132. Aswad, *To Protect Freedom of Expression*, 639, 642.
133. Douek, "The Limits of International Law," 18.
134. Cassese, *International Law*, 393.
135. Statute of the International Court of Justice, art. 38.
136. For example, see Colombian-Peruvian Asylum Case, Judgment, 1950 I.C.J. 266 (Nov. 20).
137. Jack Goldsmith & Tim Wu, *Who Controls The Internet?: Illusions Of A Borderless World* (New York: Oxford University Press, 2008) 183.
138. Douek, "The Limits of International Law," 10.
139. Sejal Parmar, "Facebook's Oversight Board: A Meaningful Turn Towards International Human Rights Standards?," Just Security, May 20, 2020, June 24, 2022. He adds, however, that the "identification of such standards in the board's basic

documents, Facebook's values, and the statements of its leading figures suggests that some of the motivation lies in minimizing potential government regulation of social media platforms in the European Union and elsewhere. The rhetoric—and any commensurate action—also may help shore up public trust and the company's reputation globally, after many well-founded criticisms." *Id.* https://www.justsecurity.org/70234/facebooks-oversight-board-a-meaningful-turn-towardsinternatio nal-human-rights-standards/, She adds, however, that the "identification of such standards in the board's basic documents, Facebook's values, and the statements of its leading figures suggests that some of the motivation lies in minimizing potential government regulation of social media platforms in the European Union and elsewhere. The rhetoric – and any commensurate action – also may help shore up public trust and the company's reputation globally, after many well-founded criticisms."

140. Douek, "The Limits of International Law," 3.
141. Schauer, "The Exceptional First Amendment," 43.
142. Schauer, "The Exceptional First Amendment," 37–38.
143. William P. Marshall, "The Truth Justification for Freedom of Speech," in *The Oxford Handbook of Freedom of Speech*, ed. Adriene Stone and Frederick Schauer (New York: Oxford University Press, 2021), 50.
144. Oversight Board, "Case decision 2021-001-FB-FBR."
145. Mark Zuckerberg, Facebook Post, January 7, 2021, https://www.facebook.com/zuck/posts/10112681480907401.
146. It looked, it said, to the following human rights standards:

The right to freedom of expression: International Covenant on Civil and Political Rights (CCPR), Articles 19 and 20; as interpreted in General Comment No. 34, Human Rights Committee (2011) (General Comment 34); the Rabat Plan of Action, OHCHR, (2012); UN Special Rapporteur on freedom of opinion and expression report A/HRC/38/35 (2018); Joint Statement of international freedom of expression monitors on COVID-19 (March, 2020).
The right to life: ICCPR Article 6.
The right to security of person: ICCPR Article 9, para. 1.
The right to non-discrimination: ICCPR Articles 2 and 26; International Convention on the Elimination of All Forms of Racial Discrimination (ICERD), Articles 1 and 4.
Participation in public affairs and the right to vote: ICCPR Article 25.
The right to remedy: ICCPR Article 2; General Comment No. 31, Human Rights Committee (2004) (General Comment 31); UNGPs, Principle 22.

147. Nossel, *Dare To Speak*, 222.
148. Nossel, *Dare To Speak*, 221.
149. Facebook's community standards define hate speech as "a direct attack on people based on what we call protected characteristics—race, ethnicity, national origin, religious affiliation, sexual orientation, caste, sex, gender, gender identity, and serious disease or disability." Prohibited content includes content that "describes or negatively targets people with slurs, where slurs are defined as words that are inherently offensive and used as insulting labels for the above characteristics." Facebook Community Standards: Hate Speech (website), Meta, last visited August 15, 2022, https://transparency.fb.com/policies/community-standards/hate-speech/.

150. Facebook's "Introduction to the Community Standards" provided that Facebook is "working to remove content that has the potential to contribute to real-world harm, including through our policies prohibiting the coordination of harm, the scale of medical masks and related goods, hate speech, bullying and harassment, and misinformation that contributes to the risk of imminent violence or physical harm." Its Community Standard on Violence and Incitement prohibits content containing "Misinformation and unverifiable rumors that contribute to the risk of imminent violence or physical harm." An article available only to Facebook users indicates that Facebook "removes content discouraging good health practices that 'public health authorities advise people to take to protect themselves from getting or spreading COVID-19.'" Oversight Board, "Case Decision, 2021-008-FB-FBR," August 19, 2021, https://oversightboard.com/decision/FB-B6NGYREK/. Compare Twitter's announced policy of removing or limiting the distribution of material "that is shared in a deceptive or confusing manner." Twitter, *How we address misinformation on Twitter* (undated), https://help.twitter.com/en/resources/addressing-misleading-info.

151. Oversight Board, "Case Decision, 2021-008-FB-FBR," August 19, 2021, https://oversightboard.com/decision/FB-B6NGYREK/.

152. There is no question that the Oversight Board was on solid ground in concluding, in the Trump case, that principles of legality in international human rights law were traduced by the imposition of an indefinite penalty. The Board seems mistaken, however, in looking to rules in treaties to which the United States had formulated relevant reservations without noting the existence and effect of those reservations. In the South Africa case, it's hard to see how the Board could find that the remedy Facebook imposed was proportional, given the Board's acknowledgment that it did not know whether the prohibited slur would be banned globally or only within a national or regional market; a global ban on the term would seemingly have been disproportionate if the term has no derogatory meaning (or any meaning at all) in many countries. The Board was mistaken in the Brazil case in finding that international law imposes a duty on public institutions and officials to tell the truth. However noble the aspiration to reshape international law to require national leaders to be truthful with their people, it cannot seriously be maintained that international law currently imposes a prohibition against government lying. International law has long distinguished the *lex lata*, the law that actually exists, from *de lege ferenda*, the law as it should be. The Board needs to do the same.

153. Monica Bickert, "Defining the Boundaries of Free Speech on Social Media," in *The Free Speech Century*, eds. Lee C. Bollinger & Geoffrey R. Stone (New York: Oxford University Press, 2019) 256.

154. Bickert, "Defining the Boundaries of Free Speech on Social Media," in Bollinger & R. Stone, 259.

155. Bickert, 258.

156. This is not to argue that U.S. First Amendment is "complete"—it is not—but it does suggest that in a world in which some legal systems are more complete than others, few if any systems are as comprehensive or detailed as U.S. constitutional jurisprudence on freedom of speech.

157. Michael Ignatieff, "Introduction," in *American Exceptionalism and Human Rights*. Ed. Michael Ignatieff (Princeton: Princeton University Press, 2005) 15.

158. Bickert, "Defining the Boundaries of Free Speech on Social Media," in Bollinger & Stone, 271.

159. Bickert, 261.

160. Bickert, 261.

161. See Goldsmith & Wu, *Who Controls The Internet?*

162. Bickert, "Defining the Boundaries of Free Speech on Social Media," Bollinger & Stone, 262.

163. Bickert, 266.

164. Bickert, 265.

165. *See* Glennon, *The Fog of Law*, 3; Michael J. Glennon, "How International Rules Die," *Georgetown Law Journal* 93 (2005): 939.

166. This was a foundational assumption of Holmes, "that people are justified in defending what they have become accustomed to," as Louis Menand put it. Holmes to Frederick Pollock, August 30, 1929, quoted in Menand, *The Metaphysical Club*, 63.

167. Stephen Breyer, *The Court and the World: American Law and the New Global Realities* (New York: Alfred A. Knopf, 2015), 145.

168. Breyer, *The Court and the World*, 146.

169. Restatement (Third) of The Foreign Relations Law of The United States §102 comment d (1987).

170. See, for example, Peter Coy, "How CEOs Become Beholden to Shareholders," Bloomberg, December 4, 2014, https://www.bloomberg.com/news/articles/2014-12-04/shareholder-value-friedman-linked-profits-social-responsibility#xj4y7v zkg, citing Milton Friedman, "A Friedman Doctrine: The Social Responsibility of Business is to Increase Its Profits" The New York Times Magazine, September 13, 1970.

171. Klaus Schwab and Peter Vanham, "What is Stakeholder Capitalism?," World Economic Forum, January 22, 2021, https://www.weforum.org/agenda/2021/01/klaus-schwab-on-what-is-stakeholder-capitalism-history-relevance/.

172. See, for example, Jeff Horwitz, "Facebook Says Its Rules Apply to All: Company Documents Reveal a Secret Elite That's Exempt," *Wall Street Journal*, September 13, 2021, https://www.wsj.com/articles/facebook-files-xcheck-zuckerberg-elite-rules-11631541353?mod=article_inline (reporting that Facebook used a tiered system for high profile users); Georgia Wells, Jeff Horwitz, and Deepa Seetharaman, "Facebook Knows Instagram Is Toxic for Teen Girls, Company Documents Show," *Wall Street Journal*, September 14, 2021, https://www.wsj.com/articles/facebook-knows-instagram-is-toxic-for-teen-girls-company-documents-show-11631620739?mod=article_inline, (reporting on Facebook's knowledge that its platform harms users); Keach Hagey and Jeff Horwitz, "Facebook Tried to Make Its Platform a Healthier Place: It Got Angrier Instead," *Wall Street Journal*, September 15, 2021, https://www.wsj.com/articles/facebook-algorithm-change-zuckerberg-11631654215?mod=article_inline (reporting on Facebook's system rewarding public outrage); Justin Scheck, Newley Purnel, and Jeff Horwitz, "Facebook Employees Flag Drug Cartels and Human Traffickers: The Company's Response Is Weak, Documents Show," *Wall*

Street Journal, September 16, 2021, https://www.wsj.com/articles/facebook-drug-cartels-human-traffickers-response-is-weak-documents-11631812953?mod=article_inline (reporting on Facebook's poor response to reported human and drug trafficking).

173. Meta, "Corporate Human Rights Policy," About Facebook (website), 2021, https://about.fb.com/wp-content/uploads/2021/03/Facebooks-Corporate-Human-Rights-Policy.pdf.

Chapter 12

1. Bob Woodward & Robert Costa, Peril, at xxvii (2021). Nuclear weapons were a particular concern. "Madam Speaker," Milley reportedly told Pelosi, "you have to take my word for it. I know the system and we're okay. The president alone can order the use of nuclear weapons. But he doesn't make the decision alone. One person can order it, several people have to launch it." *Id.* at xxiv.

2. Karoun Demirjian & John Wagner, *Biden Comes to Milley's Defense After Revelation Top General, Fearing Trump, Conferred with China to Avert War*, Wash. Post (Sept. 16, 2021), https://www.washingtonpost.com/politics/milley-defended-china-call/2021/09/15/3393fa18-1645-11ec-b976-f4a43b740aeb_story.html [https://perma.cc/WCP4-9X2L].

3. *Myers v. United States*, 272 U.S. 52, 293 (1926) (Brandeis, J., dissenting).

4. As Frederick Schauer observed, "[f]reedom of speech . . . can be an integral part of a system of government based on separation of powers and checks and balances." Frederick Schauer, Free Speech: A Philosophical Enquiry 43 (Cambridge Univ. Press 1982). "Political speech, including public deliberation of political issues and open criticism of governmental officials and policies, is an important and arguably necessary method of retaining public control over officials, preventing usurpation of power, and acting as a check on the intrinsic force of the governmental apparatus." *Id.* at 107.

5. Alexander Meiklejohn, Free Speech and Its Relation to Self-Government 6 (1948).

6. *Id.* at 5.

7. *See* Michael J. Glennon, *National Security and Double Government*, 5 Harv. Nat'l Sec. J. 1 (2014). The article is elaborated in a book, Michael J. Glennon, National Security and Double Government (Oxford Univ. Press 2015).

8. Michael H. Hunt, The American Ascendancy: How the United States Gained and Wielded Global Dominance 149 (2007) (quoting Walter LaFeber, *American Policy-Makers, Public Opinion, and the Outbreak of the Cold War, 1945-50, in* The Origins of the Cold War in Asia 60 (Yōnosuke Nagai & Akira Iriye eds., 1977).

9. *See* Glennon, *supra* note 7, at 46–60.

10. Nat'l Comm'n on Terrorist Attacks upon the U.S., 9/11 Commission Report 420 (2004).

11. Mark Mazzetti, The Way of the Knife: The CIA, A Secret Army, and a War at the Ends of the Earth 228 (2013).

12. *See, e.g.,* a 2013 briefing by State Department spokesperson Jen Psaki (asked about the continuation of military assistance to Egypt in apparent violation of the law):

QUESTION: And who ultimately made the decision not to make a determination?

MS. PSAKI: Well, obviously, there's a factor as it relates to the legal component, which our legal office here played a significant role in, and certainly this was discussed and agreed to through the interagency process.

QUESTION: But who decided? I mean, the buck stops somewhere. As Harry Truman said, it stopped with him. Does the buck stop with the President in this case, or with the Secretary, or with the acting legal advisor of the State Department, or who? Who made the decision?

MS. PSAKI: Well, I'm not going to read out who was where on what and all the players involved in this.

QUESTION: I'm not asking that. I'm asking who made the decision.

MS. PSAKI: This was agreed to by the national security team. Beyond that, I'm not going to—I don't have anything.

QUESTION: Why are you afraid to say who made the decision?

MS. PSAKI: I'm not afraid of anything, Arshad. I'm just not—I'm not getting into more specifics than that for you.

Press Briefing, U.S. Dep't of State, Daily Press Briefing (July 26, 2015), https://2009-2017.state.gov/r/pa/prs/dpb/2013/07/212484.htm [https://perma.cc/PMX8-KUEZ].

13. Portions of this chapter draw upon my earlier articles. *See* Michael J. Glennon, *Populism, Elites, and National Security*, XXXI Humanitas 35, 39 (2018), https://css.cua.edu/humanitas_journal/populism-elites-and-national-security/ [https://perma.cc/2ZX7-2USP]; Michael J. Glennon, *Security Breach: Trump's Tussle with the Bureaucratic State*, Harper's Mag. (June 2017), https://harpers.org/archive/2017/06/security-breach/ [https://perma.cc/9PLX-KNAR].

14. Donald J. Trump (@realDonaldTrump), Twitter (Apr. 13, 2018, 5:17 AM), https://media-cdn.factba.se/realdonaldtrump-twitter/984767560494313472.jpg [https://perma.cc/23TZ-MSEQ]. Trump's tweets are available only through an archive, as Trump was banned from Twitter on Jan. 8, 2021. Twitter, *Permanent Suspension of @realDonaldTrump*, Twitter Blog (Jan. 8, 2021), https://blog.twitter.com/en_us/topics/company/2020/suspension [https://perma.cc/F26X-65HU].

15. Donald J. Trump (@realDonaldTrump), Twitter (Jan. 11, 2017, 4:48 PM), https://media-cdn.factba.se/realdonaldtrump-twitter/819164172781060096.jpg [https://perma.cc/NK7E-6RRN].

16. Brandon Carter, *Trump Slams Former US Intel Leaders as 'Political Hacks'*, The Hill (Nov. 11, 2017), http://thehill.com/homenews/administration/359894-trump-slams-former-us-intel-leaders-as-political-hacks [https://perma.cc/B3BY-HVTV].

17. Greg Miller, Adam Entous & Ellen Nakashima, *National Security Adviser Flynn Discussed Sanctions with Russian Ambassador, Despite Denials, Officials Say*, Wash. Post (Feb. 9, 2017), https://www.washingtonpost.com/world/national-security/national-security-adviser-flynn-discussed-sanctions-with-russian-ambassador-despite-denials-officials-say/2017/02/09/f85b29d6-ee11-11e6-b4ff-ac2cf509efe5story.html?utm_term=.4d19880d10f9 [https://perma.cc/63B6-J72A].

18. Michael S. Schmidt, Mark Mazzetti & Matt Apuzzo, *Trump Campaign Aides Had Repeated Contacts with Russian Intelligence*, N.Y. Times (Feb. 14, 2017), https://www.

nytimes.com/2017/02/14/us/politics/russia-intelligence-communications-trump. html [https://perma.cc/RZ4T-R6U8].

19. For a detailed account of television networks' reliance upon former security officials as analysts following the search of Trump's Mar-a-Lago home, see Matt Taibbi, *Sweeps Week on FBI TV!*, TK News by Matt Taibbi (Aug. 16, 2022), https://taibbi.subst ack.com/p/sweeps-week-on-fbi-tv?utm_source=substack&utm_medium=email [https://perma.cc/9N58-JVAY].

20. The most comprehensive account appeared over forty years ago, when the Church Committee issued its report. *See* S. Select Comm. to Study Governmental Operations, Final Report of the Select Committee to Study Governmental Operations with Respect to Intelligence Activities of the United States Senate, S. Rep. No. 94-755 (1976). The report describes COINTELPRO, the FBI's program aimed at exposing and disrupting the activities of thousands of groups and individuals that were engaged in constitutionally protected conduct aimed at protesting the Vietnam War or campaigning for civil rights. The FBI mailed hundreds of anonymous letters to civil rights activists; one was sent to Martin Luther King, intending to drive him to suicide. It describes Operation Chaos, the CIA's own domestic spy program, and Operation Lingual, under which the CIA illegally opened and read thousands of international letters every year to and from American citizens. It also describes Operation Minaret, under which the NSA placed fifteen hundred individuals on a watch list and listened in on telephone conversations with no court warrants. It revealed that even the army engaged in domestic surveillance, spying on political officials, antiwar and civil rights activists, and church leaders, and sharing the information it gathered with the FBI, CIA, and local police departments. These were not rare, one-off pranks undertaken by a lone cowboy. These were painstakingly planned, deliberate operations in which America's most trusted security services, under the direction of their leaders and acting over a period of many years, "turned their dark arts against the very people they were created to protect," as Loch Johnson has written. Loch K. Johnson, Spy Watching: Intelligence Accountability in the United States xi (Oxford Univ. Press 2017). Their actions represented a violation of the public trust, an attempt to alter the people's form of government without the people's knowledge or consent.

21. Virtually every one of the newly exalted champions of morality in government—James Clapper, Michael Hayden, John Brennan, Mike Morrell, Leon Panetta, Robert Gates—lined up behind President Trump and pushed for the approval of Gina Haspel's nomination to head the CIA. Their gift to the nation was a CIA director who ran a secret prison where unspeakably gruesome practices occurred, who destroyed records of what happened, and who then continued the cover-up during her confirmation hearings. *See* Julian E. Barnes and Scott Shane, *Cables Detail C.I.A Waterboarding at Secret Prison Run by Gina Haspel*, N.Y. Times (Aug. 10, 2018), https://www.nytimes.com/2018/08/10/us/politics/waterboarding-gina-haspel-cia-prison.html [https://perma.cc/W6YD-GT6V] (detailing the cables from the prison Haspel oversaw); Annabelle Timsit, *What Happened at the Thailand 'Black Site' Run by Trump's CIA Pick*, The Atlantic (Mar. 14, 2018), https://www.theatlantic.com/ international/archive/2018/03/gina-haspel-black-site-torture-cia/555539/ [https://

perma.cc/5WGX-FPD3]; Glenn Greenwald, *Will Democrats Unite to Block Trump's Torturer, Gina Haspel, as CIA Chief? If Not, What do They #Resist?*, THE INTERCEPT (May 8, 2018), https://theintercept.com/2018/05/08/will-democrats-unite-to-block-trumps-torturer-gina-haspel-as-cia-chief-if-not-what-do-they-resist/ [https://perma.cc/5C8H-8ZJM] (documenting Clapper's and Brennan's support for Haspel). Senator Ron Wyden, a member of the Senate Intelligence Committee, said that the process by which Haspel was confirmed was "a stark failure of Senate oversight, and it is about as flagrant an example as I have ever seen. The Senate should have stood up to this self-serving abuse of power, but it did not." 164 CONG. REC. S2736 (daily ed. May 17, 2018) (statement of Sen. Wyden).

22. Mallory Shelbourne, *Schumer: Trump 'Really Dumb' for Attacking Intelligence Agencies*, THE HILL (Jan. 3, 2017), https://thehill.com/homenews/administration/312 605-schumer-trump-being-really-dumb-by-going-after-intelligence-community/ [https://perma.cc/PU8Y-KGGZ].

23. *Id.*

24. Tim Hains, *Former CIA Official Phil Mudd Warns Trump: "Think Again" About War with Intel Community, "We're Going to Win"*, REALCLEAR POLITICS (Feb. 4, 2018), https://www.realclearpolitics.com/video/2018/02/04/phil_mudd_warns_trump_ in_war_with_intelligence_community_were_going_to_win.html [https://perma.cc/ 4FYT-BVSG].

25. Bill Kristol (@BillKristol), TWITTER (Feb. 14, 2017, 8:36 AM), https://twitter.com/bill kristol/status/831497364661747712?lang=en [https://perma.cc/3QF7-VZST].

26. John Cassidy, *Trump Isolates Himself with C.I.A. Attack*, NEW YORKER (Dec. 12, 2016), https://www.newyorker.com/news/john-cassidy/trump-isolates-himself-with-c-i-a-attack?mbid=feed_ns [https://perma.cc/Z39P-4DL4].

27. Eugene Robinson, Opinion, *God Bless the 'Deep State'*, WASH. POST (July 19, 2018), https://www.washingtonpost.com/opinions/god-bless-the-deep-state/2018/07/ 19/de36bd00-8b8a-11e8-85ae-511bc1146b0b_story.html [https://perma.cc/ZB2E-ZAPT].

28. *Id.*

29. *Id.*

30. MONMOUTH UNIV. POLLING INST., NATIONAL: PUBLIC TROUBLED BY 'DEEP STATE' 2 (Mar. 19, 2018), https://www.monmouth.edu/polling-institute/documents/mon mouthpoll_us_031918.pdf/ [https://perma.cc/U9D5-LXVQ].

31. SAMUEL P. HUNTINGTON, THE SOLDIER AND THE STATE: THE THEORY AND POLITICS OF CIVIL-MILITARY RELATIONS 163 (1957).

32. *Id.* at 189–90.

33. Greer v. Spock, 424 U.S. 828, 839 (1976).

34. U.S. Dep't of Homeland Sec., *National Terrorism Advisory System Bulletin* (Feb. 7, 2022), https://www.dhs.gov/ntas/advisory/national-terrorism-advisory-system-bulletin-february-07-2022 (last visited May 9, 2022) [https://perma.cc/Y5XW-9C4Q] (abbreviating mis-, dis-, and mal-information as "MDM" and noting that "MDM" contributes to the heightened threat environment faced by the United States).

35. C-SPAN, *Biden Foreign Policy and National Security Team Announcement* (Nov. 24, 2020), https://www.c-span.org/video/?478351-1/biden-foreign-policy-national-

security-team-announcement (Sullivan addressed President Biden and the nation, stating "Sir, we will be vigilant in the face of enduring threats from nuclear weapons to terrorism, but you have also tasked us with re-imagining our national security for the unprecedented combination of crises we face at home and abroad: The pandemic, the economic crisis, the climate crisis, technological disruption, threats to democracy, racial injustice, and inequality in all forms ") [https://perma.cc/LRA6-WE3G]

36. Eric Schmitt & Helene Cooper, *Pentagon Acknowledges Aug. 29 Drone Strike in Afghanistan Was a Tragic Mistake that Killed 10 Civilians*, N.Y. TIMES (Nov. 3, 2021), https://www.nytimes.com/2021/09/17/us/politics/pentagon-drone-strike-afghanistan.html [https://perma.cc/Y8WQ-EVLP].

37. 303 Creative Ltd. Liab. Co. v. Elenis, 6 F.4th 1160, 1178 (10th Cir. 2021) *cert. granted in part*, 142 S. Ct. 1106 (2022).

38. U.S. Dep't of Homeland Sec., *supra* note 34.

39. See infra text accompanying notes 322–327 and 361–388.

40. Katherine Fung, *Elon Musk Calls Trudeau Government the Real 'Fringe Minority' in Trucker Protest*, NEWSWEEK (Jan. 31, 2022), https://www.newsweek.com/elon-musk-calls-trudeau-government-real-fringe-minority-trucker-protest-1674524 [https://perma.cc/NTH3-BK4W].

41. Other tactics include "exclusion, derogatory labelling, hostile comments and threatening statements by the media, both mainstream and social; dismissal by the respondents' employers; official inquiries; revocation of medical licenses; lawsuits; and retraction of scientific papers after publication." Yaffa Shir-Razl, Ety Elisha, Brian Martin, Natti Ronel & Josh Guetzkow, *Censorship and Suppression of Covid-19 Heterodoxy: Tactics and Counter-Tactics*, MINERVA, Sept. 28, 2022, https://doi.org/10.1007/s11024-022-09479-4 [https://perma.cc/5X9K-S8J6].

42. See Damon Linker, Opinion, *The Plausible Dystopia of a Social Credit System*, THE WEEK (Feb. 17, 2022), https://theweek.com/politics/1010271/the-plausible-dystopia-of-a-social-credit-system [https://perma.cc/5K3Z-R3R5] (arguing that "the core worry is founded in fact. The alignment of pervasive high-tech gatekeeping with an impulse to police ideological and moral conformity is not only possible but already beginning to emerge.").

43. *See generally* Shir-Razl et al., *supra* note 41.

44. John Podesta, *Need to Know: Governing in Secret, in* THE WAR ON OUR FREEDOMS: CIVIL LIBERTIES IN AN AGE OF TERRORISM 227 (Richard C. Leone & Greg Anrig Jr. eds., PublicAffairs 2003). "[I]f people are not aware of censorship, they're not upset about it." Shir-Razl et al., *supra* note 41 (detailing use of cover-up tactics such as third-party "fact-checkers" to discredit reputable sources, publishing disparaging claims about them, and dismissing them from positions of influence).

45. Joan Donovan, *Why Social Media Can't Keep Moderating Content in the Shadows*, MIT TECH. REV. (Nov. 6, 2020), https://www.technologyreview.com/2020/11/06/1011769/social-media-moderation-transparency-censorship/ [https://perma.cc/D7ZW-W2QH].

46. Thomas Barrabi, *Mark Zuckerberg Tells Joe Rogan Facebook Was Wrong to Ban the Post's Hunter Biden Laptop Story*, N.Y. POST (Aug. 25, 2022), https://nypost.com/2022/08/25/mark-zuckerberg-criticizes-twitters-handling-of-the-posts-hun

ter-biden-laptop-story/ [https://perma.cc/CCF5-VYHS]. Jack Dorsey, Twitter's CEO, later said, "Straight blocking of URLs was wrong." Avery Hartmans, *Jack Dorsey Responded to Outrage Surrounding Twitter's Handling of the New York Post's Hunter Biden Story, Saying 'Straight Blocking of URLs Was Wrong'*, Bus. Insider (Oct. 16, 2020), https://www.businessinsider.com/twitter-jack-dorsey-blocking-ny-post-hun ter-biden-story-wrong-2020-10?utm_medium=referral&utm_source=yahoo.com [https://perma.cc/Z36B-NF7D].

47. Thomas Friedman, Opinion, *The Cancellation of Mother Russia Is Underway*, N. Y. Times (Mar. 6, 2022), https://www.nytimes.com/2022/03/06/opinion/putin-ukra ine-china.html [https://perma.cc/4KPK-2BFH].

48. "If these trends continue, citizens could find themselves effectively exiled by order of corporate governors—unable to travel or go to school while also barred from espousing dissenting views on social media. They would, effectively, be 'disappeared' within a shadow state that lacks any electoral or appellate process, a dystopian brave new world that could become all too real if we allow elected officials to use corporate surrogates to control the essential aspects of our lives." Jonathan Turley, Opinion, *'Shadow State': Embracing Corporate Governance to Escape Constitutional Limits*, The Hill (July 17, 2021), https://thehill.com/opinion/judiciary/563520-shadow-state-embracing-corporate-governance-to-escape-constitutional-limits/ [https://perma. cc/4WSJ-73Y6].

49. *See, e.g.*, Amanda Holpuch, *Why Social Media Sites Are Removing Andrew Tate's Accounts*, N.Y. Times (Aug. 24, 2022), https://www.nytimes.com/2022/08/24/technol ogy/andrew-tate-banned-tiktok-instagram.html [https://perma.cc/BQ9V-QNNZ].

50. *See* Siladitya Ray, *Amazon Responds to Republican Sens. on Book Ban, Says Won't Sell Books That Frame LGBTQ+ Identities as Mental Illness*, Forbes (May 12, 2021), https://www.forbes.com/sites/siladityaray/2021/03/12/amazon-responds-to-republi can-sens-on-book-ban-says-wont-sell-books-that-frame-lgbtq-identities-as-men tal-illness/?sh=62b7e974006e [https://perma.cc/P2M4-2BE3].

51. *See* Matthew Loh, *Canada Says It Will Freeze the Bank Accounts of 'Freedom Convoy' Truckers Who Continue Their Anti-Vaccine Mandate Blockades*, Bus. Insider (Feb. 14, 2022), https://www.businessinsider.com/trudeau-canada-freeze-bank-accounts-free dom-convoy-truckers-2022-2 [https://perma.cc/RZH5-UK2Y]. De-banking—the politicization of lines of credit and the severing of basic financial services to "controversial" conservatives—is already very much here to stay. Just ask (recent congressional candidate) Laura Loomer about PayPal. Avery Anapol, *Far-Right Activist Laura Loomer Banned from PayPal*, The Hill (Feb. 5, 2019), https://thehill.com/policy/technology/ 428600-far-right-activist-laura-loomer-banned-from-paypal/ [https://perma.cc/9Q6F-KUVN]. Or ask the Canadian truckers about GoFundMe. *Freedom Convoy: GoFundMe Seizes Funds of Canada 'Occupation'*, BBC News (Feb. 5, 2022), https://www.bbc.com/ news/world-us-canada-60267840 [https://perma.cc/7HJP-7Y8T]. In recent years, moreover, conglomerates such as Bank of America have stopped lending to certain firearms manufacturers—the very defenders, in this case, of the Second Amendment. Tiffany Hsu, *Bank of America to Stop Financing Makers of Military-Style Guns*, N.Y. Times (Apr. 10, 2018), https://nytimes.com/2018/04/10/business/bank-of-america-guns.html [https://perma.cc/56QW-W8R6]. Other examples abound.

52. *See, e.g.*, Anna Merlan, *The Ivermectin Advocates' War Has Just Begun*, VICE (July 1, 2021), https://www.vice.com/en/article/y3d5gv/ivermectin-covid-treatment-advocates-rogan-weinstein-hecker [https://perma.cc/G67U-5EJJ].

53. Eugene Volokh, *PayPal Still Threatens $2500 Fines for Promoting "Discriminatory" "Intolerance" (Even if Not "Misinformation")*, REASON (Oct. 9, 2022), https://reason.com/volokh/2022/10/09/paypal-still-threatens-2500-fines-for-promoting-discriminatory-intolerance-even-if-not-misinformation/ [https://perma.cc/EJ4W-LX57]. *See also* Glenn Greenwald, *The Consortium Imposing the Growing Censorship Regime*, Substack (Oct. 28, 2022), https://greenwald.substack.com/p/the-consortium-imposing-the-growing (describing various examples of PayPal shutting down the ability for organizations to receive a donation based on dissenting causes or views ranging from WikiLeaks, "Gays Against Groomers," and left-wing anti-war news organizations Mint Press and Consortium News) [https://perma.cc/3KWP-5US].

54. *Amerithrax or Anthrax Investigation*, FED. BUREAU OF INVESTIGATION, https://archives.fbi.gov/archives/about-us/history/famous-cases/anthrax-amerithrax/amerithrax-investigation (last visited Oct. 4, 2022) [https://perma.cc/W2AN-CJVZ].

55. *The Threat of Bioterrorism and the Spread of Infectious Diseases, Hearing Before the S. Comm. on Foreign Rels.*, 107th Cong. 78 (2001) (statement of Dr. David L. Heymann, Exec. Dir., Communicable Diseases, World Health Org.).

56. WHITE HOUSE, NATIONAL SECURITY STRATEGY OF THE UNITED STATES OF AMERICA 9 (2017), https://trumpwhitehouse.archives.gov/wp-content/uploads/2017/12/NSS-Final-12-18-2017-0905.pdf [https://perma.cc/38NZ-NRKG].

57. *Id.*

58. *Id.*

59. *See* Editorial, Opinion, *The Coming Storm: America Is Not Ready for a Future Pandemic*, WASH. POST (Aug. 27, 2022), https://www.washingtonpost.com/opinions/2022/08/27/covid-pandemic-lessons-prepare/ [https://perma.cc/2ZFL-FDRC] ("The pandemic response was badly fragmented among states and localities. The nation broke into warring camps about whether to be open or to adopt restrictions and whether to mandate masks or vaccines, and a checkerboard of jurisdictions fought against each other for diagnostic tests, supplies and therapeutics."); *see generally*, ERIK J. DAHL, THE COVID-19 INTELLIGENCE FAILURE: WHY WARNING WAS NOT ENOUGH (2022).

60. U.S. Dep't of Homeland Sec., *supra* note 34.

61. *See* Ken Dilanian et al., *In a Break with the Past, U.S. Is Using Intel to Fight an Info War with Russia, Even When the Intel Isn't Rock Solid*, NBC NEWS (Apr. 6, 2022), https://www.nbcnews.com/politics/national-security/us-using-declassified-intel-fight-info-war-russia-even-intel-isnt-rock-rcna23014 [https://perma.cc/F8SN-2C9Q]. NBC has reported that the government has intentionally made false or low-confidence assertions concerning Russian requests for arms from China, plans for false flag and chemical weapons attacks, and a variety of other subjects. Ken Klippenstein & Lee Fang, *Leaked Documents Outline DHS's Plans to Police Disinformation*, THE INTERCEPT (Oct. 31, 2022), https://theintercept.com/2022/10/31/social-media-disinformation-dhs/ [https://perma.cc/UD78-NE6F (noting that censorship of dissident voices was carried out with explicit encouragement from government actors).

62. Judith Miller, Stephen Engelberg & William J. Broad, *U.S. Germ Warfare Research Pushes Treaty Limits*, N.Y. TIMES (Sept. 4, 2001), https://www.nytimes.com/2001/09/04/world/us-germ-warfare-research-pushes-treaty-limits.html [https://perma.cc/S27D-VN5S].

63. *See id.*

64. *Id.*

65. *Id.*

66. See Alison Young & Nick Penzenstadler, *Universities, Feds Fight to Keep Lab Failings Secret*, USA TODAY (May 28, 2015), https://www.usatoday.com/story/news/2015/05/28/labs-fight-for-secrecy/26530719/ [https://perma.cc/QPD4-ABKW].

67. *See infra* notes 107, 111.

68. Judith Miller, Stephen ENGELBERG & WILLIAM J. BROAD, GERMS: BIOLOGICAL WEAPONS AND AMERICA'S SECRET WAR 35 (2001).

69. LYN KLOTZ & EDWARD SYLVESTER, BREEDING BIO INSECURITY: HOW U.S. BIODEFENSE IS EXPORTING FEAR, GLOBALIZING RISKS, AND MAKING US ALL LESS SECURE 113 (2009).

70. *Id.* Biosafety level 3 laboratories are used to control infectious agents that can cause serious hazards and potentially lethal conditions within the laboratory and community through respiratory transmission of the organism. Marlon L. Bayot and Kevin C. King, *Biohazard Levels*, National Library of Medicine, National Institutes of Health, Sept. 19, 2022, https://www.ncbi.nlm.nih.gov/books/NBK535351/.

71. *Id.*

72. MILLER, ENGELBERG & BROAD, *supra* note 68, at 67.

73. *Id.* at 68.

74. *Id.* at 69.

75. *See id.*

76. KLOTZ & SYLVESTER, *supra* note 69, at 120 (defining BSL-3 and BSL-4 labs).

77. Convention on the Prohibition of the Development, Production and Stockpiling of Bacteriological (Biological) and Toxin Weapons and on Their Destruction art. I(1), Apr. 10, 1972, 26 U.S.T. 583, 1015 U.N.T.S 163.

78. *Id.* art. I(2).

79. Gary D. Solis, *The Law of Armed Conflict: International Humanitarian Law in* WAR 766 (2d ed. 2016).

80. Miller et al., *supra* note 62.

81. *Id.*

82. *Id.*

83. *Id.*

84. *Id.*

85. KLOTZ & SYLVESTER, *supra* note 69, at 111. "We were surprised it was the Ames strain," said the microbiologist who identified the anthrax used in the attack letters, Dr. Paul Keim. "And it was chilling at the same time, because the Ames strain is a laboratory strain that had been developed by the U.S. Army as a vaccine-challenge strain." Sarah Moughty, *Paul Keim: "We Were Surprised It Was the Ames Strain"*, FRONTLINE, October 10, 2010, https://www.pbs.org/wgbh/frontline/article/paul-keim-we-were-surprised-it-was-the-ames-strain/ [https://perma.cc/K83E-3DZA].

86. *See* Miller, Engelberg, & Broad, *supra* note 68, at 331.

87. *See* Klotz & Sylvester, *supra* note 69, at 111.

88. Miller, Engelberg, & Broad, *supra* note 68, at 335.

89. Klotz & Sylvester, *supra* note 69, at 111.

90. *Id.* at 112.

91. *See* Miller, Engelberg, & Broad, *supra* note 68, at 334.

92. *Id.* at 233.

93. *Id.* at 334.

94. *See generally* Klotz & Sylvester, *supra* note 69.

95. *See id.* at 172–73 (describing CDC's post-9/11 emphasis on bioterrorism and increased secrecy).

96. Nat'l Inst. of Allergy and Infectious Diseases, *NIAID Role in Biodefense and Emerging Infectious Diseases Research* (Oct. 26, 2011), https://www.niaid.nih.gov/research/bio defense-emerging-infectious-diseases-research [https://perma.cc/ZM63-H8YG].

97. Klotz & Sylvester, *supra* note 69, at 172. *Cf.* Ashley Rindsberg, *How Dick Cheney Created Anthony Fauci*, UnHerd (Aug. 29, 2022), https://unherd.com/2022/08/ how-dick-cheney-created-anthony-fauci/ [https://perma.cc/7CDA-FXCC] ("Far from being a public health expert, Fauci sits at the very top of America's biodefence infrastructure.").

98. *See* Press Release, Ctrs. for Disease Control and Prevention, Dr. Gerberding's Remarks at the National Press Club Conference (Feb. 22, 2005), https://www.cdc. gov/media/pressrel/r050222b.htm [https://perma.cc/BGV7-SHFQ].

99. Klotz & Sylvester, *supra* note 69, at 173.

100. Ctrs. for Disease Control and Prevention, *the state of the cdc, fiscal year 2004* 4, 36 (2005), https://stacks.cdc.gov/view/cdc/6496 [https://perma.cc/ JH9D-Z3EL].

101. Klotz & Sylvester, *supra* note 69, at 173.

102. Willem Marx, *COVID-19 Has Shown U.S., U.K. are Vulnerable to Biological Terrorism, Experts Say*, NBC News (May 18, 2020), https://www.nbcnews.com/polit ics/national-security/experts-covid-19-has-shown-u-s-u-k-are-n1207776 [https:// perma.cc/ZW3P-HGFQ].

103. Ewen MacAskill, *Bill Gates Warns Tens of Millions Could be Killed by Bio-Terrorism*, The Guardian (Feb. 18, 2017), https://www.theguardian.com/technology/ 2017/feb/18/bill-gates-warns-tens-of-millions-could-be-killed-by-bio-terrorism [https://perma.cc/R7K2-XLY3].

104. *Id.*

105. Barack Obama & Richard Lugar, Opinion, *Grounding a Pandemic*, N.Y. Times (June 6, 2005), https://www.nytimes.com/2005/06/06/opinion/grounding-a-pandemic. html [https://perma.cc/L2SB-EVSY].

106. "There is currently no system for the global monitoring and regulation of gain-of-function research of concern," the *Lancet* COVID-19 Commission stated. Jeffrey D. Sachs et al., *The* Lancet *Commission on Lessons for the Future from the COVID-19 Pandemic*, 400 The Lancet 1224, 1233 (Sept. 14, 2022), https://www.thelancet.com/act ion/showPdf?pii=S0140-6736%2822%2901585-9 [https://perma.cc/4YWU-3NMG].

Restrictions on "gain of function" research had actually been loosened in recent years. See David Willman & Madison Muller, *A Science in the Shadows: Controls on 'Gain of Function' Experiments with Supercharged Pathogens Have Been Undercut Despite Concerns About Lab Leaks*, WASH. POST (Aug. 26, 2021), https://www.washingtonp ost.com/nation/interactive/2021/a-science-in-the-shadows/ [https://perma.cc/ 9QBE-2XGS].

107. *See* ALINA CHAN & MATT RIDLEY, VIRAL: THE SEARCH FOR THE ORIGIN OF COVID-19 133-148 (2021) (describing accidents risking the escape of dangerous pathogens even in high-security laboratories); Mara Hvistendahl, *Experimenting With Disaster*, THE INTERCEPT (Nov. 1, 2022), https://theintercept.com/series/experi menting-with-disaster/ [https://perma.cc/L9NY-BJEX]; Alison Young, *Could an Accident Have Caused COVID-19? Why the Wuhan Lab-Leak Theory Shouldn't Be Dismissed*, USA TODAY (Mar. 22, 2021), https://www.usatoday.com/in-depth/opin ion/2021/03/22/why-covid-lab-leak-theory-wuhan-shouldnt-dismissed-column/ 4765985001/ (there is "no reason to believe" that safety lapses are not occurring at elite U.S. labs and in other countries as well) [https://perma.cc/Y2XR-MUVY]. There is "enormous reason to believe," said Dr. Jeffrey Sachs, chair of the *Lancet* COVID-19 Commission, that extremely dangerous research was going on involving the modification of viruses to make them more lethal; that the scientists who are involved in that research keep the public in the dark through misdirection ("It's like sleight of hand art. Don't look over there. Look over here."); that "they don't want any regulations on it"; that "a very extensive research program" along these lines was funded by the National Institutes of Health and the National Institute of Allergy and Infectious Diseases; that Dr. Anthony Fauci believed the scope of this research was better swept "under the rug"; that scientists at the Wuhan Institute of Virology "were trained by American scientists to use advanced bioengineering methodologies"; and that NIH is "not telling us the truth, that they had reason to fear from the start that this came out of a lab. And that to this day, they have reason to suspect it, but they're not talking." It is likely, Sachs said, that COVID "came out of U.S. lab biotechnology, not out of nature." Why is all this being kept from the public? Not simply, Sachs indicated, because of the enormous ethical, moral, and geopo- litical implications—about 18 million people have died worldwide from COVID— but because "there is so much dangerous research underway right now under the umbrella of biodefense or other things that we don't know about, that is not being properly controlled." The "technological capacity to do dangerous things using this biotechnology is extraordinary right now. . . . I want some global control over this stuff. . . . [T]his is a clear and present risk." Nathan Robinson, *Why the Chair of the* Lancet's *COVID-19 Commission Thinks the US Government Is Preventing a Real Investigation Into the Pandemic*, CURRENT AFFAIRS (Aug. 2, 2022), https://www. currentaffairs.org/2022/08/why-the-chair-of-the-lancets-covid-19-commission- thinks-the-us-government-is-preventing-a-real-investigation-into-the-pandemic [https://perma.cc/QK94-99FT] (interview with Jeffrey Sachs). In response to such comments, Sachs has been accused of dangerous "meddling and conspiratorialism." Angela Rasmussen & Michael Worobey, *Conspiracy Theories About COVID-19 Help*

Nobody, Foreign Policy (Sept. 15, 2022), https://foreignpolicy.com/2022/09/15/conspiracy-theories-covid-19-commission/ [https://perma.cc/6Q36-48HY].

108. Dan Diamond, *'Untrustworthy and Ineffective': Panel Blasts Governments' Covid Response*, Wash. Post (Sept. 14, 2022), https://www.washingtonpost.com/health/2022/09/14/lancet-covid-commission-report-who/ [https://perma.cc/KC5S-ESUT].

109. Sachs et al., *supra* note 106, at 1232.

110. *Id.* at 1233.

111. *See supra* text accompanying notes 67–76 and 85–89. *See also* Carl Zimmer, *Bat Virus Studies Raise Questions About Laboratory Tinkering*, N.Y. Times (July 15, 2022), https://www.nytimes.com/2022/07/15/science/bat-coronavirus-laboratory-experiments.html/ [https://perma.cc/7652-YY3M]. "We clearly are not safe from our own labs," Klotz and Sylvester conclude. Klotz & Sylvester, *supra* note 69, at 111 (2009); Alison Young, *Newly Disclosed CDC Biolab Failures 'Like a Screenplay For a Disaster Movie'*, USA Today (June 2, 2016), https://www.usatoday.com/story/news/2016/06/02/newly-disclosed-cdc-lab-incidents-fuel-concerns-safety-transparency/84978860/ [https://perma.cc/H4YF-G3VS]; Alison Young, *Power, Airflow, Safety Issues Plague High-Tech CDC Labs*, USA Today (July 9, 2015), https://www.usatoday.com/story/news/2015/07/09/new-cdc-lab-incidents-airflow/29920917/; Alison Young, *Reports Reveal Safety Violations at Many Bioterror Labs*, USA Today (July 16, 2014), https://www.usatoday.com/story/news/nation/2014/07/15/inspector-general-reports-violations-bioterror-labs/12664213/ [https://perma.cc/BZ2E-8LLY].

112. Sachs et al., *supra* note 106, at 1233.

113. *See, e.g.,* Bret Stephens, Opinion, *Media Groupthink and the Lab-Leak Theory*, N.Y. Times (May 31, 2021), https://www.nytimes.com/2021/05/31/opinion/media-lab-leak-theory.html/ [https://perma.cc/H52V-S2WT].

114. Nicholas Wade, *The Origin of COVID: Did People or Nature Open Pandora's Box at Wuhan?*, Bulletin of the Atomic Scientists (May 5, 2021), https://thebulletin.org/2021/05/the-origin-of-covid-did-people-or-nature-open-pandoras-box-at-wuhan/ [https://perma.cc/3243-LPPM]. Under the moratorium statute, Wade writes, gain-of-function research is defined as "'any research that improves the ability of a pathogen to cause disease.'" *Id.*

115. *See Statement by President Joe Biden on the Investigation into the Origins of COVID-19*, White House (Aug. 27, 2021), https://www.whitehouse.gov/briefing-room/statements-releases/2021/08/27/statement-by-president-joe-biden-on-the-investigation-into-the-origins-of-covid-%E2%81%A019/ [https://perma.cc/Z9H9-SXEM].

116. Adam Taylor, *WHO Covid Origins Report Says 'Lab Leak' Theory Needs Further Investigation*, Wash. Post (June 9, 2022), https://www.washingtonpost.com/world/2022/06/09/who-sago-covid-origins/ [https://perma.cc/UMM9-GTKB]; Alexander Smith, *China Slams New WHO Report Suggesting Further Investigation Into Covid 'Lab Leak' Theory*, NBC News (June 10, 2022), https://www.nbcnews.com/news/world/covid-19-urges-investigation-chinese-wuhan-lab-leak-theory-rcna32910 [https://perma.cc/EQ2E-KNCU].

117. For examples from the *New York Times, Washington Post*, and *National Public Radio* see CHAN & RIDLEY, *supra* note 107, at 304 (2021). Facebook censored or labelled as misinformation posts that discussed a laboratory origin of the virus. *Id.* at 307. "[C]ensorship," they conclude, "marked the coverage." *Id.* at 307. *See generally* Matt Ridley & Alina Chan, *What Happened to the Lab-Leak Hypothesis?*, UNHERD (June 23, 2022), https://unherd.com/2022/06/what-happened-to-the-lab-leak-hypothesis [https://perma.cc/Q69P-HZ3B] ("[B]y taking down credible moderate voices, our critics within the scientific establishment are polarising the issue and casting the lab origin-- hypothesis as one that is only championed by anti-science or uninformed groups."); Thomas Fazi, *The Lab-Leak Theory Isn't Dead*, UNHERD (Aug. 30, 2022), https://unherd.com/2022/08/the-lab-leak-theory-isnt-dead/ [https://perma.cc/2XTJ-Q7ET] ("[F]rom the beginning the very notion that the virus might have a laboratory-based origin was stifled. The hot denials came not only from the Chinese authorities and the Wuhan Institute of Virology itself, but also from the WHO and leading Western scientists, institutions and media organisations."). *See* Katherine Eban, *The Lab-Leak Theory: Inside the Fight to Uncover COVID-19's Origins*, VANITY FAIR (June 3, 2021), https://www.vanityfair.com/news/2021/06/the-lab-leak-theory-inside-the-fight-to-uncover-covid-19s-origins/ [https://perma.cc/52XK-L59X] ("In one State Department meeting, officials seeking to demand transparency from the Chinese government say they were explicitly told by colleagues not to explore the Wuhan Institute of Virology's gain-of-function research, because it would bring unwelcome attention to U.S. government funding of it."). *See* Shir-Razl et al., *supra* note 41.

118. Ari Schulman, Opinion, *Why Many Americans Turned on Anthony Fauci*, N.Y. TIMES (Aug. 30, 2022), https://www.nytimes.com/2022/08/30/opinion/why-anthony-faucis-covid-legacy-is-a-failure.html [https://perma.cc/A893-84SM].

119. *See* Eban, *supra* note 117.

120. *Id.*

121. *Id.*

122. *Id.*

123. *Id.*

124. Paulina Firozi, *Tom Cotton Keeps Repeating a Coronavirus Fringe Theory That Scientists Have Disputed*, WASH. POST (Feb. 17, 2020), https://www.washingtonpost.com/politics/2020/02/16/tom-cotton-coronavirus-conspiracy/ [https://perma.cc/MTV4-AKAY].

125. *Id.*

126. *See* Rowan Jacobsen, *Exclusive: How Amateur Sleuths Broke the Wuhan Lab Story and Embarrassed the Media*, NEWSWEEK (June 2, 2021), https://www.newsweek.com/exclusive-how-amateur-sleuths-broke-wuhan-lab-story-embarrassed-media-1596958/ [https://perma.cc/5Y3G-PC4Z].

127. Editorial, Opinion, *Facebook's Lab-Leak About-Face*, WALL ST. J. (May 27, 2021), https://www.wsj.com/articles/facebooks-lab-leak-about-face-11622154198 [https://perma.cc/2DEY-T3BS]; Cristiano Lima, *Facebook No Longer Treating 'Man-Made' COVID as a Crackpot Idea*, POLITICO (May 27, 2021), https://www.politico.com/news/2021/05/26/facebook-ban-covid-man-made-491053 [https://perma.cc/8E8N-RCD3].

128. See Martin Robinson, James Tapsfield & Rory Tingle, *Twitter REFUSES to Say if It Will Censor Coronavirus Lab Leak Theory or Considers It 'Misleading'*, DAILY MAIL (May 28, 2021), https://www.dailymail.co.uk/news/article-9629057/Twitter-REFUSES-say-censor-Coronavirus-lab-leak-theory.html [https://perma.cc/K8KP-NDP7].

129. Editorial, Opinion, *Facebook's Lab-Leak About-Face*, WALL ST. J. (May 27, 2021), https://www.wsj.com/articles/facebooks-lab-leak-about-face-11622154198 [https://perma.cc/2DEY-T3BS].

130. Daniel Funke, *Li-Meng Yan Stated On September 15, 2020 in an Interview on "Tucker Carlson Tonight": "This Virus, COVID-19 SARS-CoV-2 Virus, Actually is Not from Nature. It is a Man-Made Virus Created in the Lab"*, POLITIFACT (Sept. 16, 2020), https://www.politifact.com/li-meng-yan-fact-check/ [https://perma.cc/GQ66-WU29].

131. Angelo Fichera, *Report Resurrects Baseless Claim that Coronavirus Was Bioengineered*, FACTCHECK.ORG (Sept. 17, 2020), https://www.factcheck.org/2020/09/report-resurrects-baseless-claim-that-coronavirus-was-bioengineered/ [https://perma.cc/7YQQ-DCMX].

132. *See* CHAN & RIDLEY, *supra* note 107, at 304 ("[M]any public figures of influence" in the West "[took] their cue" from the *Lancet* letter.).

133. Charles Calisher et al., *Statement in Support of the Scientists, Public Health Professionals, and Medical Professionals of China Combatting COVID-19*, 395 THE LANCET e42, e42 (2020). The question of course had been whether a leak had occurred as the result of an accident, not as part of a conspiracy.

134. *See* Wade, *supra* note 114; Sharon Lerner & Mara Hvistendahl, *Peter Daszak Answers Critics and Defends Coronavirus Research*, THE INTERCEPT (March 11, 2022), https://theintercept.com/2022/03/11/covid-nih-ecohealth-peter-daszak-interview/ [https://perma.cc/EKW6-QCX3].

135. *Id.*

136. *See* Wade, *supra* note 114.

137. *Id.*

138. See Nickie Louise, *Vox Caught Stealth Editing an Old Article from March 2020 'Debunking' the Lab Origin of COVID-19*, TECH STARTUPS (May 24, 2021), https://techstartups.com/2021/05/24/vox-caught-stealth-editing-old-article-march-2020-debunking-lab-origin-covid-19/ [https://perma.cc/YL4L-C6VK]. *PolitiFact* quietly retracted its earlier criticisms of a Chinese whistleblower who claimed that her supervisors covered up evidence of COVID's human-to-human transmissibility. CHAN & RIDLEY, *supra* note 107, at 197-198, 307 (2021). The *Washington Post's* headline, *Tom Cotton Keeps Repeating a Coronavirus Conspiracy Theory That Was Already Debunked*, quietly became *Tom Cotton Keeps Repeating a Coronavirus Fringe Theory That Scientists Have Disputed. Id.*

139. Press Release, Meta, An Update on Our Work to Keep People Informed and Limit Misinformation About COVID-19 (May 26, 2021, 3:30 PM), https://about.fb.com/news/2020/04/covid-19-misinfo-update/ [https://perma.cc/Q48D-J57B].

140. *See* Neil L. Harrison & Jeffrey D. Sachs, *A Call for an Independent Inquiry into the Origin of the SARS-CoV-2 Virus*, PNAS (May 19, 2022), https://www.pnas.org/doi/10.1073/pnas.2202769119/ [https://perma.cc/UYQ4-WBXY].

141. *See* Emma-Jo Morris & Gabrielle Fonrouge, *Hunter Biden Emails Show Leveraging Connections with His Father to Boost Burisma Pay*, N.Y. POST (Oct. 14, 2020), https://nypost.com/2020/10/14/hunter-biden-emails-show-leveraging-connections-with-dad-to-boost-burisma-pay/ [https://perma.cc/S9JN-ZVLK].

142. *See* Emma-Jo Morris & Gabrielle Fonrouge, *Smoking-gun Email Reveals How Hunter Biden Introduced Ukrainian Businessman to VP Dad*, N.Y. POST (Oct. 14, 2020), https://nypost.com/2020/10/14/email-reveals-how-hunter-biden-introduced-ukrainian-biz-man-to-dad/ [https://perma.cc/KZJ5-GXX5].

143. *See id.* ("Photos of a Delaware federal subpoena given to The Post show that both the computer and hard drive were seized by the FBI in December, after the shop's owner says he alerted the feds to their existence.").

144. *See* Morris & Fonrouge, *supra* note 142 ("The customer who brought in the water-damaged MacBook Pro for repair never paid for the service or retrieved it or a hard drive on which its contents were stored, according to the shop owner, who said he tried repeatedly to contact the client."). It was conceivable at the time that the *New York Post* had been misled. The paper acknowledged, it had been given a copy of the hard drive by President Trump's lawyer Rudy Giuliani, who had earlier been given a copy by the shop owner before turning it over to the FBI. *Id.* ("But before turning over the gear, the shop owner says, he made a copy of the hard drive and later gave it to former Mayor Rudy Giuliani's lawyer, Robert Costello. Steve Bannon, former adviser to President Trump, told The Post about the existence of the hard drive in late September and Giuliani provided The Post with a copy of it on Sunday."). Nonetheless, considerable evidence existed to believe the claim was authentic, some of which has been compiled by the journalist who had won a Pulitzer Prize for reporting on a similar trove of documents at the heart of the Snowden surveillance revelations, Glenn Greenwald. *See* Glenn Greenwald, *Article on Joe and Hunter Biden Censored by the Intercept*, SUBSTACK (Oct. 29, 2020), https://greenwald.substack.com/p/article-on-joe-and-hunter-biden-censored/ [https://perma.cc/5ADZ-V5J6] (giving evidence proving the authenticity of the relevant emails). Persons who were included in some of the emails have also confirmed their authenticity. *See id.* ("One of Hunter's former business partners, Tony Bubolinski, has stepped forward on the record to confirm the authenticity of many of the emails and to insist that Hunter along with Joe Biden's brother Jim were planning on including the former Vice President in at least one deal in China. And GOP pollster Frank Luntz, who appeared in one of the published email chains, appeared to confirm the authenticity as well, though he refused to answer follow-up questions about it."). The emails' authenticity was not denied by either of the Bidens, even though the former vice president had claimed in 2019 that he had "never spoken to [his] son about his overseas business dealings." Aamer Madhani, *Biden: I Never Talked to Son Hunter About Overseas Business Dealings*, USA TODAY

(Sept. 21, 2019), https://www.usatoday.com/story/news/politics/elections/2019/
09/21/joe-biden-never-talked-ukraine-son-trump-needs-investigated/2401830
001/ [https://perma.cc/26T6-ENJB]. The story was, moreover, clearly relevant
to Biden's candidacy for the presidency, since it raised questions, as Greenwald
pointed out, about whether Biden knew about his son's influence-peddling and
whether Biden had taken any actions in his official capacity to benefit his son's
business interests. Greenwald, *supra*.

145. Katie Brenner, Kenneth P. Vogel, and Michael S. Schmidt, *Hunter Biden Paid Tax
Bill, but Broad Federal Investigation Continues*, N.Y. TIMES (Mar. 16, 2022), https://
www.nytimes.com/2022/03/16/us/politics/hunter-biden-tax-bill-investigation.
html [https://perma.cc/3MAD-YBE2].

146. *See, e.g.*, Ryan Lizza et al., *Double Trouble for Biden*, POLITICO (Sept. 21, 2021),
https://www.politico.com/newsletters/playbook/2021/09/21/double-trouble-for-
biden-494411 [https://perma.cc/SN49-77QF] (discussing Schreckinger's book,
asserting that the book "finds evidence that some of the purported Hunter Biden
laptop material is genuine, including two emails at the center of last October's
controversy").

147. Jim Clapper et al., Public Statement on the Hunter Biden Emails (Oct. 19, 2020),
https://www.politico.com/f/?id=00000175-4393-d7aa-af77-579f9b330000 [https://
perma.cc/QQE8-4P7W]. *See also* Shannon Larson, *Dozens of Former Intelligence
Officials Sign Letter Warning Hunter Biden Story Could be Russian Disinformation*,
BOSTON GLOBE (Oct. 20, 2020), https://www.bostonglobe.com/2020/10/20/nat
ion/dozens-former-intelligence-officials-sign-letter-warning-hunter-biden-story-
could-be-russian-disinformation/ [https://perma.cc/QN25-4652] (providing press
coverage of the public statement).

148. Clapper et al., *supra* note 147.

149. *Id.*

150. *Id.*

151. *Id.*

152. *Id.*

153. *Id.*

154. *Id.*

155. Jen Psaki (@jrpaski), TWITTER (Oct. 19, 2020, 10:45 PM), https://twitter.com/
jrpsaki/status/1318382779659411458 [https://perma.cc/6MUZ-FMLA]. In fact,
the principal source of disinformation may have been the government. Senator
Charles Grassley has advised Attorney General Merrick Garland and FBI Director
Christopher Wray of "highly credible whistleblowers" who have reported "a
scheme in place among certain FBI officials to undermine derogatory information connected to Hunter Biden by falsely suggesting it was disinformation." Letter
from U.S. Senator Charles Grassley to Attorney General Merrick Garland and FBI
Director Christopher Wray (July 25, 2022) (on file with author).

156. A basic axiom of effective information control is not to respond to unwanted speech
with counterspeech, but rather to ignore it. This was the tactic of the "conspiracy
unfolding behind the scenes" of the 2020 presidential campaign, reported in a

widely read *Time* magazine article by Molly Ball. The article describes "a well-funded cabal of powerful people, ranging across industries and ideologies, working together behind the scenes to influence perceptions, change rules and laws, steer media coverage and control the flow of information." Not swinging at most pitches is hard, one of the group's strategists said, but it wins games. "[T]he more engagement something gets," another said, "the more the platforms boost it. The algorithm reads that as, 'Oh, this is popular; people want more of it.'" The solution was to pressure platforms to remove unwanted content or accounts. Molly Ball, *The Secret History of the Shadow Campaign That Saved the 2020 Election*, TIME (Feb. 4, 2021), https://time.com/5936036/secret-2020-election-campaign/ [https://perma.cc/99GM-V7D4].

157. Glenn Greenwald, *The NYT Now Admits the Biden Laptop—Falsely Called 'Russian Disinformation'—is Authentic*, SUBSTACK (Mar. 17, 2022), https://greenwald.substack.com/p/the-nyt-now-admits-the-biden-laptop?s=r [https://perma.cc/2MUB-9CJV].

158. NPR Public Editor (@NPRpubliceditor), TWITTER (Oct. 22, 2020, 10:15 AM), https://twitter.com/nprpubliceditor/status/1319281101223940096?lang=en [https://perma.cc/NF73-V5BY].

159. Jared Gans, *FBI Says It 'Routinely Notifies' Social Media Companies of Potential Threats Following Zuckerberg-Rogan Podcast*, THE HILL (Aug. 27, 2022), https://thehill.com/policy/national-security/3618137-fbi-says-it-routinely-notifies-social-media-companies-of-potential-threats-following-zuckerberg-rogan-podcast/ [https://perma.cc/28EB-CHXN].

160. Andy Stone (@andymstone), TWITTER (Oct. 14, 2020, 11:10 AM), https://twitter.com/andymstone/status/1316395902479872000 [https://perma.cc/EC6F-BS7A]. *See also* Katie Glueck, Michael S. Schmidt, and Mike Isaac, *Allegation on Biden Prompts Pushback From Social Media Companies*, N.Y. TIMES (Oct. 14, 2020), https://www.nytimes.com/2020/10/14/us/politics/hunter-biden-ukraine-facebook-twitter.html [https://perma.cc/K8PA-HAWK] (stating that "Facebook said that soon after the story was posted it noticed the controversy around the veracity of its claims and over how The Post had obtained the evidence. As the story circulated, the company said it had moved to tamp down its potential for virality. In essence, it meant that Facebook would show fewer instances of shared posts featuring the story in users' News Feeds, the main way people view and share links and other stories across Facebook."). Zuckerberg later seemed to indicate that he regretted the decision to slow distribution of the story. Ryan King, *Mark Zuckerberg Says He Regrets Facebook Throttling Hunter Biden Laptop Story*, WASH. EXAMINER (Aug. 26, 2022) https://www.washingtonexaminer.com/policy/technology/mark-zuckerberg-regrets-facebook-throttling-hunter-biden-laptop [https://perma.cc/82CM-EP8M].

161. *See* Greenwald, *supra* note 157 (discussing Twitter locking the *New York Post*'s Twitter account).

162. Elizabeth Dwoskin, *Facebook and Twitter Take Unusual Steps to Limit Spread of New York Post Story*, WASH. POST. (Oct. 15, 2020), https://www.washingtonpost.com/technology/2020/10/15/facebook-twitter-hunter-biden/ [https://perma.cc/APS8-FFFQ].

163. *See* Greenwald, *supra* note 157 (reporting that "[t]he social media site also blocked any and all references to the reporting by all users; Twitter users were barred even from linking to the story in private chats with one another").

164. Matt Taibbi, *YouTube Censors Reality, Boosts Disinformation: Part 1*, SUBSTACK (Nov. 21, 2022), https://taibbi.substack.com/p/youtube-censors-reality-boosts-dis information?utm_source=post-email-title&publication_id=1042&post_id=85912 473&isFreemail=false&utm_medium=email1 [https://perma.cc/45G9-8VDD]. "YouTube," he writes, "has become a place that censors true content but traffics in official and quasi-official deceptions. It's become indistinguishable from a state censorship bureau." *Id.*

165. *Debate Transcript: Trump, Biden Final Presidential Debate Moderated by Kristen Welker*, USA TODAY (Oct. 23, 2020), https://www.usatoday.com/story/news/polit ics/elections/2020/10/23/debate-transcript-trump-biden-final-presidential-deb ate-nashville/3740152001/ [https://perma.cc/RR6Q-GDWJ].

166. *Id.*

167. *Id.*

168. *See, e.g.,* Johnathan Easley, *Poll: Biden Builds Bigger Lead Nationally*, THE HILL (Oct. 29, 2020), https://thehill.com/homenews/campaign/523462-poll-biden-builds-big ger-lead-nationally/ [https://perma.cc/AK8Z-PRX6] (finding that "[a] slim majority, 51 percent, believe the discovery of Hunter Biden's laptop at a pawn shop is Russian disinformation," and opining that this is despite the fact that "there is no evidence for that"). Nearly two years later, 50% of Democrats and 47% of independents continued to believe that the Hunter Biden laptop is "Russian disinformation." Harvard CAPS Harris Poll, HARVARD UNIVERSITY CENTER FOR AMERICAN POLITICAL STUDIES 46, Sept. 7–8, 2022, https://harvardharrispoll.com/wp-content/ uploads/2022/09/HHP_Sept2022_KeyFindings.pdf (50% of polled Democrats believe that the Hunter Biden laptop is "Russian Disinformation" whereas in aggregate; Tom Bevan (@TomBevanRCP), TWITTER (Sept. 13, 2022, 12:04 PM), https://twitter. com/tombevanrcp/status/1569718637551828993 [https://perma.cc/X9XE-HXGC].

169. *See* Domenico Montanato, *President-Elect Joe Biden Hits 80 Million Votes in Year of Record Turnout*, NPR (Nov. 25, 2020), https://www.npr.org/2020/11/25/937248659/ president-elect-biden-hits-80-million-votes-in-year-of-record-turnout [https:// perma.cc/PGG4-KWJP].

170. *See, e.g.,* Univ. Mass. Amherst, Toplines and Crosstabs December 2021 National Poll: Presidential Election & Jan 6th Insurrection at the US Capitol (Dec. 28, 2021), https://polsci.umass.edu/toplines-and-crosstabs-december-2021-national-poll-presidential-election-jan-6th-insurrection-us [https://perma.cc/B5NW-RXWW] (poll finding 11% of respondents believe that Joe Biden's victory was "probably not legitimate," 22% believe that the victory is "definitely not legitimate" and 9% were unsure.).

171. In 2021, roughly three-fourths of American adults had Facebook accounts. Cato Inst./YouGov Poll, Cato Institute (Aug. 2021), https://www.cato.org/sites/cato.org/ files/2021-12/cato-social-media-survey-report-toplines.pdf [https://perma.cc/ 4PPF-8DCT].

172. SUZANNE NOSSEL, DARE TO SPEAK: DEFENDING FREE SPEECH FOR ALL 234 (HarperCollins Publishers 2020).

173. This is, to be sure, not the first time the lines between the public and private spheres have blurred. *See* ROBERTO UNGER, LAW IN MODERN SOCIETY 202 (1976) (arguing that "the increasing recognition of the power these [corporate] organizations exercise, in a quasi-public manner . . . makes it even harder to maintain the distinction between state action and private conduct.").

174. Daphne Keller, *Who Do You Sue?: State and Platform Hybrid Power Over Online Speech* 7 (Hoover Working Grp. on Nat'l Sec., Tech. & Law, Aegis Series Paper No. 1902, 2019), https://www.hoover.org/sites/default/files/research/docs/who-do-you-sue-state-and-platform-hybrid-power-over-online-speech_0.pdf [https://perma.cc/K2NF-69TV] (describing the "snarl" of "state and private power").

175. As succinctly summarized by Jack Goldsmith, the NSA "set up a system to collect huge quantities of intelligence information, not just by breaking into foreign networks but also by (among other means) demanding information from Google, Yahoo, Facebook, and other American firms that themselves collected data from abroad, especially communications of individuals." Jack Goldsmith, *The Failure of Internet Freedom, in* THE PERILOUS PUBLIC SQUARE: STRUCTURAL THREATS TO FREE EXPRESSION TODAY 238–47 (David E. Pozen ed., 2020). Contrary to popular belief, mass surveillance has not ended. Between December 2020 and November 2021, "[t]he FBI searched emails, texts and other electronic communications of as many as 3.4 million U.S. residents without a warrant over a year." Chris Strohm, *FBI Searched Data of Millions of Americans Without Warrants*, BLOOMBERG (Apr. 29, 2022), https://www.bloomberg.com/news/articles/2022-04-29/fbi-searched-the-data-of-millions-of-americans-without-warrants?leadSource=uverify%20wall [https://perma.cc/WLG7-EHAG].

176. *See* Klippenstein & Fang, *supra* note 61 (reporting on the relationship between government agencies and Facebook that "[t]here is also a formalized process for government officials to directly flag content on Facebook or Instagram and request that it be throttled or suppressed through a special Facebook portal that requires a government or law enforcement email to use. At the time of writing, the "content request system" at facebook.com/xtakedowns/login is still live.").

177. *See, e.g.*, Jeff Nesbit, *Google's True Origin Partly Lies in CIA and NSA Research Grants for Mass Surveillance*, QUARTZ (Dec. 8, 2017), https://qz.com/1145669/googles-true-origin-partly-lies-in-cia-and-nsa-research-grants-for-mass-surveillance/ [https://perma.cc/ZR4S-U9GS] (finding that as a graduate student, one of Google's founders, Sergey Brin, met regularly with two intelligence-community managers while researching how search functions could be used to pull precise information from very large data sets; the CIA was interested in using such data to identify and track individual users who might pose security threats).

178. Gerrit De Vynck, *Government Has Key Role in Tech Investing, Google Board Member Says*, WASH. POST (Aug. 17, 2022), https://www.washingtonpost.com/politics/2022/08/17/government-has-key-role-tech-investing-google-board-member-says/ [https://perma.cc/RY7B-VQHN].

179. *See* Aaron Gregg, *CIA Long Relied Exclusively on Amazon for its Cloud Computing*, WASH. POST (Apr. 2, 2019), https://www.washingtonpost.com/business/2019/04/02/cia-long-relied-exclusively-amazon-its-cloud-computing-now-it-is-seeking-multiple-providers-massive-new-contract/ [https://perma.cc/BJR6-JGPB]; Frank Konkel, *The Details About the CIA's Deal With Amazon*, THE ATLANTIC (Jul. 17, 2004), https://www.theatlantic.com/technology/archive/2014/07/the-details-about-the-cias-deal-with-amazon/374632/ [https://perma.cc/B3GX-AKEZ] (describing how in 2013, the CIA awarded a $600 million contract to Amazon's cloud computing division, later announcing its intent to enter into similar contracts with other tech giants).

180. *See infra* text accompanying note 339.

181. 47 U.S.C. § 230 (c)(1) ("no provider or user of an interactive computer service shall be treated as the publisher or speaker of any information provided by another information content provider.").

182. Barbara Ortutay, *AP Explains: The Rule that Made the Modern Internet*, AP NEWS (Oct. 28, 2020), https://apnews.com/article/what-is-section-230-tech-giants-77bce70089964c1e6fc87228ccdb0618 [https://perma.cc/3K87-ZZ2Z].

183. *Does Section 230's Sweeping Immunity Enable Big Tech Bad Behavior?: Hearing Before the S. Comm. on Com., Sci., & Transp.*, 116th Cong. 2 (2020) (statement of Mark Zuckerberg, CEO, Facebook Inc.).

184. NOSSEL, *supra* note 172, at 240.

185. *Disinformation Nation: Social Media's Role in Promoting Extremism and Misinformation: Hearing Before the H. Comm. on Energy & Com.*, 117th Cong. 10 (2021) (statement of Sundar Pichai, CEO, Alphabet Inc.).

186. Daisuke Wakabayashi, *Legal Shield for Social Media Is Targeted by Lawmakers*, N.Y. TIMES (May 28, 2020), https://www.nytimes.com/2020/05/28/business/section-230-internet-speech.html [https://perma.cc/2LYN-BGER]. *See also* Eric Johnson, *Nancy Pelosi Says Trump's Tweets "Cheapened the Presidency" — and the Media Encourages Him*, VOX (Apr. 12, 2019), https://www.vox.com/2019/4/12/18307957/nancy-pelosi-donald-trump-twitter-tweet-cheap-freak-presidency-kara-swisher-decode-podcast-interview [https://perma.cc/2F3F-39CH] (podcast transcript for Nancy Pelosi: "I do think that for the privilege of 230, there has to be a bigger sense of responsibility on it. And it is not out of the question that that could be removed.").

187. *See* James Clapper et al., Open Letter from Former Defense, Intelligence, Homeland Security, and Cyber Officials for National Security Review of Congressional Tech Legislation (Apr. 18, 2022), https://punchbowl.news/open-letter-cyber-intel-defense-hs-1/ [https://perma.cc/RHP6-2EZT].

188. *See* Emily Birnbaum, *12 Former Security Officials Who Warned Against Antitrust Crackdown Have Tech Ties*, POLITICO (Sept. 22, 2021), https://www.politico.com/news/2021/09/22/former-security-officials-antitrust-tech-ties-513657 [https://perma.cc/JX9G-FSGH]. Several were among the signers of the "Hunter Biden letter" suggesting that his emails were Russian disinformation. *Compare* Letter from Robert Cardillo, et al., to Nancy P. Pelosi and Kevin O. McCarthy (Sept. 15, 2021), https://www.documentcloud.org/documents/21062393-national-security-letter-on-antitr

ust?responsive=1&title=1 [https://perma.cc/7VLB-7FKV] *with* Public Statement from Jim Clapper, et. al (Oct. 19, 2022), https://www.politico.com/f/?id=00000175-4393-d7aa-af77-579f9b330000 [https://perma.cc/6Q55-4B73].

189. Matt Stoller (@matthewstoller), TWITTER (Apr. 12, 2022, 2:05 PM), https://twitter.com/matthewstoller/status/1513941334666665986 [https://perma.cc/RJH4-M58A].

190. Donald Trump's Truth Social platform, for example, founded after Trump was banned from Twitter and patterned after it, had 513,000 active daily users in April 2022, compared to Twitter's 217 million. Nicole Lyn Pesce, *Two Truth Social Execs Quit as Trump's Social Media App Struggles to Take Off*, MARKETWATCH (Apr. 4, 2022), https://www.marketwatch.com/story/two-truth-social-execs-quit-as-tru mps-social-media-app-struggles-to-take-off-report-11649090306 [https://perma. cc/4GNL-78Y9]. The *Washington Post* reported that the Truth Social "website is facing financial challenges as its traffic remains puny" and that "Trump, the site's most popular user, has fewer than 4 million followers, and the site's most active trending topics, including #DefundTheFBI, have shown only a few thousand people posting to them in recent days, data from the site shows. For comparison, Twitter says it has about 37 million people in the U.S. actively using the site every day." Drew Harwell, *Truth Social Faces Financial Peril as Worry About Trump's Future Grows*, WASH. POST (Aug. 27, 2022), https://www.washingtonpost.com/technology/2022/08/27/trump-truth-social-mar-a-lago-fbi/ [https://perma.cc/PU8K-7KUG].

191. *See* Glenn Greenwald, *How Silicon Valley, in a Show of Monopolistic Force, Destroyed Parler*, SUBSTACK (Jan. 12, 2021), https://greenwald.substack.com/p/how-silicon-valley-in-a-show-of-monopolistic. [https://perma.cc/P3ER-9ZM8].

192. NetChoice, LLC v. Paxton, 49 F.4th 439, 476 (5th Cir. 2022) (quoting Biden v. Knight First Amend. Inst., 141 S. Ct. 1220, 1225 (2021) (Thomas, J., concurring)).

193. *See* Whizy Kim, *Ex-Google CEO Eric Schmidt's New Investment Fund Deepens His Ties to National Security Interests*, VOX (June 9, 2022), https://www.vox.com/rec ode/2022/6/9/23160588/eric-schmidt-americas-frontier-fund-google-alphabet-tech-government-revolving-door [https://perma.cc/KZD5-4DKK] (describing a "public-private, deep-tech fund" that would receive government funding alongside private money funded by Michael Schmidt, former Google CEO, "a go-to liaison between the tech industry and the military").

194. A 2021 *Newsweek* investigation reported the existence of a "secret army" of sixty thousand people gathered by the Pentagon, working under masked identities and under civilian cover, "who assume false personas online, employing 'nonattribution' and 'misattribution' techniques to hide the who and the where of their online presence while they . . . engage in campaigns to influence and manipulate social media." William M. Arkin, *Exclusive: Inside the Military's Secret Undercover Army*, NEWSWEEK (May 17, 2021), https://www.newsweek.com/exclusive-inside-milita rys-secret-undercover-army-1591881 [https://perma.cc/XDU7-ET9X].

195. For comprehensive analysis, *see* Shir-Razl et al., *supra* note 41. Among their conclusions: "Some governments and tech corporations, such as Facebook, Google, Twitter and LinkedIn, have taken measures to censor contrary viewpoints,

arguing that views challenging government policies are dangerous misinformation. . . . This heavy censorship was done with the encouragement of governments, which cooperated with tech companies such as Facebook, Twitter, and Google. . . . [G]overnment officials directly coordinated with tech companies like Twitter and Facebook to censor doctors, scientists and journalists. . . . [I]nformation technology companies such as Google and Facebook play a prominent role in the attempts of governments and authorities to censor dissenting positions on COVID-19." *Id* (citations omitted). *See also* Klippenstein & Fang, *supra* note 61. Glenn Greenwald, *The Consortium Imposing the Growing Censorship Regime*, SUBSTACK, Oct. 28, 2022 https://greenwald.substack.com/p/the-consortium-imposing-the-growing (underscoring the collaboration between government and private actors to silence speech and the use of financial services of blacking out dissenters such as WikiLeaks) Contrary to popular impression, cooperation is reportedly not limited to social media. *See* Tad Galen Carpenter, Opinion, *How the National Security State Manipulates the News Media*, CATO INSTITUTE (March 9, 2021), https://www.cato.org/commentary/how-national-security-state-manipulates-news-media [https://perma.cc/SN9F-GS6K] (describing investigative journalism that details continuing ties between mainstream media and the intelligence community).

196. *See, e.g.*, Keller, *supra* note 174 (describing the indirect pressure of government "jawboning," which "in its subtler forms makes state action much harder to trace."); Shir-Raz et al., *supra* note 41 (describing the recommendations and guidance provided for censoring Covid information); Editorial, *Climate-Change Censorship: Phase Two*, WALL ST. J. (June 13, 2022) (remarks of the senior White House climate adviser urging "the tech companies to really jump in" to silence criticism of green energy), https://www.wsj.com/articles/climate-censorship-phase-two-gina-mccarthy-social-media-biden-white-house-11655156191?mod=hp_opin_pos_3 [https://perma.cc/QYT8-GC7P]. *See also* Michael Shellenberger, *Why the Biden Admin Wants Censorship of Renewable Energy Critics*, SUBSTACK (June 14, 2022), https://michaelshellenberger.substack.com/p/why-the-biden-admin-wants-censorship?s=r [https://perma.cc/CK3M-YNN9]. *See also* Jacob Sullum, *Biden Is Trying to Impose Online Censorship by Proxy*, REASON (July 21, 2021), https://reason.com/2021/07/21/biden-is-trying-to-impose-online-censorship-by-proxy/ [https://perma.cc/K7G5-8MVX].

197. Keller, *supra* note 174, at 10.

198. WHITE HOUSE, *supra* note 56.

199. WHITE HOUSE, INTERIM NATIONAL SECURITY STRATEGIC GUIDANCE 12 (2021), https://www.whitehouse.gov/wp-content/uploads/2021/03/NSC-1v2.pdf [https://perma.cc/RHK6-W8RC].

200. U.S. Dep't of Homeland Sec., *supra* note 34.

201. *See MIS, DIS, MALINFORMATION*, CYBER & INFRASTRUCTURE SEC. AGENCY, https://www.cisa.gov/mdm [https://perma.cc/3B7Z-T5EJ] ("Misinformation, disinformation, and malinformation make up what CISA defines as 'information activities'. . . . When this type of content is released by foreign actors, it can be referred to as foreign influence. Definitions for each are below. Misinformation is false, but not created or shared with the intention of causing harm. Disinformation is deliberately

created to mislead, harm, or manipulate a person, social group, organization, or country. Malinformation is based on fact, but used out of context to mislead, harm, or manipulate.").

202. U.S. Dep't of Homeland Sec., *supra* note 34.

203. *Id.*

204. *Id.*

205. *Id.*

206. *See* Amanda Seitz, *Disinformation Board to Tackle Russia, Migrant Smugglers*, AP News (Apr. 28, 2022), https://apnews.com/article/russia-ukraine-immigration-media-europe-misinformation-4e873389889bb1d9e2ad8659d9975e9d   [https://perma.cc/M2J5-TSE8].

207. Press Briefing, White House, Press Briefing by Secretary Jen Psaki (Apr. 28, 2022), https://www.whitehouse.gov/briefing-room/press-briefings/2022/04/28/press-briefing-by-press-secretary-jen-psaki-april-28-2022/ [https://perma.cc/C5P5-YBWS]. The "disinformation expert" appointed to head the Disinformation Governance Board had earlier proclaimed that the Hunter Biden laptop story was "a Trump campaign product." *See* Eric Tucker and Stephen Braun, *AP Explains: Trump Seizes on Dubious Biden-Ukraine Story*, AP News (Oct. 14, 2020), https://apnews.com/article/election-2020-joe-biden-donald-trump-ukraine-elections-134406f28e826380924bbcf773d2c05a [https://perma.cc/37Q2-TD9V].

208. John Hamilton & Kevin Kosar, *Why Biden Is in Danger of Replicating Woodrow Wilson's Propaganda Machine*, Politico Mag. (May 5, 2022), https://www.politico.com/news/magazine/2022/05/05/disinformation-propaganda-war-board-biden-woodrow-wilson-00030098 [https://perma.cc/3WB4-T638].

209. *See* Rebecca Beitsch, *DHS To Pause Work of Disinformation Board*, The Hill (May 18, 2022), https://thehill.com/news/state-watch/3493070-dhs-to-pause-work-of-disinformation-board/ [https://perma.cc/9V5H-7P2M].

210. Steven Lee Meyers, *A Panel to Combat Disinformation Becomes a Victim of It*, N.Y. Times (May 18, 2022), https://www.nytimes.com/2022/05/18/technology/disinformation-governance-board.html [https://perma.cc/3933-FACS].

211. For example, a year-old CDC press release remained live on its website throughout the DHS Disinformation Board controversy. *See* Press Release, Ctrs. for Disease Control and Prevention, CDC COVID-19 Study Shows mRNA Vaccines Reduce Risk of Infection by 91 Percent for Fully Vaccinated People (June 7, 2021), https://www.cdc.gov/media/releases/2021/p0607-mrna-reduce-risks.html [https://perma.cc/6QKV-NTPV].

212. *See infra* text accompanying notes 258–281. Justin Monticello writes, "The CDC has . . . been a superspreader of COVID misinformation. To justify universal mask mandates, Walensky spent months citing a junk study on their efficacy in schools, exaggerating the risks of breakthrough infections among the vaccinated, and misrepresenting a study on outdoor COVID transmission, according to its author. The CDC claimed the delta variant was as transmissible as chickenpox, which isn't true—it turns out the agency had used inaccurate data from a New York Times infographic. It also promoted an infographic on cloth masks using data that were not statistically significant. Meanwhile, the CDC has not run a single randomized

controlled trial on the efficacy of masking since the beginning of the pandemic. In the vaccine rollout, the CDC told the elderly they needed to wait in line behind essential workers, including young and healthy school support staff, corporate tax lawyers, and magazine fashion editors. In its noble zeal to convince parents to get their children vaccinated, the CDC used old data that the agency knew were no longer valid to falsely claim hospitalizations were rising among adolescents; it misrepresented a study to exaggerate the dangers faced by unvaccinated children, and it falsely claimed that kids who get COVID are more likely to develop diabetes. Under both the Trump and Biden administrations, the CDC publicly cast doubt on the value of N95 masks, vaccines, and diagnostic tests at times when there were supply shortages or when it was politically expedient. Both presidents even used the CDC to exert federal control over state-level housing policy, repeatedly extending an unconstitutional ban on evictions based on junk science." Justin Monticello, *COVID-19 Exposed the Truth About the CDC*, REASON (June 28, 2022), https://reason.com/video/2022/06/28/covid-19-exposed-the-truth-about-the-cdc/ [https://perma.cc/35Y2-7VEX].

213. Keller, *supra* note 174, at 2.

214. Complaint at 20–33, Missouri v. Biden, No. 3:22-cv-01213 (W.D. La. Jul. 2, 2022) (listing recent examples).

215. David E. Pozen, *Straining (Analogies) to Make Sense of the First Amendment in Cyberspace*, in THE PERILOUS PUBLIC SQUARE: STRUCTURAL THREATS TO FREE EXPRESSION TODAY 141 (David E. Pozen ed. 2020).

216. *See* Complaint at 1, Missouri v. Biden, No. 3:22-cv-01213 (W.D. La. Jul. 2, 2022). The New Civil Liberties Alliance joined the action on behalf of authors of the Great Barrington Declaration, described in *infra* text accompanying notes 282–88. *See* Press Release, New C. L. All., NCLA Clients Join Missouri and Louisiana Suit Challenging Gov't-Directed Social Media Censorship (Aug. 2, 2022), https://nclale gal.org/2022/08/ncla-clients-join-missouri-and-louisiana-suit-challenging-govt-directed-social-media-censorship/ [https://perma.cc/JHA8-H7SR].

217. *See* The Parties' Joint Statement on Discovery Disputes at 9, Missouri v. Biden, No. 3:22-cv-01213 (W.D. La. Aug. 31, 2022) (hereinafter "Joint Statement"); Jacob Sullum, *These Emails Show How the Biden Administration's Crusade Against 'Misinformation' Imposes Censorship by Proxy*, REASON (Sept. 1, 2022), https://reason.com/2022/09/01/these-emails-show-how-the-biden-administrations-crusade-against-misinformation-imposes-censorship-by-proxy/?itm_source=parsely-api [https://perma.cc/8G9Q-8KXG].

218. Brief for the Petitioner at 3, Missouri v. Biden, No. 3:22-cv-01213 (W.D. La. Aug. 31, 2022).

219. Editorial, *How the Feds Coordinate with Facebook on Censorship*, WALL ST. J. (Sept. 9, 2022), https://www.wsj.com/articles/how-the-feds-coordinate-with-facebook-twit ter-white-house-social-media-emails-covid-instagram-11662761613?mod=hp_opin_pos_1 [https://perma.cc/MCP8-T8NP].

220. Jeffery Tucker describes this relationship as an "obsequious friendship": "What you see here is not antagonism but obsequious friendship: ongoing, relentless, guileless,

as if nothing could be wrong here. They knew what they believed to be the problem voices and were determined to stamp them out. . . . Finally we see courts coming around to the view that government needs to be held accountable for its actions. It is happening far too little and far too late but at least it is happening." Jeffrey A. Tucker, *Judge Orders Fauci to Cough It Up*, BROWNSTONE INST. (Sept. 8, 2022), https://brownstone.org/articles/judge-orders-fauci-to-cough-it-up/ [https://perma.cc/E63W-EANK].

221. Joint Statement, *supra* note 217, Exhibit 3 at 1. (Emails sent on July 20, 2021).

222. *See* Jessica Bursztynsky, *White House Says Social Media Networks Should Be Held Accountable for Spreading Misinformation*, CNBC (Jul. 20, 2021), https://www.cnbc.com/2021/07/20/white-house-social-networks-should-be-held-accountable-for-spreading-misinfo.html [https://perma.cc/J7NX-D8HN] (noting that Biden said giants like Facebook were "killing people" on July 16, 2020, before later backtracking on his comments).

223. Eric Schmitt, *Missouri and Louisiana Attorneys General Ask Court to Compel Department of Justice to Produce Communications Between Top Officials and Social Media Companies*, MO. ATT'Y GEN. OFF. (Sept. 1, 2022), https://ago.mo.gov/home/news/2022/09/01/missouri-and-louisiana-attorneys-general-ask-court-to-compel-department-of-justice-to-produce-communications-between-top-officials-and-social-media-companies [https://perma.cc/7W92-3GLX].

224. Joint Statement, *supra* note 217, Exhibit 8 at 86–87.

225. Joint Statement, *supra* note 217, Exhibit 5, at 4.

226. *Id.*

227. Joint Statement, *supra* note 217, Exhibit 9 at 69–72.

228. *Id.* at 67–68.

229. *Id.* at 69.

230. *Id.* at 10. *See also* Kristie Cangello, *How Google and YouTube are Working to Protect the 2020 U.S. Census*, GOOGLE (Dec. 11, 2019), https://www.blog.google/technology/safety-security/how-google-and-youtube-are-working-protect-2020-us-census/ [https://perma.cc/F2JJ-X7T5].

231. Joint Statement, *supra* note 217, at 3.

232. *Id.*

233. *See* Will Duffield, *Jawboning against Speech How Government Bullying Shapes the Rules of Social Media*, CATO INSTITUTE (Sept. 20, 2022), *https://www.cato.org/policy-analysis/jawboning-against-speech?utm_source=social&utm_medium=email&utm_campaign=Cato%20Social%20Share* (the sixty-two examples are set out in Annex A) [https://perma.cc/GP2Z-H4UP].

234. Craig Timberg, Hamza Shaban & Elizabeth Dwoskin, *Fiery Exchanges on Capitol Hill as Lawmakers Scold Facebook, Google and Twitter*, WASH. POST (Nov. 1, 2022), https://www.washingtonpost.com/news/the-switch/wp/2017/11/01/fiery-exchanges-on-capitol-hill-as-lawmakers-scold-facebook-google-and-twitter/ [https://perma.cc/DY75-2UQQ].

235. Alexander Hall, *Biden Climate Adviser Demands Tech Companies Censor 'Disinformation' to Promote 'Benefits of Clean Energy'*, FOX NEWS (June 14, 2022),

https://www.foxnews.com/media/biden-climate-advisor-tech-companies-censor-disinformation-promote-benefits-clean-energy [https://perma.cc/7JHT-C4JP].

236. *See* Press Briefing, White House, Press Briefing by Press Secretary Jen Psaki and Surgeon General Dr. Vivek H. Murthy (Jul. 15, 2021), https://www.whitehouse.gov/briefing-room/press-briefings/2021/07/15/press-briefing-by-press-secretary-jen-psaki-and-surgeon-general-dr-vivek-h-murthy-july-15-2021/ [https://perma.cc/VQ5W-49XZ].

237. *Id.*

238. *Id.*

239. Bloomberg Live, *Bloomberg Tech Summit*, YOUTUBE (Dec. 14, 2021, 01:19:08), https://youtu.be/ke6YAOFi6HE [https://perma.cc/X6SG-AKQ2].

240. *Event Highlights: Bloomberg Technology Summit—December 14-15, 2022—Day 1*, BLOOMBERG LIVE (Dec. 14, 2021), https://www.bloomberglive.com/blog/event-highlights-bloomberg-technology-summit-dec14-15-day1/ [https://perma.cc/XD6E-GDWE].

241. Press Briefing, White House, Press Briefing by Press Secretary Jen Psaki (Feb. 1, 2022), https://www.whitehouse.gov/briefing-room/press-briefings/2022/02/01/press-briefing-by-press-secretary-jen-psaki-february-1-2022/ [https://perma.cc/A6JD-TGYM].

242. *Id. See also* Eugene Scott & Adela Suliman, *White House Wades Into Spotify Controversy as India.Arie, David Crosby, Stephen Stills and More Artists Pull Music*, WASH. POST (Feb. 2, 2022), https://www.washingtonpost.com/arts-entertainment/2022/02/02/spotify-rogan-white-house-covid-misinformation/ [https://perma.cc/XJ6B-B7XX].

243. *See* Vivek Ramaswamy & Jed Rubenfeld, *Save the Constitution from Big Tech*, WALL ST. J. (Jan. 11, 2021), https://www.wsj.com/articles/save-the-constitution-from-big-tech-11610387105 [https://perma.cc/XUA3-4JKT] (reporting that "in April 2019, Louisiana Rep. Cedric Richmond warned Facebook and Google that they had 'better' restrict what he and his colleagues saw as harmful content or face regulation: 'We're going to make it swift, we're going to make it strong, and we're going to hold them very accountable.' New York Rep. Jerrold Nadler added: 'Let's see what happens by just pressuring them.' "); Tony Romm, *House to Grill Facebook, Google, Twitter CEOs as Washington Seeks to Crack Down on Disinformation, Antitrust*, WASH. POST (Feb. 18, 2021), https://www.washingtonpost.com/technology/2021/02/18/house-antitrust-amazon-apple-facebook-google/ [https://perma.cc/M4QJ-PS57] (reporting that the House Energy and Commerce Committee, which had scheduled testimony from social media CEOs, intended to "take fresh aim at the tech giants for failing to crack down on dangerous political falsehoods and disinformation about the coronavirus."); Press Release, House Comm. on Energy and Com., E&C Comm. Announces Hearing With Tech CEOs on the Misinformation and Disinformation Plaguing Online Platforms (Feb. 18, 2021), https://energycommerce.house.gov/newsroom/press-releases/ec-committee-announces-hearing-with-tech-ceos-on-the-misinformation-and [https://perma.cc/ZE9B-RC4J] (the leaders of the Committee promised to "continue the Committee's work of holding online platforms accountable for the growing rise of misinformation and

disinformation."); Letter from Anna G. Eshoo and Jerry McNerney, Members of Congress to John T. Stankey, CEO, AT&T (Feb. 22, 2021), https://mcnerney.house. gov/sites/mcnerney.house.gov/files/McNerney-Eshoo%20TV%20Misinfo%20Lett ers%20-%202.22.21.pdf [https://perma.cc/M43C-NAYV] (asking cable companies if they plan to continue carrying Fox News, which they claimed was a "hotbed" of disinformation);. Abby Ohlheiser, *Kamala Harris Wants Trump Suspended from Twitter for 'Harassment'*, WASH. POST (Oct. 2, 2019), https://www.washingtonp ost.com/technology/2019/10/02/kamala-harris-wants-trump-suspended-twitter- harassment-these-loopholes-protect-him/ [https://perma.cc/S38L-4CJM] (as a Senator, Harris called on Twitter to suspend President Donald Trump's account.); Rep. Frank Pallone (@FrankPallone), TWITTER (Jan. 8, 2021, 7:21 PM), https:// twitter.com/frankpallone/status/1347699874670772230 [https://perma.cc/THC2- MVCM] (Representative Frank Pallone tweeted that "Trump is losing the platform he used to foment outright insurrection and violence. Finally he will be barred from so openly fanning the flames of hate. I've long called on Twitter to take action, and tonight I'm relieved that it has."); Adam Schiff (@RepAdamSchiff), TWITTER (Jan. 8, 2021, 11:09 PM), https://twitter.com/repadamschiff/status/1347757310257504259 [https://perma.cc/QJL5-DEVH] ("Donald Trump spent years demagoguing, lying, spreading hate, and propagating conspiracies on Twitter. And worse, inciting vio- lence. Social media companies have allowed this vile content to fester for too long, and need to do much more. But banning him is a good start.").

244. Editorial, *Joe Biden*, N.Y. TIMES (Jan. 17, 2020), https://www.nytimes.com/interact ive/2020/01/17/opinion/joe-biden-nytimes-interview.html [https://perma.cc/ WBJ3-CLJ9]. *See also* Casey Newton, *Everything You Need to Know About Section 230*, THE VERGE (Dec. 29, 2020), https://www.theverge.com/21273768/section-230- explained-internet-speech-law-definition-guide-free-moderation [https://perma. cc/CD7U-SBZB].

245. Zolan Kanno-Youngs & Cecilia Kang, *'They're Killing People': Biden Denounces Social Media for Virus Disinformation*, N.Y. TIMES (Jul. 19, 2021), https://www. nytimes.com/2021/07/16/us/politics/biden-facebook-social-media-covid.html [https://perma.cc/ZQL7-PQMK].

246. White House, *supra* note 236.

247. *See* Bursztynsky, *supra* note 222; comments of House Speaker Nancy Pelosi, *supra* text at note 186.

248. FACEBOOK,TAKINGACTIONTOCOMBATCOVID-19VACCINEMISINFORMATION4(Jul. 2021), https://about.fb.com/wp-content/uploads/2021/07/Combating-COVID-19- Vaccine-Misinformation.pdf [https://perma.cc/R9JW-X3GV].

249. Alexandria Ocasio-Cortez (@AOC), TWITTER (Jan. 8, 2021, 5:59 PM), https:// twitter.com/aoc/status/1347679332014161920?lang=en [https://perma.cc/ZYY6- TDHS]

250. Alexandria Ocasio-Cortez (@AOC), TWITTER (Jan. 8, 2021, 6:04 PM), https://twit ter.com/aoc/status/1347680648778153984 [https://perma.cc/4TAP-AH7P].

251. *See* Glenn Greenwald, *Congress Escalates Pressure on Tech Giants to Censor More, Threatening the First Amendment*, SUBSTACK (Feb. 20, 2021), https://greenw ald.substack.com/p/congress-escalates-pressure-on-tech?s=r [https://perma.cc/

XVQ3-RB4C]; Duffield, *supra* note 233 ("Asking 'what steps have you taken to address X content' is not merely a request for information. It is premised upon the assumption that the identified content is a problem that should be addressed. In most cases, 'addressed' implies algorithmic deprioritization or removal.")

252. Jack Nicas & Davey Alba, *Amazon, Apple and Google Cut Off Parler, an App That Drew Trump Supporters*, N.Y. TIMES (Jan. 9, 2021), https://www.nytimes.com/2021/01/09/technology/apple-google-parler.html [https://perma.cc/34TX-863C].

253. Twitter, *supra* note 14.

254. *See* Naomi Nix, *Facebook Removed 18 Million Misleading Posts on COVID-19*, BLOOMBERG (May 19, 2021), https://www.bloomberg.com/news/articles/2021-05-19/facebook-removed-18-million-misleading-posts-on-covid-19 [https://perma.cc/A98U-55UG].

255. *See* Davey Alba, *YouTube Bans All Anti-Vaccine Misinformation*, N.Y. TIMES (Sept. 29, 2021), https://www.nytimes.com/2021/09/29/technology/youtube-anti-vaxx-ban.html [https://perma.cc/MS55-P6Y8].

256. *See* Jordan Boyd, *Facebook Censors Article About Dangers of COVID Censorship*, THE FEDERALIST (Dec. 15, 2021), https://thefederalist.com/2021/12/15/facebook-censors-article-about-dangers-of-covid-censorship/ [https://perma.cc/9D5L-T4PY].

257. *See, e.g.,* Politifact's flagging as "false information" accusations that the government has attempted to change the definition of a recession. Robby Soave, *Facebook, Instagram Posts Flagged as False for Rejecting Biden's Recession Wordplay*, REASON (July 29, 2022), https://reason.com/2022/07/29/recession-facebook-fact-check-biden-politifact/ [https://perma.cc/52VD-J62P].

258. Craig Whitlock, *At War with the Truth*, WASH. POST (Dec. 9, 2019), https://www.washingtonpost.com/graphics/2019/investigations/afghanistan-papers/afghanistan-war-confidential-documents/ [https://perma.cc/2TPL-892G].

259. *Id.*

260. *Id.*

261. *Id.*

262. Olivier Knox, *The Daily 202: Biden Said U.S. Officials Lied About Afghanistan. It's Not Clear Whether They'll Be Held to Account*, WASH. POST (Aug. 18, 2021), https://www.washingtonpost.com/politics/2021/08/18/daily-202-biden-said-us-officials-lied-about-afghanistan-its-not-clear-whether-theyll-be-held-account/ [https://perma.cc/598X-H5JW].

263. Editorial, *Joe Biden*, N.Y. TIMES (Jan. 17, 2020), https://www.nytimes.com/interactive/2020/01/17/opinion/joe-biden-nytimes-interview.html [https://perma.cc/WBJ3-CLJ9].

264. For examples of the government's misrepresentations on COVID-19, see Kerrington Powell & Vinay Prasad, *The Noble Lies of COVID-19*, SLATE (July 28, 2021), https://slate.com/technology/2021/07/noble-lies-covid-fauci-cdc-masks.html [https://perma.cc/4K39-W6M8]; *see also supra* note 216.

265. McKenzie Beard, *Covid is No Longer Mainly a Pandemic of the Unvaccinated. Here's Why*, WASH. POST (Nov. 23, 2022), https://www.washingtonpost.com/politics/2022/11/23/vaccinated-people-now-make-up-majority-covid-deaths/ ("Fifty-eight

percent of coronavirus deaths in August were people who were vaccinated or boosted.") [https://perma.cc/FSH7-X7CX].

266. *See, e.g., Remarks by President Biden Marking the 150 Millionth COVID- 19 Vaccine Shot*, WHITE HOUSE (Apr. 6, 2021), https://www.whitehouse.gov/briefing-room/ speeches-remarks/2021/04/06/remarks-by-president-biden-marking-the-150- millionth-covid-19-vaccine-shot/ [https://perma.cc/3LXD-VQ6C]; David Z. Morris & Sy Mukherjee, *It's Official: Vaccinated People Don't Spread COVID-19*, FORTUNE (Apr. 1, 2021), https://fortune.com/2021/04/01/its-official-vaccinated- people-dont-transmit-covid-19/ [https://perma.cc/Q3R3-67BE].

267. Jordan Schachtel, *Memory Hole: Virtually Every Major Health Official in the United States Has Claimed That COVID Shots Stop the Virus*, SUBSTACK (Dec. 18, 2021), https://dossier.substack.com/p/memory-hole-virtually-every-major [https:// perma.cc/665E-H4CW].

268. *Remarks by President Biden in a CNN Town Hall with Don Lemon*, WHITE HOUSE (July 21, 2021), https://www.whitehouse.gov/briefing-room/speeches-remarks/ 2021/07/22/remarks-by-president-biden-in-a-cnn-town-hall-with-don-lemon/ [https://perma.cc/S9KG-ZXFH].

269. *Transcript: Dr. Anthony Fauci on 'Face the Nation,' May 16, 2021*, CBS NEWS (May 16, 2021), https://www.cbsnews.com/news/transcript-dr-anthony-fauci-face-the-nat ion-05-16-2021/ [https://perma.cc/2CST-23X2].

270. Apoorva Mandavilli, *Can Vaccinated People Spread the Virus? We Don't Know, Scientists Say*, N.Y. TIMES (Apr. 1, 2021), https://www.nytimes.com/2021/04/01/hea lth/coronavirus-vaccine-walensky.html [https://perma.cc/3HQS-QQLF].

271. *See* Jeffrey A. Tucker, *Is YouTube Now Presuming to Be in Charge of Science?*, BROWNSTONE INST. (Dec. 2, 2021), https://brownstone.org/articles/is-youtube- now-presuming-to-be-in-charge-of-science/ [https://perma.cc/CNW6-QB7S].

272. *See Science Brief: COVID-19 Vaccines and Vaccination*, CTRS. FOR DISEASE CONTROL AND PREVENTION (Sept. 15, 2021), https://www.cdc.gov/coronavirus/ 2019-ncov/science/science-briefs/fully-vaccinated-people.html [https://perma.cc/ 82HN-APFG].

273. *See* Kaitlyn Tiffany, *A Prominent Vaccine Skeptic Returns to Twitter*, THE ATLANTIC (Aug. 24, 2022), https://www.theatlantic.com/technology/archive/2022/08/alex- berenson-twitter-ban-lawsuit-covid-misinformation/671219/ [https://perma.cc/ HL77-BQAZ].

274. Maria Cramer & Knvul Sheikh, *Surgeon General Urges the Public to Stop Buying Face Masks*, N.Y. TIMES (Feb. 29, 2020), https://www.nytimes.com/2020/02/29/hea lth/coronavirus-n95-face-masks.html [https://perma.cc/S5UF-XUN6]. Ten days earlier, Fauci gave the same advice: "Now, in the United States, there is absolutely no reason whatsoever to wear a mask." The danger posed by COVID, Fauci advised, is "just minuscule." Jayne O'Donnell, *Top Disease Official: Risk of Coronavirus in USA Is 'Minuscule'; Skip Mask and Wash Hands*, USA TODAY (Feb. 19, 2020), https://www. usatoday.com/story/news/health/2020/02/17/nih-disease-official-anthony-fauci- risk-of-coronavirus-in-u-s-is-minuscule-skip-mask-and-wash-hands/4787209 002/ [https://perma.cc/K2FD-XQJ4].

275. Brett Samuels, *Surgeon General Urges Widespread Mask Use: 'It Is Not a Suppression of Your Freedom'*, THE HILL (Jun. 30, 2020), https://thehill.com/policy/healthcare/505354-surgeon-general-urges-widespread-mask-use-it-is-not-a-suppression-of-your/ [https://perma.cc/UP6P-GV7D].

276. The tweet, now since removed, was not removed at the time the statement in question was made. *See* Miriam Fauzia, *Fact check: Trump Surgeon General Initially Dismissed Mask-Wearing, But Then Endorsed*, USA TODAY (Feb. 17, 2021), https://www.usatoday.com/story/news/factcheck/2021/02/17/fact-check-ex-surgeon-general-jerome-adams-reversed-position-masks/6765301002/ [https://perma.cc/KJM6-9BSH].

277. *See* Media Statement, Ctrs. for Disease Control and Prevention, Vaccination Offers Higher Protection than Previous COVID-19 Infection (Oct. 29, 2021), https://www.cdc.gov/media/releases/2021/s1029-Vaccination-Offers-Higher-Protection.html [https://perma.cc/4HMS-7QWS].

278. *See* Tomas M. Leon et al., *COVID-19 Cases and Hospitalizations by COVID-19 Vaccination Status and Previous COVID-19 Diagnosis—California and New York, May-November 2021*, CTRS. FOR DISEASE CONTROL AND PREVENTION MORBIDITY AND MORTALITY WKLY. REP. (Jan. 28, 2022), https://www.cdc.gov/mmwr/volumes/71/wr/mm7104e1.htm [https://perma.cc/VRK8-TMGP].

279. *CDC Reports Fewer COVID-19 Pediatric Deaths After Data Correction*, REUTERS (Mar. 18, 2022), https://www.reuters.com/business/healthcare-pharmaceuticals/cdc-reports-fewer-covid-19-pediatric-deaths-after-data-correction-2022-03-18/ [https://perma.cc/9DPL-9QEA].

280. *See* Melody Schreiber, *CDC Coding Error Led to Overcount of 72,000 Covid Deaths*, THE GUARDIAN (Mar. 24, 2022), https://www.theguardian.com/world/2022/mar/24/cdc-coding-error-overcount-covid-deaths [https://perma.cc/WE3E-DXTP].

281. *See* Apoorva Mandavilli, *The C.D.C. Isn't Publishing Large Portions of the Covid Data It Collects*, N.Y. TIMES (Feb. 22, 2022), https://www.nytimes.com/2022/02/20/health/covid-cdc-data.html [https://perma.cc/TP56-VBTT].

282. *The Great Barrington Declaration* (Oct. 4, 2020), https://gbdeclaration.org/ [https://perma.cc/3D57-R4DP].

283. *Id.*

284. Editorial, Opinion, *How Fauci and Collins Shut Down Covid Debate*, WALL ST. J. (Dec.21,2021),https://www.wsj.com/articles/fauci-collins-emails-great-barrington-declaration-covid-pandemic-lockdown-11640129116 [https://perma.cc/Q9AN-F6UE].

285. Sunetra Gupta, *A Contagion of Hatred and Hysteria*, AM. INST. FOR ECON. RSCH. (Nov. 1, 2021), https://www.aier.org/article/a-contagion-of-hatred-and-hysteria/ [https://perma.cc/FZE7-Z5HP].

286. Corky Siemaszko, *YouTube Pulls Florida Governor's Video, Says His Panel Spread Covid-19 Misinformation*, NBC NEWS (Apr. 9, 2021), https://www.nbcnews.com/news/us-news/youtube-pulls-florida-governor-s-video-says-his-panel-spread-n1263635 [https://perma.cc/R856-Y84G].

287. *Id.*

288. *Id.*

289. Shir-Razl et al., *supra* note 41.

290. *Budget*, Nat'l Inst. of Health (Aug. 18, 2022), https://www.nih.gov/ABOUT-NIH/WHAT-WE-DO/BUDGET (last visited Nov. 1, 2022) [https://perma.cc/3PR8-ULZV].

291. Ridley & Chan, *supra* note 117.

292. The dynamic is not limited to government funding of science. It is one reason why some academics resist accepting donations from businesses with a political agenda, such as fossil fuel companies. As a former Cambridge professor put it, "[F]unding can exert a subtle influence on research and the researchers themselves." Huw Price, *Universities Must Wean Themselves Off Fossil Fuel Funding*, Fin. Times (Apr. 11, 2022), https://www.ft.com/content/b80d9715-4204-4592-a135-067878dc589e? [https://perma.cc/J72X-DKVK]. He continued, "As one young engineering colleague put it: 'Ostensibly, fossil fuel dollars at universities fund research, but that money also buys influence, conscious or unconscious—over academics and thus also over students. In my experience, academics funded by fossil fuels were faster to defend, and slower to criticise, big oil.'" *Id.* The dynamic is understood by internet companies. The *New York Times* reported a leading privacy advocate's observation: "Google's willingness to spread cash around the think tanks and advocacy groups focused on internet and telecommunications policy has effectively muted, if not silenced, criticism of the company over the past several years." Kenneth P. Vogel, *Google Critic Ousted from Think Tank Funded by the Tech Giant*, N.Y. Times (Aug. 30, 2017), https://www.nytimes.com/2017/08/30/us/politics/eric-schmidt-google-new-america.html [https://perma.cc/H63V-7Y8B].

293. *The Invasion of Ukraine Is Not the First Social Media War, But It Is the Most Viral*, The Economist (Apr. 2, 2022), https://www.economist.com/international/the-invasion-of-ukraine-is-not-the-first-social-media-war-but-it-is-the-most-viral/21808456 [https://perma.cc/7LRY-WYF7].

294. Jennifer Jacobs, *White House Reaches Out to Social Media Influencers on Ukraine*, Bloomberg (Mar. 12, 2022), https://www.bloomberg.com/news/articles/2022-03-12/white-house-reaches-out-to-social-media-influencers-on-ukraine [https://perma.cc/4DEN-GSH2].

295. Taylor Lorenz, *The White House is Briefing TikTok Stars About the War in Ukraine*, Wash. Post (Mar. 11, 2022), https://www.washingtonpost.com/technology/2022/03/11/tik-tok-ukraine-white-house/ [https://perma.cc/K2GD-UUWB].

296. *See* Ryan Mac, Mike Isaac & Sheera Frenkel, *How War in Ukraine Roiled Facebook and Instagram*, N.Y. Times (Mar. 31, 2022), https://www.nytimes.com/2022/03/30/technology/ukraine-russia-facebook-instagram.html [https://perma.cc/4UHW-FMQ7].

297. *Id.*

298. *Id.*

299. *Id.*

300. *See, e.g.*, Press Briefing, White House, Press Briefing by Press Secretary Karine Kean-Pierre (Sept. 1, 2022), https://www.whitehouse.gov/briefing-room/press-briefi

ngs/2022/09/01/press-briefing-by-press-secretary-karine-jean-pierre-7/ [https://perma.cc/5WUV-PG7M] (In response to a question about whether the president thought the effort to restrict abortion was "semi-fascism," White House Press Secretary Karine Jean-Pierre stated, "And so, when you are not with where a majority of Americans are, then, you know, that is extreme. That is an extreme way of thinking.").

301. Evelyn Douek, *The Rise of Content Cartels*, KNIGHT FIRST AMEND. INST. (Feb. 11, 2020), https://knightcolumbia.org/content/the-rise-of-content-cartels [https://perma.cc/J5MH-EXU2].

302. *See, e.g.*, Faiza Patel & Mary Pat Dwyer, *Facebook's New Dangerous Individuals and Organizations Policy Brings More Questions Than Answers*, JUST SECURITY (Jul. 20, 2021), https://www.justsecurity.org/77503/facebooks-new-dangerous-individuals-and-organizations-policy-brings-more-questions-than-answers/ [https://perma.cc/BG4Y-KTH6] (discussing Facebook's DIO policy).

303. Tony Romm & Ellen Nakashima, *U.S. Officials Huddle with Facebook, Google and Other Tech Giants to Talk About the 2020 Election*, WASH. POST (Sept. 4, 2019), https://www.washingtonpost.com/technology/2019/09/04/us-officials-huddle-with-facebook-google-other-tech-giants-talk-about-election/ [https://perma.cc/WA4C-KA9E].

304. Patel & Dwyer, *supra* note 302.

305. *Tech Innovation*, GLOB. INTERNET F. TO COUNTER TERRORISM, https://gifct.org/tech-innovation/ (last visited Oct. 13, 2022) [https://perma.cc/NV5V-TPWQ] (describing the technical process).

306. *Governance*, GLOB. INTERNET F. TO COUNTER TERRORISM, https://gifct.org/governance/#government (last visited Oct. 13, 2022) [https://perma.cc/B57E-2BRG].

307. *A Note from Nicholas Rasmussen, Inaugural Executive Director*, GLOB. INTERNET F. TO COUNTER TERRORISM (Oct. 3, 2022), https://gifct.org/2022/10/03/note-from-nicholas-rasmussen/ [https://perma.cc/F58C-BHJT]; *Nicholas Rasmussen*, MCCAIN INST., https://www.mccaininstitute.org/about/fellows/nicholas-rasmussen/ (last visited October 13, 2022) [https://perma.cc/UQ25-FR88].

308. GLOB. INTERNET F. TO COUNTER TERRORISM, *supra* note 306.

309. *See* Douek, *supra* note 301.

310. Keller, *supra* note 174, at 7.

311. *Id.* at 6.

312. Douek, *supra* note 301.

313. *Joint Letter to New Executive Director, Global Internet Forum to Counter Terrorism*, HUM. RTS. WATCH (Jul. 30, 2020), https://www.hrw.org/news/2020/07/30/joint-letter-new-executive-director-global-internet-forum-counter-terrorism [https://perma.cc/RF2X-MBGM].

314. *Id.*

315. *Id.*

316. Douek, *supra* note 301.

317. *Artificial Intelligence and Counterterrorism: Possibilities and Limitations, Hearing before the House Subcomm. on Intel. and Counterterrorism*, 116th Cong. 10 (Jun.

25, 2019) (written testimony of Alexander Stamos, Director, Stanford Internet Observatory), https://homeland.house.gov/imo/media/doc/Testimony-Stamos.pdf [https://perma.cc/J7P2-R9YS]).

318. Chandelis Duster, *Kamala Harris Defends Her Push to Get Trump's Twitter Account Suspended*, CNN (Oct. 16, 2019), https://www.cnn.com/2019/10/16/politics/kamala-harris-trump-twitter-suspension-cnntv/index.html [https://perma.cc/4BSS-75CJ].

319. Douek, *supra* note 301.

320. ANDREW DOYLE, FREE SPEECH: AND WHY IT MATTERS 13 (2021). *See also* Josh Hammer, Opinion, *The Biden Regime Collapses the 'Public'-'Private' Distinction*, NEWSWEEK (Sept. 2, 2022), https://www.newsweek.com/biden-regime-collapses-public-private-distinction-opinion-1739197 [https://perma.cc/R6PE-APZ5] (stating that "[t]hese technology platforms . . . have proven themselves to not be 'private' actors in any meaningful sense of the term. They are now direct appendages of the state, and they must be constitutionally treated and regulated as such . . . . Applying a First Amendment speech standard to Big Tech is manifestly fair—and simply bespeaks the reality of what these platforms have become.").

321. Vincent Blasi, *Free Speech and Good Character: From Milton to Brandeis to the Present*, *in* ETERNALLY VIGILANT: FREE SPEECH IN THE MODERN ERA 73 (Lee C. Bollinger & Geoffrey R. Stone eds., 2002).

322. Johanns v. Livestock Mktg. Ass'n, 544 U.S. 550, 553 (2005).

323. Reed v. Town of Gilbert, 576 U.S. 155, 178 (2015) (Breyer, J., concurring).

324. Walker v. Tex. Div., Sons of Confederate Veterans, Inc., 576 U.S. 200, 207 (2015).

325. Matal v. Tam, 137 S. Ct. 1744, 1757 (2017).

326. *See id.* at 1758.

327. *Walker*, 576 U.S. at 207.

328. *See* Va. State Bd. of Pharmacy v. Va. Citizens Consumer Council, 425 U.S. 748, 770 (1976).

329. Burwell v. Hobby Lobby Stores, Inc., 573 U.S. 682, 706–07 (2014).

330. NetChoice, LLC v. Paxton, 2021 WL 5755120, at *7 (W.D. Tex. Dec. 1, 2021).

331. Complaint for Plaintiffs at 31, NetChoice, LLL v. Paxton, 2021 WL 5755120 (W.D. Tex. Dec. 1, 2021).

332. *Id.* at 16.

333. Barack Obama, Keynote Address at Stanford Univ.'s Challenges to Democracy in the Digit. Info. Realm (Apr. 21, 2022), https://barackobama.medium.com/my-remarks-on-disinformation-at-stanford-7d7af7ba28af [https://perma.cc/U5SR-G2M5].

334. "[T]he state action doctrine is an absurd basis for choosing between two liberties. The concept of state action completely ignores the competing rights at stake and chooses based entirely on the identity of the actors." Erwin Chemerinsky, *Rethinking State Action*, 80 Nw. U. L. REV. 503, 537 (1985).

335. For one of the earliest critiques of the single-actor approach to state action, see generally Robert J. Glennon Jr. & John E. Nowak, *A Functional Analysis of the Fourteenth Amendment "State Action" Requirement*, 1976 SUP. CT. REV. 221 (1976).

336. Donald J. Trump v. Twitter, Inc., 2022 WL 1443233, at *2 (N.D. Cal. May 6, 2022).

337. NetChoice, LLC v. Paxton, 2022 WL 4285917, at *2 (5th Cir. 2022).

338. The court said, "They've told their users: 'We try to explicitly view ourselves as not editors. . . . We don't want to have editorial judgment over the content that's in your feed.' They've told the public that they 'may not monitor,' 'do not endorse,' and 'cannot take responsibility for' the content on their Platforms. They've told Congress that their 'goal is to offer a platform for all ideas.' And they've told courts—over and over again—that they simply 'serv[e] as conduits for other parties' speech.'" *NetChoice*, 2022 WL 4285917, at *13.

339. Section 230(c)(1) of the Communications Decency Act, the statute that immunizes the platforms from liability for content posted by their users, provides that the platforms "shall [not] be treated as the publisher or speaker" of content developed by other users, undercutting the claim that the platforms' content moderation constitutes protected speech. *NetChoice*, 2022 WL 4285917, at *18. This provision, the court said, "reflects Congress's judgment that the Platforms are not acting as speakers or publishers when they host user-submitted content." *Id.* at 20.

340. As Eugene Volokh pithily put it, "there's more to actual freedom of speech than just the freedom from government retaliation." Eugene Volokh, *Freedom of Speech ≠ The Free Speech Clause*, REASON (Jul. 21, 2021), https://reason.com/volokh/2021/07/21/freedom-of-speech-%e2%89%a0-the-free-speech-clause/ [https://perma.cc/4E64-YR26].

341. Nossel stated it well: "Many of the fears we associate with government controls over speech—that dissent will be suppressed, that the open exchange of ideas will shrivel or skew, and that power over speech will be abused to benefit those that wield it—are as applicable to conglomerates as they are to a national government. While a tech company doesn't have the authority to arrest and prosecute you, its ability to delete your posts and shut down your account is a potent form of social control, and not subject to the appeals and other constraints of our legal system." NOSSEL, *supra* note 172, at 215. Nearly four decades ago Erwin Chemerinsky forcefully made the same point concerning the effect of private infringement of speech freedom: "Freedom of speech, privacy, and equality—this society's most cherished values—are trampled without any redress in the courts. Certainly, such private infringements of basic freedoms can be just as harmful as governmental infringements. Speech can be chilled and lost just as much through private sanctions as through public wants." Erwin Chemerinsky, *Rethinking State Action*, 80 Nw. U. L. REV. 503, 510 (1985). Jonathan Turley observes that the vast new power of social media dwarfs that of earlier state censors: "Recent years have shown that a uniform system of corporate censorship can be far more effective than the classic model of a central ministry in controlling information. . . . [T]hese companies have direct control over a far greater range of speech than would any state apparatus. The dangers posed by private censorship for a political system are the same as government censorship in the curtailment of free speech." Jonathan Turley, *Harm and Hegemony: The Decline of Free Speech in the United States*, 45 HARV. J. L. & PUB. POL'Y 571, 613–14 (2022).

342. Audience and recipient interests are particularly relevant with respect to information. "Restrictions on the free flow of political information are suspect because they

invade the audience's interests in having enough material before it to make informed choices and to participate fully in the democratic process." ERIC BARENDT, FREEDOM OF SPEECH 25 (2005). "We protect free speech," Alexander Meiklejohn argued, "to give every voting member of the body politic the fullest possible participation in the understanding of those problems with which the citizens of a self-governing society must deal." MEIKLEJOHN, *supra* note 5, 26.

343. Lamont v. Postmaster General, 381 U.S. 301, 302 (1965).

344. BURT NEUBORNE, MADISON'S MUSIC: ON READING THE FIRST AMENDMENT 102 (2015).

345. *See Lamont*, 381 U.S. at 307.

346. Va. State Bd. of Pharmacy v. Va. Citizens Consumer Council, 425 U.S. 748, 756 (1976).

347. Bd. of Educ. v. Pico, 457 U.S. 853, 867 (1982).

348. *Id. See also* Marsh v. Alabama, 326 U.S. 501 (1946), discussed *infra* at notes 398–401.

349. N.Y. Times Co. v. Sullivan, 376 U.S. 254, 270 (1964).

350. Requiring major social media platforms (perhaps those advantaged by Section 230) to provide optional access to one channel moderated pursuant to First Amendment principles would not preclude their offering additional channels moderated with different filters. Companies could offer a menu with different options, including one under which content is moderated under their own standards, or another applying standards such as those imposed under the European Union's limits. The companies could go further and allow users to filter content individually, blocking categories of content such as racial slurs, pornography, or depictions of violence. Artificial intelligence, in response to pressing a "dislike" button, might block even more particularized content. This type of technology is already in use today, not only with respect to individuals but entire countries in which internet companies employ geoblocking to tailor content to comply with local legal limits. Employing it, companies could still offer users the same content they do today— provided they also offer unfiltered, "First Amendment" content to those who want it. *See* Vivek Ramaswamy & Jed Rubenfeld, Opinion, *How Elon Musk Can Liberate Twitter*, WALL ST. J. (Apr. 26, 2022), https://www.wsj.com/articles/how-elon-musk-can-liberate-twitter-censorship-fact-check-free-speech-buy-website-platform-takeover-content-moderation-hate-speech-misinformation-disinformation-1165 0983718?mod=mhp [https://perma.cc/38AU-2YBL].

351. Neuborne, *supra* note 344, at 99.

352. *Id.* at 98.

353. Packingham v. North Carolina, 137 S. Ct. 1730, 1737 (2017) (citing Reno v. ACLU, 521 U.S. 844, 870 (1997)).

354. Neuborne, *supra* note 344, at 118. "It's time to turn 'borrowed' corporate speech rights into a hearer-centered doctrine." *Id.* at 117.

355. "[T]he most important role for state action in the area of free speech," Jonathan Turley writes, "is to protect the entire 'marketplace of ideas'—both physical and virtual forums for the expression of viewpoints." Turley, *supra* note 341, at 641.

356. United States v. Carolene Prods. Co., 304 U.S. 144, 152 n.4 (1938).

357. John Hart Ely, Democracy and Distrust 76 (1980).

358. Palko v. Connecticut, 302 U.S. 319, 327 (1937).

359. Heightened scrutiny of restrictions that clog the channels of political change suggests the propriety of similarly heightened scrutiny of restrictions on the speech interests of listeners and bystanders whose access to those channels is blocked by speakers engaged in expression that is immunized from review by the state action or government speech doctrines. *See Carolene Prods. Co.*, 304 U.S. at 152 n.4.

360. Matal v. Tam, 137 S. Ct. 1744, 1758 (2017). A moment's reflection reveals the doctrine's insidious threat. Government normally acts through words. If all governmental words were immunized from judicial review, judicial invalidation of unconstitutional government action would come to an end. *Marbury v. Madison*, 5 U.S. 137 (1803) would be history.

361. Walker v. Tex. Div., Sons of Confederate Veterans, Inc., 576 U.S. 200, 208 (2015).

362. *Id.*

363. Bantam Books, Inc. v. Sullivan, 372 U.S. 58 (1963).

364. *Id.* at 72.

365. *Id.* at 61.

366. *Id.* at 62–63.

367. *Id.* at 63.

368. *Id.* at 68.

369. *Id.* at 70–72.

370. *Id.* at 67.

371. Backpage.com v. Dart, 807 F.3d 229 (7th Cir. 2015).

372. *Id.* at 230.

373. *Id.*

374. *Id.*

375. *Id.* at 231.

376. *Id.* at 236.

377. *Id.* at 231 (citing *Sullivan*, 372 U.S. at 64–72).

378. *Id.* at 238.

379. *Id.*

380. *Id.* at 230.

381. Okwedy v. Molinari, 333 F.3d 339, 340–41 (2d Cir. 2003).

382. *Id.* at 339–341.

383. *Id.* at 344.

384. *Id.* at 340–341.

385. *Id.* at 343. The case was X-Men Sec., Inc. v. Pataki, 196 F.3d 56 (2d Cir. 1999).

386. Tim Wu proposes a parallel approach based not on an assumed agency relationship but on a theory of independent liability under which, for example, "[i]f the president or other officials order private individuals or organizations to attack or publish critics of the government," the courts could find state action based on concepts akin to accomplice or secondary liability. Tim Wu, *Is the First Amendment Obsolete?*, *in* The Free Speech Century 272, 286–87 (Lee C. Bollinger & Geoffrey R. Stone eds., 2019).

387. *See* Norwood v. Harrison, 413 U.S. 455, 465 (1973) ("'[A] state may not induce, encourage or promote private persons to accomplish what it is constitutionally forbidden to accomplish.'" (quoting Lee v. Macon County Board of Education, 267 F. Supp. 458, 475–76 (M.D. Ala. 1967))); Vivek Ramaswamy & Jed Rubenfeld, Opinion, *Twitter Becomes a Tool of Government Censorship*, WALL ST. J. (Aug. 17, 2022), https://www.wsj.com/articles/twitter-becomes-a-tool-of-government-cens ors-alex-berenson-twitter-facebook-ban-covid-misinformation-first-amendm ent-psaki-murthy-section-230-antitrust-11660732095?mod=opinion_lead_pos5 [https://perma.cc/8NBV-SS5A].

388. Shurtleff v. City of Boston, 142 S. Ct. 1583, 1590 (2022). The three justices joining a concurring opinion written by Justice Samuel Alito drew a similar line. The inquiry, they indicated, is "whether the government is actually expressing its own views or the real speaker is a private party and the government is surreptitiously engaged in the 'regulation of private speech.'" *Id.* at 1596 (quoting Pleasant Grove City v. Summum, 555 U.S. 460, 467 (2009)).

389. *See, e.g.*, Lugar v. Edmondson Oil Co., 457 U.S. 922, 924 (1982) ("Because the Amendment is directed at the States, it can be violated only by conduct that may be fairly characterized as 'state action.'"); Peterson v. Greenville, 373 U.S. 244, 250 (1963) (Harlan, J., concurring in the result) ("Freedom of the individual to choose his associates or his neighbors, to use and dispose of his property as he sees fit, to be irrational, arbitrary, capricious, even unjust in his personal relations are things all entitled to a large measure of protection from governmental interference. This liberty would be overridden, in the name of equality, if the strictures of the Amendment were applied to governmental and private action without distinction. Also inherent in the concept of state action are values of federalism, a recognition that there are areas of private rights upon which federal power should not lay a heavy hand and which should properly be left to the more precise instruments of local authority.").

390. Blum v. Yaretsky, 457 U.S. 991, 1004 (1982).

391. In *Blum* itself, the Court found it was not the choice of the state to discharge or transfer nursing home residents, who claimed they were denied due process. *See id.* at 991.

392. *Id.* at 466.

393. ERWIN CHEMERINSKY, CONSTITUTIONAL LAW: PRINCIPLES AND POLICIES 578 (6th ed. Aspen Publ'g 2019).

394. Burton v. Wilmington Parking Auth., 365 U.S. 715, 725 (1961).

395. Brentwood Acad. v. Tenn. Secondary Sch. Athletic Ass'n, 531 U.S. 288, 288 (2001).

396. *Id.* at 305 (Thomas, J., dissenting).

397. Packingham v. North Carolina, 137 S. Ct. 1730, 1737 (2017) (citing Reno v. Am. C.L. Union, 521 U.S. 844, 870 (1997)).

398. Marsh v. Alabama, 326 U.S. 501 (1946). *See also* PruneYard Shopping Center v. Robbins, 447 U.S. 74 (1980) (upholding the right under the California Constitution of students to solicit signatures in a privately-owned shopping center). "[W]e can plausibly analogize Facebook, Google, and Twitter to the shopping center in *Pruneyard* [sic]." Pozen, *supra* note 215 at 136. "[I]f government is not favoring

any point of view and if it is genuinely improving the operation of democratic processes," Cass Sunstein writes, "it is hard to find a legitimate basis for complaint. Indeed, the Supreme Court has expressly held that the owner of shopping centers—areas where a great deal of speech occurs—may be required to keep their property open for expressive activity [citing *PruneYard*]." Cass Sunstein, *The Future of Free Speech, in* ETERNALLY VIGILANT: FREE SPEECH IN THE MODERN ERA 305 (Lee C. Bollinger & Geoffrey R. Stone eds., 2002). "[I]n *PruneYard*, the speech of the shopping mall owner was not hindered in the slightest by the public's pamphleteering right." NetChoice v. Paxton, 49 F.4th 439, 457 n.7 (5th Cir. 2022) (internal quotations omitted). The shopping center was a business establishment that was open to the public, the *NetChoice* Court noted. *See* NetChoice, 49 F.4th at 491.

399. *Marsh*, 326 U.S. at 503.

400. *Id.* at 507.

401. *Id.* at 508.

402. Packingham v. North Carolina, 137 S. Ct. 1730, 1735 (2017).

403. Geoffrey R. Stone, *Reflections on Whether the First Amendment Is Obsolete, in* THE PERILOUS PUBLIC SQUARE: STRUCTURAL THREATS TO FREE EXPRESSION TODAY 45 (David E. Pozen ed., 2020).

404. *Id.*

405. *Marsh*, 326 U.S. at 506.

406. *Id.*

407. *See* Biden v. Knight First Amend. Inst., 141 S. Ct. 1220, 1223 (2021) (Thomas, J., concurring).

408. *Id.* at 1224.

409. *See, e.g.*, Turley, *supra* note 341, at 644 ("The regulation of social media companies as akin to a telephone company would allow the government to impose public forum protections from censorship.").

410. NetChoice v. Paxton, 49 F.4th 439, 473–74 (5th Cir. 2022).

411. An early example cited by the court is *State ex rel. Webster v. Nebraska Telephone Co.*, in which the Supreme Court of Nebraska ordered a telephone company to put a telephone in a lawyer's office. *NetChoice*, 49 F.4th at 471 (citing State *ex rel.* Webster v. Neb. Tel. Co., 22 N.W. 237 (Neb. 1885)).

412. *See* Chemerinsky, *supra* note 341, at 538.

413. N.Y. Times v. Sullivan, 376 U.S. 254, 270 (1964).

414. *See supra* notes 343–344 (discussing Lamont v. Postmaster General, 381 U.S. 301 (1965)).

415. Milwaukee Pub. Co. v. Burleson, 255 U.S. 407, 437 (1921) (Holmes, J., dissenting).

416. Lamont v. Postmaster General, 381 U.S. 301, 305 n.3 (1965) (quoting Pike v. Walker, 121 F.2d 37, 39 (D.C. Cir. 1941)).

417. *Lamont*, 381 U.S. at 308 (Brennan, J., concurring).

418. *See supra* note 386.

419. *See* Glennon, *supra* note 7, at 86.

420. For a fine account of the drafting of Eisenhower's January 17, 1961 speech, *see generally* JAMES LEDBETTER, UNWARRANTED INFLUENCE: DWIGHT D. EISENHOWER AND THE MILITARY-INDUSTRIAL COMPLEX (Yale Univ. Press 2011).

421. *See* United States v. Carolene Prods. Co., 304 U.S. 144, 152 n.4 (1938). *See generally* John Hart Ely, *supra* note 357.

422. Learned Hand's admonition is widely accepted: "Liberty lies in the hearts of men and women; when it dies there, no constitution, no law, no court can save it." Learned Hand, The Spirit of Liberty 190 (Irving Dillard ed., 3d ed. 1960).

423. Article III, Section 2 of the Constitution empowers federal courts to decide "all cases . . . arising under this Constitution" and all "controversies to which the United States shall be a party." U.S. Const. art. III, § 2, cl. 1.

424. "In a fully developed bureaucracy there is nobody left with whom one can argue, to whom one can present grievances, on whom the pressures of power can be exerted. Bureaucracy is the form of government in which everybody is deprived of political freedom, of the power to act; for the rule by Nobody is not no-rule, and where all are equally powerless, we have a tyranny without a tyrant." Hanna Arendt, On Violence 81 (1970).

425. New State Ice Co. v. Liebmann, 285 U.S. 262, 311 (1932) (Brandeis, J., dissenting).

Chapter 13

1. *Debs v. United States*, 249 U.S. 211 (1919).

2. *Brandenburg v. Ohio*, 395 U.S. 444 (1969).

3. *Missouri v. Biden*, No. 23-30445 at 61-62 (5th Cir.), Sept. 8, 2023 (quoting the district court in *Missouri v. Biden*, No. 3:22-01213, memorandum ruling on request for preliminary injunction (Western District of Louisiana, Monroe Division), July 4, 2023), chrome-extension://efaidnbmnnnibpcajpcglclefindmkaj/https://www.ca5.uscourts.gov/opinions/pub/23/23-30445-CV0.pdf.

4. William Henry Seward, "The Irrepressible Conflict" (1858), in *The Works of William H. Seward,* University of Michigan Digital Library, 2005, 289, 292, https://quod.lib.umich.edu/g/genpub/ABT5537.0001.001/297?rgn=full+text;view=image.

5. *Missouri* at 72 (5th Cir.).

Index

For the benefit of digital users, indexed terms that span two pages (e.g., 52–53) may, on occasion, appear on only one of those pages.